Grace for All

GRACE FOR ALL

The Arminian Dynamics of Salvation

—

Clark H. Pinnock and **John D. Wagner**
Editors

RESOURCE *Publications* · Eugene, Oregon

GRACE FOR ALL
The Arminian Dynamics of Salvation

Resource Publications
An Imprint of Wipf and Stock Publishers
199 W. 8th Ave., Suite 3
Eugene, OR 97401

www.wipfandstock.com

ISBN 13: 978–1–4982–0012–7

Manufactured in the U.S.A.   05/01/2015

Published in previous form in Clark H. Pinnock, ed. *Grace Unlimited* (Minneapolis: Bethany House Publishers, 1975), republished by Wipf and Stock Publishers

To Our Precious Wives,

Dorothy Pinnock and Wendy Wagner

Contents

The Contributors

David J.A. Clines, Honorary Doctorate, University of Amsterdam, is Emeritus Professor of Old Testament at University of Sheffield, England. He has also served as President of the Society for Old Testament Study and the Society of Biblical Literature. His published works include: *The Theme of the Pentateuch*, *Job* (3 vols.), and *The Concise Dictionary of Classical Hebrew*.

Jack Cottrell, PhD, Princeton Theological Seminary, is Professor of Theology at Cincinnati Christian University, Ohio. Among his many books are *Set Free! What the Bible Says About Grace*, *What the Bible Says About God the Creator*, *What the Bible Says About God the Redeemer*, and *What the Bible Says About God the Ruler*.

Vernon Grounds (1914–2010), PhD, Drew University, served as Academic Dean and then President of Conservative Baptist Theological Seminary (now Denver Seminary) in Colorado. His books include: *The Reason for Our Hope*, *Emotional Problems and the Gospel*, and *Evangelicalism and Social Responsibility*.

William G. MacDonald, PhD, Southern Baptist Theological Seminary, is former Professor of Biblical and Theological Studies at Gordon College in Wenham, Mass. He has also served as President of the Society for Pentecostal Studies. His books include *Glossolalia in the New Testament* and *Greek Enchiridion: A Concise Handbook of Grammar for Translation and Exegesis*.

I. Howard Marshall, PhD, University of Aberdeen, Scotland, is Professor Emeritus of New Testament Exegesis, at the University of Aberdeen. His many books include: *Kept by the Power of God*, *The Acts of the Apostles: An Introduction and Commentary*, and *The Origins of New Testament Christology*.

Roger Olson, PhD, Rice University, is Professor of Theology at Baylor University in Waco, Texas. His books include, *Arminian Theology: Myths and Realities*, *The Mosaic of Christian Belief*, and *The Westminster Handbook to Evangelical Theology*.

Grant Osborne, PhD, University of Aberdeen, Scotland, is Professor of New Testament at Trinity Evangelical Divinity School, in Deerfield, Ill. His published works include: *The Hermeneutical Spiral*, *Three Crucial Questions About the Bible*, and *The Resurrection Narratives*.

Robert Picirilli, PhD, Bob Jones University, served as Academic Dean and Professor of Greek and New Testament Studies at Free Will Baptist Bible College (now Welch College) in Nashville, Tenn. His published works include: *Grace Faith Free Will*; *Teacher, Leader, Shepherd: The New Testament Pastor*; and *Discipleship: The Expression of Saving Faith*.

Clark Pinnock (1937–2010), PhD, University of Manchester, was Professor Emeritus of Systematic Theology at McMaster Divinity College in Vancouver, Canada. His many books include *The Scripture Principle*, *Reason Enough: A Case for the Christian Faith*, and *Three Keys to Spiritual Renewal*.

J. Matthew Pinson, EdD, Vanderbilt University, is President of Welch College in Nashville, Tenn. His published works include *The Washing of the Saints' Feet* and *A Free Will Baptist Handbook*.

Vic Reasoner, DMin, Asbury Theological Seminary, is President of Southern Methodist College in Orangeburg, S.C. He has served as General Editor of Fundamental Wesleyan Publications since 1993. His published works include: *A Fundamental Wesleyan Commentary on Revelation*, *The Importance of Inerrancy*, and *The Hope of the Gospel: An Introduction to Wesleyan Eschatology*.

Glen Shellrude, PhD, University of St. Andrews, is Professor of New Testament at Alliance Theological Seminary, in New York. His published articles include: "Imputation in Pauline Theology: Christ's Righteousness or a Justified Status" and "All are Elect, Few are Elect: Understanding New Testament Election Language" (both in the *Scottish Bulletin of Evangelical Theology*).

James D. Strauss (1929–2014), DMin, Eden Theological Seminary, was Professor of Theology and Philosophy at Lincoln Christian University in

Lincoln, Ill. He has been described as the "Einstein" of the Restorationist Movement. His published works include: *Pardon and Power: A Biblical Theology of Grace, The Shattering of Silence: Job, Our Contemporary,* and *Restoration: The Stone-Campbell Movement from the Enlightenment to Post-Modernism.*

John D. Wagner, MA, University of Arizona, is a Biblical Studies student with Trinity Theological Seminary in Newburgh, Ind. He is the editor of *Redemption Redeemed: A Puritan Defense of Unlimited Atonement, Freedom of the Will: A Wesleyan Response to Jonathan Edwards,* and *Arminius Speaks: Essential Writings on Predestination, Free Will and the Nature of God.*

Steve Witzki, MA, Grand Rapids Baptist Seminary, is ordained in the Free Methodist Church Southern Michigan Conference, and has served as Associate and Senior Pastor in Michigan, Ohio, and Missouri. His articles include: "Calvinism and John Six: An Exegetical Response" Parts 1 and 2 (both in *The Arminian* magazine). He is currently working on a revised version of Robert Shank's classic work, *Life in the Son.*

Preface

This work is an updated and revised version of *Grace Unlimited*, a 1975 collection of scholarly articles assembled by the late Clark H. Pinnock of McMaster Divinity College. His intent was to produce a treatise defending the Arminian perspective and tactfully disagreeing with Calvinism. This was also long before he embraced his controversial "open theism."

Much has happened during the forty years since that time. I believe a new and fresh version of Dr. Pinnock's book will benefit the theological world.

Of the articles I have retained, I have included some editing and updating. I have also invited six scholars to contribute new articles on various aspects of this controversy. They include Robert Picirilli, Matthew Pinson, Vic Reasoner, Steve Witzki, Glen Shellrude, and Roger Olson.

My thanks to Dr. Pinnock for his work on GU, and to his wife Dorothy and daughter Sarah for their consent on this project.

John D. Wagner
Altadena, Calif.

Foreword

The meaning of our Savior's name Jesus is "Yahweh saves!" It sums up in a single word the central theme of the whole Bible: the triumph of grace in the salvation of sinners, with that grace abounding for all. The attention of our international symposium is directed to this extraordinary truth. We wish to articulate the doctrine of grace in the most biblical and coherent way possible. We therefore offer this powerful anthology of Arminian essays toward that purpose.[1]

Defending this doctrine leads us to focus on the universality of grace, on the all-inclusive scope of God's salvific will. The most important theological presupposition of all writing in this volume is our conviction that God is good in an unqualified manner, and that he desires the salvation of all sinners. To each human being, God offers forgiveness in Jesus Christ and the gift of becoming children of God. We delight in our Lord's words in Scripture to all people: "Come to Me all who are weary and heavy laden and I will give you rest" (Matt 11:28); "For God did not send His Son into the world to condemn the world, but that the world through Him might be saved" (John 3:17). We reject all forms of theology that deny this truth and posit some secret abyss in God's mind that contradicts his revealed will.

We rejoice in Paul's judgment that God "desires all men to be saved and to come to the knowledge of the truth" and to Peter's conviction that God is "not wishing that any should perish, but that all should reach repentance" (1 Tim 2:4, 2 Pet. 3:9). If it seems controversial to assert this conviction boldly and unashamedly, then it ought at least to be admitted that here is a truth far more deserving of controversy than many debated. On it hangs, we

1. The term "Arminian" stems from the name of Dutch theologian James Arminius (1559–1609), who challenged the prevailing Calvinism of his day. Please see Roger Olson's article at the beginning of this book refuting the myth that Arminianism is "man-centered theology," and J. Matthew Pinson's article, "Jacobus Arminius: Reformed and Always Reforming." Depending on the source, Arminius's first name varies between James, Jacob and Jacobus.

believe, the validity of the universal offer of the gospel, and the possibility of Christian assurance. If we do not know that God loves all sinners, we do not know that he loves us, and we do not know that he loves all those to whom we take the gospel.[2]

In the cross of Christ we see the will of God for the salvation of all sinners perfectly exemplified. As Paul says, "For the love of Christ controls us, having concluded this: that one died for *all* . . . and He died *for all*" (2 Cor 5:14–15). In Romans, the Apostle draws a parallel between Christ and Adam in these words: "Consequently, just as the result of one trespass was condemnation for all men, so also the result of one act of righteousness was justification that brings life *for all men*" (5:18). It is difficult to imagine how the Bible could have made things more clear. Christ's saving work is pertinent to the whole race, as Adam's work was, and is therefore offered to all sinners. Or, again, Paul says, "God was in Christ reconciling the world to himself " (2 Cor 5:19). According to John, "He is the expiation for our sins, and not for ours only but also for the sins of the whole world" (1 John 2:2). The universal salvific will of the Father has become objectified in the atoning work of the Son according to all these texts so that no sinner can now doubt that God loves him and desires to save him. We take vigorous exception, therefore, to any theology that denies Jesus's bold declaration: "This bread is my flesh that I will give for the life of the world" (John 6:51). We are implacably opposed to any attempt to limit grace and the atonement. It is because he died for all that we can claim for ourselves and confidently extend to others the right and title to sonship and salvation through Christ, and live in a state of blessed assurance.[3]

Although most of the essays in this book are not written in a polemical manner, its thesis gives the book a controversial character. While the contributors do have differences on some points[4], all are united in believing God's grace is for everyone and that God desires the salvation of all people.

---

2. Most authors defending double predestination, according to which God is said to elect some to salvation and reprobate the rest to damnation, seek to defend their position against these charges. But we do not think it is possible, considering the contents of this book.

3. In defense of Christ dying for all people, we offer the essay "The Intent and Extent of Christ's Atonement" by Robert Picirilli. Consult also on this matter Norman F. Douty, *Did Christ Die Only for the Elect?* (Eugene, Ore.: Wipf and Stock, 1998); and John Goodwin, *Redemption Redeemed: A Puritan Defense of Unlimited Atonement* (Eugene, Ore; Wipf and Stock, 2004).

4. This is also true among Calvinists. For a source that cites a large number of their in-house differences, see Laurence Vance, *The Other Side of Calvinism* (Pensacola, Fla.: Vance Publications, 1999).

There has in recent years been a resurgence of interest in Calvinism, including what has been called the "New Calvinism," described by Time magazine as one of "10 Ideas Changing the World Right Now."[5] Its youthful adherents have been called the "young, restless and Reformed."[6] All of this is a powerful effort in Protestant orthodoxy to limit the gospel and to cast a dark shadow over its universal availability and intention.[7] This theology, in its dreadful doctrine of double predestination, calls into question God's desire to save all sinners and as a logical consequence, it denies Christ died to save the world at large. This is simply unacceptable exegetically, theologically, and morally, and to it we must say an emphatic "No!"

According to the Westminster Confession of Faith: "By the decree of God, for the manifestation of his glory, some men and angels are predestinated unto everlasting life, and others foreordained to everlasting death." And with particular reference to the nonelect, we read: "The rest of mankind God was pleased, according to the unsearchable counsel of his own will, whereby he extendeth or withholdeth mercy as he pleaseth, for the glory of his sovereign power over his creatures, to pass by, and to ordain them to dishonor and wrath for their sin, to the praise of his glorious justice" (W.C. III). Calvinists themselves have often admitted of course that this is "an unpleasant doctrine."[8] Calvin himself referred to it as a "decretum horribile." Indeed it is so. It is hard to see on the basis of it how the gospel can be preached at all or why in that case it should be called "good" news. For further elaboration, Glen Shellrude offers an insightful summary in this book on the problems of Calvinism. We also note that Calvinist author Edwin Palmer writes the following:

> Reprobation as condemnation is conditional in the sense that once someone is passed by, then he is condemned by God for his sins and unbelief. Although all things—belief and sin

---

5. David Van Biema, "The New Calvinism," Time, March 12, 2009.

6. Collin Hansen, *Young, Restless, Reformed: A Journalist's Journey with the New Calvinists* (Wheaton, Ill: Crossway, 2008); and see the dissenting work, Austin Fischer, *Young, Restless, No Longer Reformed* (Eugene, Ore.: Cascade, 2014).

7. This book is one of a number in response to the rising interest in Calvinism. See also, James Arminius, *Arminius Speaks* (Eugene, Ore.: Wipf and Stock, 2011); Roger Olson, *Arminian Theology: Myths and Realities* (Downers Grove, Ill: InterVarsity, 2006); Robert Picirilli, *Grace Faith Free Will* (Nashville: Randall House, 2002); and F. Leroy Forlines, *Classical Arminianism*, (Nashville: Randall House, 2011).

8. Loraine Boettner, *The Reformed Doctrine of Predestination* (Philadelphia: Presbyterian and Reformed, 1965), 108.

included—proceed from God's eternal decree, man is still to blame for his sin. He is guilty; it is his fault and not God's.[9]

This is a theology burdened with extraordinary difficulties of every kind, and we believe it important to show the Christian public that it is not the only way Holy Scripture can be read. Exegetically, it stumbles over the great universal texts of Scripture. Theologically, it impugns the goodness of God and casts a dark shadow over the gospel. Morally, far from glorifying his justice, it calls it into question and raises very serious doubts about it. The theology underlying this volume, on the other hand, exults in the free offer of grace and bears joyous testimony to God's loving kindness. Truly, "the grace of God has appeared, bringing salvation to all men" (Titus 2:11).

It is not necessary, strictly speaking, to go any further. If Scripture speaks of the universal salvific will of God, as it does repeatedly, the matter is settled. We need hardly give any theology that limits the gospel a second look. Nevertheless, it is important to probe more deeply, and seek to discover the impetus that lies behind this desire to limit it. Why would a theologian like Augustine or Calvin, conceive of the idea that God does not desire to save all and that Jesus did not die to redeem them? It is because several re-lated scriptural ideas have been seriously misinterpreted, and which, if not corrected, will continue to result in the same theological distortions. Four of the most important of these concepts receive a thorough examination in our symposium: election, faith, predestination, and perseverance of the saints.

With respect to *election*, if a person believed that God has chosen only a limited number of people to be saved out of the entire race, he would have to conclude *either* that the universal texts do not mean what they appear to say, *or* that God has two wills in the matter, one which is well disposed toward all sinners, and another secret will which purposes only to be gra-cious to a few. So long as the premise regarding election is not corrected, however unsatisfactory the conclusions undoubtedly are, a person would be compelled to select one of them.[10] That is, he would be compelled either to deny the universal texts (e.g. 1 Tim 2:4–6) outright, or accept the exceed-ingly paradoxical notion of two divine wills regarding salvation. Therefore,

9. Edwin H. Palmer, *The Five Points of Calvinism* (Grand Rapids: Baker, 1972), 105–106, quoted in Roger Olson, *Against Calvinism* (Grand Rapids: Zondervan, 2011), 106. Olson adds, "This is enough to make anyone's head spin." (Ibid.)

10. Belief in limited election and what it entails is as old as Augustine, though no older, and is expounded with characteristic clarity and rigor in B. B. Warfield, *The Plan of Salvation* (Grand Rapids: Eerdmans, 1955). Among more recent works, see Sam Storms, *Chosen for Life: The Case for Divine Election* (Wheaton, Ill.: Crossway, 2007).

it is imperative that we not only bear witness to the universal grace of God, but also explain this doctrine of election in such a way that the consistency of the Bible's teaching in this area is vindicated.

The contributors to this volume are all convinced that belief in a limited unconditional election is mistaken, and does not represent fairly the biblical doctrine. Therefore we present the essay "Conditional Election" by Jack W. Cottrell, which is designed to open up for the reader possibilities of interpretation passed over in the Calvinistic rendering.[11] Like H. H. Rowley, Cottrell points to election to service such as with Israel and its corporate nature. And like biblical theologians in general, to the election of the church and of individuals in regard to salvation. Beyond that, he defends his own view of individual election to salvation based on the foreknowledge of God of those who are "in Him" i.e. in Christ.

Though there remain questions as to emphasis and orientation, and a need to continue the theological discussion, we are convinced that the biblical doctrine of election presents no threat and exists in no tension with the scriptural doctrine of universal grace. God desires to save all peoples and Jesus Christ has died for them all. The path is therefore open for them to return to the Father from whom they have rebelled. Only when it is misrepresented does the doctrine of election suggest any contradiction to this biblical truth.[12] With respect to *faith*, if a person believed as Augustine did, that saving grace is an irresistible operation of God's Spirit that overwhelms the unbeliever and creates faith in him, he would have to conclude either that all will be saved, or if not, that saving grace is not made universally available.

Evangelicals, wanting to take seriously the biblical doctrine of final judgment, will have to opt for the limitation of grace, therefore, if they accept the Augustinian premise. But, again, it is the premise which is faulty. Augustine's view of irresistible grace was a new theology in the early Christian church. Before that time all her teachers including Irenaeus, Origen, Jerome, and Justin Martyr among them had emphasized the universality of grace and the possibility of declining it.[13] We believe this is also the biblical

11. We dispute Calvin's bold assertion that there is no other way to handle the biblical doctrine of election than his own in his *Institutes of the Christian Religion* (Peabody, Mass: Hendrickson, 2007), 3.22.1.

12. Ancillary to Cottrell's essay we present one by James D. Strauss and John D. Wagner, "God's Promise and Universal History" on Romans 9, and two by Grant R. Osborne, "Soteriology in the Epistle to the Hebrews," and "Exegetical Notes on Calvinist Texts." See also, Steve Witzki's "Saving Faith: The Act of a Moment or the Attitude of a Life?"

13. On the novelty of Augustine's theology, see Paul Marston and Roger Forster,

view. Two articles in particular here explore the dynamic understanding of universal grace: "God's Universal Salvific Grace" by Vernon Grounds, and "The Spirit of Grace," by William G. MacDonald and John D. Wagner.

Scripture makes it quite clear that the love and grace of God offered to us in the gospel is an overture that can be accepted or rejected, welcomed or repudiated. Although grace is certainly prevenient, it is not coercive.[14] In a comparison of the church with the ancient people of Israel, the writer to the Hebrews declares, "For good news came to us just as to them; but the message which they heard did not benefit them, because it did not meet with faith in the hearers" (Heb 4:2). God's grace may be genuinely extended to people, but unless it meets the response of faith, the only response that pleases God, it has no saving effect. Stephen declared to the Jews of his day, "You stiff-necked people, uncircumcised in heart and ears, you always resist the Holy Spirit" (Acts 7:51).

Personal fellowship of the kind envisioned in the gospel only exists where consummated in a free decision. If we wish to understand God's grace as a personal address to his creatures, we must comprehend it in dynamic, nonmanipulative, noncoercive terms, as the Bible does. The standard criticism leveled against a theology of this kind is synergism. It is supposed to bring into the event of salvation a decisive human work, and thereby destroy its purely gracious character. But this is simply not the case. Faith is not a work at all (Rom 3:28; 4:5). It is not an achievement and has no merit attaching to it. It is simply surrender of the will to God, the stretching out of an empty hand to receive the gift of grace. In the decision of faith, we renounce all our works, and repudiate completely every claim to self righteousness. Far from encouraging conceit and self-esteem, faith utterly excludes them (Rom 3:27).

Even when we speak of faith as a "condition," let us not misrepresent the meaning of this expression. Faith is not the condition of grace, which originates in the counsels of eternity, and comes to us first (John 16:8). Faith is rather the *response* to grace God calls for through which salvation becomes a reality to the individual concerned. We are saved by God's grace *through faith*.

In Daane's book on election, he affirms God's universal salvific will and rejects vigorously the election/reprobation pattern of classical decretal

---

God's Strategy in Human History (Eugene, Ore: Wipf and Stock, 2000), 305–344. See also the book's appendix with quotes from numerous early church fathers advocating free will.

14. R. C. Sproul actually describes the Calvinistic concept of irresistible grace as "a holy rape of the soul" (R. C. Sproul, *Thy Brother's Keeper* [Brentwood, Tenn.: Wolgemuth & Hyatt, 1988], 58).

theology. He points out the weakness in some versions of Arminian theology insofar as election is supposedly turned into a human act. But after that Daane's position becomes unclear. Early in the book he criticizes Arminian theology for supposing that the sinner possesses the ability to reject God's elective choice.[15] But later on states himself that in his judgment the Bible teaches "he who rejects God, God rejects."[16] Daane really needs to make up his mind. Is the grace that saves sinners irresistible or not? If it is and not all are saved, it must be because it was not universally available, and this in turn raises a doubt about the universal decree of election, as both Daane (and Barth) want to interpret it. If the grace that saves sinners is resistible as Daane seems to believe, then he ought to stop criticizing Arminianism which has always stood up for this truth.

The point is this: if God's grace is truly intended for all sinners, and if all sinners are not in the end saved, it must be (there is no other possibility) that the grace of God in the gospel is resistible. Or to put it positively and more adequately, personal in character, so that the choice before mankind to choose between life and death is an eternally real one. This is of course the assumption underlying every such exhortation in Scripture. With regard to *predestination*, if a person believed that the concept of the divine plan and purpose entailed a smothering determinism in which everything that occurs takes place because God has decreed that it should, he would have to conclude that those who are saved and those who are lost are so as the result of God's ordination, and that the glorious message of God's free grace for all sinners is fundamentally misleading.

By a faulty understanding of predestination, many have faltered in their convictions about God's universal salvific will, with grievous results of every kind. Therefore, we present two important essays on this subject, one on predestination in the Old Testament by David J. A. Clines, and another on predestination in the New Testament by I. Howard Marshall. These essays by two prominent British biblical scholars should do much to correct our thinking on this important matter. We have referred already to *soteriological* predestination, the view of election first developed by Augustine that is part of a double predestination of human beings— either to eternal life or to eternal death. Such a view, as we noted, contradicts the biblical teaching about universal grace and precludes a sincere offer of the gospel to all men. Moreover, it represents God as unjustly partial and a respecter of persons, and describes him acting in a manner which would never be pleasing to

---

15. James Daane, *The Freedom of God: A Study of Election and the Pulpit* (Grand Rapids: Eerdmans, 1973), 15.

16. Ibid., 200.

God if we did it. We heartily reject this view of election, and rejoice that such an idea is not to be found in Holy Scripture.

Often associated with soteriological predestination in Calvinism is the notion of cosmic predestination as well. In an important essay entitled, "Predestination," B. B. Warfield speaks of cosmic and soteriological predestination as the two foci of the idea.[17] Everything that occurs in time and in eternity, from the falling of a stone to the torments of the damned, has been ordered and ordained by God's eternal decree. According to this view, in the words of Herman Hoeksema, the counsel of God is "the eternal reality of all things in God's conception, of which the creatures are but the revelation in time and space."[18] Such a notion, indistinguishable from fatalism, is inconsistent with human freedom and undermines the reality of history and man's moral responsibility. Worse still, it makes God the author of sin, since every act of rebellion, including the fall of Adam and since then was, as every event is, ordained in the secret counsels of God. It is with no small relief that we inform our readers of our conviction that Scripture teaches no such doctrine.

Although we can appreciate the concern of Classical Calvinism to call attention to the purpose of God being worked out in all of history, we must also emphasize the reality of the created order, and its relative autonomy. God can create such creatures as he pleases, and he has chosen in fact to give to man the power to love him freely, or to rebel and oppose his plan. Luke says that in their rejection of John's message, the Pharisees and the lawyers "rejected the purpose of God for themselves" (Luke 7:30). Does that sound shocking? Men actually have sufficient power and freedom (in certain instances) to oppose, and in a measure to frustrate, God's will! In one of Jesus's parables, a question was asked as to why tares appeared in the field alongside the wheat. The Master did not attribute their presence to the sovereign decree of God. He said simply, "An enemy has done this" (Matt 13:28). By creating a finite world in which there are personal wills other than his own, God made possible relationships between creatures and himself that are freely chosen and fully personal. Possible also is the misuse of freedom that has led historically to the sin of man and the fall of angels. In speaking of an

17. B. B. Warfield. *Biblical and Theological Studies* (Philadelphia: Presbyterian and Reformed, 1948), 270–333.

18. Herman Hoeksema, *Reformed Dogmatics* (Grand Rapids: Reformed Free, 1966), 155. It is amusing to find Boettner as he enumerates how widely spread belief in predetermination is, should find satisfaction in the fact that forms of fatalism have been held in heathen nations and secular deterministic theories in Western lands. For us, these associations are more likely to damn the theory! (Boettner, *Reformed Doctrine of Predestination*, 2)

"enemy," Jesus is acknowledging that events occur in the world which God does *not* will and actions which he will eventually punish. It is an understanding of the world completely incompatible with determinism.

The idea that God's will is something which is always and infallibly accomplished does not derive from biblical teaching. God's purpose according to Scripture is not a blueprint encompassing all future contingencies. It is a dynamic program for the world, the outworking of which depends in part upon man's decisions. When the term predestination is used in relation to salvation, it concerns the believer's future destiny which is to be conformed to Jesus Christ, not to his becoming be converted from nonbeliever to believer. We are "predestined" to be conformed to "the image of his Son" (Rom 8:29) and "to be adopted as his sons through Jesus Christ" (Eph 1:5). There is no predestination to salvation or damnation in the Bible. There is only a predestination for those who accept Christ in faith with respect to certain privileges out ahead of them. It means that God's will for those who have been redeemed is that they become adopted and will one day be conformed to Jesus Christ. It is a pity that a doctrine intended to communicate hope has been turned into such a fearful concept. The two essays by Marshall and Clines should do much to dispel the misconceptions of this doctrine and the fears associated with them.[19]

We believe that the majority of Christians recognize and believe the truth about the wideness of God's mercy and the generous offer of grace to all sinners, and do not embrace the malformed theological theories we find it necessary to oppose in this volume. It has become more and more common to run across "Calvinists without reserve," today especially the previously mentioned "young, restless and Reformed," a development we lament. However, we are compelled to admit that the Calvinistic tradition whose theology we are constrained to reject has placed a great value on systematic theological study and learning with the result that it has produced many works of highest quality, though more and more are coming out supporting our position as well.

Thus it is that the Calvinistic position on grace and salvation is becoming well known.[20] We have called forth this volume because of the need for

19. In addition to the twelve essays of a theological nature, we have included two historical articles, dealing with figures of great importance in connection with these subjects: Pinson's already-mentioned article on Arminius and Vic Reasoner on the history and theology of John Wesley.

20. Sadly, Calvinists have achieved a near monopoly on the terms "Reformed," and "Sovereignty of God." This need not be so. In particular, certain Arminians today term themselves "Reformation Arminians," taking the position that Arminius's doctrines were an alternate branch of Reformed theology. See Olson, *Arminian*

scholarly expositions of what we take to be the more biblical position. We hope in turn that its appearance will spark further research and writing until it will be possible for Christian people at large to have a fair opportunity to make an intelligent decision on these matters.

Theology and Picirilli, *Grace Faith Free Will*, both of which strongly argue this point, along with Pinson's article in this volume. Furthermore, Arminians completely accept the idea of God's sovereignty. See Marston and Forster, *God's Strategy in Human History*, and Jack Cottrell, *What the Bible Says About God the Ruler*, (Eugene, Ore.: Wipf and Stock, 2000).

1

Arminianism is God-Centered Theology

Roger Olson

One of the most common criticisms aimed at Arminianism by its opponents is that it is "man-centered theology."[1] One Reformed critic of Arminianism who frequently levels this charge is Michael Horton, Professor of Theology at Westminster Theological Seminary (Escondido campus) and editor of *Modern Reformation* magazine. I have engaged Horton in protracted conversations about Classical Arminianism and his and other Reformed critics' stereotypes of it, but to date he still says it is "man-centered."

Almost every article in the infamous special "Arminianism" issue of *Modern Reformation* repeats this caricature. Horton's is no exception. In his article "Evangelical Arminians," where he says "an evangelical cannot be an Arminian any more than an evangelical can be a Roman Catholic,"[2] the Westminster theologian and magazine editor also calls Arminianism "a human-centered message of human potential and relative divine impotence."[3]

Horton is hardly the only critic who has made this accusation against Arminianism. Several authors of articles in that same issue do the same thing. For example, Kim Riddlebarger, following B. B. Warfield, claims

---

1. I will occasionally use the gender-exclusive phrase because it is used so often by Arminianism's critics. It means, of course, "humanity-centered."

2. Michael Horton, "Evangelical Arminians" *Modern Reformation* 1 (May/June 1992): 18.

3. Ibid., 16.

that human freedom is the central premise of Arminianism, its "first principle" that governs everything else.[4] That is simply another way of saying it is "man-centered." Lutheran theologian Rick Ritchie lays the same charge against Arminianism in that issue as well.[5] And theologian Alan Maben quotes Charles Spurgeon as saying that "Arminianism [is] a natural, God-rejecting, self-exalting religion and heresy" and man is the principle figure in its landscape.[6]

Another evangelical theologian who accuses Arminianism of being man-centered is the late James Montgomery Boice, one of my own seminary professors. The late pastor of Tenth Presbyterian Church of Philadelphia wrote that under the influence of Arminianism, contemporary evangelical Christianity is "focused on ourselves and. . .[its adherents are] in love with their own supposed spiritual abilities."[7] According to him, Arminians cannot give glory to God alone and must reserve some glory for themselves because they believe the human will plays a role in salvation. He concludes "A person who thinks along these lines does not understand the utterly pervasive and thoroughly enslaving nature of human sin."[8]

Reformed theologian Sung Wook Chung of Korea, trained in theology at Princeton Theological Seminary, writes that Arminianism "exalts the autonomous power and sovereign will of human beings by denying God's absolute sovereignty and his free will. Arminianism also regards man as the center of the universe and the purpose of all things."[9] Southern Baptist Theological Seminary President Al Mohler writes in *The Coming Evangelical Crisis* about the "human-centered focus of the Arminian tradition."[10] In the same volume Gary Johnson calls Arminianism a "man-centered faith" and says that "When theology becomes anthropology, it becomes simply a form of worldliness."[11]

Perhaps the most sophisticated way of saying the same thing is provided by scholar of Protestant orthodoxy Richard Mueller[12] in his volume

---

4. Ibid., 23.

5. Ibid., 12.

6. Ibid., 21.

7. James Montgomery Boice, *Whatever Happened to the Gospel of Grace* (Wheaton: Crossway, 2001), 168.

8. Ibid., 167.

9. Sung Wook Chung, "Recovering God's Sovereign Grace: The Arminian Captivity of the Modern Evangelical Church," *Modern Reformation* 4 (Jan/Feb 1995): 2–3.

10. R. Kent Hughes, John H. Armstrong, eds., *The Coming Evangelical Crisis: Current Challenges to the Authority of Scripture and the Bible* (Chicago: Moody, 1997), 34.

11. Ibid., 63.

12. Richard Mueller, *God, Creation and Providence in the Thought of Jacob Arminius*

on Arminius. Mueller writes that "Arminius's thought evinces. . .a greater trust in nature and in the natural powers of man. . .than the theology of his Reformed contemporaries."[13] He goes on to accuse Arminius of confusing nature and grace and of placing creation at the center of theology to the neglect of redemption. He writes that Arminius tended "to understand creation as manifesting the ultimate purpose of God."[14] A close reading of Mueller's interpretation of Arminius's theology will reveal that he is charging it with being anthropocentric or man-centered rather than God-centered and focused on grace.

A close reading of Arminius, on the other hand, will reveal how wrong this assessment is. What do these and other critics mean when they accuse Arminianism of being "man-centered" or "human-centered?" And what would it mean for a theology to be God-centered as they claim theirs is? Especially in today's Calvinist resurgence of "young, restless, Reformed" Christians it's important to clarify these terms as one often hears it said, as a mantra, that non-Calvinist theologies are man-centered whereas Reformed theology is God-centered. Their main guru, John Piper, frequently talks about the "God-centeredness of God" and refers everything in creation and redemption to God's glory as the chief end. His implication, occasionally stated, is that Arminianism falls short of this high view of God. Too often without any consideration of what these appellations mean, today's new Calvinists toss them around as clichés and shibboleths. It seems that when critics of Arminianism accuse it of being man-centered, they mean primarily three things.

First, it focuses too much on human goodness and ability in the realm of redemption. That is, it does not take seriously enough the depravity of humanity and prizes the human contribution to salvation too much. Another way of putting that is that Arminian theology does not give God all the glory for salvation. Second, they mean that Arminianism limits God by suggesting that God's will can be thwarted by human decisions and actions. In other words, God's sovereignty and power are not taken sufficiently seriously. Third, they mean that Arminianism places too much emphasis on human fulfillment and happiness to the neglect of God's purpose which is to glorify himself in all things. Another way of expressing this is that Arminianism allegedly has a sentimental notion of God and humanity in which God's chief end is to make people happy and fulfilled.

(Grand Rapids: Baker, 1991).

13. Ibid., 233.

14. Ibid.

Certainly there is some truth in these criticisms, but their target is wrong when aimed at Classical Arminian theology. Unfortunately, all too seldom do the critics name any Arminian theologians or quote from Arminius himself to support these accusations. When they say "Arminianism" they seem to mean popular folk religion which is, admittedly, by and large semi-Pelagian. Some, most notably Horton, name nineteenth-century revivalist Charles Finney as the culprit in dragging American Christianity down into human-centered spirituality. Whether Finney is a good example of an Arminian is highly debatable. I agree with Horton and others that too much popular Christianity in America, including much that goes under the label "evangelical," is human-centered. I disagree with them, however, about Classical Arminianism, about which I suspect most of them know very little.

What would count as truly God-centered theology to these Reformed critics of Arminianism? First, human depravity must be emphasized as much as possible so that humans are not capable, even with supernatural, divine assistance, of cooperating with God's grace in salvation. In other words, grace must be irresistible. Another way of saying that is that God must overwhelm elect sinners and compel them to accept his mercy without any cooperation, even non-resistance, on their parts. This is part and parcel of high Calvinism, otherwise known as five-point Calvinism. According to Boice and others, theology is only God-centered if human decision plays no role whatsoever in salvation. The downside of this, of course, is that God's selection of some to salvation must be purely arbitrary and God must be depicted as actually willing the damnation of some significant portion of humanity that he could save because salvation in this scheme is absolutely unconditional. In other words, Calvinism may be God-centered, but the God at the center is morally ambiguous and unworthy of worship.

Second, apparently, for the Reformed critics of Arminianism, God-centered theology must view God as the all-determining reality including the one who ordains, designs, governs and controls sin and evil which are then imported into God's plan, purpose and will. God's perfect will is always being done, even when it paradoxically grieves him to see it (as John Piper likes to affirm). The only view of God's sovereignty that will satisfy these Reformed critics of Arminianism is meticulous providence in which God plans everything and renders it all certain down to the minutest decisions of creatures. Most notably this includes the Fall of humanity and all its consequences including the eternal suffering of sinners in hell. The downside of this, of course, is that the God at the center is, once again, morally ambiguous at best and a monster at worst.

Theologian David Bentley Hart expresses it thus: One should consider the price of this God-centeredness: "It requires us to believe in and love a God whose good ends will be realized not only in spite of—but entirely by way of—every cruelty, every fortuitous misery, every catastrophe, every betrayal, every sin the world has ever known; it requires us to believe in the eternal spiritual necessity of a child dying an agonizing death from diphtheria, of a young mother ravaged by cancer, of tens of thousands of Asians swallowed in an instant by the sea, of millions murdered in death camps and gulags and forced famines (and so on). It is a strange thing indeed to seek [God-centered theology]. . .at the cost of a God rendered morally loathsome."[15]

Third, to satisfy Arminianism's Reformed critics, God-centeredness requires that human beings are mere pawns in God's great scheme to glorify himself; their happiness and fulfillment cannot be mentioned as having any value for God. But this means, then, that one can hardly mention God's love for all people. One must first say with John Piper and others that God loves people because he loves himself and that Christ died for God more than for sinners. The down side of this is that the Bible talks much about God's love for people—in John 3:16 and numerous similar verses—and explicitly says that Christ died *for sinners* (Romans 5:8). While not canonical, early church father Irenaeus's saying that "The glory of God is man fully alive" ought to be considered to have some validity. Surely it is possible to have a God-centered theology without implying that people created in the image and likeness of God and loved by God so much that he sent his Son to die for them are of no value to God.

In fact, some Reformed theologians such as John Piper ironically do violate the third principle of God-centeredness as it is required by some critics of Arminianism. His so-called "Christian hedonism" says that human happiness and fulfillment *are* important to theology even if not to God. His mantra is "God is *most* glorified in us when we are *most* satisfied in him." In spite of this saying and his Christian hedonism, overall and in general Piper follows the typical Calvinist line of thinking that human happiness and fulfillment should be of little or no value compared with God's glory. Another down side of this, besides the Bible's emphasis on God's love and care for people, is the picture of God it delivers. In this theology, the God at the center is the ultimate narcissist, the greatest egoist who finds glory in displaying his naked power even to the point of consigning millions to hell just to manifest his attribute of justice.

---

15. David Bentley Hart, *The Doors of the Sea* (Grand Rapids: Eerdmans, 2005), 99.

The point of all this is simply this: It accomplishes very little to construct a God-centered theology if the God at its center is sheer, naked power
of ambiguous moral character. "Glory" is an ambiguous term. When di-
vorced from virtue it is unworthy of devotion. Many of the monarchs of
history have been "glorious" while at the same time being blood-thirsty and
cruel. True glory, the best glory, the right glory worthy of worship and honor
and devotion necessarily includes goodness. Power without goodness is not
truly glorious even if it is called that. What makes someone or something
worthy of veneration is not sheer might but goodness. Who is more worthy of imitation and even veneration, Mother Teresa or Adolf Hitler? The
latter conquered most of Europe. The former had little power outside of
her example. And yet, most people would say that Mother Teresa was more
"glorious" than Adolf Hitler. God is glorious because he is *both* great *and*
good and his goodness, like his greatness, must have some resonance with
our best and highest notions of goodness or else it is meaningless.

All that is to say that Arminianism's critics are the proverbial people
casting stones while living in glass houses. They talk endlessly about God's
glory and about God-centeredness while sucking the goodness out of God
and thus divesting him of real glory. Their theology may be God-centered
but the God at its center is unworthy of being the center. Better a man-
centered theology than one that revolves around a being hardly distinguishable from the devil.

In spite of objections to the contrary, I will argue that Classical Arminian theology is just as God-centered as Calvinism if not more so. The God
at its center, whose glory, to the contrary of critics' claims, is the chief end
or purpose of everything is not morally ambiguous. That is the main point
of Arminianism. Somehow Arminian theology has been stuck with the bad
reputation of believing most strongly in human freedom above all else. That
has never been true. Real Arminianism has always believed in human freedom for one main reason—to protect the goodness of God and thus God's
reputation in a world filled with evil. There is only one reason Classical Arminian theology emphasizes free will, but it has two sides. First, to protect
and defend God's goodness; second to make clear human responsibility for
sin and evil. It has nothing whatever to do with any humanistic desire for
creaturely autonomy or credit for salvation. It has never been about boasting
except in the goodness of the God who creates, rules and saves.

Why did Arminius reject and why do Classical Arminians reject Calvinism? Certainly not because it is God-centered. As I will demonstrate,
Arminius's own theology was fully God-centered in every sense. Arminius
and his followers rejected Calvinism because, as Arminius himself put it, it

is "repugnant to the nature of God."[16] How so? According to Arminius (and all Classical Arminians agree) Calvinism implies that "*God really sins.* Because (according to this doctrine), he moves to sin by an act that is unavoidable, and according to his own purpose and primary intention, without having received any previous inducement to such an act from any preceding sin or demerit in man."[17] Also, "From the same position we might also infer *that God is the only sinner.* For man, who is impelled by an irresistible force to commit sin (that is, to perpetrate some deed that has been prohibited), cannot be said to sin himself."[18] Finally, "As a legitimate consequence it also follows, *that sin is not sin,* since whatever that be which God does, it neither can be sin, nor ought any of his acts to receive that appellation."[19]

Anyone who has read John Wesley's sermons "On Free Grace" and "Predestination Calmly Considered" knows very well that he rejected Calvinism for the same reason given by Arminius before him. In the former sermon he described double predestination (which he rightly argued is necessarily implied by Classical Calvinist unconditional election) as "Such a blasphemy . . . as one would think might make the ears of a Christian tingle."[20] According to him, that doctrine "destroys all [God's] attributes at once" and "represents the most Holy God as worse than the devil, as both more false, more cruel, and more unjust."[21] In "Predestination Calmly Considered," Wesley rejected Calvinism for one reason only: not because it denied the free will of man but because it "overthrows the justice of God." He preached as if to a listening Calvinist "you suppose him [viz., God] to send them [viz., the reprobate] into eternal fire, for not escaping from sin! That is, in plain terms, for not having that grace which God had decreed they should never have! O strange justice! What a picture do you draw of the Judge of all the earth!"[22] Anyone who has read later Classical Arminians knows that their main reason for rejecting Calvinism is the same: it impugns the goodness of God and sullies God's reputation. It has nothing at

16. James Arminius, "A Declaration of Sentiments" *The Works of James Arminius,* (Grand Rapids: Baker, 1996 [These three volumes were originally published in London in 1825, 1828 and 1875 respectively], 1: 623.

17. Ibid., 630.

18. Ibid.

19. Ibid.

20. Robert Cochrane, ed., *The Treasury of British Eloquence* (Edinburgh: William P. Nimmo, 1881), 131.

21. Ibid.

22. John Wesley, *The Works of the Rev. John Wesley A.M.* (London: Wesleyan Conference Office, 1872), 221.

all to do with valuing human free will in and for itself and I challenge critics
to demonstrate otherwise.

To explain and defend Arminianism's God-centeredness let's begin
with the first issue mentioned above as a reason critics give for claiming that
Arminian theology is man-centered: the human condition and participation in salvation. Classical Arminian theology, defined by Arminius's own
thought and by the thoughts of his faithful followers, has always emphasized
human depravity just as strongly as Calvinism and it has always given all
the credit for salvation to God alone. Anyone who has read Arminius for
himself or herself cannot dispute this. The editor of *The Works of James
Arminius* says rightly that "Were any modern Arminian to avow the sentiments which Arminius himself has here maintained, he would be instantly
called *a Calvinist!*"[23]

In that context Arminius wrote about the human condition "under
the dominion of sin": "In this state, the Free Will of man towards the True
Good is not only wounded, maimed, infirm, bent, and. . .weakened; but
it is also. . .imprisoned, destroyed, and lost: And its powers are not only
debilitated and useless unless they be assisted by grace, but it has no powers
whatever except such as are excited by Divine grace."[24] Lest anyone misunderstand, he drives home his point saying of man that in the state of nature,
due to the fall, he is "altogether dead in sin."[25] This is not the only place in
his voluminous writings where Arminius describes the human condition
apart from supernatural grace this way. In virtually every essay, oration and
declaration he says the same and abundantly! There can be no doubt that
Arminius believed in total depravity every bit as much as do Calvinists.

What about free will? What about the human contribution to salvation? Did not Arminius attribute some good to the human person that
causes God to save him or her? I'll allow Arminius to speak for himself on
this matter also. Immediately after describing the divine cure for human
depravity, which is what is commonly known as "prevenient grace" which
awakens the person dead in sin to awareness of God's mercy, Arminius says
that even "the very first commencement of every good thing, so likewise
the progress, continuance and confirmation, nay even the perseverance
in good, are not from ourselves, but from God through the Holy Spirit."
This is not an isolated quote taken out of context. Everywhere, Arminius
constantly refers all good in man to God as its source and attributes every
impulse and capacity for good to grace. I cannot resist offering one more

---

23. Editor's notes, Arminius "Twenty-five Public Disputations," *Works* 2:189.

24. Ibid., 192.

25. Ibid., 194.

example. In his "A Letter Addressed to Hippolytus A Collibus" Arminius speaks of grace and free will:

> I confess that the mind of . . . a natural and carnal man is ob-
> scure and dark, that his affections are corrupt and inordinate,
> that his will is stubborn and disobedient, and that the man him-
> self is dead in sins. And I add to this, that teacher obtains my
> highest approbation who ascribes as much as possible to Divine
> Grace; provided he so pleads the cause of Grace as not to inflict
> an injury on the Justice of God, and not to take away *the free will
> to do that which is evil.*[26]

The context of this statement makes clear that Arminius's concern for free will is to avoid doing injury to God's goodness by making him the author of sin and evil. For him, human free will is always the cause of sin and evil and God is never their cause even indirectly. (Although, it should be noted that in his doctrine of providence Arminius affirms that a creature cannot do anything without God's permission and even concurrence.) This is the only reason he affirms free will.

What about later Arminians such as the Remonstrants? Sometimes critics of Arminianism allege that the true meaning of Arminianism is to be found in the theology of the Remonstrants who were Arminius's followers after his death. Of course, that is like saying the true meaning of Calvinism is to be found in the theology of the Reformed scholastics after Calvin. The truth is that both "Arminianism" and "Calvinism" must be defined by both their namesakes and their most faithful followers. I argue that true, Classical Arminian theology was always faithful to and consistent with Arminius's thought and vice versa. I have demonstrated that in one of my own books.[27]

The normative expression of Remonstrant theology may be found in *The Arminian Confession of 1621* written by Simon Episcopius, founder of the Remonstrant Seminary in Holland. In complete harmony with Ar- minius, the *Confession* affirms that the fallen human person is completely incapable of saving faith and that he or she is totally dependent on grace for any and every good. In the article on the creation of the world, angels and men it says (Confession 5.6), "whatever good [man] has, he owes all solidly to God and. . .he is obligated. . .to render and consecrate the same wholly to him."[28] As for the human condition, the *Confession* says of grace that "with-

26. Arminius, *Works*, 2: 700–701.

27. Roger Olson, *Arminian Theology: Myths and Realities* (Downers Grove: Inter-Varsity, 2006)

28. Mark A. Ellis, ed., *The Arminian Confession of 1621* (Eugene, Ore.: Wipf & Stock, 2005), 56.

out it we could neither shake off the miserable yoke of sin, nor do anything truly good in all religion, nor finally ever escape eternal death or any true punishment of sin. Much less could we at any time obtain eternal salvation without it or through ourselves."[29] There is nothing "man-centered" about this *Confession*. Later Remonstrants such as Philip Limborch, who fits Alan Sell's category of "Arminian of the head" as opposed to "Arminian of the heart," veered off toward a man-centered, semi-Pelagianism. But most Arminians followed the path of Arminius and Episcopius and Wesley and the nineteenth-century Methodist theologians such as Richard Watson who averred that even repentance is a gift of God.[30]

Anyone who reads these Classical Arminians with a hermeneutic of charity rather than a hermeneutic of suspicion and hostility cannot help but see their God-centeredness in emphasizing the absolute dependence of human persons on God's grace for everything good. All of them repeat this maxim frequently and attribute all of salvation from its beginning to end to God's supernatural grace. Of course, most Reformed critics will not be satisfied with this. They will still say, as does Boice, that if the sinner, however enabled by prevenient grace, makes a free choice to accept God's mercy unto salvation, that is man-centered rather than God-centered. All I can say is that this is ludicrous. The point Boice and other critics continually make is that in the Arminian system the saved person can boast because he or she did not resist God's grace and others did. All Arminian theologians from Arminius to Wesley to Wiley have pointed out that a person who receives a life-saving gift cannot boast if all he or she did was accept it. All the glory for such a gift goes to the giver and none to the receiver.

The second issue raised by critics of Arminianism has to do with God's alleged limitations and lack of sovereignty and power. Southern Baptist Theological Seminary president Al Mohler writes in *The Coming Evangelical Crisis* that "The Arminian God ultimately lacks omniscience, omnipotence, and transcendent sovereignty."[31] I argue that this objection carries no weight at all. Anyone who reads Arminius or his faithful followers, Classical Arminians, cannot come away with this impression. All emphasize the sovereignty of God over his creation including specific providence and all underscore God's power limited only by his goodness. What throws off Reformed (and perhaps other) critics is the underlying Arminian assumption of God's voluntary self-limitation in relation to humanity. However, that God lim-

---

29. Ibid., 68–69.

30. Richard Watson, *Theological Institutes, Or, a View of the Evidences, Doctrines, Morals and Institutions of Christianity* (New York: Lane & Scott, 1851), 99.

31. Hughes, Armstrong, *Coming Evangelical Crisis*, 34.

its himself by no means implies that he *is essentially limited*. According to Arminian theology God is sovereign over his sovereignty and his goodness conditions his power. Otherwise, he would be sheer naked power without character. As I argued earlier, that would make him unworthy of worship.

I will begin as before with Arminius himself. What did he believe about God's sovereignty and power? First, he rightly pointed out that, although he did affirm God's absolute dominion over creation, "The declaration of *dominion* has no glory by itself, unless it has been justly used."[32] In his "Private Disputations" and "Public Disputations," Arminius went to great lengths to affirm and endorse what is called classical Christian theism with all the traditional attributes attached to it including omnipotence and sovereignty. A stronger statement of God's incommunicable attributes could not be found anywhere. As for sovereignty, Arminius confessed that "Satan and wicked men not only cannot accomplish, but, indeed, cannot even commence anything except by God's permission."[33]

Even some Arminians might find some of Arminius's statements about God's sovereignty perplexing if not troubling. He attributed every power to God and denied that any creature has the ability to accomplish anything, including evil, independently of God. To critics who accused him of limiting God and exalting human autonomy, Arminius wrote: "I openly allow that God is the cause of all actions which are perpetrated by the creatures. But I merely require this, that that efficiency of God be so explained as that nothing whatever be derogated from the liberty of the creature, and that the guilt of sin itself be not transferred to God: that is, that it may be shown that God is indeed the *effector of the act*, but only the *permitter of the sin* itself; nay, that God is at the same time the effecter and permitter of one and the same act."[34]

This is an expression of Arminius's doctrine of divine concurrence in which the creature cannot act without God's permission and aid. God wills creaturely free will and therefore must reluctantly concur with creatures in their sinful acts because they cannot act independently of him. He does not, however, plan or propose or render certain any sin or evil.

To drive the point home further: In his "A Letter Addressed to Hippolytus A. Collibus" Arminius went to great lengths to affirm divine sovereignty, power and providential control over creation. He speculates that he was accused of holding "corrupt opinions respecting the Providence of

32. Arminius, "Examination of the Theses of Dr. Franciscus Gomarus Respecting Predestination," *Works*, 3:632.

33. Arminius, *Works*, 3:369.

34. Ibid., 415.

God" because he denied that "with respect to the decree of God, Adam nec-essarily sinned."[35] In other words, he rejected the typical Calvinist view that God foreordained and rendered certain Adam's sin. However, he averred that, in spite of his rejection of the necessity of Adam's fall, he did teach a strong and high view of God's providence:

"I most solicitously avoid two causes of offence, — that God be not proposed as the author of sin, — and that its liberty be not taken away from the human will: These are two points which if anyone knows how to avoid, he will think upon no act which I will not in that case most gladly allow to be ascribed to the Providence of God, provided a just regard be had to the divine pre-eminence."[36]

What is absolutely clear from the context is that his insistence that liberty be not taken away from the human will has only one motive—that God should not be proposed as the author of sin. He had no vested interest in human autonomy or free will for its own sake. His God-centeredness revolved around two foci: God's untarnished goodness and absolute crea-turely dependence on God for everything good. These cannot be missed as they appear on almost every page of his writings.

What about the Arminian Confession of 1621[37], the normative statement of Remonstrant belief after Arminius? Did it fall into human-centeredness as critics claim? In its chapter "On the providence of God, or his preservation and government of things," the Confession avers that "nothing happens anywhere in the entire world rashly or by chance, that is, God either not knowing, or ignoring, or idly observing it, much less looking on, still less altogether reluctantly even unwillingly and not even willing to permit it."[38] The practical conclusion of the doctrine of providence, the *Confession* affirms, is that the true believer "will always give thanks to God in prosperity, and in addition, in the future. . .freely and continuously place their greatest hope in God, their most faithful Father."[39]

As for God's omnipotence, the Confession says that God "is omnipo-tent, or of invincible and insuperable power, because he can do whatever he wills, even though all creatures be unwilling. Indeed he can always do more than he really wills, and therefore he can simply do whatever does not involve contradiction, that is, which are not necessarily and of themselves

35. Arminius, *Works*, 2:698
36. Ibid., 697–698.
37. Ellis, *The Arminian Confession of 1621*.
38. Ibid., 63.
39. Ibid.

repugnant to the truth of certain things, nor to his own divine nature."[40] What more can anyone ask of a doctrine of omnipotence? Oh, yes. . .certain Reformed critics can and so seem to ask for *divine omnicausality*. The problem with that, of course, is that it entangles God in evil. Again, the God at the center of that system is not worthy of being central to a belief system that values virtue and goodness. The fact is, that Arminius's and the Remonstrants's doctrines of God's sovereignty and power are as high and strong as possible short of making God the author of sin and evil.

What about later Arminians? Did they remain true to this high doctrine of God's supremacy in and over all things? While affirming everything Arminius and the early Remonstrants taught about this doctrine, including God's control over all things in creation, Richard Watson rightly cautioned that "the sovereignty of God is a Scriptural doctrine no one can deny; but it does not follow that the notions which men please to form of it should be received as scriptural."[41] For example, he avers that God could have prevented the fall of Adam and all its evil consequences but regarded it as better to allow it.[42] That God merely allowed it and did not foreordain or cause it is where Watson's doctrine of providence parts ways with the typical Reformed view. However, he rejects any notion that God is in any way the author of sin as incompatible with God's goodness.[43] The very fact that he affirms that God *could have prevented* the Fall points to his strong view of God's omnipotence and sovereignty. Again, in Watson, we see a subtle but definite assumption of God's voluntary self-limitation in order to keep the God who stands at the center of theology good and worthy of worship.

The upshot of all this so far is that Classical Arminian theology *does not* have a man-centered emphasis. Arminius's main concern was not to elevate humanity alongside or over God; no one can read him fairly and get that impression. His main concern was to elevate God's goodness alongside or even over God's power without in any way diminishing God's power. The way he accomplished that was by means of the idea of voluntary divine self-limitation—something he everywhere assumes and hints at without explicitly expounding. Reformed theologian Richard Mueller has rightly discovered and brought this element of Arminius's thought to light. He acknowledges the two equally important impulses in Arminius's thought: God's absolute right to exercise power and control and God's free limitation of his power for the sake of the integrity of creation:

40. Ibid., 48.

41. Watson, *Theological Institutes*, 442.

42. Ibid., 435.

43. Ibid., 429.

Both in the act of creation and in the establishment of covenant, God freely commits himself to the creature. God is not, in the first instance, in any way constrained to create, but does so only because of his own free inclination to communicate his goodness; nor is God in the second instance, constrained to offer man anything in return for obedience inasmuch as the act of creation implies a right and a power over the creature. Nonetheless, in both cases, the unconstrained performance of the act results in *the establishment of limits to the exercise of divine power.* Granting the act of creation, God cannot reprobate absolutely and without a cause in the creature; granting the initiation of covenant, God cannot remove or obviate his promises.[44]

The point is that any and all limitations of God's power and sovereign control to dispose of his creatures as he wills is self-imposed either by his nature or by his covenant promises. This hardly amounts to a man-centered theology! In fact, one could rightly argue that certain Reformed doctrines of the necessity of creation, including redemption and damnation, for the full manifestation of God's attributes and the full display of God's glory amount to a creation-centered theology that robs God of his freedom and makes the world necessary for God.

The third charge laid against Arminianism that allegedly demonstrates its man-centeredness is its focus on human happiness and fulfillment to the detriment of God's glory. Some Reformed theologians claim that Arminianism's God is a weak, sentimental God who exists to serve human needs and wants and that in Arminian theology man is made glorious at the expense of God's glory. This is nothing more than vicious calumny that needs to be exposed as such. It may be true of a great deal of American folk religion, but it has nothing whatever to do with Classical Arminian theology in which the chief end of all things is God's glory.

As always, I will begin with Arminius himself. Anyone who reads his "Private Disputations," his "Public Disputations" or his "Orations" cannot deny that he makes God's glory the ultimate purpose of everything including creation, providence, salvation, the church and the consummation. In his "Private Disputations" Arminius stated clearly that God is the cause of all blessedness *and* that the "end" of this blessedness is twofold: "(1.) a demonstration of the glorious wisdom, goodness, justice, power, and likewise the universal perfection of God; and (2.) his glorification by the beatified."[45] Lest anyone think that he makes God dependent on creation or creation necessary to God, Arminius declares in his "Apology or Defence" that everything God does *ad extra* is absolutely free, even his self-glorifi-

---

44. Mueller, *God, Creation, and Providence,* 243.

45. Arminius, *Works:* 2:321.

cation through creation and redemption: "God *freely* decreed to form the world, and did *freely* form it: And, in this sense, *all things are done contingently in respect to the Divine decree;* because no necessity exists why the decree of God should be appointed, since it proceeds from his own pure and free . . . will."[46] In other words, *only* Arminius's belief in libertarian freedom, both in God and creatures, protects the absolute contingency and therefore gratuitousness of creation. Which is more glorious? A God who creates to glorify himself absolutely freely or one who, like Jonathan Edwards's God, cannot do otherwise than he does?

It's difficult to know from which context to quote Arminius's numerous affirmations of the glory of God as the chief end of all his works. Here, however, is a typical example from his "Private Disputations" where he covers all the loci of theology and almost always concludes that everything in heaven and earth is for the glory of God. This one has to do with sanctification although his words are nearly identical with regard to justification and everything else God does. Sanctification, Arminius declares, "is a gracious act of God . . .[that] man may live the life of God, to the praise of the righteousness and of the glorious grace of God . . . ."[47] Then, also, "The End [purpose] is, that a believing man, being consecrated to God as a Priest and King, should serve Him in newness of life, to the glory of his divine name. . . ."[48] Similarly, the "end" of the church is "the glory of God"[49] and the "end" of the sacraments is "the glory of God"[50] and "The principle End [of worship] is, the glory of God and Christ. . . ."[51] In his "Public Disputations," Arminius repeats the pattern of describing everything blessed and good as God's work and its end or purpose as the glory of God.

Earlier, I said that Arminius *almost* always concludes that everything in heaven and earth is for the glory of God. There is *one* and *only one* exception. In his discussion of sin he concludes, specifically here with respect to the first sin, that "There was no End for this sin."[52] Man who sinned and the devil both proposed an end or purpose for it, but ultimately it could not have a purpose which would be to import it into God's will which would make it not sin. Rather, the first sin, like all sin, was absurd, something inexplicable—except by appeal to man's misuse of free will. However, God had

46. Ibid., 1:758.
47. Ibid., 2:408.
48. Ibid., 409.
49. Ibid., 412.
50. Ibid., 436.
51. Ibid., 447.
52. Ibid., 373.

an end in allowing it: "acts glorious to God, which might arise from it."[53] In other words, while sin does not glorify God, God's redemption of sinners does.

Time and space prohibit a lengthier and more detailed account of Arminius's emphasis on the glory of God as the chief end or purpose of every good in creation. All I can do is urge skeptics to read his "Orations" in *Works I* where he constantly repeats the refrain for "the glory of God and the salvation of men." Lest anyone think he puts these two ends on the same level of importance he says in *Oration II* that all salvation has the single purpose that "we might sing God's praises to him forever."[54]

One finds no hint anywhere in Arminius of any concern for human autonomy for its own sake. Arminius's only reason for affirming libertarian free will is to disconnect sin from God and make the sinner solely responsible for it. His one overriding concern is for God's glory in all things. There can be no doubt that he would agree wholeheartedly with the answer to the first question of the *Westminster Shorter Catechism*: "What is the chief end of man?" "The chief end of man is to glorify God and enjoy him forever."

Space prohibits me from citing a litany of Arminian affirmations of the glory of God after Arminius. Suffice it to say that all Classical Arminians have always agreed with Arminius about this matter. I challenge critics of Armininism to display one example of a Classical Arminian theologian who has elevated humanity to an end in itself or in any way made God's chief end the glory of man. It doesn't exist.

I conclude with this observation. The difference between Arminian and Calvinist theologies does not lie in man-centeredness versus God-centeredness. True Arminianism is as thoroughly God-centered as Calvinism. A fair reading of Classical Arminian theologians from Arminius to Thomas Oden cannot avoid finding in them a ringing endorsement of the God-centeredness of all creation and redemption. The difference, rather, lies in the nature and character of the God who stands at the centers of these two systems.

The God who stands at the center of classical, high Calvinism of the TULIP variety is a morally ambiguous being of power and control who is hardly distinguishable from the devil. The devil wants all people to go to hell whereas the God of Calvinism wants some, perhaps most, people to go to hell. The devil is God's instrument in wreaking havoc and horror in the world—for God's glory. The God who stands at the center of Classical Arminianism is the God of Jesus Christ, full of love and compassion as well

53. Ibid.

54. Ibid., 1:372.

as justice and wrath who voluntarily limits his power to allow creaturely rebellion but is nevertheless the source of all good for whose glory and honor everything except sin exists.

2

God's Universal Salvific Grace

Vernon C. Grounds

Behind, beneath, beyond, and yet within the evanescent phenomena of space-time, we Christians believe, is God—the ultimate reality, the eternal, infinite, perfect, self-subsistent being—a trinity of three persons all of whom cohere in an indivisible unity of essence and purpose. God, we believe, is the source and sustainer of whatever exists, the life in all life, the truth in all truth, the goodness in all goodness, the beauty in all beauty, the love in all love.

For in that corpus of writings we call the Holy Scriptures and which we hold to be God's medium of self-revelation, this being behind and beneath and beyond and yet within all being defines himself as love. Hence we further believe that in the unending process of self-impartation and self-communication of his triune fellowship, God must be the embodiment of unending beatitude. All of this is for his glory.

We believe, moreover, that because he is love, God freely chooses to expand the orbit of beatitude by creating persons who are centers of consciousness and choice whom he wills to share his own eternal fellowship of love through the convicting, drawing, and salvation of God's grace. This purpose, inexplicable except on the ground of God's free decision, is announced by Paul at the beginning of his Ephesian letter:

> Grace be to you, and peace, from God our Father, and from the
> Lord Jesus Christ. Blessed be the God and Father of our Lord

Jesus Christ, who hath blessed us with all spiritual blessings in
heavenly places in Christ: according as he hath chosen us in him
before the foundation of the world, that we should be holy and
without blame before him in love; having predestinated us unto
the adoption of children by Jesus Christ to himself, according
to the good pleasure of his will, to the praise of the glory of
his grace, wherein he hath made us accepted in the beloved: in
whom we have redemption through his blood, the forgiveness
of sins, according to the riches of his grace; wherein he hath
abounded toward us in all wisdom and prudence; having made
known unto us the mystery of his will, according to his good
pleasure which he hath purposed in himself: that in the dispen-
sation of the fullness of times he might gather together in one
all things in Christ, both which are in heaven, and which are
on earth; even in him: in whom also we have obtained an inheritance, being predestinated according to the purpose of him
who worketh all things after the counsel of his own will: that we
should be to the praise of his glory, who first trusted in Christ.
(Eph 1:2–12)

This purpose, explicable solely on the inexplicable ground of God's
grace and focusing in Jesus Christ, is the *raison d'etre* of everything in nature
and history. As Samuel Mikolaski says:

Put into a real definition, God's purpose is the creation of free
men who will experience the bliss of divine fellowship and service. The creation narrative of Genesis teaches that man lost this
freedom through sin, but the promise of grace in both Testaments is the restoration of freedom by redemption and forgiveness. God intends that man shall share with Him a common
life, spirit, and aim. Grace means that God is determined to
accomplish His good and righteous purpose.[1]

Motivated by grace, then, freely electing to share his experience of infinite
love with finite experients, God has created *ex nihilo* all that is. Grace is
thus the revealed explanation of the whole space-time complex. The act of
creation, like everything the triune God does, James Daane reminds us, has
grace as its dynamic.

If we regard it from the point of view of the reality of God, the
creation of the world is an amazing decision. God is God alone.
Beside him there is none else. He necessarily exists. He needs
nothing. The creation of finite, contingent, unnecessary reality,

1. Samuel J. Mikolaski, *The Grace of God* (Grand Rapids: Eerdmans, 1966), 96.

then, in order that man, who is not God, might share in, know, love, and live with God, staggers the human mind. The truth of creation evades man's every rational attempt to comprehend. Philosophy may try to eliminate our sense of wonder at this; science may do the same by dissolving all the mystery of the universe. But true religion begins with wonder and never loses it. For creation is the wonder of God, the new and novel surprise of his freedom to extend and share his love —that is, to share himself.[2]

History, too, which from the biblical perspective pivots on the incarnation of God in Jesus Christ, has grace as its dynamic. In fact, from the biblical perspective, all the events occurring anywhere and everywhere, no matter when, are teleologically related to the Christ event. Daane again helps us to appreciate the significance of what we may be in danger of overlooking:

Nowhere is God's freedom more fully expressed than in his resolve to become himself historical, a man existing in space and time in Jesus Christ, and in his Son to become involved in a world of sin and death, and through death to conquer and eliminate sin and death. God is so free that he can, in order to achieve the intention that man know him, love him, and live with him in eternal blessedness, deliver his own Son to the power of sin and death. God is so free that he can elect his own Son for the cross so that, in spite of all man's sin and evil, man may still share God's eternal life, beauty, glory, and joy.[3] Or in the complementary words of Karl Rahner: grace is not simply the intermittent chance of salvation of an individualist kind granted to a few only and restricted in time and place, but that it is ultimately the dynamism of all human history everywhere and always, and indeed of the world generally, even though it remains a question put to the free decision of each and every individual.[4]

Yet what is grace, anyway, this dynamic of all God's action? How can it be explicated? To set forth its quintessence we must put it over against sin, man's defiant misuse of his finite freedom which has estranged him from God and now renders him liable to divine judgment. Sin has negated any claim which as a creature he might have levied on the Creator's blessing. Grace, therefore, stands in antithesis to sin. It is God's utterly inscrutable

2. James Daane, *The Freedom of God* (Grand Rapids: Eerdmans, 1973), 171.

3. Ibid., 111.

4. Karl Rahner, *The Christian of the Future* (London: Burns and Oates, 1967), 96.

attitude of mercy and kindness which motivates His self-sacrifice in Jesus Christ, a redemptive action for which no reason can be assigned. Contradicting and nullifying all norms of logic and justice, grace offers forgiveness and reconciliation where wrath and exile are properly merited.

Notice a text like Rom 3:23, "For all have sinned, and come short of the glory of God." Notice also a text like Rom 4:4, "Now to him that worketh is the reward not reckoned of grace, but of debt." Notice once more a text like Eph 2:8–9, "For by grace are ye saved through faith; and that not of yourselves: it is the gift of God: not of works, lest any man should boast." Grace, then, viewed negatively, baffles reason totally and completely. Viewed positively, however, it is the omnipotent help which God in His freedom chooses to give through Jesus Christ and by his Spirit, liberating man from his self-incurred bondage and misery, reestablishing a right relationship with himself. "The first and primary meaning of grace," says Mikolaski,

> is the generous love of God, His goodwill, lovingkindness, or favor, by which His blessings are bestowed on mankind and a new era opened. *God's grace is His unmerited favor by which He saves an unworthy world.*[5]

Grace, consequently, must not be regarded as if it were some impersonal entity, akin to a force or a fluid, operating apart from God. Rather, grace is God redemptively in action through Jesus Christ and by His Holy Spirit. Personal through and through, grace, let it be repeated, is God acting. John 1:14 stresses the Christocentric personalism of grace: "And the Word was made flesh, and dwelt among us, (and we beheld his glory, the glory as of the only begotten of the Father,) full of grace and truth."

Acts 15:11 carries the same stress, "But we believe that through the grace of the Lord Jesus Christ we shall be saved, even as they." And this stress on Christocentric personalism is repeated in 2 Cor 8:9, "For ye know the grace of our Lord Jesus Christ, that, though he was rich, yet for your sakes he became poor, that ye through his poverty might be rich." Karl Rahner is therefore correct when he affirms that

> Grace is God himself, his communication, in which he gives himself to us as the divinizing loving kindness which is himself. Here his work is really *himself*, as the one communicated. From the very first this grace cannot be conceived as separable from God's personal love and man's answer to it. This grace must not be thought of "materialistically"; it is only put "at man's disposal"

---

5. Mikolaski, *The Grace of God*, 49.

by letting itself be used as is the way with the freest grace of all, the miracle of love.[6]

Grace, which is God freely, lovingly and savingly at work in the lives of fallen and self-frustrated human beings, has existential effects which cannot be psychologically analyzed: God working through Jesus Christ and by his Holy Spirit enables a man to be and do what otherwise tantalizes him as merely an impossible possibility. Paul, for example, bears this witness in 1 Cor 15:10, "By the grace of God I am what I am: and his grace which was bestowed upon me was not in vain: but I laboured more abundantly than they all: yet not I but the grace of God which was with me."

In Eph 3:8 the same apostle disclaims any credit for the success of his ministry, attributing his effectiveness entirely to grace: "Unto me, who am less than the least of all saints, is this grace given, that I should preach among the Gentiles the unsearchable riches of Christ." So Paul would no doubt have endorsed the comment made by W. H. Griffith-Thomas: "Grace is, first, a quality of graciousness in the Giver, and then, a quality of gratitude in the recipient, which in turn makes him gracious to those around."[7] Concerning the nature of grace, then, there is a fairly broad consensus among Christians of all theological alignments. But when its outworking and outreach are under discussion, heated disagreement flares up.

Theologians who align themselves with John Calvin, proudly naming fourth-century Saint Augustine and others such as twenty-first century R. C. Sproul as representative spokesmen, contend that divine grace, though unlimited in its sufficiency, is nevertheless limited in its efficiency—and limited by God himself. According to this major tradition in Christian thought, grace does not universally and indiscriminately provide every human being with an opportunity for a redemptive relationship to God that includes the forgiveness of sin and the promise of eternal beatitude.

Instead, as Calvinistically interpreted, grace in its effective outworking and outreach avails only for elect individuals, those human beings whom God in his sovereignty has predestined from all eternity to be the recipients of his mercy. Whatever linguistic and logical *legerdemain* is employed to mitigate the inescapable corollaries of this position, it maintains that non-elect individuals are outside the orbit of God's effective grace. Extreme in his statement of the Calvinist position, Herman Hoeksema, until his death the foremost theologian of the Protestant Reformed Churches, uncompromisingly developed the implications of the Canons of Dordt (such at least was his self-appraisal):

6. Karl Rahner, *Nature and Grace* (New York: Sheed & Ward, 1964), 128.

7. Quoted by Mikolaski, *The Grace of God*, 42.

God loves the elect because they are righteous in Christ; he hates the reprobate because they are sinners. The elect alone are the object of grace; for them alone the gospel is good news. For the reprobate God has no blessing at all, but only an eternal hatred. Rain and sunshine, the hearing of the gospel, the sacrament of baptism (if administered to a person as an infant)— all are curses heaped on the reprobate.[8]

Other theologians of what Daane calls the decretal school, adhering as they do to some formulation of an alleged *gestalt* of destiny-determining divine decrees, urge

that God is the ultimate cause and the primary source of sin, that the function of the proclamation of the gospel is to make some men ripe for judgment; that God created sin. . .; that God takes pleasure in the death of sinners; that preaching is *per se* a curse for the reprobate; that every thing that occurs is a divine wish—fulfillment, for if anything were to occur contrary to what God wills, God would not be sovereign but a godling who had created more world than he can take care of. . . .[9]

Daane, himself a Calvinist, has so justly excoriated this position that he deserves to be heard at length:

How pervasively this view has penetrated and shaped Reformed theology! Here is the theological bottomland from which has arisen what is often regarded as the correct Reformed understanding of God's immutability and of sovereignty. Here is the source of the assertion that God is the cause and source of sin, yet not responsible for it. Here is the root of an unconditional theology that not only rightly rejects Arminian theology (although with wrongly formulated reasons) but which also insists that God is so imperturbable that he is not free to be moved with compasssion for the plight of man. Here is the origin of the position that reprobation is ultimately not an act of divine justice *in response* to sin, but something that has its ground in God himself. Here arises Reformed theology's tendency to cast a threatening shadow over all reality.[10]

Despite the wide acceptance of this position, especially among contemporary evangelicals, it quite flatly contradicts the overwhelming testimony of

8. Quoted by Daane, *The Freedom of God*, 24.

9. Ibid., 79.

10. Ibid., 160.

Scripture to the universality of God's salvific grace. A mere *catena* of passages discloses the fact, for fact it is, that the divine purpose in Jesus Christ embraces not a segment of the human family but the race *en toto*:

> Behold the Lamb of God, which taketh away the sin of the world (John 1:29). For God so loved the world, that he gave his only begotten Son, that whosoever believeth in him should not perish, but have everlasting life (John 3:16). For if by one man's offence death reigned by one; much more they which receive abundance of grace and of the gift of righteousness shall reign in life by one, Jesus Christ. Therefore, as by the offence of one judgment came upon all men to condemnation; even so by the righteousness of one the free gift came upon all men unto justification of life. For as by one man's disobedience many were made sinners, so by the obedience of one shall many be made righteous. Moreover the law entered, that the offence might abound. But where sin abounded, grace did much more abound: That as sin hath reigned unto death, even so might grace reign through righteousness unto eternal life by Jesus Christ our Lord (Rom 5:17–21).

(Note the repetition of the phrase "much more" which asymmetrically outbalances the ruin of humanity in Adam by the race's redemption in Christ. Since all humanity came under judgment in Adam, all humanity must come into at least the possibility of eternal life through Christ.)

> For God hath concluded them all in unbelief, that he might have mercy upon all (Rom 11:32). Who gave himself a ransom for all, to be testified in due time (1 Tim 2:6). But we see Jesus, who was made a little lower than the angels for the suffering of death, crowned with glory and honour; that he by the grace of God should taste death for every man (Heb 2:9). The Lord is not slack concerning his promise, as some men count slackness; but is longsuffering to us-ward, not willing that any should perish, but that all should come to repentance (2 Pet 3:9). And he is the propitiation for our sins: and not for ours only, but also for the sins of the whole world (1 John 2:2).

It takes an exegetical ingenuity which is something other than a learned virtuosity to evacuate these texts of their obvious meaning; it takes an exegetical ingenuity verging on sophistry to deny their explicit universality. A Protestant may—no, must!—criticize Karl Rahner sharply for many of the views which he ingeniously espouses. But a Protestant—in other words, a Biblicist—can applaud Rahner's insistence on the all-inclusiveness of grace. So one finds himself wishing that decretal theologians might catch a glimpse of the vision that enthralls Rahner and which ought, eliminating Rahner's dogmatic mirages, likewise enthrall every Biblicist:

> If we wish to be Christians, we must profess belief in the universal and serious salvific purpose of God towards all men which is true even within the post-paradisean phase of salvation dominated by original sin. We know, to be sure, that this proposition of faith does not say anything certain about the *individual* salvation of man understood as something which has in fact been reached. But God desires the salvation of everyone. And this salvation willed by God is the salvation won by Christ, the salvation of supernatural grace which divinizes man, the salvation of the beatific vision. It is a salvation really intended for all those millions upon millions of men who lived perhaps a million years before Christ —and also for those who have lived after Christ— in nations, cultures and epochs of a very wide range which were still completely shut off from the viewpoint of those living in the light of the New Testament.[11]

And if redemptive particularism be argued against redemptive universalism, the argument loses its cogency in the light of a principle which runs throughout Scripture: redemptive particularism subserves the ends of redemptive universalism. Thus E. Y. Mullins, discussing God's loving purpose for the race, rightly maintains that Abraham's election and through him Israel's election were not individual or national hut racial in their ultimate design. God, Mullins writes,

> had in view not one family or nation, but the whole of mankind. There were chosen families and a chosen nation. But these were not only ends in themselves, they were also means toward a larger end. At one crisis in the world's history Noah and his family were chosen as the channel of God's blessing to mankind. Later God chose Abraham, whose descendants became the nation of Israel. God's promise to Abraham was the disclosure of his purpose toward mankind: "I will make of thee a great nation, and I will bless thee and make thy name great; and be thou a blessing; and I will bless them that bless thee, and him that curseth thee will I curse; and in thee shall all the families of the earth be blessed" (Gen 12:2, 3). This promise was repeated to Abraham many times in substantially the same form. We do

---

11. Karl Rahner, *Theological Investigations* (London: Darton, Longman and Todd, 1966), 5: 122–123.

not rightly understand the calling of Abraham unless we see in him the manifestation of God's world-wide purpose of grace.[12]

The universality of grace, it must be made clear, does not mean universalism! It means merely that God is at work in Jesus Christ and by his Holy Spirit sovereignly and sincerely —yes, and seriously, as Rahner points out—providing the potential of salvation for every human being. But that potential depends for its actualization on a believing response. Kenneth J. Foreman, a Presbyterian and thus a Calvinist, has said emphatically what needs to be said:

> On God's side, all barriers were down. There was nothing else that even God could do to restore the broken bond. Nothing else? One thing only: to force man's will, compel his assent, reconcile him against his will. One thing—but God would not do it. He would not treat man like a tree trunk or a rock. Not a single writer in the New Testament, not a converted person depicted on its pages, thinks of his conversion as of a tidal wave that washed him ashore without his choice or against his will. Paul, in whose case the hand of God was clearly in evidence, said years later to King Agrippa: "I was not disobedient to the heavenly vision." The vision was a bolt from the blue; it had the effect of an attack with a deadly weapon. Yet in retrospect, Paul can speak of it as something to which he could have been disobedient. Peter's sermon at Pentecost addresses persons whom he later describes as "born anew" (1 Peter 1:3), but he does not address them there in Jerusalem as logs and rocks. The very fact that the Christians used the words *kerygma, kerusso, euangelion*, to describe their missionary efforts, suggests that the news could be understood, the heralding heeded. But it was more than an announcement, it was a summons. "God. . . commands all men everywhere to repent" (Acts 17:30). . . If it be objected that this leaves too much to man's decision, we can only say that to control man as one would a log or a rock is to treat him as something less than a man, and this God does not do. God deals personally with personal beings, as Dr. Oman laid it out so beautifully years ago. Grace that left no option whatever would not be grace, it would be something else. We should have to say. By force were ye saved, and not of yourselves.[13]

---

12. Edgar Mullins, *The Christian Religion in Its Doctrinal Expression* (Philadelphia: Judson, 1917), 340–341.

13. Kenneth Foreman, *Identification: Human and Divine* (Richmond: John Knox , 1963), 116–117.

That the truth of universal grace—"all of grace and grace for all"—is shot through with mystery, we unhesitatingly confess. It needs to be safeguarded against the dangers of semi-Pelagianism and the hazards of a modified Arminianism that John Wesley would repudiate; it needs to be safeguarded as well against the enticements of the universalism to which Karl Barth nearly succumbs. It needs, moreover, to be rethought and resystematized if it is to function as a corrective of the sub-biblical decretalism which largely dominates evangelicalism today.

The truth of God's universal grace needs to be proclaimed with adoring fervor, a grace that springs from a love which cannot be limited temporally (Matt 28:20), geographically (Mark 16:15), racially, religiously, economically, sexually (Gal 3:28), or culturally (Rom 1:16), a love which has no limits except the limits which unbelief imposes. It is this universal salvific grace, which, if preached in the Spirit's power, may bring in our time another evangelical awakening like that which had John Wesley as its herald. And if and as it does, Charles Wesley's hymn "Free Grace" will once more express the praise of a church set free by grace from any view of grace that would make grace less inclusive than God's all-inclusive love.

> Come let us join our friends above.
> The God of our salvation praise,
> The God of everlasting love.
> The God of universal grace.
>
> 'Tis not by works that we have done;
> 'Twas grace alone His heart inclined.
> 'Twas grace that give His only Son
> To taste of death for all mankind.
>
> For every man He tasted death;
> And hence we in His sight appear.
> Not lifting up our eyes beneath,
> But publishing His mercy here.
>
> By grace we draw our every breath;
> By grace we live, and move, and are;
> By grace we 'scape the second death;
> By grace we now Thy grace declare.
>
> From the first feeble thought of good
> To when the perfect grace is given,
> 'Tis all of grace; by grace renew'd
> From hell we pass through earth to heaven.
>
> We need no reprobates to prove

That grace, free grace, is truly free;
Who cannot see that God is love,
Open your eyes and look on me;

On us, whom Jesus hath call'd forth
To assert that all His grace may have.
To vindicate His passion's worth
Enough ten thousand world's to save.[14]

14. Mildred Wynkoop, *A Theology of Love* (Kansas City, Mo.: Beacon Hill, 1972), 93.

3

Calvinism and Problematic Readings of New Testament Texts Or, Why I Am Not a Calvinist

Glen Shellrude

Theological determinism affirms that everything that happens does so because God has ordained it to happen that way.[1] Augustine introduced this concept into Christian theology, though determinism is more commonly identified with John Calvin and the tradition of Reformed theology that he initiated.[2] For many, Calvinism is associated primarily with the doctrines

1. In the words of the Westminster Confession (1646): "God from all eternity, did, by the most wise and holy counsel of His own will, freely, and unchangeably ordain whatsoever comes to pass; yet so, as thereby neither is God the author of sin, nor is violence offered to the will of the creatures; nor is the liberty or contingency of second causes taken away, but rather established." If everything that happens does so because God has ordained it to happen that way, then it follows that not only has God ordained the eternal suffering of most of those he created, but in the present world God has, through the mechanics of second causes, choreographed down to the smallest detail every murder, every rape, every genocide, every act of child abuse, every famine, every serial killing, every instance of child prostitution, every terrorist atrocity, every expression of racism, every addiction, every sin.

2. Cf. Robert Peterson, Michael Williams. *Why I Am Not An Arminian* (Downers Grove, Ill.: InterVarsity, 2004), 141. John Feinberg, "God Ordains All Things" in David Basinger, Randall Basinger, eds., *Predestination and Free Will: Four Views on Divine Sovereignty and Human Freedom* (Downers Grove: InterVarsity, 1986), 19–43;

of election and perseverance. Election is understood as God's selection of a subset of humanity for salvation and only those elected can respond to the Gospel. Those selected for salvation will necessarily persevere in the faith and therefore cannot commit apostasy. However Calvinism also affirms a theology of "specific sovereignty," i.e. everything that happens does so because God has choreographed it to happen that way. As Peterson and Williams put it, God ordains everything down to "the trajectory of the smallest raindrop."[3] Calvinism must deny that people have any free will ("libertarian freedom") as this would mean that choices could be made which run counter to what God has ordained for them at every moment. Instead, Calvinists work with the concept of "compatibilistic freedom," meaning that people will always willingly make the choices which God ordains that they make.

Many lay Calvinists prefer to say that God "permits" evil rather than "ordains" it. It feels better to say that while God intentionally wills what is good, he reluctantly permits many evils.[4] However, mainstream Calvinist theologians do not take this view and Calvin himself was critical of those who used this language: ". . .how foolish and frail is the support of divine justice afforded by the suggestion that evils come to be, not by His will but by His permission. . .It is a quite frivolous refuge to say that God indirectly permits them, when Scripture shows Him not only willing, but the author of them. . . .it is quite clear from the evidence of Scripture that God works in the hearts of men to incline their wills just as he will, whether to good. . .or to evil. . . ."[5]

Paul Helm, "Classical Calvinist Doctrine of God" in Bruce Ware, ed. *Perspectives on the Doctrine of God: Four Views* (Downers Grove: InterVarsity, 2008), 5–52; Bruce Ware, "A Modified Calvinist Doctrine of God," in *Perspectives on the Doctrine of God*, 76–120.

3. Peterson and Williams, *Not An Arminian*, 141. As expressed by the Westminster Confession, Calvinists do not believe that God is the immediate cause of sin and evil but instead argue that God works through "second causes" to ordain sin and evil. Thus, for example, if God wants someone to become a serial killer, he will bring influences to bear on the person so that they will willingly and without any direct coercive prompting from God become a serial killer.

4. Some Calvinist theologians do use the language of "permission" as a way of saying that God works through secondary causes when he scripts evil events. However, they still believe that God intentionally wills that these evils occur and it is not a matter of reluctant permission.

5. John Calvin, *Concerning the Eternal Predestination of God*, J.K.S. Reid, trans. (Louisville: Westminster John Knox, [1552]1961), 176–177. A theological axiom undergirding Calvinist theology is that God's grace is always irresistible. This has a much broader application then the irresistible character of grace with respect salvation and perseverance. It applies to every moment of the life of every person, believer and unbeliever. Many lay Christians who identify themselves as Calvinists appear to be "cafeteria Calvinists," believing that the grace which enables salvation and perseverance is irresistible while in the daily outworking of the Christian life they have some degree

Calvinist theologians and New Testament scholars commonly develop their theology in relation to those texts which speak to the issues of salvation and perseverance. They rarely discuss the implication of a deterministic theological framework for the interpretation of other New Testament texts. This paper will explore some of the implications for reading a whole range of texts within the framework of theological determinism.[6]

Many Christians who think of themselves as Calvinists will protest my descriptions of Calvinist interpretations of New Testament texts and say that is not what they believe. In effect, they assume that in the daily outworking of the Christian life they have free will. However, no Calvinist theologians take this view and they acknowledge that I am correctly representing the consequences of mainstream Calvinist theology for reading various types of material in the New Testament. Many Christians selectively embrace those ideas which they like, e.g. 1. that they are one of the privileged elect; 2. that they cannot lose their salvation; 3. as long as things are going well, God has ordained all the good things that happen to them. However, consistent Calvinist theology affirms much more than this and to that I now turn.

MORAL EXHORTATIONS IN THE NEW TESTAMENT

Every text in the New Testament contains a wealth of moral exhortations as to how God's people are to live, e.g. remain committed to their marriages (e.g. Matt 5:31–32), forgive those who wrong them (e.g. Matt 6:14–15), be other focused rather then self centered (Phil 2:1–4), love and care for their wives (e.g. Eph 5:25–33), live worthy of the Gospel (e.g. Phil 1:27), resist sin (e.g. Rom 6:12). These moral exhortations are comprehensible on the assumption that God has gifted his people with libertarian freedom and extends the grace that enables them to obey. God's people are challenged to respond to God's grace by daily striving to live obediently.

If these exhortations are read within the framework of theological determinism, then the implication is that the extent of the believer's obedience

---

of free will. However no Calvinist theologians take this view.

6. Roger Olson, *Against Calvinism* (Grand Rapids: Zondervan, 2011), is now the single best critique of Calvinist theology. Jerry Walls and Joseph Dongell, *Why I Am Not A Calvinist* (Downers Grove/Leicester: InterVarsity, 2004), is also exceptional. Cf. Roger Olson, "The Classical Free Will Theist Model of God" in *Perspectives on the Doctrine of God*, 148–172, for an excellent summary of a theological framework that affirms libertarian freedom. As Olson points out, Arminian-Wesleyans do not believe that we have "absolute" free will in that there are a range of forces that shape and influence our will: e.g. our sinful humanity; culture and our personal biography; the work of God in a person's life (151).

is determined by what God has ordained for them at any moment; it is never by the person in his exercise of the gift of grace-empowered libertarian freedom. Since God's grace is always "irresistible," when Christians sin it is ultimately because God withheld the grace that would have enabled obedience.[7] When Christians divorce their spouses, refuse to forgive, are self-centered, give in to temptation, bring shame on the Gospel, and abuse their wives or children, then the explanation must be that in these instances God has withheld the grace enabling obedience to the moral exhortations of Scripture because he wanted these sins to be committed.[8]

It would appear that the positive function of moral exhortations is to inform believers what obedience will look like in those times when God ordains that they will be obedient. In those times when God withholds the grace that would enable obedience, the moral exhortations function as an indictment on the behavior which God ordains. The necessary implication is that God exhorts believers to obedience while simultaneously withholding the grace that would enable obedience in those situations where Christian obedience would result in outcomes which run counter to what God has determined should happen. Or, to put it another way, if Christian obedience resulted in an outcome that God did not ordain, e.g. that a marriage remain intact, then God would withhold the grace that would enable obedience, with the result that in this example he would render the divorce certain. These conclusions are necessary deductions from the Calvinist view that God ordains everything that happens and that God's grace is always irresistible. As Williams and Peterson put it, "God sovereignly directs and ordains . . . our *sinful acts* as well as the good that we do."[9]

---

7. Terrance Tiessen, *Who Can Be Saved?* (Downers Grove: InterVarsity, 2004), 230–258, makes a distinction between "sufficient grace" and "effective grace." When applied to God's work in the life of the believer, "effective grace" is for those times when obedience is the desired outcome. When God ordains that the believer sins, he only extends "sufficient grace" so that the believer can be held accountable for her disobedience. However, if God intentionally withholds the grace which would enable obedience so as to render the sin certain, it is problematic to call this "sufficient grace."

8. To take another set of examples, when Christians grieve the Spirit (Eph 4:30), lack moral discernment (Phil 1:10; Rom 12:2), succumb to sexual sin (1 Thess 4:3), choose evil rather than good (1 Thess 5:21–22), fail to share with those in need (Rom 12:13), are untruthful (Matt 5:33–37), are gripped with fear and anxiety (Matt 6:25–34), are judgmental (Matt 7:1–5), are unfaithful in prayer (Rom 12:12), are hearers but not doers of Jesus's teaching (Matt 7:21–23), deny their faith when persecuted (Matt 10:16–20), are catalysts for dividing and destroying the church (1 Cor 10:10–17), or cause other believers to sin (Matt 18:6–7), this is ultimately due to the fact that God withheld the grace which would have enabled obedience to his will and thus rendered these outcomes certain.

9. Peterson and Williams, *Not an Arminian*, 161. To restate an earlier point, this is a

GOD'S PURPOSES FOR THE BELIEVER

Closely related to the previous point are the frequent New Testament statements of the purposes or goals God has for believers. These include believers are to bring God glory (Eph 1:12), to do good works (Eph 2:10), to do what pleases God (Phil 2:13); to be holy (1 Thess 4:3–7), to love God and others (Luke 10:27), and to be conformed to the image of Christ (Rom 8:29). Theological determinism requires that extent to which these purposes are realized in the life of individual believers and churches is determined entirely by God, never by the person in her exercise of the gift of grace-empowered libertarian freedom. God is the one who determines the extent to which believers bring glory to God or do good works. When believers fail to love God and others it is because God has withheld the grace that would enable love. God is the one who determines the specific path for each person with respect to their progress in the Christian life and being "conformed to the image of Christ." When some Christians make no progress in spiritual development while others evidence significant growth, this can only be explained in terms of what God has ordained for each person with respect to his progress in the Christian life.

GOD'S DAILY WORK IN THE LIFE OF THE BELIEVER

To come at this from another angle, there are a number of statements in the New Testament that focus directly on God's ongoing work in the life of the believer: e.g. enabling the Philippians to be partners with Paul in spreading the Gospel (Phil 1:6), empowering believers to live righteous lives (Phil 1:11), enabling them to both will and do what pleases him (Phil 2:13). This language makes sense on the assumption of grace-enabled libertarian freedom. God is at work to empower the believer to break free from the conditioning of "the flesh" (their fallen humanity) so that they have the ability both to desire what is right and then to do it. In modern terminology, God grants the believer the gift of grace-empowered libertarian freedom. The moral exhortations which occur in the context of these affirmations encourage the believer to embrace and live out the gift of grace empowered libertarian freedom each day.

There is a problem with interpreting these statements within the framework of compatibilistic freedom. How does one explain those times when believers are disobedient? The failure cannot be traced to the misuse of libertarian freedom. The problem must be that when believers sin it is

---

mainstream Calvinist position, not some extreme "hyper-Calvinism."

because God did not extend sufficient grace "to enable them to will and do what pleases God."[10] To take a specific Pauline example, in 1 Cor 10:13 Paul tells the Corinthians that when tempted, in this context to attend temple meals, God will provide the grace which will enable them to resist temptation (="a way out"). This makes sense on the assumption of libertarian freedom, i.e. grace is not irresistible and therefore believers must exercise their "grace-enabled libertarian freedom" to take "the way out." It is harder to make sense of this on the assumption of compatibilistic freedom.

If God always extends the grace to resist the temptation to attend temple meals, why do some Christians fail to embrace that grace and resist temptation? The answer for a Calvinist must be that God ordained that the person succumb to temptation and attend temple meals. In these circumstances God simultaneously extends the grace to provide a "way out of temptation" and ordains that the believer give in to temptation.

One way a theological determinist might rationalize this would be to argue that when tempted, some Christians receive "general grace" while others receive "effectual grace."[11] "General grace" is for those situations when God ordains that believers do not resist temptation and therefore sin; "effectual grace" is for those situations when God ordains that believers resist temptation and do not sin.

CRITIQUES OF THE SINS OF BELIEVERS

In many New Testament texts, churches are rebuked for embracing sin and erroneous theological and ethical perspectives. The Corinthian epistles provide a glimpse into a church which had embraced a remarkable concentration of problematic positions. Examples include they wanted to marginalize the message of the Cross (1 Cor 1:18), tried to demonize Paul using a variety of strategies (e.g. 2 Corinthians 10), argued that there was no ethical objection to using prostitutes (1 Cor 6:12–20), concluded that sex between

---

10. Peterson and Williams, *Not an Arminian*, 146–147, use Phil 2:12–13 as a proof text to support a compatibilistic understanding of freedom. The necessary implication of this reading is that Paul in fact means that God is *sometimes* at work to enable us to will and to do what pleases him, i.e. to do what is in alignment with his "revealed will." Phil 2:12–13 would not be true in those instances when God had ordained that believers sin and therefore withheld the grace that would enable obedience, i.e. there are many times in the life of the believer when God is in fact not at work to enable us to will and do what pleases him.

11. As Calvinists will recognize, this is a play on the Calvinist distinction between a "general call" versus an "effectual call." When the Gospel is preached, those whom God has predestined to damnation hear it only as a "general call" while the elect hear it as an "effectual call," i.e. God enables them to respond.

believers was inappropriate (1 Corinthians 7), advocated attending meals at pagan temples where drunkenness and sex with prostitutes was the norm (1 Cor 8:10; 10:1–22), used tongues as a means of self-promotion (1 Corinthians 12–14), allowed the Lord's Supper to be an occasion where the elites met early in the dining room to overeat and get drunk (1 Cor 11:17–33), and defined Christian leadership using Greco-Roman cultural values such as rhetorical ability, a strong physical appearance, the ability to avoid suffering, and a willingness to engage in patronage relationships (2 Corinthians 10–13). In response to these and other problems, Paul labored strenuously to try to correct their flawed perspectives. If Paul were a theological determinist, then he believed: 1. that God choreographed each of these sins in the Corinthian church; 2. that God ordained all the specifics of Paul's response; 2. that whether or not the Corinthian church responded to Paul's appeals would be determined entirely by what God wanted to happen in Corinth so that if the Corinthian church was unresponsive it would ultimately be because God had ordained this outcome.[12]

In Revelation 2—3, Jesus dictates letters to seven churches in Asia Minor. Depending on what was true for each church, the letters blend commendation and/or censure. Where circumstances require words of censure, an opportunity is given for repentance. Finally there are promises of eschatological salvation and/or judgment depending on how believers respond to Jesus's words. If these letters are read within the framework of theological determinism, then Jesus dictates these letters with full awareness that God has ordained 1. the precise pattern of obedience and disobedience in each church, 2. the specifics of the sins of each church, 3. whether and to what extent each church will respond to his call to repentance and change. In the case of Rev 3:20, for example, Jesus knows that the Father has ordained both that the church shut Jesus out and that he would plead with the church for a restoration of relationship. He also knows that God, not the church, is the one who determines whether or not the church will respond to Jesus' call to be invited into their midst.

James 4:2–3 states that there are times when believers do not receive from God either because they fail to pray and/or because their prayers are self-seeking and self-indulgent. A Calvinist understanding must conclude that God himself ordained the failure to pray and/or the self-indulgent focus of prayers.

12. Ezek 24:13–16 provides an illuminating O.T. parallel: "You mix uncleanness with obscene conduct.14 *I tried to cleanse you*, 15 *but you are not clean.* You will not be cleansed from your uncleanness16 until I have exhausted my anger on you." In a Calvinist reading, God simultaneously tried to cleanse Israel and prevented them from being cleansed because he wanted to judge them. Cf. also Jer 7:12–14.

WARNINGS TO BELIEVERS

Related to the above point are the frequent warnings in the New Testament about embracing erroneous teaching. Jesus warns about false prophets (e.g. Matt 7:15-20), Paul warns the Philippian church about the dangers of both Judaizers and libertines (Phil 3:2-21), and the Colossian church about a theology that is somewhat difficult to reconstruct precisely (Col 2:16-23). Galatians rebukes Christians for embracing a Judaizing theology; and the Johannine epistles those who embrace a theology which again is difficult to reconstruct precisely. When these texts are read within the framework of theological determinism, the conclusion is that God choreographed all the details of these heretical theologies as well as the extent to which believers would resist false teaching, embrace it, or realign themselves with truth when they stumbled. In Rev 14:9-13, believers are warned not to compromise with an Antichrist order when persecuted.

Those who fail to heed this warning and deny their faith will come under eschatological judgment while those who remain faithful to the point of death will "rest from their labor," i.e. will experience eschatological salvation. Elsewhere Revelation explicitly states that God extends the grace that will enable believers to remain faithful in a tribulation context (e.g. Rev 7:1-8; 11:1-2). The language of Rev 14:9-13 assumes that the believers can exercise their grace-empowered libertarian freedom by choosing either to remain faithful or to deny their faith. However on Calvinist assumptions, God is the one who decided "before the foundation of the world" how each believer would choose.

WELL-INTENTIONED DIFFERENCES AMONG CHRISTIANS

The New Testament contains a number of texts that acknowledge Christians differ among themselves on various issues. In Rom 14:1—15:4 Paul instructs Christians how to handle those situations where Christians differ on issues which Paul believes lack intrinsic moral significance (the strong and the weak). Acts reflects the fact that there were differences of opinion about the Gentile mission and the conditions for Gentile acceptance as believers (Acts 15). Gal 2:11-13 describes a situation where Paul strongly disagreed with Peter and Barnabas. The Jerusalem Council stipulated that Gentile Christians not eat market-place meat that originated in pagan sacrifices (Acts 15), but about six to seven years later Paul says that this meat can be eaten by any Christian (1 Cor 10:23-33). In Phil 3:15 Paul acknowledges that Christians will have different perspectives on some issues. Paul develops a strong theological argument for women wearing head coverings in public worship, but acknowledges that not all will agree with him (1 Cor 11:2–15, 16). Theological determinism requires the conclusion that God has ordained all these differences of opinions as well as the specifics of whether Christians will handle their differences well or poorly.[13]

STATEMENTS ABOUT THE CHRISTIAN LIFE

In Rom 5:3–4 Paul states that God uses adversity as a catalyst for the character development of a believer. The question is whether this statement is conditional in that believers must respond appropriately to difficult circumstances in order for it to be character building. Schreiner will argue that ultimately this is not conditional because God will always overcome the believer's temptation to respond poorly to adversity.[14] The unstated assumption is that when believers respond poorly to suffering, and adversity has an ultimately negative impact on their personal and spiritual formation, this is because God has ordained this situation. The character building function of adversity is now conditioned not upon how the person responds but on what God ordains for the person in any particular experience of adversity.

Paul understands that the Christian life is one where there is a tension between what God wants for us and our desires rooted in our fallen humanity.[15] In Rom 7:14–25, Paul explores those times in the experience of the believer when "the flesh" rather than "the Spirit" wins. There are times when the believer wants to do what is right but instead does what he or she knows is wrong. On the assumption of libertarian freedom, Paul is saying that there are times when in spite of the fact that in his grace God is at work to enable him "to will and to do" what pleases God, Paul chooses wrongly and sins. The failure lies with Paul's exercise of his grace empowered libertarian freedom.

---

13. Down through the centuries, Christians have differed on countless points of theology and Biblical interpretation. Theological determinism assumes that God ordained each and every concept, no matter how outrageous, erroneous and destructive. Furthermore God ordained all the conflicts and divisions within the church that resulted from these differences. It is impossible to reconcile this conclusion with Paul's affirmation that "God is not a God of disorder but of peace" (1 Cor 14:33. the context being a statement about worship).

14. Thomas Schreiner, *Romans (Baker Exegetical Commentary on the New Testament)* (Grand Rapids: Baker Academic, 1998), 256.

15. E.g., the conflict between the flesh and Spirit in Gal 5:16–17.

On the assumption of compatibilistic freedom, Paul is saying that there are times when God extends sufficient grace which enables Paul to desire to do the right thing but not enough grace which would enable him to carry out this intention. The result is that Paul chooses wrongly and sins. On this assumption the problem is ultimately that God withheld the grace that would have enabled Paul to translate God-ordained intentions into actions (which God did not ordain for those circumstances). Or, to put it another way, God extends the "general grace" which enables the believer "to will to do the good" but withholds the "effectual grace" which would enable the person "to do what pleases God."

In Rom 8:10–17, Paul says that the Spirit bears witness to our spirit that we are sons and daughters of God. Some believers have a deep and consistent experience of this witness of the Spirit. However other believers have no experiential sense of being loved and accepted by God. Some experience deep anguish and torment at this lack. On the deterministic assumptions, God is the one who ordains what will be true for each believer. In 1 Cor 3:10–17, Paul differentiates three ways that Christians can contribute to shaping the church: 1. a constructive one ("building with gold and silver"); 2. an anemic one ("building with wood and hay"); 3. a destructive one ("if anyone destroys God's Temple"). When read within the framework of theological determinism, God determines what will be true for any given individual. In Matt 18:16–17, Jesus speaks to a situation where a disciple refuses to repent of their sin when confronted. On a Calvinist reading, God is the one who ordains that the person be unresponsive to discipline.

Jesus states that God is responsive to the prayers of his people (e.g. Luke 11:5–13; 18:1–8). On the assumption of theological determinism, this could only be true if God choreographed the specifics of the believer's prayer so that they petitioned precisely what God had already determined would happen. God would "respond" in the sense that there was a one-to-one correspondence between what was prayed and what transpired because God had ordained that it happen "before the foundation of the world." Once again this is counterintuitive in that this is not how people understand the concept of God's responsiveness to prayer, was not how divine responsiveness to prayer was understood in contemporary Judaism, and there is no contextual evidence that this is how Jesus meant his words to be understood.[16]

A number of New Testament texts promise "rewards" or "blessing" for faithful discipleship and service (e.g. Matt 6:4; 6, 18; 10:41–42; Luke 6:35; 1

---

16. Cf. David Crump, *Knocking on Heaven's Door: A New Testament Theology of Petitionary Prayer* (Grand Rapids: Baker, 2006), 129–130, 289–291, critiques the Calvinist reading of petitionary prayer along similar lines. This is especially remarkable because he is Professor of Theology and Religion at Calvin Seminary.

Cor 3:8; 4:5; Gal 6:9). The intent of these statements is to motivate believers to use their "grace-empowered libertarian freedom" in faithful discipleship. This idea is expressed broadly in 2 Cor 5:10 where Paul says that each believer will stand before Christ and give an accounting of their discipleship. Each person will "receive what is due them for the things done. . .whether good or evil." On Calvinist assumptions, God has determined before the foundation of the world what will be true for each believer with respect to the quality of their discipleship and therefore the "rewards" or "rebukes" they will receive. God then uses these promises of reward as a catalyst for motivating obedience in those believers that he wants to bless. When God ordains that some believers will receive eschatological rebukes, the promises will not be a catalyst for motivating obedience and therefore the believer will receive their God ordained rebuke.[17]

OTHER NEW TESTAMENT TEXTS

The Matthean version of the Lord's prayer has the petition "your will be done on earth as it is in Heaven" (Matt 6:10). The assumption behind the statement would appear to be that in the present age God's will is not fully realized on earth in the same way that it is in heaven. This would appear to contradict the Calvinist assumption whatever happens in this age does so because God has ordained it and therefore his will is always done "on earth as it is in heaven."[18]

If Jesus worked with a deterministic theology, then when he critiqued the failures of the Pharisees he would have done so with the realization that God ordained each of these sins (e.g. Matt 23:1–36). The same would be true of his words of judgment spoken with respect to the unresponsive Galilean village (e.g. Matt 11:20–24). After exploring options for understanding the reasons for Israel's unbelief, Paul concludes in Rom 10:21 that the real problem is stubborn disobedience in spite of the fact that from his side God has been continuously "holding out his hand" to Israel. A Calvinist reading of this requires that God himself ordains the stubborn disobedience. Therefore

17. For these promises of reward and rebuke to have a motivational function for most people, the hearer must read them on the assumption of libertarian freedom, i.e. it is within their power to make right or wrong choices that lead to these different outcomes. If Calvinists are right, then it seems to me that these statements are necessarily communicated within a misleading and even deceptive framework in order to be effective. I will restate this point in the concluding section.

18. The Calvinist solution is to distinguish God's revealed moral will and his "secret ordaining will." The latter is always done on earth. Thus the petition is a prayer that God's revealed moral will would be done on earth.

he is "holding out his hand" to Israel while simultaneously withholding the grace that would enable them to respond.[19]

The Biblical concept of "divine grief" is inexplicable on the assumptions of theological determinism. The Gospels record Jesus's grief over the unresponsiveness of Jerusalem and the people of God (e.g. Matt 23:37–39). If Jesus were a theological determinist then he believed that God himself had ordained this unresponsiveness. But if God had choreographed this unbelief, why grieve over it?[20] Human expressions of moral outrage (e.g. Gal 2: 14–21) are also problematic on the assumptions of theological determinism. Why be angry about realities which God has in fact ordained? On Calvinist assumptions, when believers are distressed at evil in the world and church, God has ordained that they express moral outrage about realities which God himself choreographed. God is also the one who decides whether an expression of moral outrage is a catalyst for correcting problems or an exercise in futility.

In my experience theological determinists do not normally try to explain the types of texts discussed to this point from the perspective of God's ordination of all things. However, Calvinists commonly discuss New Testaments texts which affirm God's universal salvific will and warn believes about apostasy. The question is whether the interpretations of these texts are plausible.

GOD'S UNIVERSAL SALVIFIC WILL

The New Testament contains many affirmations that God desires the salvation of every person.[21] These statements challenge the Calvinist understanding of election language as meaning that God unconditionally selects a subset of humanity for salvation and only these individuals can respond

19. Schreiner, *Romans*, 520, argues with respect to this text that God does simultaneously invite people into relationship while simultaneously withholding the grace which would enable them to respond.

20. This is also problem for reading the Old Testament texts which portray God's grief and anger over the sins of Israel with profound intensity (e.g. Jer 13:15–17; Isa 1:10–15). If God has "morally sufficient reasons" to ordain the sins of his people, why would he grieve over the fact that they are doing precisely what he has scripted for them? Sanders, *Perspectives on the Doctrine of God*, 142, points out that Augustine and Calvin were consistent on this point and argued that God is never grieved.

21. Matt 22:14; Luke 2:10; John 1:7, 9, 29; 3:16; 4:42; 5:23; 6:45; 11:48; 12:32; Acts 17:30; 22:15; Rom 5:15–19; 10:11–13; 11.32; 2 Cor 5:19; Phil 2:11; Col 1:20; 1 Tim 2:4; Titus 2:11; 2 Pet 3:9; 1 John 2:2; Rev 22:17. Cf. I. Howard Marshall, "For all, for all my Saviour Died," Stanley Porter and Anthony Cross, eds., *Semper Reformandum: Studies in Honour of Clark H. Pinnock* (Carlisle: Paternoster, 2003), 322–346.

to the Gospel.[22] Calvinist interpreters use a variety of strategies to deal with the texts stating that God desires that all be saved: 1. restricting the "all" to "all the elect"; 2. defining "all" as "all kinds of people" from every sector of society; 3. interpreting the intention as being that salvation is not just for the Jew but also the Gentile. Each of these interpretations is counter-intuitive and lacks any contextual support. Thomas Schreiner recognizes this and concedes that texts such as 2 Pet 3:9 do indeed affirm that God *desires* the salvation of every person. However he argues that while God does *desire* the salvation of all, he *ordains* to make salvation possible only for a limited number.[23]

In addition to being a counter-intuitive way of reading the relevant texts, it raises the logical question of why God would desire one thing but ordain something else.[24] To put it more starkly, why would God *desire* that all of humanity experience the glory of his presence for eternity but then choose to *ordain* that the majority of people experience the horror of eternal separation? And why in his self-revelation would he say that he desires that all be saved when he knows that he is going to ordain something completely different? And where is the contextual evidence that this is how the Jesus, John, Paul and Peter understood these affirmations of God's universal salvific will?

22. For a Calvinist understanding of election cf. e.g. Bruce Ware, "Divine Election to Salvation: Unconditional, Individual, and Infralapsarian," in *Perspectives on Election*, 1–58. For an understanding of election that gives full weight to God's universal salvific will and libertarian freedom cf. Glen Shellrude, "All are Elect, Few are Elect: Understanding New Testament Election Language," *Scottish Bulletin of Evangelical Theology* 30/2 (Autumn, 2012)

23. Thomas Schreiner, *The New American Commentary: 1, 2 Peter, Jude* (Nashville: Broadman, 2003), 380–383. Cf. also Ware, *Divine Election*, 32–35. John Piper, "Are There Two Wills in God?" in *Still Sovereign*, 107–113, has developed the fullest defense of this construct. Schreiner, *1, 2 Peter, Jude*, 381–382, acknowledges that "Many think this approach is double-talk and outright nonsense." I would add that this interpretive approach is counterintuitive, contextually unsupported and ahistorical in that there is no evidence that this is how these statements would have been read in a first century context.

24. John Piper argues that God ordains both the damnation of the majority of humanity as well as the evil and carnage so pervasive in human experience for the express purpose of magnifying his glory in that these realities are necessary prerequisites for the elect to understand the depth of God's holiness, majesty and glory. For a critique of this construct along with a response from Piper cf. Thomas McCall, "I Believe in Divine Sovereignty," *Trinity Journal* 29:2 (Fall 2008), 205–226; John Piper, "I Believe in God's Self-Sufficiency: A Response to Thomas McCall" Ibid., 227–234; Thomas McCall, "We Believe in God's Sovereign Goodness: A Rejoinder to John Piper" Ibid., 235–246.

WARNINGS AGAINST APOSTASY

The New Testament contains numerous warnings against believers falling away and losing their salvation.[25] These texts are a problem for Calvinists since they affirm that apostasy is impossible for the elect.[26] However, if this were true then why warn against it? Once again theological determinists must resort to counterintuitive and contextually unsupported interpretations which do not take account of the historical context in which the warnings were given. The three main approaches to the warning texts used by Calvinist interpreters are: 1. the warnings have to do with the loss of rewards, not salvation; 2. the warnings have in view those who are not genuine believers; 3. the warnings are the means God uses to ensure that the elect do not commit apostasy.

The first approach fails to take account of the contexts and language of the warnings. The problem with the second approach is that if the real problem is that some are deluded about being genuine believers, why not speak to that issue directly rather than address them as believers and warn them about the possibility of apostasy? The warnings should be about the danger of being self-deluded that one is a believer rather than about the danger of apostasy. The problem with the third approach is that it requires the logically and ethically challenged assumption that God warns about something that could not happen as a means of ensuring that it doesn't happen. It calls in question the moral integrity of God that he would warn about something as though it were a real possibility when in fact this was not the case. The bigger problem for all these approaches is that they fail to take account of the historical context in which the warnings about apostasy were spoken and written. Second Temple Judaism had no theology of the assured "perseverance of the saints" and believed that apostasy was always a real possibility and danger. If Jesus and the early church took a different view of this issue then one would expect it to be clearly expressed. As the texts are written, the

25. I. Howard Marshall, *Kept by the Power of God: A Study of Perseverance and Falling Away* (Minneapolis: Bethany House, 1969), is the best analysis of the relevant texts. Stephen Ashby, "A Reformed Arminian View" J. Matthew Pinson, ed., *Four Views on Eternal Security* (Grand Rapids: Zondervan, 2002), 137–187, has an excellent, concise discussion of the issues (cf. 170–180 for a summary analysis of the Biblical texts). For a Calvinist perspective cf. Thomas Schreiner, *The Race Set Before Us: A Biblical Theology of Perseverance and Falling Away* (Downers Grove: InterVarsity, 2001).

26. Theological determinism does not necessarily require "eternal security." Augustine believed that it was possible that a person could be truly regenerate and then fall away, the assumption being that God ordained that the person be a believer for a limited period of time. However, since Calvin, a theology of assured perseverance has been axiomatic in Calvinist theology.

New Testament warnings about apostasy would have been understood by any first-century hearer as assuming that it was a real possibility and danger to be avoided.[27]

SEVEN CONCLUDING OBSERVATIONS

First, there is a the lack of historical and contextual evidence that would validate interpreting the New Testament within the framework of theological determinism. There is no evidence that mainstream Second Temple Judaism embraced exhaustive theological determinism. If Jesus, Paul and other writers of the New Testament had a different view on this matter then one would expect this to be clearly expressed. In order to be understood correctly, they would need to distinguish their theological framework from the traditional Jewish construct of reality which assumed libertarian freedom.[28] However there are no contextual indicators that they departed from

27. Calvinists claim that Scriptural affirmations of God being for us (e.g. John 10:27–30; Rom 8:28–39) provide the contextual indicators that Jesus and the early church believed that apostasy was impossible. But these texts simply cannot mean what Calvinists want them to mean. These texts affirm that God is working to sustain the believer's perseverance and that nothing external to them can separate them from God's work on their behalf. However this does not mean that grace is irresistible and that the individual cannot choose to separate themselves from Christ. This is especially clear when the same texts which affirm that God is completely on the side of believers also warn against the possibility of apostasy (e.g. John 10:27–30 & 15:6; Rom 8:28–39 & 8:13; 11:22). The Essene texts from Qumran also affirm that God is working to enable the perseverance of his people while simultaneously and explicitly affirming the possibility of apostasy (cf. I. Howard Marshall, *Kept by the Power of God*, 38–43).

28. The lack of evidence that either mainstream Second Temple Judaism or Jesus and the early church were theological determinists is an important consideration when considering Old Testament texts which Calvinists take as proof texts for theological determinism (e.g. Gen 50:20; Exod 8:15, 32; 9:12; 10.1; Deut 32:39; Job 1:21; 2:10; Eccles 7:14; Lam 3:38; Prov 16:9; 21:1; 1 Sam 2:6–7; Isa 45:7; Amos 3:6). If this was how the original authors intended their statements to be understood, then one would expect that this would be reflected in Second Temple Jewish literature or the New Testament. The lack of evidence for theological determinism in this literature suggests that neither Second Temple Jews or Jesus and the early church understood these Old Testament texts in the way that Calvinists propose. However the real problem for using these texts as Scriptural evidence for theological determinism is that when viewed in the total context of the OT, a Calvinist interpretive framework is contextually unsupported and results in counterintuitive and ahistorical readings of thousands of Old Testament texts and many different kinds of material (precisely the same problem as reading the N.T. within the framework of theological determinism). Crump, *Knocking on Heaven's Door*, 290–291, note 16, points out that the use Calvinist theologians make of these texts ignores the meaning of the texts in their original context. For an historically and contextually based interpretation of these texts, cf. Fredrik Lindstrom, *God and the Origin*

Jewish thinking on this point and embraced comprehensive theological determinism.[29] Christians in the early centuries would have been familiar with a deterministic world view in light of the pervasive impact of Stoic philosophy. It is therefore remarkable no theologian, pastor or scholar in the early church prior to Augustine found theological determinism in the New Testament.[30] This is not what one would expect if the New Testament contained significant contextual indicators that the writers conceptualized reality within a deterministic theological framework.

Second, theological determinism conflicts with the natural, intuitive reading of so many Scriptural texts. A good hypothesis is one that accounts for the largest amount of data with the fewest number of residual challenges. It is not the case that reading the New Testament within the framework of theological determinism creates the occasional tension that may require a somewhat counterintuitive interpretation of scattered texts. The challenges are monumental in that a Calvinist reading requires counterintuitive and ahistorical interpretations of thousands of texts and many different kinds of material.

A Calvinist reading of the various kinds of New Testament material discussed in this paper is in the end an exercise in eisegesis on a grand scale which in turn generates an enormous amount of textual destruction. One must impose a deterministic theological framework on texts through the use of consistently counterintuitive and ahistorical interpretive strategies.[31]

---

of Evil: A Contextual Analysis of Alleged Monistic Evidence in the Old Testament (Lund, Sweden: Gleerup, 1983).

29. Rom 9:6-23 is the text most commonly cited by Calvinists to prove that Paul was a theological determinist. Statements like "I will have mercy on whom I will have mercy" (9:15) and "he has mercy on whom he wishes and hardens whom he wishes" (9:18) do sound like an expression of theological determinism. These statements must be read within the context of Paul's entire argument in Romans 9—11. There are numerous statements in Romans 9—11 that clearly demonstrate that Paul was not a theological determinist. Cf. Glen Shellrude, "The Freedom of God in Mercy and Judgment: A Libertarian Reading of Romans 9:6-29," *Evangelical Quarterly* 81.4 (2009), 306–318.

30. Augustine would have been familiar with determinism from both Manichaeism and Stoicism. However it appears that his determinism is rooted in the Platonic and neo-Platonic concept that an absolutely perfect being (God) must be "impassible or immutable," i.e. could not experience any inward changes. Cf. John Sanders, *The God Who Risks* (2nd ed; Downers Grove: InterVarsity, 2007), 149–153.

31. When reading online responses to books debating the Calvinist-Arminian issue (e.g. on Amazon.com), I often notice lay Calvinists pointing out that Arminians argue from a more philosophical perspective while Calvinists argue from Scripture and have the upper hand with respect to Scriptural proof texts. They conclude from this that Calvinism is the more "Scriptural theology." In reality, Calvinism is deeply and profoundly contradicted by the Scripture in that theological determinism requires the exegetical abuse of "countless" Biblical texts. This is not immediately apparent to most people

Third, in a Calvinist reading of Scripture, the motivational effectiveness of many Scriptural statements is dependent on the reader being deceived. God's people are motivated to faithful service and discipleship with the promise of eschatological blessing when in fact God has already determined the precise experience of blessing and rebuke that will be true for each person. Believers are promised that God will enable them to resist temptation when in reality he has already determined that in many situations they will give in to temptation and sin. The warnings against apostasy motivate believers to persevere in their faith when in reality apostasy is a theoretical impossibility. God assures his people that he will enable them to be renewed in their thinking while simultaneously ordaining that they embrace a wide range of erroneous ideas. The promise is made that the Spirit will enable obedience when in reality God only intends that believers have a very limited experience of obedience. In these and many other instances, the effectiveness of Scriptural affirmations is dependent on the reader being deceived, i.e. reading them on the assumption of libertarian freedom.

Fourth, one needs to account for the chasm between what God says about his moral will for humanity and the way God actually choreographs human experience. God is opposed to evil and the champion of goodness and truth but writes a script for human history in which evil and carnage are the dominate realities. In order to account this, Calvinists must distinguish between God's "revealed will" ("preceptive will") and his "secret/hidden or ordaining will" ("decretive will"). God's "revealed will" is the expression of his moral will for humanity while his secret or ordaining will is what God in fact ordains will be the experience of each person. God reveals that he is responsive to prayer while in his secret will ordains that only those petitions which he ensures correlate with the script he wrote before creating the world will "appear" to have been "answered."

God has revealed that believers should align themselves with truth while simultaneously ordaining that believers embrace a wide range of erroneous thinking. God has revealed that believers are "to be perfect as he is perfect" while simultaneously ordaining the precise expression and degree of sin which will characterize each believer. God has revealed that believers should not divorce their spouses but in his secret will has ordained that believers divorce their spouses with about the same frequency as is true in secular society.

God has revealed that he cares about children while simultaneously ordaining that vast numbers of children are abused, neglected, and sexually

because they don't reflect on the implications of consistent theological determinism for reading each Scriptural statement.

exploited. God has revealed that believers are to honor and delight him while ordaining that much of the time believers deeply grieve him and bring shame on the Gospel. God has revealed that he is uncompromisingly opposed to sin and evil while in his ordaining will has scripted a staggering level of sin and evil in human history. God's "secret will" is fully knowable with respect to the present and past since all that happens corresponds precisely to what he has ordained. What cannot be known are the disparities between God's "revealed will" and "secret will" as it relates to future events. One implication of this construct is that Christians are often simultaneously working on the side of God's revealed will but against God's secret will. Thus, for example, Christians who give themselves to working with the suffering children of the world can be assured that their goals are in complete alignment with God's revealed will. However it is possible that they are working against God's secret/ordaining will. If this is the case then their work will bear little or no results. This is true for every aspect of Christian ministry. The result is a view of God that represents him as having two distinct wills which are deeply conflicted and contradictory.

Fifth, Calvinists use language and concepts in ways unparalleled in human experience. They typically affirm that God loves each and every person (though some dissent on this point) while simultaneously ordaining that the majority of those he "loves" will have no opportunity to avoid the horror of eternal separation. Calvinism affirms that God is pure holiness while simultaneously ordaining and rendering certain all the sins and evils in human experience. Calvinists claim that God holds people responsible for their choices even though every single choice has been choreographed by God and people can never do other than what God has ordained they do. This theology affirms that God is in no way responsible for sin and evil even though he has structured reality and human experience in such a way that people willingly commit the sins God has ordained for them. Calvinism claims that God has choreographed all the evils and horrors which will characterize human experience for the purpose of enhancing his own glory. Each of these positions is logically and morally offensive as well as being without parallel in human experience. If human parents were to act with respect to their children in any way similar to how Calvinists claim God acts then those parents would be declared moral monsters.[32]

Edwin Palmer acknowledges the absurdity of what Calvinism affirms: "He [the Calvinist] realizes that what he advocates is ridiculous. . . .The Calvinist freely admits that his position is illogical, ridiculous, nonsensical and

32. Olson, *Against Calvinism*, develops and illustrates these ideas at many points, cf. especially pp. 166f; 175–179.

foolish."[33] However he argues that the Scriptural evidence requires one to embrace this intrinsically absurd view of God. If God has created us with a rational and moral discernment which to some extent mirrors his own, then the cluster of logical and moral absurdities inherent in the Calvinist system suggests that there is a problem with the theology itself. The appropriate response is not to celebrate absurdity, or as is more commonly done, to appeal to mystery, but rather to rethink the theology in light of the totality of the Scriptural evidence.

Sixth, the Calvinist view of God is contradicted by God's self-revelation in Scripture, e.g. God reveals an uncompromising opposition to sin and evil, but Calvinism argues that God has in fact decreed every expression of sin and evil in human experience. God reveals a universal salvific will, but Calvinism affirms that God has an extraordinarily restrictive salvific will. God challenges his people to obedience on the assumption that they can make meaningful choices to be obedient, but Calvinism argues that God has ordained the choices believers will make in every situation. Calvinists justify God's ordination of the monumental scale of evil and sin in human experience by arguing that God has "morally justified reasons" for acting in this way in that some greater good, fully known only to God, is served by all the carnage.

The difficulty with challenging this argument is the claim that "the reasons are known only to God." However given the magnitude of sin and evil in human experience, if the Calvinist argument were true, then it should be obvious that in many cases that these evils served some demonstrable good. Furthermore, since on Calvinist assumptions God can script history as he chooses, he could have accomplished the same good results with much less evil and ambiguity. In any case, it is easier to evaluate the argument with respect to the eternal destiny of men and women. What are the "morally justified reasons" for God's decision that the vast majority of people will be unable to respond to God because he has ordained that their destiny will be one of eternal torment? How can this reconciled with God's self-revelation as one characterized by absolute love, mercy and holiness? This is especially problematic for Calvinists who take the position that God does indeed desire the salvation of every person but chooses to ordain that the majority of humanity will experience the horror of eternal separation. Given the Calvinist denial of free will, there would be nothing to prevent God from ordaining the salvation of all and then so working in each person so that they ultimately respond to him.

Because these things are part of our experience now, many find it difficult to come to terms with the idea that God has choreographed all

---

33. Edwin Palmer, *The Five Points of Calvinism* (Grand Rapids: Baker, 1972), 106.

the evil and carnage that characterizes human experience, e.g. genocides, rapes, murders, abuse of children, etc. However this suffering is in reality completely inconsequential in comparison with the thought that God has ordained the damnation of the vast majority of the human race. Suffering in this world is for an infinitesimally short period of time when compared to eternal suffering. If one accepts that God has predestined the eternal damnation of most of those he created then it should be easy to accept that God has scripted all the evil we see in human experience here and now. "Cafeteria" Calvinists who stumble at the thought that God has scripted all the evil and sin in present human experience need to ask themselves why they find it easier to accept that God has ordained the eternal suffering of the vast majority of humanity.

It is evident that the scale of evil and carnage in the world is truly monumental. The question can be asked as to which worldview best accounts for this phenomena: 1. atheism; 2. a deterministic theism; 3. a theistic perspective which affirms the reality of libertarian freedom. I personally believe an atheistic view of reality is more plausible than theological determinism. On atheistic assumptions the explanation might be that humans are the product of natural evolutionary forces and what we chose to describe as evils are all part of the natural evolutionary process. On the assumptions of theological determinism, God could just as easily have constructed a script for human history in which there was no evil or far less evil than is actually the case.

However on Calvinist assumptions, God intentionally chose to write a script with all the evil and carnage that we observe. It is impossible to reconcile this with God's self-revelation as one characterized by love, mercy, holiness and an uncompromising opposition to sin and evil. A theistic world view constructed on the assumption that God has created men and women with genuine libertarian freedom provides a much more plausible account of reality in that the explanation for a great deal of what is wrong with the world can be traced to the sinful abuse of the gift of libertarian freedom.[34]

Calvinists like to claim that their theology serves to highlight the holiness and glory of God. In reality Calvinism denigrates God's holiness and glory with its claim that God has choreographed every expression of sin and evil in human experience.[35] Seventh, theological determinism in effect

34. I realize that the affirmation of libertarian freedom does not explain everything and leaves plenty of room for "mystery."

35. In his sermon *Free Grace*, John Wesley said that Satan might as well take a permanent leave of absence since God does Satan's work far more effectively: "You, with all your principalities and powers, can only so assault that we may resist you; but He can irresistibly destroy both body and soul in hell! You can only entice; but his unchangeable decrees to leave thousands of souls in death, compels them to continue in sin, till

denies the Scriptural affirmation that God desires to be in relationship with the women and men who he created. If one day we are able to actualize the science fiction notion of creating artificial intelligence that replicates human behaviors, it is difficult to imagine that people would find joy in relationships with those who are following their programming 100 percent of the time. It is also impossible to imagine that the God who created men and women for relationship would find joy in relationship with those who were simply following their divine programming at every point.

Why would God find delight in human responses to his grace which were completely ordained by him and never freely chosen? Are we to believe that God takes delight in expressions of love, worship and praise which he himself has scripted? What would we think of a novelist or script writer who restricted their relationships to mental ones with the characters they had created in literary works and movies? A good movie is one that creates tension and drama by conveying the impression that people are making real decisions and therefore the outcome is in doubt. But in fact it is all an illusion as every action and word has been scripted in advance. Calvinism affirms that this is also true of real life and that, by implication, God delights in relationships with the characters who are playing out their divinely scripted roles.

In the modern world, determinism is a dominant paradigm in secular philosophy as honest atheists can find no logical basis for libertarian free will on the assumption that humans are product of natural evolutionary forces. By contrast, Christians should celebrate the fact that there is a Scriptural basis for libertarian free will. The triune God who is the perfect embodiment of libertarian freedom chose to create people in his image who are endowed with grace-enabled libertarian freedom so that they could enter into a relationship of reciprocal love with their Creator.

"The Minister's Daughter"
John Greenleaf Whittier

Then up spoke the little maiden,

---

they drop into everlasting burnings. You tempt; He forces us to be damned; for we cannot resist his will. You fool, why do you go about any longer, seeking whom you may devour? Have you not heard that God is the devouring lion, the destroyer of souls, the murderer of men?" http://new.gbgm-umc.org/umhistory/wesley/sermons/128/ (I have modernized the language.) In reality the God of Calvinism requires Satan to stay on the job in order "to keep his hands clean." God choreographs evil and sin in human experience through "second causes" and Satan is a major source of "second causes." Roger Olson, *Perspectives on the Doctrine of God*, 163, points out that Arminius himself argued that on Calvinist assumptions the only real sinner in the universe is God. It is striking how in the present, many Christians go ballistic over the "gnat" of open theism but happily embrace the "camel" of Calvinism.

Treading on snow and pink:
"O father! These pretty blossoms
Are very wicked, I think.
"Had there been no Garden of Eden
There never had been a fall;
And if never a tree had blossomed
God would have loved us all."
"Hush, child!" the father answered,
"By his decree man fell;
His ways are in clouds and darkness,
But he doeth all things well.
"And whether by his ordaining
To us cometh good or ill,
Joy or pain, or light or shadow,
We must fear and love him still.
"O, I fear him!" said the daughter,
"And I try to love him too;
But I wish he was good and gentle
Kind and loving as you."[36]

36. John Greenleaf Whittier, *The Complete Poetical Works of John Greenleaf Whittier* (Boston: Houghton Mifflin, 1848, 1894), 459–460.

4

The Intent and Extent of Christ's Atonement

Robert E. Picirilli

Frederick W. Faber's 1862 hymn begins, *There's a wideness in God's mercy Like the wideness of the sea.* Nothing in human history testifies to the wideness of God's mercy or the breadth of his love (third verse of the hymn) like the atoning death of Christ. John 3:16 directly connects God's love for the world with the giving of his unique Son to provide for us eternal life.

If access to God's grace is indeed for all, as the title of this book intentionally claims, we ought to be able to see it here before anywhere else. The question that covers all the issues is this: What did God intend to achieve by the redemptive acts of Jesus?

WHAT GOD INTENDED THE ATONEMENT TO ACHIEVE, AND FOR WHOM: A BIBLICAL THEOLOGY

During the history of the church, there have arisen different views of what Jesus accomplished by his death. I cannot deal with these here, except to note that discussion of them has intensified in recent years. I proceed on the assumption that the atonement was substitutionary (vicarious) and that it accomplished a full satisfaction of a holy God's demands for the punishment of sin (penal satisfaction).[1] Even so, other views of the atonement flesh out important truths; no single view expresses the whole meaning of this gracious, self-giving work of God.

The New Testament itself provides more than one perspective. Three of these—all metaphors, to some degree—seem most important, with each illuminated by at least one key passage that speaks of a universal dimension, i.e. for humanity. These concepts provide the most important answers to the question what God intended by the atonement.

JESUS DIED AS RANSOM OR REDEMPTION

These two words represent cognates in the original. *Ransom* appears in two passages, both in reference to Jesus's death.

> 1 Tim 2:5, 6: There is one God, and there is one mediator between God and men, the man Christ Jesus, who gave himself as a ransom for all.[2]

> Matt 20:28; Mark 10:45: The Son of Man came not to be served but to serve, and to give his life as a ransom for many.

In Timothy, *ransom* is the compound *antilutron*. Matthew and Mark use the simple *lutron*, but the *anti* appears as a preposition immediately following. In both, the *anti* "accents" the "idea of substitution."[3] The root points to "the means or instrument by which release or deliverance is made possible."[4] It is thus "the 'price of release' for the liberation of a prisoner or debtor" [or slave].[5]

Redemption (*lutrōsis*) occurs in Luke 1:68 and 2:38, where Zechariah and Anna greet the coming of the Messianic era. "Blessed be the Lord God of Israel," said Zechariah, "for he has visited and redeemed [lit., "wrought redemption for"] his people." Anna "began to give thanks to God and to speak of him to all who were waiting for the redemption of Jerusalem."

1. For an excellent presentation of atonement as "penal substitution," see J. I. Packer, *What Did the Cross Achieve? The Logic of Penal Substitution* (Leicester, England: Centaprint of Leicester, n.d.; reprinted from *Tyndale Bulletin* 25/1974).

2. Unless otherwise noted, all citations of the Bible are from the *English Standard Version*.

3. Karl Kertelge, *lutron*, in Horst Balz and Gerhard Schneider, eds., *Exegetical Dictionary of the New Testament*; three vols. (Grand Rapids: Eerdmans , 1991), 2:366.

4. Johannes P. Louw and Eugene A. Nida, eds., *Greek-English Lexicon of the New Testament Based on Semantic Domains*, 2nd ed., two vols. (New York: United Bible Societies, 1988, 1989), 1:488.

5. Kertelge, *lutron*, 2:365.

Then, in a theological statement, Heb 9:12 adds that Jesus "entered once for all into the holy place, . . . by means of his own blood, thus securing an eternal redemption." In other words, the sacrificial death of Jesus was the instrument or price by which the deliverance was accomplished. Louw and Nida appropriately suggest that the word (and the cognate compound noun, below) has "the implied analogy to the process of freeing a slave."[6]

The verb cognate to these nouns is *lutroomai* and means to set free, liberate, ransom, or deliver; the need for a means or price is implicit in the background. It appears three times.

> Luke 24:21: We [the two disciples on the Emmaus road] had hoped that he was the one to redeem Israel.

> Titus 2:14: [Jesus Christ] gave himself for us to redeem us from all lawlessness and to purify for himself a people for his own possession.

> 1 Pet 1:18,19: You were ransomed from the futile ways inherited from your forefathers, not with perishable things such as silver or gold, but with the precious blood of Christ, like that of a lamb without blemish or spot.

The last is the most explicit: redemption was by means of the sacrificial death of Jesus, whose death was both the means and the "price" required.

The cognate compound *apolutrōsis* (apparently a synonym of the simple noun) occurs ten times in the New Testament (Luke 21:28; Rom 3:24; 8:23; 1 Cor 1:30; Eph 1:7, 14; 4:30; Col 1:14; Heb 9:15; 11:35). Most of these refer to our redemption without indicating the means, but two are pointed.

> Eph 1:7: We have redemption through his blood, the forgiveness of our trespasses.

> Heb 9:15: A death has occurred that redeems them from the transgressions committed under the first covenant.

Both identify how and from what the redemption is obtained:

Another pair of Greek verbs is nearly synonymous: namely, *agorazō* and the compound *exagorazō*, meaning to buy or redeem. The simple verb is used most often for ordinary purchases, but a few instances speak specifically of Jesus's death as "buying" us (1 Cor 6:20; 7:23; 2 Pet 2:1; Rev 5:9; 14:3, 14). The two verses in 1 Corinthians say that believers were "bought with a price," and the two in Revelation 14 speak of believers as "redeemed." Two verses are especially significant:

---

6. Louw and Nida, *Greek-English Lexicon*, 1:488.

Rev 5:9: By your blood you ransomed people for God from every tribe and language and people and nation.

Gal 3:13: Christ redeemed us from the curse of the law by becoming a curse for us.

Here are both vicarious atonement and redemption by means of Jesus's dying under the curse of our sins. There is no need, then, to abandon the idea of a price paid in redemption.

That Jesus's atoning death served as ransom or redemption does not suggest that a ransom was paid to Satan. Indeed, it does not need to suggest a financial transaction at all. Analogies with a kidnapper's ransom demands, for example, only go so far in illuminating the concept. At root, the idea of ransom or redemption has two important facets: a need for liberation and the requirement that something must be done to effect it. "As a metaphor ransom commonly points to a price paid, a transaction made, to obtain the freedom of others," ideas "rooted in the ancient world where slaves and captured soldiers were given their freedom upon the payment of a price."[7]

The most important thing, then, is that by means of the death of Jesus we were delivered from our sins. His dying under the curse of our sins (Gal 3:13) was the means, the "price" paid, for our liberation. And it was a price he could not pay *for* us without doing so in our place.

Was the provision of ransom/redemption intended to be universal? First Tim 2:1–6 is a key passage for this. Three times we meet "all":

v. 1: Pray for all, including specifically the governing authorities.

v. 4: God desires that all be saved and come to know the truth.

v. 6: Jesus "gave himself as a ransom for all." God's provision for *all* matches his desire for all and is the ground of our prayers for all.

Calvinists typically claim this means "all kinds" of human beings, rather than all persons. Berkhof, for example, refers to "the revealed will of God that both Jews and Gentiles should be saved,"[8] although nothing in the context suggests a Jew-Gentile tension. Nicole focuses on all classes of people, "even rulers who seem to be such unlikely objects of divine grace."[9] But the passage as a whole makes better sense if God's universal desire for

7. R. W. Lyon, "Ransom," in Walter A. Elwell, ed., *Evangelical Dictionary of Theology* (Grand Rapids: Baker, 1984), 907.

8. Louis Berkhof, *Systematic Theology* (Grand Rapids: Eerdmans, 1949), 396–397.

9. Roger Nicole, "The Case for Definite Atonement," *Bulletin of the Evangelical Theological Society* 10:4 (1967), 204.

the salvation of all and Christ's ransom for all provide the basis for our prayers for all, including kings as a special case. The universal *all* includes the particular *kings* whose good graces are needed for believers to live in piety and pursue the mission of the God who desires that all be saved.

Others, adopting the more obvious meaning of *all*, suggest that the passage refers to the *sufficiency* of the atonement for all, rather than to its intended extent. Thus, Shedd cites Owen to say "that Christ's blood was sufficient *to be made* a ransom for all." Shedd appears to agree, saying: "Atonement must be distinguished from redemption," that "atonement is unlimited, and redemption is limited," and that redemption "includes the *application* of the atonement."[10] Credit Owen and Shedd with recognizing the meaning of *all* in the passage, even if they go on to argue for limited atonement on other grounds. Indeed, Shedd apparently agrees that Christ died for (made atonement for) all men individually but that it is applied (redemption) only to some.

All occurs again in a similar context in 1 Tim 4:10, referring to "the living God, who is the Savior of all people, especially of those who believe." This language shows exactly how he can be both the Savior of all, in providing a universal atonement, and at the same time *especially* the Savior of believers, as those to whom alone the provision is applied. This strengthens the case for understanding 1 Tim 2: 4, 6 as universal: God the Savior of all desires that all be saved, and Jesus the mediator between God and men gave himself as a ransom for them all.

Titus 2:11, apparently written at about the same time as 1 Timothy, compares directly and adds confirmation: "The grace of God has appeared, bringing salvation for all people."

JESUS DIED AS A PROPITIATION

This word appears three times in our English tradition: Rom 3:25; 1 John 2:2, 4:10. The two instances in 1 John translate *hilasmos*, "expiation, propitiation" or "sin-offering"[11] or, more weakly, "the means of forgiveness, expiation"[12]—depending on which lexicon one consults. There is a real

10. W. G. T. Shedd, *Dogmatic Theology*, 2 vols. (Grand Rapids: Zondervan, n. d.), 2:469–470.

11. William F. Arndt and F. Wilbur Gingrich , eds., *A Greek-English Lexicon of the New Testament and Other Early Christian Literature* (Chicago: University of Chicago Press, 1957, 1964), 376.

12. Louw and Nida, *Greek-English Lexicon*, 2:504.

difference of opinion here, given that Louw and Nida say that the word and its cognate "denote the means of forgiveness and *not* propitiation."[13]

Rom 3:25 has the cognate *hilastērion*, "that which is expiatory or propitiatory or pertains thereto." The question is whether this means the *place* or the *means* of accomplishing this. In Heb 9:5, its only other occurrence in the New Testament, it clearly means the place, the *mercy-seat*. Rom 3:25, however, is not so clear. Roloff, for example, reads "the *place of expiation* through faith in his blood," but he acknowledges that exegetes like Käsemann, Schlier, and Lohse render "an expiation (or expiatory sacrifice)."[14]

The cognate verb *hilaskomai* occurs twice, in Luke 18:13 and Heb 2:17. The former uses the passive form of the verb, the tax-collector praying that God will "show mercy" ("be propitiated") to him. The latter explicitly views Jesus's death (v. 14) as the means by which he would "make propitiation for the sins of the people."

As a whole, then, and especially in Rom 3:25 and Heb 2:17, it is clear that the propitiation or expiation for our sins was accomplished by the sacrificial, atoning death of Jesus. It also seems clear that the stronger meaning is justified. Although we need not think in crass, materialistic terms, we should understand that propitiation involves the lifting of God's holy sentence against sin, and that this lifting was accomplished by his satisfaction with the penalty paid by Jesus on the cross. We can properly think of this in terms of the bearing of God's wrath in such a way that he was appeased, even if we must be aware that God's wrath is not like ours. As Packer puts it, "By undergoing the cross Jesus expiated our sins, propitiated our Maker, turned God's 'no' to us into a 'yes,' and so saved us."[15]

Was the provision for propitiation intended to be universal? 1 John 2:2 holds the key: "He is the propitiation for our sins, and not for ours only but also for the sins of the whole world." The text presents special difficulty for any reading of limited atonement precisely because it speaks of propitiation both for *us* and for the whole *world.*

Calvinists explain the contrast between the *us* and *the world* in ways that differ from what seems to be the plain meaning. Berkhof, for example, defines "world" to mean that, in contrast to "Old Testament particularism," "the blessings of the gospel were extended to all nations."[16] Nicole agrees,

13. Ibid. (emphasis added).

14. Jurgen Roloff, *hilastērion*, in Balz and Schneider, *Exegetical Dictionary*, 2:186.

15. Packer, *What Did the Cross Achieve?*, 21.

16. Berkhof, *Systematic Theology*, 396.

regarding the *us* as "a small group, perhaps of Jewish Christians," in contrast to "the redeemed elected out of every nation and category."[17]

The question, of course, is not whether such construals as these *can* be placed on the text but whether they will stand the test of careful exegesis. For this reason, it is necessary to analyze the way John uses the first plural and the word *world* in the rest of the letter.

World (*kosmos*) occurs twenty-two more times in 1 John: in 2:15–17 (6 times); 3:1, 13, 17 (3 times); 4:1–5 (6 times), 9, 14, 17 (3 times); 5:4–5 (3 times), 19 (once)—consistently in a sense antipathetic to the church or Christians. (Only in four instances—3:17; 4:9, 14, 17—is it even possible that this negative sense is not intended.) In 2:15–17 the contrast is emphatic, warning John's readers that they must choose between loving the world and the love of God because the world is passing away. In several places there is a clear contrast between the *us* and the world, as in 3:1 ("the world does not know us") and 5:4 ("our faith has overcome the world"). Furthermore, only in 5:19 does John again use (as in 2:2), the phrase "the whole world," and the comparison is significant: "We are of God, and *the whole world* lies in the power of the evil one."

In other words, if "the whole world" in 2:2 stands as some sort of shorthand for "the elect of all nations or classes," it is the *only* instance of this in the entire letter. One cannot avoid comparing 4:14: "We have seen and testify that the Father has sent his Son to be the Savior of the world." In both 2:2 and 4:14, then, "the world" has the negative implications of all the rest of the personal uses of the word in the letter and takes on the sense it has in John 3:16.[18] Indeed, Calvin himself, in commenting on John 3:16 said:

> Both points are distinctly stated to us: namely that faith in Christ brings life to all, and that Christ brought life, because the heavenly father loves the human race, and wishes they should not perish. . . .And he has employed the universal term *whosoever*, both to invite all indiscriminately to partake of life, and to cut off every excuse from unbelievers. Such is also the import of the term *World*, which he formerly used; for though nothing

17. Nicole, "The Case for Definite Atonement," 206. Editor's note: On the other side, see Norman Douty, *Did Christ Die Only for the Elect? A Treatise on the Extent of Christ's Atonement* (Eugene, Ore.: Wipf and Stock, 1998). Of particular interest are p. 41–45, in which the author surveys seventeen lexicons, theological dictionaries and theological encyclopedias, on their definitions of "kosmos" and "world." None of those sources listed those words as ever meaning believers or the elect.

18. The extensive use of *world* in John's Gospel will support this claim. Indeed, John uses *world* more than the other three Gospels combined, and 1 John more than any other epistle. See, for examples, John 1:29; 3:17; 7:7; 8:23; 9:39; 12:31; 14:17, 30; 15:18–19; 16:8, 11; 17:14–18.

will be found in *the world* that is worthy of the favor of God, yet he shows himself to be reconciled to the whole world, when he invites all men without exception to the faith of Christ, which is nothing else than an entrance into life.[19]

Furthermore, 1 John's frequent use of the first person plural—*we, us, our*—does not support the idea that it means a limited group of Jewish or first generation Christians. A careful analysis yields two conclusions. (1) The only part of 1 John where *we* may be limited is in the prologue (1:1–5), where it can sensibly be read as "we apostles." (2) None of the other uses support limitation to a defined circle of homogeneous believers, to be read as "we in our particular group." For a few examples of typical usage see 1:7, 9; 2:3; 3:1, 2, 14; 4:6; 5:11, 14. All of these refer to John and his fellow believers and indicate what is characteristic of the Christian community. The comparison between 2:2 and 5:19, drawn above, shows both the identity of "the whole world" in the two passages and the identity of the "we/our" in tension with it.

One also notes the parallelism between 2:2 and 4:10, which says that God "loved us and sent his Son to be the propitiation for our sins." There is such close correspondence that the phrase "the propitiation for our sins" has the ring of a standard Christian confession, thus tending to confirm the "our" as applying to all believers and pointing up the contrast with the "world."

19. John Calvin, *Commentary on the Gospel of John*, William Pringle, trans., (Grand Rapids: Baker reprint, 1981), 1:123, 125. (My thanks to John D. Wagner, editor of this volume, for pointing me to this.) I do not propose to enter the discussion as to whether Calvin actually believed in limited or unlimited atonement. That issue has been treated ably by scholars of both opinions. For the view that he did not hold to limited atonement, see R. T. Kendall, *Calvin and English Calvinism to 1649* (Oxford, U.K.: Oxford University Press, 1979); for the view that he did, see Paul Helm, *Calvin and the Calvinists* (Edinburgh: Banner of Truth, 1982). See also Charles Bell, "Calvin and the Extent of the Atonement," *Evangelical Quarterly* 55:2 (1983): 115–123; and Kevin Dixon Kennedy, *Union With Christ and the Extent of the Atonement in Calvin* (New York: Peter Lang, 2002). The problem stems from the fact that Calvin did not address the issue systematically in his *Institutes*, although he did say there, "And the first thing to be attended to is, that so long as we are without Christ and separated from him, nothing which he suffered and did *for the salvation of the human race* is of the least benefit to us" 3.1.1 (emphasis added). In the commentaries, it is clear that sometimes Calvin understood *all* and *the world* to be universal; quotations in this chapter substantiate that.

JESUS DIED AS RECONCILIATION

Rom 5:8–11 is basic for this. Paul makes two points especially clear. First, we *were* God's enemies (v. 10), and this involved (as in the preceding) being objects of his wrath (v. 9). Second, by means of Jesus' death (v. 10)—the sacrificial shedding of his blood (v. 9)—we have been reconciled to God (vv. 10, 11).

The key words are the verb *katallassō* and its cognate noun *katallagē*. Louw and Nida suggest that four elements of meaning are involved: (1) "disruption of friendly relations" between two parties, (2) "presumed or real provocation" on the part of one or the other, (3) "overt behavior designed to remove hostility," and (4) "restoration of original friendly relations.[20]

Other New Testament statements assume and reiterate what is found in Romans 5. Indeed, both the noun and the verb occur twice each in 2 Cor 5:18–20, another key text for this concept. While the death of Jesus is not specifically identified as the means of reconciliation, that meaning is self-evident; and v. 21 makes clear that this is grounded in God making his Son "to be sin" for us so that we might "become the righteousness of God." This is what Luther called "*a wonderful exchange* [by which] our sins are no longer ours but Christ's: and the righteousness of Christ is ours."[21]

A compound verb, *apokatallassō*, means essentially the same thing and appears three times: in Eph 2:16 and Col 1:20, 22. The first indicates, again, that reconciliation to God is "by the cross" (v. 16). Col 1:21–22 is especially pointed: "You, who once were alienated and hostile in mind, doing evil deeds, he has now reconciled in his body of flesh by his death, in order to present you holy and blameless and above reproach before him." As in Romans 5, the notion of prior hostility is once again present, and the means of reconciliation is the death of Jesus.

Interpreters have argued whether the reconciliation has effect only on man or on both God and man. While it is clear that the vicarious self-sacrifice of Jesus is aimed at reconciling sinners to God, it is likewise clear, given the reference in Romans 5 to God's wrath, that the propitiation or expiation offered for our sins satisfies his just demands and so renders him favorable to those to whom the benefits of that atonement are applied. In other words, the offense between God and man is removed (John 1:29) and they are reconciled. In different senses, both sides are affected.

Was the provision for reconciliation intended to be universal? Second Cor 5:19 gives a positive answer to this question.

20. Louw and Nida, *Greek-English Lexicon*, 2:502.

21. Martin Luther, *Selected Works of Martin Luther* (London: T. Bensley, 1826), 4:369.

We will also examine Rom 5: 12–19, which is more debatable. After focusing on reconciliation in vv. 10–11, Paul compares the results of Adam's sin and Jesus's reconciling death. The climactic part of the discussion is in vv. 18–19: "Therefore, as one trespass led to condemnation for all men, so one act of righteousness leads to justification and life for all men. For as by the one man's disobedience the many were made sinners, so by the one man's obedience the many will be made righteous."

It is certainly possible to regard those on whom the consequences of Adam's sin have fallen as all mankind, and those on whom the consequences of Jesus's redemptive work have fallen as all the redeemed. Each is the head of a company of people: Adam of the human race, Jesus of the saved. A number of interpreters take this approach, indicating that "all" in Rom 5:18 "includes only those who are in Christ, as contrasted with all who are in Adam."[22] Indeed, some Arminians agree: "The words 'upon all men unto justification of life' must be understood as 'all who are identified with Christ.'"[23]

However, it is possible that "all men" includes the whole human race both times it appears in v. 18, and "the many" means the same thing as "all men" both times it appears in v. 19. Douglas Moo, listing the options, reports: "Others argue that what is universal in v. 18b is not the actual justification accomplished in the lives of individuals, but the *basis* for this justification in the work of Christ. Christ has won for all 'the sentence of justification' . . . , and this is now offered freely (*eis*) to all who will 'receive the gift.'" He cites, as supporters of this view, Prat, Denney, Godet, Stuart, Lenski, Meyer, Gifford, Beasley-Murray, and Hughes[24]—an impressive list.

Although at one time I thought otherwise,[25] recent analysis has inclined me to understand Paul to mean that the *provision* or *basis* for justification and life is made for all, so that *all* encompasses all humanity. As I will show later in this chapter, the New Testament can (as can any of us in normal discourse) speak of an event as *accomplishing* what is more technically said to be *made possible* by or *grounded in* it. Calvin himself, commenting on v. 18, apparently viewed the *all* this way: "He makes this favor common to all, because it is propounded to all, and not because it is in reality extended to all; for though Christ suffered for the sins of the whole world, and is offered

22. Berkhof, *Systematic Theology*, 396.

23. Leroy Forlines, *The Randall House Bible Commentary: Romans* (Nashville: Randall House, 1987), 143.

24. Douglas Moo, *The Wycliffe Exegetical Commentary: Romans 1–8* (Chicago: Moody, 1991), 355.

25. Robert Picirilli, *The Book of Romans* (Nashville: Randall House, 1975), 103.

through God's benignity indiscriminately to all, yet all do not receive him."[26] It is clear how he understands *all*.

Whatever one's conclusion about Rom 5:12–19, 2 Cor 5:18–19 is not so debatable: "All this is from God, who through Christ reconciled us to himself and gave us the ministry of reconciliation; that is, in Christ God was reconciling the world to himself, not counting their trespasses against them, and entrusting to us the message of reconciliation." Here Paul says both that in Christ's redemptive work God reconciled *us* and that he was reconciling the *world* to himself. Paul emphasizes this right after twice declaring in vv. 14 and 15 that "one has died for all" and "he (Christ) died for all" and describes the "us" as "that those who live might no longer live for themselves but for him. . ."

The contrast between *us* and the *world*, as in 1 John (above), seems clearly to be a contrast between believers and the world at large. Second Cor 5:21 appears to make clear who is meant by *us*: "For *our* sake he made him to be sin who knew no sin, so that in him *we* might become the righteousness of God."

Furthermore, the *world*, as in Paul's usual usage, does not lend itself to mean something like "the elect of the nations" in contrast to Jews.[27] Nothing in the context of 2 Corinthians 5 suggests a contrast between a narrow Jewish particularism and a broader concern for Gentiles. *Kosmos* occurs twice more in 2 Corinthians, in 1:12 and 7:10, and both are in contrast to what is true for believers. It occurs twenty-one times in 1 Corinthians, none of which comes anywhere close to meaning God's people among the nations. All of them are either neutral, as in 14:10 ("different languages in the world"), or clearly negative, as in 11:32 ("that we may not be condemned along with the world"), most in the latter category.

As a result of this study of Christ's atonement as ransom/redemption, propitiation, and reconciliation, what seems most biblical is to say that God's intention was to provide atonement for all mankind and to apply it savingly to those who would accept that provision by faith.

26. John Calvin, *Commentaries on the Epistle of Paul the Apostle to the Romans*, trans. and ed. John Owen, (Grand Rapids: Baker, 1981 reprint), 211.

27. See Berkhof, *Systematic Theology*, 396, for this view; he cites Shedd as holding the same.

SYSTEMATIC THEOLOGY AND GOD'S INTENTION FOR THE ATONEMENT

While "exegetical theology" seems more weighty to me than systematic theology, one cannot avoid the arguments over the extent of the atonement in the latter field. There is only space here for attention to the most important of these.

The Question of Accomplishment in the Divine Intention

The strongest argument for limited atonement is probably to point to Scripture as affirming that whatever the death of Christ intended was actually *accomplished* thereby. Those who offer this perspective insist that the New Testament is better read to say that the atonement actually saved those it was intended for, rather than simply providing for the possibility of salvation for all human beings.

Indeed, some of the same key words used above to explain the nature of the atonement appear to speak of accomplishment. Matt 20:28 indicates that Jesus came "to give his life as a *ransom* for many," not just as a means of making ransom possible. First John 4:10 affirms that God "sent his Son to be the *propitiation* for our sins," not just to provide for propitiation. Second Cor 5:19 says that "in Christ God was *reconciling* the world to himself," not that he was performing a work that could result in reconciliation.

These and similar passages appear to say that Jesus actually redeemed or ransomed persons, that he made the propitiation, that he accomplished the reconciliation. He did not just make salvation possible, he *saved*. Roger Nicole has argued this case strongly:

> What kind of redemption would this be where the redeemed are still under the power of the enemy? What kind of propitiation, where God still deals in wrath? What kind of reconciliation where estrangement continues to exist and is even sealed for eternity? These three terms, severally and jointly, bear witness to the fact that the Scripture views the work of Christ as bringing about the effectuation of salvation.[28]

Therefore, the argument goes, these affirmations show that Jesus did *not* die to make atonement for the non-elect, or else they would mean that he actually effected the salvation of the reprobate! As Berkhof expressed this, to say that Jesus died for the purpose of saving all men "logically leads

---

28. Nicole, "The Case for Definite Atonement," 201.

to absolute universalism, . . . It is impossible that they for whom Christ paid the price, whose guilt He removed, should be lost on account of that guilt."[29]

J. I. Packer, in an otherwise excellent presentation of atonement as penal substitution, likewise emphasizes this point: "If we are going to affirm penal substitution for all without exception we must either infer universal salvation or else, to evade this inference, deny the saving efficacy of the substitution for anyone."[30] He concludes his discussion of the point by asking, rhetorically, "Is there any good reason for finding difficulty with the notion that the cross *both* justifies the 'free offer' of Christ to all men *and also* guarantees the believing, the accepting and the glorifying of those who respond, when this was precisely what Paul and John affirmed?"[31] But if Jesus did not die for the non-elect, the cross does not justify the offer of salvation to them.

Given the weight of the argument based on accomplishment, a careful response is required. One important consideration is the way humans use language: we typically speak of some action as actually accomplishing what it led to. In other words, the *potential* of an act is often spoken of as the act itself. To illustrate, one may say that a doctor's diagnosis, on such a date, *saved* his life. In fact, what saved the person's life was what the correct diagnosis led to in the way of treatment. Whatever critical thing leads to or provides for or makes possible a given result is frequently spoken of as accomplishing that result.

Shedd, one of the important Reformed theologians, although he holds to a limited atonement, appears to have recognized that the making of atonement in itself does not save. He said, "Atonement in and by itself, separate from faith, saves no soul . . . this sacrifice in itself, and apart from its vital appropriation, is useless. . . . It is only when the death of Christ has been actually confided in as atonement, that it is completely 'set forth' as God's propitiation for sin."[32]

Again, he says: "Vicarious atonement without faith in it is powerless to save. It is not the *making* of this atonement but the *trusting* in it, that saves the sinner. . . . Unless his objective work is subjectively appropriated, it is useless, so far as personal salvation is concerned."[33] "When a particular person trusts in this infinite atonement, and it is imputed to him by God, it

29. Berkhof, *Systematic Theology*, 395.

30. Packer, *What Did the Cross Achieve?*, 37.

31. Ibid., 39.

32. Shedd, *Dogmatic Theology*, 2:477.

33. Ibid., 2:440–441.

then becomes his atonement for judicial purposes as really as if he had made it himself, and then it naturally and necessarily cancels his personal guilt."[34]

With these observations, Shedd has shown us how to understand when the Scriptures appear to say that the atonement accomplished redemption, and it is good that he has done so. I say this because if, in fact, the events at Calvary then and there had *accomplished* salvation for anyone yet unborn, then that person would *never* be an unredeemed sinner, not even before regeneration. The Bible, however, speaks of Christians as having previously lived under the wrath of God and in a state of estrangement from him; see Eph 2:3, 13 among many examples.

Furthermore, some of the passages that seem to speak of salvation accomplished speak of "all men" or "the whole world." If the natural exegesis of these expressions to mean all humanity is accepted (as above), understanding the passages to speak of effective application would indeed lead to universal salvation, and that is manifestly unbiblical. (I may add that it is Shedd's solution, understood in the light of human usage of words to incorporate the results of an action into statements of the action, that affects the discussion of Rom 5:18–19 above. In this light, the *all* in that passage may really mean all.)

I would add that Shedd's treatment makes a strong case for the atonement as both substitutionary and penal, and with that conviction I heartily concur. I suspect that the reason some interpreters have avoided the *penal satisfaction* view of the atonement and substituted a *governmental* view is the very argument being treated here: namely, that the New Testament seems to say that the intention of the atonement, whatever it was, was actually *accomplished*. But once we see that such statements include the *application* along with the event itself, and that the application is dependent on personal faith, there remains no reason to avoid the satisfaction view. Arminius himself, a staunch defender of the penal satisfaction view, fully recognized this in his reply to William Perkins: "You confound the result with the action and passion, from which it exists . . . the obtainment of redemption with its application. . . . reconciliation made with God by the death and sacrifice of Christ, with the application of the same, which are plainly different things."[35]

As a final observation on this topic I add that in a real sense the argument on the basis of accomplishment ultimately resolves into an affirmation that Christ, on the cross, effectively saved those whom he effectively saved. Indeed, Shedd's solution, just discussed, leads him to this: "Atonement must

34. Ibid., 2:438.

35. James Arminius, *The Works of James Arminius*, James Nichols and W.R. Bagnall, trans., 3 vols. (Grand Rapids: Baker, 1956), 3:456.

be distinguished from *redemption*. The latter term includes the *application* of the atonement. . . . Atonement is unlimited, and redemption is limited. This statement includes all the Scripture texts: those which assert that Christ died for all men, and those which assert that he died for his people."[36] "In saying that Christ's atonement is limited in its application, and that redemption is particular not universal, it is meant that the number of persons to whom it is effectually applied is a fixed and definite number."[37] Who could disagree?

Again, then, the biblical way to state what God intended in the atonement is that he intended to provide a basis for the salvation for every person and to apply it to all who receive that provision by faith. The following two sections develop this briefly.

Did God intend the atonement to save his people? Yes, and this explains all the passages, frequently used to support the doctrine of a limited atonement, that say that Jesus died to save those who are in fact saved. Indeed, some passages speak directly to the fact that Jesus died for believers—as, of course, he did! Among the most significant of these are Matt 1:21 ("his people"), John 10:15 ("the sheep"); Acts 20:28; Eph 5:25 ("the church"); Rom 8:32; Titus 2:14 ("us").

The obvious response to such statements is that they do not—not even by implication—serve to justify denying that Jesus died for all. It is always appropriate for those who have believed to ground their deliverance in the death of Christ for them. On one occasion, Paul said that Christ "loved me and gave himself for me" (Gal 2:20). By no means does this mean that he did not love and give himself for others.

Did God intend the atonement for the whole world? Again, yes. This does not mean, of course, that by the atonement he intended, effectively, to save all mankind. He intended to apply it only to those who appropriate its provision by faith.

The only real issue for Scripture, then, is whether the New Testament teaches that Jesus' death was atonement for all human beings. The discussion above has already treated some of the key passages that affirm so, including 2 Cor 5:19 (and probably Rom. 5:18–19); 1 Tim 2:6; and 1 John 2:2. Other significant passages include:

> John 3:16–18: God so loved *the world* that he gave his son, in order that *the world* may be saved through him.

> 2 Cor 5:14, 15: He died for all.

36. Shedd, *Dogmatic Theology*, 2:479–480.
37. Ibid., 3:474.

1 Tim 4:10: . . . the living God, who is the Savior of *all people*, especially of those who believe.

Titus 2:11: The grace of God that brings salvation to *all men* has appeared.

Heb 2:9: Jesus tasted death for *every man*.

1 John 4:14: The Father has sent his Son to be the Savior of *the world*.

Such passages teach us that atonement has been made for all mankind. The provision stands and is offered to all. As Shedd has taught us (above), there is a difference between the making of atonement and its application. First Tim. 4:10 neatly expresses the difference between the two.

It is customary, among those who propose a limited atonement, to speak of the *sufficiency* of the atonement for all the world, as though that satisfies the universal dimension of the gospel.[38] What seems to me to escape their notice is that if no provision has been made, in the atonement, for the non-elect, it is by no means sufficient for their salvation. To be sufficient means, by definition, to be equal to or adequate for what is required for some objective or need. Especially is it so, then, that an atonement that was intended by God to *accomplish* salvation for all for whom it was made, is not adequate to save those for whom it was not made.

Did God intend the atonement for some who perish? The previous point includes within it this clear implication, since Jesus died for all and not all are saved, that he died for those who perish. Is there more than implication here? Does the Scripture say such a thing?

Three passages indicate that this is the case. Two of them are on the same subject: namely, what believers ought to be careful about when deciding whether to participate in disputed practices.

1 Cor 8:11: And so by your knowledge this weak person is destroyed, the brother for whom Christ died.

Rom 14:15: By what you eat, do not destroy the one for whom Christ died.

In both discussions, Paul is warning the so-called stronger brothers that they must not be indifferent to the conscience of a weaker brother. To set aside the weaker brother's welfare and insist on the exercise of one's liberty regardless of the consequences may be to cause the weaker brother to

---

38. See Berkhof, *Systematic Theology*, 393; Shedd, *Dogmatic Theology*, 2:464.

stumble into sin and, ultimately, to perish—in spite of the fact that Christ died for him.[39]

The other passage is 2 Pet 2:1, where the apostle warns against the certain coming of false teachers into the Christian community. One characteristic that Peter uses to describe them is, "even denying the Master who bought them, bringing upon themselves swift destruction." The buying referred to is most certainly that which was paid for in the atonement, and the swift destruction is surely eternal.

If, indeed, Christ died for some who perish, there is no reason to doubt that he died for all who perish.

CONCLUSIONS

There are other logical and Biblical evidences for a universal atonement, of course, but space allows only a brief statement of them. They include: (1) passages affirming God's desire that all be saved—2 Pet 3:9; 1 Tim 2:4; (2) passages offering the gospel to all and commanding that it be preached to all—Luke 24:47; Acts 17:30; Eph 3:7–9; 2 Cor 5:18–20; and (3) passages blaming the wicked not just for their sins but for the rejection of the gospel and the atonement proclaimed in that gospel—1 John 5:10, 11; John 3:18; 2 Thess 2:10–12.

These may not seem as important to the discussion as the things treated up to this point, but they add significant considerations that are more coherent with a view of universal atonement. All of them complement better the view that in the redemptive work of Christ God intended to provide a basis for the salvation of all. That fits well with his desire, with the universal offering and preaching of the gospel, and with the responsibility people have for rejecting Christ.

What, then, did God intend for the atoning, redemptive work of Jesus Christ to achieve? The biblical answer seems clear enough, and two-fold. First, he intended to provide a basis for the salvation of all humanity and did, in fact, achieve this in the general atonement of Christ for the world. That atoning work made possible the salvation of anyone and everyone who will receive the gospel in the loving, trusting obedience of faith. That good news—the *gospel*—is preached to all persons without discrimination,

---

39. If, indeed, the one for whom this danger exists is a *brother* in Christ, this implies the possibility of apostasy. The discussion of that possibility lies beyond the scope of this chapter. But even if apostasy is not in view, here, the possibility remains that *someone* for whom Christ died may perish after all. See also the warning passages against falling away in Heb. 3:12; 6:4–6; 10:26–31.

because all have sinned and have exactly the same need before God (Rom 3:22–23).

Second, God intended the atonement, effectively, to save all those who exercise this obedient faith. It did, in fact, achieve this by the application of the fruits of the atonement according to the condition the sovereign God unconditionally established: namely, faith. This has taken place in time but is anchored in eternity, because it "was the (eternal) good pleasure of God . . . to save the ones believing" (1 Cor 1:21: *eudokēsen ho theos . . . sōsai tous pisteuontas*).

There is, indeed, a wideness in God's mercy, demonstrated by the most gracious and costly sacrifice ever offered. The eternal God himself, in the person of his beloved Son, has become one of us and taken our sins on himself. Christ has satisfied all that the holy God requires as atonement for our sins—and not for ours only but for the whole world—by dying in our place. Nothing that we can offer him, then, can contribute to such a self-giving act of love. The atonement is most certainly not a provision through which *we* achieve anything; it is a finished work of God, in Christ, that provides for us, no other grounds required, saving grace. We can only hold out empty hands, in faith, to receive this unspeakable gift.

5

Conditional Election

Jack W. Cottrell

Since the Reformation era, no biblical doctrine has been more misrepresented and maligned than the doctrine of soteriological predestination (or election). Many people do not consider the idea of predestination to be biblical at all. This is because they have equated it in their minds with a particular interpretation of predestination, namely, the one developed by Augustine and made popular through the influence of John Calvin. Recognizing Calvinistic predestination to be alien to the Bible, they dismiss it or explain it away altogether.

This is extremely unfortunate, since the doctrine of predestination is definitely scriptural; and when rightly understood, it is one of the most significant and rewarding teachings of the Bible. It enhances the majesty, wisdom, love and faithfulness of God; and it strengthens the heart of the believer. The whole counsel of God is not proclaimed when this doctrine is ignored. The main concern of this chapter is to present the positive biblical teaching about election or predestination. This will require, however, some consideration of false or inadequate ideas of predestination, especially those which arise from the Calvinistic tradition.

I. THE BIBLICAL DOCTRINE OF ELECTION

The New Testament terms that are especially relevant are the words *proorizō,* meaning "to predestine, to predetermine, to decide beforehand"; and *eklogomai,* meaning "to elect, to choose, to select." Related terms are the adjective *eklektos,* meaning "elect" or "chosen"; and the noun *eklogē,* meaning "the election." In the context of the doctrine of election there is no significant theological distinction between the words *predestine* and *elect.* The word *predestine* includes a time element by means of its prefix, and it may be a more general term;[1] but no doctrinal point can be made by drawing a sharp distinction here. In this chapter the word *elect* will ordinarily be used, since it is the more common, versatile, and convenient of the two.

A. The Structure of Election

It is very important to see that the biblical doctrine of election is much broader in scope than election to eternal glory. Its broadest context is the total redemptive purpose of God. In choosing the cast for the grand drama of redemption, the sovereign God selected certain people to fill certain roles or to accomplish specific limited tasks.

1. THE ELECTION OF JESUS

The primary character in the drama is the Redeemer himself, the one who must do what is necessary in order to set humanity free from sin's guilt and bondage. The one chosen for this role is Jesus of Nazareth, son of a humble Jewish maiden. He alone is qualified to accomplish this task, because he alone, by God's plan, is the incarnate Son of God. This election of Jesus is the central and primary act of election. All other aspects of election are subordinate to it and dependent upon it. It is the very heart of the redemptive plan.

Through Isaiah the prophet, the Lord speaks of Jesus as the elect one: "Behold, My Servant, whom I uphold; my chosen one in whom my soul delights"[2] (Isa 42:1). Matt 12:18 quotes this passage and refers it to Jesus. At the transfiguration God spoke directly from heaven and announced the election of Jesus in these words: "This is My Son, My Chosen One; listen to Him!" (Luke 9:35). As Peter says, Jesus is the elect cornerstone (1 Pet 2:4, 6)

---

1. It refers to events as well as to persons. See Acts 4:28.
2. All Scripture quotations are from the New American Standard Bible.

and further, "He (Christ) was chosen before the creation of the world but was revealed in these last times for your sake" (1 Pet 1:20). The election of Jesus was part of the divine plan even in eternity, before the worlds were created. Foreknowing both the obedience of the Redeemer and the disobedience of his enemies, God predetermined the accomplishment of redemption through Jesus of Nazareth (Acts 2:23; 1 Pet 1:20). Jesus was predestined or foreordained to die for the sins of the world (Acts 4:28).

2. THE ELECTION OF ISRAEL

Although Jesus has the leading role in the drama of redemption, there is a large cast of supporting characters. These are necessary in order to prepare the way for Christ's appearance upon the stage of history.

The primary element of God's preparatory plan was the election of Israel as the people who would produce the Christ. Deut. 7:6 says, "For you are a holy people to the LORD your God; the LORD your God has chosen you to be a people for His own possession out of all the peoples who are on the face of the earth." (See Deut 14:2.) The Israelites were God's "chosen ones" (1 Chron 16:13). Paul begins his sermon in the synagogue at Antioch by reminding his fellow Jews that "the God of this people Israel chose our fathers, and made the people great during their stay in the land of Egypt" (Acts 13:17).

Several significant points about the election of Israel must be noted. In the first place, it was a sovereign election to service. Being chosen as the people from whom the Christ would come carried with it some of the highest privileges known to man (Rom 9:4, 5), but salvation was not automatically among them. Whether an Israelite was saved or not did not depend simply on his membership in the chosen people. The nation could serve its purpose of preparing for the Christ even if the majority of individuals belonging to it were lost.

This leads to a second point, namely, that the election of Israel was the election of a group or a corporate body, not the election of individuals. As Daane says, "Divine election in its basic Old Testament form is collective, corporate, national. It encompasses a community of which the individual Israelite is an integral part."[3] Calvinist theologian Berkouwer grants that even Romans 9 must refer to the nation of Israel and not to the eternal destiny of individuals.[4] In other words, God's purpose of preparing for the

---

3. James Daane, *The Freedom of God: A Study of Election and Pulpit* (Grand Rapids: Eerdmans, 1973), 104.

4. G. C. Berkouwer, *Divine Election,* Hugo Bekker, trans. (Grand Rapids: Eerdmans,

Messiah was served through the nation as such, not necessarily through the individual members of the nation.

In the third place, however, it must be noted that at times certain individuals connected with Israel were chosen for special roles in order to facilitate the purpose of the nation as a whole. In order to create Israel, God chose Abraham, Isaac and Jacob (see Neh 9:7; Rom 9:7, 13). He chose Moses (Ps 106:23) and David (Ps 78:70), among others; he even chose certain Gentile rulers to help carry out his purpose for Israel (e.g., Pharaoh: Rom 9:17; Cyrus: Isa 45:1).

The fact that God elected these individuals for specific service in the history of salvation does not, however, mean that they were elected to personal salvation (or condemnation, as the case may be). Since Israel was chosen specifically to prepare the way for the Messiah's appearance, her purpose was accomplished and her destiny fulfilled in the incarnation, death and resurrection of Jesus Christ (Acts 13:32, 33).[5]

3. THE ELECTION OF THE CHURCH

The drama of redemption was not complete, of course, when Israel had finished her role. Neither was it complete even when Christ had accomplished his saving work in history. Christ was chosen in order to redeem sinners and to bring them back into fellowship with God. Thus the drama is not complete until his redemptive work has borne its fruit, until there is a body of redeemed persons. These, too, are included in the historical enactment of the drama.

God had already decided to create on this side of the cross a new nation, a new Israel. Her role differs from that of Old Testament Israel. Her purpose is not the preparation for the coming of Christ, but rather participation in his saving work and the proclamation of it. This new elect body is the church.

As was the case with Old Testament Israel, the election of the church is a corporate or collective election. The church as a body is now God's elect people, chosen to complete God's purpose of redemption. This corporate election of the church is reflected in Peter's reference to the "chosen race" (1 Pet 2:9) and in John's description of local congregations as the "chosen lady" and her "chosen sister" (2 John 1, 13). As with Old Testament Israel, the

1960), 210ff. His main concern is to avoid the conclusion of individual reprobation as a symmetrical counterpart of individual election.

5. "God's election of Jesus does fulfill the purpose of Israel's election . . ." (Daane, *Freedom of God*, 107).

election of the church is an election to service. The church is God's vehicle for the proclamation of the good news of redemption in Christ. When Peter describes the church as a "chosen race," he adds this purpose for the choosing: "that you may proclaim the excellencies of Him who has called you out of darkness into His marvelous light" (1 Pet 2:9).

Just as God chose certain individuals for special service in relation to Israel, so did he select a group of individuals who would be his instruments in establishing the church. From among his disciples Jesus "chose twelve of them, whom He also named as apostles" (Luke 6:13). Later he asked them, "Did I Myself not choose you, the twelve. . .?" (John 6:70). Christ is speaking to the apostles when he says, "You did not choose Me, but I chose you, and appointed you, that you should go and bear fruit . . ." (John 15:16; see 13:18; 15:19). Likewise was the Apostle Paul chosen for special service (Gal 1:15, 16). In many ways, then, Old Testament Israel and the New Testament church are parallel with respect to God's electing purpose. The election of each is a corporate election; each is elected to service (Israel for preparation, the church for proclamation); and certain individuals are chosen for special roles in connection with each.

B. The Election of Individuals to Salvation

In addition to these similarities, however, there is one important difference. With the establishment of the church, a new dimension is added to the purpose of election. For now, it is not only election to service but also election to salvation. The church is elected not only for the proclamation of, but also for participation in, the saving work of Christ. The church is the very object of Christ's love and redemptive sacrifice (Acts 20:28; Eph 5:25). We are chosen unto salvation (2 Thess 2:13).

This raises the most controversial question associated with the whole subject of election, namely, what is the relationship of individuals to the process of election to salvation? Are individuals elected or predestined to salvation? If so, in what way? These important questions will now be discussed in detail.

1. THE UNCONDITIONAL ELECTION OF INDIVIDUALS

Probably the best-known view of individual election is the one associated with Calvinistic theology.[6] Calvinism teaches that certain individuals are

6. The Calvinistic system of theology did not actually originate with John Calvin,

unconditionally elected or predestined to become believers in Jesus Christ and thus be saved. From among the total mass of sinful humanity, even before it has been created, God chooses which individuals he wants to respond to the gospel call. When the call is issued, those who have been chosen are irresistibly enabled to answer it.

These are saved, while the rest of mankind is condemned to hell forever. On what basis does God choose the ones whom he saves? This is known only to God himself, and he has determined not to reveal it. God has his own reasons for the decisions which he makes, but they cannot be known by men.[7] Thus from the standpoint of human knowledge, the election is totally unconditional. There are no established conditions one may meet in order to qualify for being chosen. This view was taught by John Calvin. In the *Institutes* he says:

> As Scripture, then, clearly shows, we say that God once established by his eternal and unchangeable plan those whom he long before determined once for all to receive into salvation, and those whom, on the other hand, he would devote to destruction. We assert that, with respect to the elect, this plan was founded upon his freely given mercy, without regard to human worth; but by his just and irreprehensible but incomprehensible judgment he has barred the door of life to those whom he has given over to damnation. . . .[8]

Also to the point is Calvin's statement that "God was moved by no external cause—by no cause out of Himself—in the choice of us; but that He Himself, in Himself, was the cause and the author of choosing His people."[9] The Westminster Confession of Faith explains it thus:

> Those of mankind that are predestinated unto life, God, before the foundation of the world was laid, according to his eternal and immutable purpose, and the secret counsel and good pleasure of his will, hath chosen in Christ, unto everlasting glory, out of his mere free grace and love, without any foresight of faith or good works, or perseverance in either of them, or any other thing in the creature, as conditions, or causes moving him thereunto; and all to the praise of his glorious grace. (III:5)

---

but rather with Augustine.

7. Berkouwer, *Divine Election*, 60.

8. John Calvin, *Institutes of the Christian Religion* (Peabody, Mass: Hendrickson, 2007), 3.11.7

9. John Calvin, "A Treatise on the Eternal Predestination of God," in *Calvin's Calvinism*, Henry Cole, trans. (Grand Rapids: Eerdmans, 1956), 46.

According to Calvinism, then, specific individuals are the object of election; and they are chosen unconditionally.

2. THE CONDITIONAL ELECTION OF A CLASS OF INDIVIDUALS

A major part of Christendom has never been able to accept unconditional election of individuals as biblical. They declare that Scripture just does not teach such an idea, which appears to be unjust and arbitrary on God's part and seems to lead to pessimism and quietism on man's part. Many who oppose this concept assert instead that election is based on certain conditions which anyone may meet; and it is the election of a certain class or group, not the election of specific individuals.

This view is held by many Arminians and is sometimes thought to be *the* Arminian view on the subject. Emphasizing the corporate character of election, Dr. H. Orton Wiley, the eminent Nazarene theologian, has stated, "I hold, of course, to *class* predestination."[10] He finds it objectionable to say that "God has determined beforehand whether some should be saved or not, applied to individuals."[11]

Another Nazarene theologian, Mildred B. Wynkoop, states that theories about predestination are the watershed between Calvinism and Wesleyan Arminianism.[12] She traces the origin of the idea of personal, particular, individual predestination to Augustine.[13] Arminius's theory of predestination, she says, is just the opposite: "Individual persons are not chosen to salvation, but it is Christ who has been appointed as the only Saviour of men. *The way of salvation is predestined.*"[14]

Robert Shank, in his book, *Elect in the Son,* presents a similar view. Election, he says, is primarily corporate and only secondarily particular.[15] Individuals become elect only when they identify with or associate themselves with the elect body.[16] He summarizes his view of election as

---

10. H. Orton Wiley and others, "The Debate Over Divine Election," *Christianity Today* 4 (Oct. 12, 1959), 3.

11. Ibid., 5.

12. Mildred Bangs Wynkoop, *Foundations of Wesleyan-Arminian Theology* (Kansas City, Mo.: Beacon Hill, 1967), 14.

13. Ibid., 30,31.

14. Ibid.,53.

15. Robert Shank, *Elect in the Son* (Springfield, Mo: Westcott, 1970), 45.

16. Ibid., 50, 55.

"potentially universal, corporate rather than particular, and conditional rather than unconditional."[17]

3. THE CONDITIONAL ELECTION OF INDIVIDUALS

The views just discussed are deliberate efforts to present a biblical alternative to the Calvinistic doctrine of unconditional, particular election. Such an alternative is necessary, for the Calvinistic view as a whole is definitely contrary to Scripture. However, election is not limited to a "way" or class election. Biblical election to salvation is indeed conditional, but it is also individual or personal.

The distinctive element in Calvinistic election is its unconditional nature, not its particularity. Only the former must be rejected; to reject the latter also is an overreaction and a distortion of the Bible's own teaching.

What is the biblical doctrine of election? As understood here, it is the idea that God predestines to salvation those individuals who meet the gracious conditions which he has set forth. In other words, election to salvation is conditional and particular.[18]

a. *Individual election.* A popular belief among non-Calvinists is that "God predestined the plan, not the man." The Scriptures, however, show that it is always *persons* who are predestined and not *just* a plan.[19] This is so obvious that it hardly seems necessary to mention it. In Rom 8:29, 30 Paul is speaking of *persons.* The same persons who are predestined are also called, justified and glorified. In 2 Thess 2:13 he says that "God has chosen you," the Christian people of Thessalonica, "for salvation." Eph 1: 4, 5, 11 speaks of God's predestination in relation to his plan, but it is specifically stated that God predestined *us* (persons) to adoption as sons *in accordance with* his purpose and plan.

Election, then, is not limited to a divine plan but applies to persons as well. But does it apply to *particular* persons? Are specific individuals predestined to salvation? The answer is yes. No other view can do justice to biblical teaching in several respects.

---

17. Ibid., 122. See also William Klein, *The New Chosen People* (Eugene, Ore.: Wipf and Stock, 2001)

18. See Jack Cottrell, "Conditional Election," *The Seminary Review,* XII (Summer 1966), 57–63; also, Cottrell, "The Predestination of Individuals," *Christian Standard,* CV (Oct. 4, 1970), 13–14.

19. The plan, of course, is predetermined by God. This applies both to the redemptive work of Christ (Acts 4:28) and to the establishment of the church. But this is not the point of predestination to salvation.

First, it should be noted that the Bible often speaks of predestination in terms that specify particular individuals. Many passages do refer to the elect in general, but other references focus upon specific persons. In Rom 16:13, Rufus is identified as an elect person. In 1 Pet 1:1, 2 the apostle greets the elect Christians in certain specific geographical locations. A very clear statement of the predestination of individuals to salvation is 2 Thess 2:13. Here Paul says to the Thessalonian brethren that "God has chosen you from the beginning for salvation." This statement cannot be generalized and de-personalized. Another point that should be noted is that Rev 17:8 speaks of those "whose names have not been written in the book of life from the foundation of the world." This is a negative statement; but it would be meaningless to say that some persons' names have *not* been written in the book of life since the beginning unless there are others whose names *have* been written there from the beginning.

There is some question as to whether names can be blotted out of the book of life (see Exod 32:32, 33; Ps 69:28; Rev 3:5). If so, these would not be the names written there from the foundation of the world, but those having the status, perhaps, of the seeds that sprouted in rocky or weedy soil (Matt 13:20–22). Those who overcome are specifically promised that their names will not be blotted out (Rev 3:5), and these are in all probability the ones written from the foundation of the world.

In any case, there are certain individuals whose names have been in the book of life since the foundation of the world, and whose names will not be blotted out. Who can these be except those whom God has predestined individually to salvation? And the point here is that their very *names* have been known to God from the beginning. What can this be but individual predestination? "Rejoice that your names are recorded in heaven" (Luke 10:20)!

How is it possible that God could determine even before the creation which individuals will be saved, and could even write their names in the book of life? The answer is found in the fact and nature of God's foreknowledge. The Bible explicitly relates predestination to God's foreknowledge, and a correct understanding of this relationship is the key to the whole question of election to salvation. Rom 8:29 says, "For whom He foreknew, He also predestined to become conformed to the image of His Son, that He might be the first-born among many brethren." Peter addresses his first epistle to those "who are chosen according to the foreknowledge of God the Father" (1 Pet 1:1, 2). In other words, God's foreknowledge is the means by which he has determined which individuals shall be conformed to the image of his Son (in his glorified resurrection body).

To say that God has foreknowledge means that he has real knowledge or cognition of something before it actually happens or exists in history. This is the irreducible core of the concept, which must be neither eliminated nor attenuated. Nothing else is consistent with the nature of God.[20] One of the basic truths of Scripture is that God is eternal. This means that when time is considered as a linear succession of moments with a *before* and a *now* and an *after*, God is infinite in both directions. He has existed before now into infinite past time (i.e., eternity) without ever having begun, and he will exist after now into infinite future time (again, eternity) without ever ending.

"Even from everlasting to everlasting, You are God" (Ps 90:2). But to say that God is eternal means more than this. God's eternity is not just a quantitative distinction between him and his creation. Eternity is also also qualitatively different from time. That God is eternal means that he is not bound by the restrictions of time; he is above time. At any given moment, what is both past and future to a finite creature is present to God's knowledge. It is all *now* to God, in a kind of panorama of time; he is the great "I AM" (Exod 3:14).

To get some idea of the majesty of the infinite and eternal Creator, as contrasted with the finiteness of all creatures, one must read the Lord's challenges to the false gods and idols in Isa 41–46. The very thing that distinguishes God as God is that he transcends time, and sees it from beginning to end at one and the same moment. Therefore, God's "foreknowledge," is really his sovereign *eternal knowledge*.

God challenges the false gods to recite past history and to foretell the future. They cannot, but he can, because he is God; and his knowledge of past and future *proves* he is God. Here is what he says:

> "Present your case," the LORD says. "Bring forward your strong arguments," The King of Jacob says. Let them bring forth and declare to us what is going to take place; As for the former events, declare what they were. That we may consider them, and know

20. Most Calvinists try to avoid the clear implications of God's foreknowledge by changing the meaning of it from "foreknow" to "forelove" or something similar. The idea of cognition is made subordinate to some other concept. For instance, Roger Nicole says, "The passages dealing with foreknowledge are not at all difficult to integrate, inasmuch as the term foreknowledge in Scripture does not have merely the connotation of advance information (which the term commonly has in nontheological language), but indicates God's special choice coupled with affection" (H. Orton Wiley and others, "Debate Over Divine Election," 16). This is an arbitrary definition, however, and is not consistent with the use of the term in Acts 2:23, where it can mean no more than prescience. See Samuel Fisk, *Election & Predestination: Keys to a Clearer Understanding* (Eugene, Ore.: Wipf and Stock, 1997), 71–82.

their outcome. Or announce to us what is coming. Declare the things that are going to come afterward, That we may know that you are gods; Indeed, do good or evil, that we may anxiously look about us and fear together. Behold, you are of no account. And your work amounts to nothing; He who chooses you is an abomination (Isa 41:21–24).

"Who has declared *this* from the beginning/that we might know? Or from former times, that we may say, "*He* is right!"? Surely there was no one who declared, Surely there was no one who proclaimed, Surely there was no one who heard your words (Isa 41:26).

"Thus says the LORD, the King of Israel And his Redeemer, the LORD of hosts: 'I am the first and I am the last. And there is no God besides Me. And who is like Me? Let him proclaim and declare it; Yes, let him recount it to Me in order, From the time that I established the ancient nation. And let them declare to them the things that are coming And the events that are going to take place. Do not tremble and do not be afraid; Have I not long since announced *it* to you and declared *it*? And you are My witnesses. Is there any God besides Me, Or is there any *other* Rock? I know of none'" (Isa 44:6–8).

"Remember the former things long past, For I am God, and there is no other; *I am* God, and there is no one like Me, Declaring the end from the beginning, And from ancient times things which have not been done. Saying, 'My purpose will be established, And I will accomplish all My good pleasure'; Calling a bird of prey from the east, The man of My purpose from a far country. Truly I have spoken; truly I will bring it to pass. I have planned it, *surely* I will do it" (Isa 46:9–11).

In light of the biblical teaching concerning God's eternity and foreknowledge, and the relation between this foreknowledge and predestination, it should be evident that predestination must be of individuals. Surely God foreknows everything about the life of every individual. He cannot help but foreknow, because he is God. He sees the entire scope of every individual's destiny—even before the foundation of the world.[21]

b. *Conditional election.* Many Arminians affirm God's foreknowledge while at the same time denying individual predestination. Some just ignore the inconsistency involved, while others dismiss it with a kind of embarrassed mumbling.[22] The reason why they are so determined to reject individual election is that they believe it to be inseparable from the Calvinistic doctrine of election. This is not the case, however. Calvinism does teach individual predestination, but this is not what makes it Calvinism. The essence of the Calvinistic doctrine, as noted earlier, is that election is unconditional. The watershed is not between particular and general, but between conditional and unconditional election. The Calvinistic error is avoided by affirming *conditional* election.

The foreknowledge of God has been emphasized. God elects individuals according to his foreknowledge. But the question may well be asked, foreknowledge of what? The answer is that he foreknows whether an individual will meet the *conditions* for salvation which he has sovereignly imposed. What are these conditions? The basic and all-encompassing condition is whether a person is *in Christ,* namely, whether one has entered into a saving union with Christ by means of which he shares in all the benefits of Christ's redeeming work. Whom God foreknew to be in Christ ("until death"—Rev 2:10), he predestined to be glorified like Jesus himself.

---

21. Calvin acknowledged that this was the view of the early church fathers, and even of Augustine for a time. But he suggests that we "imagine that these fathers are silent" *(Institutes,* 3.22.8). Berkouwer notes that "Bavinck goes so far as to call this solution 'general,' for it is accepted by the Greek Orthodox, Roman Catholic, Lutheran, Remonstrant, Baptist, and Methodist churches" (Berkouwer, *Divine Election,* 37).

22. For instance, Wiley objects to applying predestination to individuals, yet grants that God has foreknowledge of who will believe in Christ (Wiley and others, "Debate Over Divine Election," 5, 15) . Shank's treatment of foreknowledge is puzzling: "Thus it is evident that the passages positing foreknowledge and predestination must be understood as having as a frame of reference *primarily* the corporate body of the Israel of God and *secondarily* individuals, not unconditionally, but only in association and identification with the elect body. . ." (Shank, *Elect in the Son,* 154). It is as if corporate election were the opposite of unconditional election. Further, Shank says that "whether God has actively foreknown each individual—both the elect and the reprobate—may remain a moot question. The Biblical doctrine of election does not require such efficient particular foreknowledge, for the election is primarily corporate and objective and only secondarily particular. The passages positing foreknowledge and predestination of the elect may be understood quite as well one way as the other" *(Ibid.,*155*).*

This is the import of Eph 1:4, which says that "He chose us in Him"—in Christ—"before the foundation of the world." The elect are chosen in (Greek: *hen*) Christ, that is, because they are in Christ; they are not chosen *into* (*eis*) Christ, that is, in order that they may be in Christ. They are in Christ before the foundation of the world not in reality but in the foreknowledge of God.

That the basic condition for election is our being *in Christ* preserves the Christocentric character of election, which seems to be a major concern for many.[23] It must not be forgotten that Jesus Christ is *the* elect one, and that all other redemptive election is in him. Thus even though election is conditional, it all depends upon Christ and the gracious benefits of his saving work.

Of course, there are also conditions which one must meet in order to *be* in Christ, i.e., in order to enter into saving union with Him and to remain in this union. The basic condition, of course, is faith (Gal 3:26; Eph 3:17; Col 2:12). Other related conditions are repentance and baptism (Acts 2:38; Gal 3:27; Col 2:12). These conditions are in no way to be interpreted as meritorious on man's part, since they are graciously and sovereignly imposed by God himself. Thus having set forth these conditions for being in Christ, God foreknows from the beginning who will and who will not meet them. Those whom he foresees as meeting them are predestined to salvation.

How, then, is biblical predestination to be described? The Calvinist says, "God unconditionally selects certain *sinners* and predestines them to become *believers*." This is contrary to the teaching of Scripture, however, which instead says, in effect, that God selects all *believers* and predestines them to become his *children* in glory.[24]

In other words, it is important to see exactly what it is to which individuals are elected. They are predestined to salvation itself, not to the means of salvation. They are not predestined to become believers; they are not predestined to faith. Their choice of Jesus Christ is not predestined; the

23. See Shank, *Elect in the Son*, 27ff.; Berkouwer, *Divine Election*, 132ff.

24. The Calvinistic mind sees election as bringing about the transition from unbelief to belief, hence making unbelievers the object of election. The Arminian says that this transition is made by a free act of will; election then is an act of God directed toward the believer after the transition has been made. Ignoring this important distinction, Daane criticizes the Arminian view of election as being unpreachable in that "it turns God's election into a human act." It makes election to be merely "a description of the possibilities of human freedom." Thus "Arminianism cannot preach election because it does not regard election as an act of God and, therefore, as an action of his Word; election is merely a possible response the sinner may make to the Word" (Daane, *Freedom of God*, 15–18). His criticism misses the mark, however, since election is not something directed toward unbelievers but toward believers. See Fisk, *Election and Predestination*, 37–40. True, the transition from unbelief to belief is influenced by God's prevenient grace, but it is not the result of election.

choice is foreknown, and the subsequent blessings of salvation are then predestined.[25]

The Bible is quite clear about this. Rom 8:29 says that those whom he foreknew were predestined by God "to become conformed to the image of His Son, that He might be the first-born among many brethren." The reference to Christ's being the "first-born" is a reference to his resurrection from the dead into a glorified state (Col 1:18; Rev 1:5). Our being conformed to his image here refers to our glorification (Rom 8:30), when we will receive a resurrection body like his own (Phil 3:21). Thus we are chosen to become God's glorified children, Christ being the first-born among many brethren. (Similar to this is Eph 1:5, which states that we are predestined unto adoption as children.)

Believers are predestined not just to receive future glory, but also to enjoy the present benefits of Christ's saving work. As 2 Thess 2:13 says, "God has chosen you from the beginning for salvation (*eis soterian*)." In 1 Pet 1:2 this salvation is seen to include a life of good works and justification by the blood of Christ ("chosen . . . that you may obey Jesus Christ and be sprinkled with His blood").

The biblical doctrine of election, then, definitely includes the conditional election of individuals to salvation. Through his foreknowledge, God sees who will believe upon Christ Jesus as Savior and Lord, and become united with him through faith. Then even before the creation of the world he predestines these believers to share the glory of the risen Christ.

II. ELECTION AND RELATED DOCTRINES

We now propose to show that the doctrine of election outlined above is consistent with biblical teaching as a whole. Attention will be focused on two related doctrines in connection with which objections are often raised, namely, the doctrine of God and the doctrine of man. This will show that conditional, individual election is most consistent with these two doctrines.

25. The supralapsarian-infralapsarian controversy is misplaced. It argues whether God's decree to elect is prior to or subsequent to his decree regarding the Fall. But the focal point of election is not man's decision to sin, but rather his decision with regard to God's offer of grace. The crucial question is whether God's decree to elect is prior to man's decision to accept Christ or whether it follows it. The latter is the biblical view.

A. The Nature of God

The strongest objection to this understanding of election is that it violates the biblical teaching concerning the nature of God. This objection, which is raised most often by Calvinists, must be taken very seriously. We shall see, however, that it is without basis, since conditional, individual election is perfectly consistent with the sovereignty, grace and justice of God.

1. THE SOVEREIGNTY OF GOD

No doctrine is more important than the sovereignty of God. Wynkoop has rightly said:

> . . . God's total sovereignty is the basis of the whole of Christian theology. No philosophical theory which permits the slightest break in that sovereignty can be permitted. Every Christian doctrine hangs on this doctrine. . . . A less than sovereign God cannot support Christian faith.[26]

One of the most common objections to conditional election is that it necessarily violates God's sovereignty. Berkouwer sums up the objection thus: "In such a notion God's decision is made dependent on man's decision."[27] It is clear, he says, that predestination according to foreknowledge "casts shadows on the sovereignty of God's election and is a flagrant contradiction of the nature of Christian faith."[28] This is why it was rejected by both John Calvin[29] and the Synod of Dort.[30] Calvin's rejection of foreseen faith, as summarized by Berkouwer, is as follows:

> . . .He sees in it an attack against God's greatness. It supposes a waiting God whose judgment and final act depend on and follow upon man's acceptance and decision, so that the final and principal decision falls with man; it teaches self-destination instead of divine destination. *(Inst.* [1.18.1])[31]

This is basically the same objection voiced by Roger Nicole:

---

26. Wynkoop, *Foundations of Wesleyan-Arminian Theology*, 87–88.

27. Berkouwer, *Divine Election*, 42.

28. Ibid., 35.

29. Ibid.,36.

30. Ibid.,26.

31. Ibid., 36.

> I find it objectionable that in the Arminian position the ultimate
> issues seem to depend upon the choice of man rather than upon
> the choice of God. And it seems to me that both the Scriptures
> and a proper understanding of divine sovereignty demand that
> the choice be left with God rather than with man . . .[32]

Herman Hoeksema's idea of divine sovereignty, according to James Daane, is that "nothing God does is a *response* to what man has done. God is never conditioned by man. Man's actions cannot become conditions for God's responses."[33] Thus divine sovereignty must rule out conditional election.

In response to such an objection, it is freely admitted that conditional election does mean that in some sense God reacts to a decision made by man. But it must be insisted that this in no way violates the sovereignty of God.[34] This is supported by two considerations.

In the first place, an arrangement under which God reacts to man's choices would violate his sovereignty *only* if God were forced into such an arrangement, only if it were a necessity imposed upon God from without. But this is not the case. It was God's sovereign choice to bring into existence a universe inhabited by free-willed creatures whose decisions would to some extent determine the total picture.[35] When God established the system of conditional election, it was God alone who sovereignly imposed the conditions.[36] God's freedom to decree whatever he pleases is the proof and essence of his absolute sovereignty. Samuel Fisk points out that God's free and voluntary decision to allow man a measure of self-determination "is something which only a great and omnipotent God would do."[37] Rather than detract from his sovereignty, it actually enhances it and glorifies it more.

32. Wiley and others, "Debate Over Divine Election," 5.

33. Daane, *Freedom of God*, 25.

34. For a fuller discussion see Jack Cottrell, "Sovereignty and Free Will," *The Seminary Review*, IX (Spring 1963), 39–51.

35. See C. S. Lewis, *Letters to Malcolm: Chiefly on Prayer* (London: Geoffrey Bles, 1964), 72. He says, "Yet, for us rational creatures, to be created also means 'to be made agents.' We have nothing that we have not received; but part of what we have received is the power of being something more than receptacles."

36. Daane presents an irresponsible and totally false caricature of conditional election when he says, "Reformed theology rejects Arminianism because it makes God comply with *human* conditions. It rejects the notions that God is not free to operate except within conditions laid down by man and that God cannot save man unless man first decides to believe and choose God" (Daane, *Freedom of God,* 127). He then refers to "the Arminian's imposition of restrictions on God." (Ibid.)

37. Fisk, *Election & Predestination*, 51.

In the second place, to deny conditional election in principle because it presents God as reacting to man's action ignores the fact that God has reacted and does react to human decisions in even more basic ways than this.

Of primary importance is the fact that man's decision to sin is a contingent factor to which God has reacted. This is the very essence of Christianity: because man has sinned, God has provided redemption. Virtually every action of God recorded in the Bible after Gen 3:1 is a *response* to human sin. The Abrahamic covenant, the establishment of Israel, the incarnation of Jesus Christ, the death and resurrection of Christ, the establishment of the church, the Bible itself—all are part of the divine reaction to man's sin. As C. S. Lewis has pointed out, God would not forgive sins if man had committed none. "In that sense the Divine action is consequent upon, conditioned by, elicited by, our behaviour."[38]

Likewise, God's judgment on unrepentant sinners is a reaction to human sin. It is very interesting that Berkouwer himself argues for this point,[39] even though in so doing he undermines his whole case against conditional election. His inconsistency here is the result of his inability to accept an unconditional reprobation that is symmetrical to unconditional election. Thus he says that "Scripture repeatedly speaks of God's rejection as a divine answer in history, as a reaction to man's sin and disobedience, not as its cause." God's rejection of sinners "is clearly His holy reaction against sin."[40] It is "a reactive deed, a holy, divine answer to the sin of man."[41]

In light of such affirmations as this, how can Berkouwer or any Calvinist continue to argue that conditional election is a violation of the sovereignty of God? If God can maintain his sovereignty while reacting to man's sin, he surely can do so while reacting to man's (foreseen) faith. Another area in which God reacts to human decisions is prayer. Lewis argues in his *Letters to Malcolm* that if God can react to sin, he certainly can react to prayer.[42]

We may press this question further and ask, if God can react to sin and prayer without compromising his sovereignty, why can he not so react to foreseen faith? The answer, of course, is that he can and does. To say that this makes God dependent on man or that man is thereby *causing* God to do something is an unfounded caricature. The whole idea that unconditional

---

38. Lewis, *Letters to Malcolm*, 72.

39. Berkouwer, *Divine Election*, 183ff.

40. Ibid., 183.

41. Ibid., 184.

42. Lewis, *Letters to Malcolm*, 72.

election is the *sine qua non* of the sovereignty of God is, as Shank says, "theological humbug" and "one of the great fallacies of Calvinism."[43]

2. THE GRACE OF GOD

Another equally strong objection to conditional election is that it violates the grace of God. That is, if God elects by means of his foreknowledge of faith, this would make man to some extent the cause or source of his own salvation. Where, then, is grace?[44]

Both Augustine and Calvin rejected conditional election as inconsistent with grace and as implying justification by works.[45] This was due in part to the fact that many people whom they opposed still taught some kind of salvation by merit, and therefore they taught predestination on the basis of foreseen *merit*. Ambrose, for instance, commenting on Rom 8:29, says that God "did not predestinate before he foreknew, but to those whose merit he foreknew, he predestinated the rewards of merit."[46] One of Calvin's main opponents, Pighius, was, as Wendel says, "the inheritor of a long tradition which had endeavoured to make predestination dependent upon foreknowledge of merits."[47] This certainly prejudiced Calvin's formulation of the problem, as shown in the following statement:

> . . . But it is a piece of futile cunning to lay hold on the term foreknowledge, and so to use that as to pin the eternal *election* of God upon the *merits* of men, which election the apostle everywhere ascribes to the alone purpose of God . . .[48]

It is quite proper to reject foreseen merit as incompatible with grace. But the Calvinist does not stop here. Even when one rejects all notions of merit and insists on foreseen *faith*, not works, the Calvinist still cries that

43. Shank, *Elect in the Son*, 143–144.

44. Daane says that "Arminians held that God decreed to elect all men and then, in response to the unbelief of many men, decreed to elect only those who believe. Reformed thought found this unacceptable, for it surrenders the truth of man's salvation by grace alone" (Daane, *Freedom of God,* 54).

45. Berkouwer, *Divine Election.*, 36. See Wynkoop, *Foundations of Wesleyan-Arminian Theology*, 56.

46. Ambrose, *De Fide,* lib. 5. n. 83, cited by Harry Buis, *Historic Protestantism and Predestination* (Philadelphia: Presbyterian and Reformed, 1958), 9.

47. Francois Wendel, *Calvin: The Origins and Development of His Religious Thought,* Philip Mairet, trans. (New York: Harper and Row, 1963), 271.

48. John Calvin, "The Eternal Predestination of God," 48; cf. 64. See also the *Institutes,* 3.12.3, where Calvin speaks of the foresight of holiness and good works.

grace is vitiated. This is because he cannot see the biblical distinction be-tween faith and works. Berkouwer asserts that "election does not find its basis in man's works and *therefore* not in his foreseen faith."[49] Whether it be merit or faith that is foreseen, "God's decision is made dependent on man's decision. The initiative and the majesty of God's grace is overshadowed."[50] Grace is thus "limited and obscured."[51]

This kind of objection to conditional election overlooks one of the most basic principles in the system of grace, namely, that faith and works are qualitatively different. Grace is consistent with *faith* as a condition, but not with *works* as a condition (Rom 4:4, 5, 16; 11:6). "For by grace you have been saved through faith," but "not as a result of works" (Eph 2:8, 9). In these passages Paul clearly shows that faith is not in the category of works. They are qualitatively distinct.

Thus we must agree that foreseen works, merit, or holiness as a con-dition for election would be contrary to grace. But must we say the same about foreseen faith? Of course not. Faith by its very nature is consistent with grace, whether foreseen or not. If God can *give* salvation on the condi-tion of faith *post facto,* then he can predestine a believer to salvation as the result of his foreknowledge of that faith.[52] Thus to say that election is of grace does not mean that it is unconditional; it simply means that it is not conditioned on works.

One of the basic problems here and with the Calvinistic system in general is the notion of *sovereign grace.* Berkouwer's thesis is that election according to foreseen faith is simply synergism and is just another way of opposing "the sovereignty of God's grace."[53] He speaks of the "*skandalon* of sovereign grace."[54]

The idea of sovereign grace indeed is a *skandalon,* but it is one that was created by man when the concepts of God's sovereignty and God's grace were fused and confused together. Surely God is sovereign in all things, but his sovereignty does not absorb and cancel out his other attributes. His wisdom, his love, and his grace are not just synonyms for his sovereignty. God's sovereignty expresses itself in terms of absolute power, the power of sheer might and strength, the power to create and to destroy. But his grace is expressed in a totally different kind of power, namely through the drawing

---

49. Berkouwer, *Divine Election.,* 42; italics supplied.

50. Ibid.

51. Ibid., 43.

52. Fisk, *Election and Predestination,* 77–78; Shank, *Elect in the Son,* 125,144–145.

53. Berkouwer, *Divine Election,* 47.

54. Ibid., 8.

power of the Spirit's love and compassion and self-sacrifice (see John 6:44; 12:32) along with God's conviction of the hearts of humanity (John 16:8).

In the concept of sovereign grace, sovereignty dominates and overwhelms grace, so that grace is not allowed to be grace. The shepherd is dressed unnaturally in the garb of the warrior.

We must let grace come to us on its own terms. Grace does not want to force its way. Like Christ, it stands at the door and knocks (Rev 3:20). The Bible teaches very plainly that the gifts of grace are appropriated by faith. If by works, then grace is no longer grace. On this all agree. But likewise, if it is by sovereign imposition, then grace is also no longer grace.

Conditional election, then, is quite consistent with grace; it opposes only the false hybrid *of sovereign* grace.

3. THE JUSTICE OF GOD

Finally it should be noted that the conditional election of individuals is consistent with the justice of God. God's justice leads him to treat all persons alike, and to bestow no special favors with respect to salvation.

This is the point of the Bible's teaching that God is no respecter of persons. (See Acts 10:34; Rom 2:11; Eph 6:9; Col 3:25; 1 Pet 1:17.) The Calvinist often quotes this biblical teaching to prove unconditional election. This is done by taking it to mean that God does not take account of anything in the person himself (i.e., no certain conditions) when selecting him to receive the gift of faith and salvation. The principle is given in Scripture, however, to show exactly the opposite, namely, that God *does* reward and punish *only* on the basis of what he finds in the person himself. The contexts in which the principle is asserted establish this. It is meant to teach God's justice and fairness in judgment.

The very thing that would violate this principle of justice would be deciding on an individual's eternal destiny without taking account of anything in him. But this is exactly what the doctrine of unconditional election asserts. Only the doctrine of conditional election, where God elects to salvation those who comply with his graciously given and announced terms of pardon, can preserve the justice and the impartiality of God.[55]

---

55. Fisk, *Election and Predestination*, 47. Wiley makes an unfortunate statement when he says that "it impugns God's justice, for him to decide—regardless of whether a man believes or not—whether he can, whether he will be saved" (Wiley and others, "*Debate Over Divine Election*," 5). Wiley means this as a criticism of unconditional, individual predestination; but it does not accurately represent that position nor anyone else's.

B. The Nature of Man

Since conditional election is seen to be consistent with the biblical doctrine of God, does it follow that there is now no reason to reject it? No, because the nature of man is also at issue here. In fact, the basic reason for Augustinianism's rejection of conditional election and affirmation of unconditional election lies in this area. Thus it remains to be shown that conditional election is consistent with the biblical doctrine of man.

1. TOTAL DEPRAVITY

Why does the Calvinist continue to insist on unconditional predestination, even when sovereignty and grace are not at stake? What is the imperative which necessitates it? The answer is the doctrine of total depravity, which in its essence means that all persons as the result of Adam's sin are from birth unable to respond in any positive way to the gospel call. There is a total inability to come to the decision to put one's trust in Christ. This point is truly the keystone in the Calvinistic system. This is what makes unconditional election logically and doctrinally necessary.

This is shown in the frequent objection that foreseen faith solves nothing, since God gives the faith to whomever he chooses.[56] Why must *God* choose the ones to whom he will give faith? Not in order to preserve his sovereignty, but because no one in the sinful mass of mankind is able to respond when the gospel is preached. Therefore if any at all are going to respond, God must decide which ones to make able to believe.

The situation is like that of a doctor who has perfected a technique that will restore sanity to the most mentally deranged persons. For some reason he cannot use it on all such persons, so some must be selected and others rejected. Since the individuals in question are too insane even to know what is going on, the doctor himself simply views the patients and decides on the basis of reasons wholly unknown to them which ones shall be made sane again.

The fact is, however, that the Bible does not picture man as *totally* depraved.[57] Man as a sinner is truly depraved and corrupted (Jer 17:9), even to the point of being dead in his trespasses and sins (Eph 2:1, 5; Col 2:13). This does not mean, however, that he is unable to respond to the gospel

---

56. Carl Bangs, *Arminius: A Study in the Dutch Reformation* (Nashville: Abingdon, 1971), 219.

57. Even Calvinist R.C. Sproul says *"Total Depravity* is a very misleading term" (*Chosen by God* [Wheaton, Ill., Tyndale House, 1986], 103).

call. The parallel between Eph 2:1–10 and Col 2:11–13 shows that even the person who is dead in his sins is regenerated *through his faith* in Christ, i.e., he believes before he is regenerated, though the Holy Spirit also "draws" him beforehand. (John 6:44)

His regeneration or his coming to life depends upon his faith. This is seen in Col 2:12, which says that in baptism a person is risen with Christ (i.e., made alive, regenerated) through faith in the working of God. Thus a person cannot come to faith without the gospel (Rom 10:17), but he *is* able to respond to the gospel in faith. God foreknows who will make such a response, and these he predestines to salvation.

2. HUMAN RESPONSIBILITY

Conditional election alone preserves the integrity of free will and thus of human responsibility, without which a moral system is impossible. God does not force man to sin; man chooses to sin of his own free will. Thus the individual is responsible for his sin and for his rejection of grace, and he justly suffers the punishment for it. Just as God does not force a person to sin, neither does he force anyone to accept grace. A person chooses to accept grace when he decides to meet the conditions which God has established for receiving it. Of course, there is no merit in making the decision, for the condition is one of grace and not of works. Nevertheless, a person is responsible for making the decision himself. If he does not make it, he has only himself to blame.

One other point must be emphasized, namely, that the authentic, free-will character of an individual's decision is not nullified by God's foreknowledge of it. Some Arminians object to individual predestination on such a basis. How can human choices be truly free, they say, if God knows them in advance? In order to preserve human freedom, they are compelled to diminish the majesty of God's foreknowledge. Some argue that God has voluntarily limited his own foreknowledge.[58] The idea is that God, by his own choice, does not know in advance who will accept Christ; he must wait until the actual decision is made.

This view, however, ignores the biblical teaching concerning God's eternity. The idea that God has voluntarily limited his knowledge has no biblical basis, and it is simply unthinkable in view of the majestic portrait of the eternal God discussed earlier. But to think that God would *have* to limit his foreknowledge in order to preserve human freedom is precluded

58. For instance, Thomas W. Brents, *The Gospel Plan of Salvation* (Nashville: Gospel Advocate, 1966), 92ff.

likewise by the eternity of God. For after all, even the free-will decisions of men are made within the framework of time.

They are truly free decisions, but they are the decisions of time-bound creatures. But God is eternal, above time, knowing the end from the beginning. To say that God could not foreknow truly free human decisions is either to exalt man too highly or to reduce God to a creaturely status.

A similar objection is this: if human decisions are foreknown, then they are certain to occur. But if they are certain, how can they be free and contingent? This again ignores the distinction between time and eternity, and overlooks the reality of history. True, every decision is certain as far as God's foreknowledge is concerned, but foreknowledge is not foredetermination. Every decision must be made in the arena of history. It is not *real* until produced by a human will in history. The fact that God foreknows what that choice will be does not mean he caused it. He simply knew in advance what would be freely decided. He can do this because he is God, not man.

Only the conditional predestination of individuals, then, can preserve the majesty of the eternal God and the integrity of free will and human responsibility.

CONCLUSIONS

In summary the doctrine of predestination with regard to salvation and damnation may be described thus: (1) There *is* an absolute, unconditional predestination, made without reference to foreknowledge. This is general or group predestination, corporate predestination, the predestination of the plan and of classes of men. In Scripture, this includes Israel and the church. As for the plan, by absolute sovereign decree God determined to save whoever responds to his free offer of salvation and to damn whoever rejects it. (2) There is also a conditional predestination, made by means of God's foreknowledge. This is particular predestination, the election of believing individuals to salvation or the reprobation of individuals to damnation. Because God foreknows each person's decisions, he predetermines each person's destiny. This is the doctrine of predestination as taught by Arminius himself. Bangs summarizes one of Arminius's statements thus:

> By an absolute predestination God wills to save those who believe and to damn those who persevere in disobedience; by a conditional predestination God wills to save those individuals

whom he foresees as believing and persevering and to damn those whom he foresees as not believing.[59]

But it is only incidental that Arminius taught this view of predestination. Of infinitely greater importance is the fact that the Bible teaches it.

59. Bangs, *Arminius,* 221.

6

"... The Spirit of Grace" (Heb. 10:29)

William G. MacDonald and John D. Wagner

The most complicating factor for system building in theology is the person-hood of God. Non-Christian theistic philosophers routinely reject the truth that God is personal, and thereby they simplify their theological constructs. A force, idea, or principle is far more consistent and controllable in thought than a living personality, so they fabricate philosophical systems unencumbered by the vagaries of will, sensitivity, responsiveness and the various other features of dynamic personhood. When something impersonal or something less than a complete personality is centralized as the universal "God," the resultant theology inevitably collides with the Christian faith.

Christian theology that is true to the whole revelation of God includes not only the personal vision of God, but also guards the doctrine of God from every deadly impersonal determinism. As for evangelical theology, while it contends objectively for "the faith which was once for all handed down to the saints," (Jude 3) it is sure that the object of that faith is none other than the *living* God. His "living" depicts not only inexhaustible vitality but his anthropomorphic accommodation of himself to temporal and even spatial (the "Most High") relatedness to mankind. It means that the "life" of him who is perfect in himself is over against mankind in such a way as evincing a measure of *undeterminedness*. That is, having contingency in matters of decision, and flexibility, compensatory adjustment, and real openness to meaningful prayer in the reciprocity of "I-Thou" relationships with man.

The concept, "person," in the normal modern sense of that word is found nowhere in the Bible under that terminology. The Bible nevertheless uses the term "spirit" to disclose God's inner self. God *is* spirit, and man *has* a spirit. Both man and God have common ground of being, inasmuch as man—unlike the animals—was given a spirit that "imaged" God. To think of God as spirit is to view him as personal, that is, as a self, and in this case as one corresponding on a colossal scale to man's personal selfhood. In saying this, we are not thereby constructing God in man's image, but merely consenting to the biblical revelation that teaches the eternal nature of God's Spirit and the derived character of man's spirit, fashioned in God's image.

A deterministic principle (e.g., evolutionary process, behaviorism, dialectical materialism, historical fate) may be conceptualized by the god-makers as "god," or as the ground under some more popular image of the deity. But it must never be thought as identical with the God whose revelation came in full in Christ and is preserved for us in the biblical writings.

Moving in closer to the situation in Christian theology, we must caveat against the construction of any theological system, however well-meaning, the culmination of which would remain unchanged had God—to speak hypothetically and foolishly— "died" before, at, or just after the creation. Such a condition would leave the world to run down determinatively through time according to God's "first-and-last will and testament."

Calvinism is a more well-known version of Christian determinism. If everything that is or ever shall be, and all that will ever happen, is predetermined from the beginning, the world's fate is sealed. And man, having no decisive say in his destiny, is deprived of his individual significance except in relationship to other human beings. Such a teaching jeopardizes both the personhood of God and of man.

Since men would rather not expose themselves to intimate contact with the self-revealing God, they consequently are prone to retreat into determinisms that shield them from direct dealings with God, and the awesome responsibilities of such encounters. In the non-Christian religious world Islam (lit., "surrender") is a most pronounced exemplification of deterministic theology. Islamic theology makes the supreme Will of Allah the all-important determinant of the affairs of men, and the Spirit of God seems at best aloof and remote. Christians should be alerted by this to the fact that a transbiblical view of the will of God can be propounded at the expense of the love of God. Making sovereignty the center and circumference of a theological system is no guarantee in itself that the system will be biblical and reveal the God who rules in love, as opposed to a god who merely loves to rule. In the Bible we read that "God is spirit," "God is love," "God is good." Never do we read "God is will" (though God certainly "wills"), nor "God is power" (though God has all-sufficient might), nor "God is mystery" (although his ways are past finding out by human means alone).

Now we know that the Spirit of God is his complete self, extending from the depths of God to every place he chooses to touch or reside. We are not to understand the Spirit as some kind of tritheistic "third God," in the same manner Justin Martyr denominated the Logos as a "second God." The Spirit is God himself in his invisible holy reality presenting himself. In the living God, therefore, there are analogical components we recognize in ourselves. God knows, God wills, and God feels (apart from physical sensation). Excepting physical sensibilities and sin, God is all that we are metaphysically— and even more so! (The personhood of man was not lost in the Fall; the holiness of his personhood was surrendered.) Evangelical theology is confined happily to thinking of the metaphysical personhood of God in anthropomorphic categories legitimatized by God's creating man in his own image.

Paul Tillich, the most celebrated philosophical theologian in the United States in the 1950s and 60s, sought to move beyond the personal concept of God—while including it dialectically as a symbol—by postulating a transpersonal or suprapersonal God. He is "being itself," above the traditionally conceived "God,"[1] to whom one would not pray or speak as if he were a Being. In so doing, Tillich ultimately broke the essential point of correspondence between God and man-in-his-image. If God is ultimately "the transpersonal One," the lines of correspondence and communication between God and man become inoperable, whatever games the unenlightened may play in prayer, using the personal symbol. But in biblical theology man is presented as in God's image with faculties of communication appropriate to use "in spirit" when truth is appropriated for worship of God. This holds true for sinning Samaritans (John 4:23–24) or anyone else who will respond to the divine call.

---

1. Paul Tillich, *Systematic Theology* (Chicago: University of Chicago Press, 1957), 2:11–12; *Biblical Religion and the Search for Ultimate Reality* (same publisher, Phoenix edition, 1964), 25–34; *Christianity and the World Religions* (New York: Columbia University Press, 1963), 88; *The Courage to Be* (New Haven: Yale University Press, 1952), 186–190.

I. THE DOCTRINE OF GRACE AS THE HEART OF BIBLICAL REVELATION

The concept of the grace of God is grounded in the doctrine of God's holy Self, his personhood, his metaphysical "spirituality." This personal understanding of grace is exemplified preeminently in the incarnate Lord. And since "grace" is at the center of God's activities in the world as the superlative statement of his intimate Self, we cannot expect to fathom the depths of that grace except as the Spirit leads us there, to an ever-deepening experience of God's engulfing us in his expressed love.

Let the writers call the reader to a task at this point and inquire for his working definition of grace. And what do you have? My guess is that the first concept that came to your mind was the well-worn catechetical phrase, "unmerited favor." This cliché of ours is deficient precisely where all the determinisms are unacceptable. The personal "involvement" of God is not required. That definition of grace stresses something good that comes to man and the undeserved character of that good. But nothing in the definition demands that the giver give any of himself in or with his gift or "favor." The rain falling on the farmland of the selfish, build-a-bigger-barn farmer, the welfare check left regularly in the alcoholic's mailbox, the "wheel of fortune's" selection of a monetary winner are all forms of "favor"—some would say "fate"—that were not merited. In light of the New Testament we cannot settle, however, for a concept of grace that would be capable of being handled through a computer without personal interaction.

"Unmerited favor" may well be a serviceable term for explicating the factitious term, "common grace," but it falls short of the glory of "the grace of God . . . for . . . salvation." To proceed in the manner of defining grace as is often done in terms of its minimal essence divisible into two kinds—"common" grace and "special" grace—rigs a jig on the theological worktable that is bound to distort either the one or the other. It is not merely a matter of classifying one as impersonal and the other personal. For it is possible to attach God's name to "unmerited favor," to give it a personal handle. To declare that the agency of grace is personal, i.e., an agent, the personal God, still leaves too much unsaid. This is because the whole term, "God's unmerited favor," under such conditions must be equally as applicable to common grace as to special grace, but not antithetical in terms of what makes one common and the other uncommon. My point is this: The difference between the *action* of God in so-called common grace and that in special grace is so deep-seated as to make inappropriate the quest for a least-common denominator of grace that is compatible with the theological classifications of "common" and "special."

A major thesis propounded in this chapter can be stated in a few words: The grace of God flowers into expression in the New Testament and is uniquely spiritual. But the explication of this statement about grace must be delayed momentarily, while consideration is made of the phenomena that reveal God's providential goodness in stocking the world with good things for man's benefit and giving man potentials for making the most of life in the world. All that God has given man in nature and in the constitution of his own being—the structures of the old creation—are to be attributed to the goodness/kindness/love of God for his creatures. The theological term "beneficence of God" as providentially expressed in the multiplexity of the harmonious systems of creation and in sustaining man as the crown of creation. It is thus a useful term for this in that it preserves the biblical idea without compromising the uniqueness of grace. Or, to put the cause for the effect, one does well to use the biblical term "the goodness of God" to categorize the outpouring of God's loving care on all men, sending sunshine and rain on good and bad men alike, giving man food and enjoyment, and supplying him with the various life-fuels needed to sustain his journey through time as a natural man.

When John the Baptist was queried as to the relative merits of John's and Jesus's ministries, he replied with a generalization that is apropos to this discussion of the goodness of God to all men. The prophet said, "A man can receive nothing unless it has been given him from heaven" (John 3:27). All the resources God placed in nature, the vitality God gave man, the position he gave man as co-regent with him in ruling the created world, and all the potentials and possibilities for a good life can be described as certainly having a "gift" character. But this goodness of God as expressed in impersonal gifts should not be doubled in terminology with the word that is central in the New Testament for God's giving us himself in his Son and Spirit. Even though the basic words "gift" and "grace" are paronymous in the original *(charisma* and *charis),* and even if we attach the somewhat pejorative qualifier "common" to the word "grace," we flatten out the majesty of that most central salvific word in the New Testament by making it commensurate with another concept.

Invariably, the gifts of creation are something (food, resources, places to live, etc.) or someone (parents, friends, companions, etc.) or some specific of permuted circumstances, but in no such gifts or good times does God give *himself!* God's goodness can be extended to man without God's inclusion of himself in the package, that is, *without God giving the Spirit.* God supplies man with consumables and possibilities and "new mercies" every day. But under this old-creation shower of blessings depicted in the Old Testament and New Testament, he does not admit man to the tree of life. He does not share with him the sacred stuff of which eternal life is made—his own spiritual life!

As stated above there is no single salvific word, other than a proper name, that sums up the New Testament so well as "grace." It is used in such a way that it is distinguishable from love. Love can be one-directional and un-requited even as *agape*. Grace in the New Testament means love given and getting through to its object by being received. Specifically, it means love's giving oneself to one who welcomes the giver as "gift." *God's* grace, then, is God's giving us himself in Jesus Christ (objectively), and (subjectively) it is the Holy Spirit received as the Spirit of Jesus Christ. This conception of grace does not set up a polarity between love and grace. On the contrary, there is a continuity between them in that grace is the fulfillment of love. "God is [as to his nature] love," (1 John 4:16) and God is, in the expression of his love to believers-receivers, "the God of all grace" (1 Pet 5:10). As the presence of God's love in man, the Spirit is "the Spirit of grace" (Heb 10:29). Jesus himself incarnated the grace of God in an immensurable *pleroma* (John 1:14, 16), so that in a programmatic sense it can be said that "grace and truth came through Jesus Christ" (John 1:17).

Whatever secrets God may have kept to himself under the administration of Moses and the law (Deut 29:29), the new administration of grace is one of open disclosure of God's love for mankind and of his will to relate to man on the basis of grace: "For the grace of God *has appeared,* bringing salvation to all men" (Titus 2:11). God has revealed his whole heart; *he loves man*—all men, everywhere, all nations, everyone (John 3:16; Titus 3:4)! God the Savior "desires all men to be saved" (1 Tim 2:4), "not wishing that any should perish, but that all should reach repentance" (2 Pet 3:9), and he made it possible to "have mercy upon all" (Rom 11:32). Indeed, "the mystery of his will" (Eph 1:9) concerning "the riches of his grace" (Eph 1:7) "he *has made known* to us" (Eph 1:9).

Paul spoke of a past day when the Colossians "*heard. . . and understood the grace of God in truth*" (Col 1:6). The carryover mystery that had to wait until the New Testament to be divulged was this: God would unite by his grace the Jews and Gentiles from every segment of world society together in one body in Christ (Eph 1:4—3:20). That mystery of God's universal love and plan was fully disclosed in the gospel. That which in the mid-60s of the first century was totally obscure in the Pharisaic synagogues of Jerusalem was basic knowledge to the Gentile believers far away in Colosse and in many other places as well.

When scripture says God "works all things after the counsel of his will" (Eph 1:11), it means that he has no one but himself to consult in matters of decision and is responsible only to himself for what he does. It does not mean that all operations of "will" in the universe are nothing less than the expression of one *absolute* Will. That would destroy the concept of "person," since generically there would be only *one* Will at work in the universe, absorbing all others into itself. God's will is limited by two factors: (1) his holy, loving nature that determines his will; (2) his granting of miniature sovereignty within the limits of finitude to man.

A theology built on the "decrees" of God that have to be interpolated between the lines of scripture, instead of clarifying God's plan, ultimately wraps up the will of God in inscrutability. Such unintelligibility of the will of God results in grace being clouded over, too. No one can be sure that God indeed loves *him,* if God has willed by eternal decision to love some and reject others according to an undisclosed schema as Calvinism advocates. Jesus, on the other hand, expressed God's gracious will to *everyone* who wanted, that is, "is willing" to follow God's gracious plan (John 7:17). Moreover, he was candid as to whom God's grace would be hidden and unavailing, viz., to the self-righteous, the stingy rich, the unforgiving, and the self-satisfied. These groups of people exclude themselves from God, not vice versa.

The will of God is this: that where sin reigns, grace will reign instead. The will of God for man, therefore, is *grace.* His will is gracious, but grace is not another name for will, much less irresistible will. Grace, having personal dimensions of comity, flows from God's whole personality to man's whole personality without violating man's right by creation to choose his destiny.

II. THE MEETING OF SPIRIT AND SPIRIT, OF GRACE AND FAITH

Will can be imposed on others less powerful than oneself without the concurrence of their wills. But grace is never imposed. Grace can only be received. Grace is a *spiritual* transaction and a continuing relationship. Justification came in the Old Testament in the name of God and took the external form of a promise. Justification comes in the New Testament "in the name of the Lord Jesus Christ *and in the Spirit of our God*" (1 Cor 6:11), and fulfilled God's gracious promise (Gal 3:14).

God has freedom to love man precisely because he is love, and not raw unconditional power. He is almighty in respect to his creation, but he is not absolute power because he cannot violate his own perfection. He cannot commit deicide; he is immortal. He cannot deny himself; he is faithful. He cannot lie; he is the truth. He cannot be unfair; he is just. His being the Almighty is not to be pressed to the absurd asseveration that God can do absolutely anything. God's sovereignty, therefore, is his administrative *role* or *work* to which his nature is perfectly suited. His sovereignty is his *rightful relationship* to his creation. It is derived from his nature as the One best suited to rule as well as the One whose sole right it is to rule by virtue of being Creator.

If one insists that sovereignty is of the very essence of God, an attribute of his nature without which he could not be God, then his very deity itself is imperiled. For such a position requires someone other than God from eternity for him to rule. Creation, then, would have been necessary to his very existence or being, and would not have been the gratuitous overflow of his love and glory. We would be compelled to posit always something other than God, ancillary to him. He would no longer be the first and last, the eternal, but a co-eternal with "governees."

God is free, therefore, to be the sovereign Lord; he is not free to lie. This means that he can delegate—surrender if you please—a small part of his sovereignty *without ceasing to be God*. On the other hand, God cannot surrender, relinquish, give up, or otherwise divest himself of his truth for any moment of time, for truth is eternal, or else it is not true. Hence, God was free to hand over to the first man the role of ruler over all creation below him in the created order, viz., his children, the earth, sea (fish), and sky (birds) (Gen 1:28). For this task God became Adam's counselor, and until sin entered, they conferred regularly each day. Adam had "dominion" and God supported him in this delegated rulership.

Now when we ask the question of the nature of man's freedom, we must look first at the first man. To him, God gave the right to make himself independent as well as the privilege of staying with God and living forever. If the opening chapters of Genesis mean anything, they mean that God actually— not speciously—gave Adam the freedom to determine his own destiny. *If* it were true that God made eternal decrees by which he decided the destiny of every individual he would create, decreeing eternal life for some and foreordaining by decree eternal damnation for the others,[2] then we would have to accept the following ineluctable implications:

(1) God is the only one who is real; men are God's toys.
(2) God is Will.
(3) God is impassible [and some would say "impossible," too!], and the tears of Jesus over the unbelieving chosen people at Jerusalem were either: (a) hypocritical, or (b)

---

2. Whether this position be called hyper-Calvinism or not, it was the plain and clear teaching of John Calvin in his most influential theological work: *Institutes of the Christian Religion* (Peabody, Mass.: Hendrickson, 2007) 3.21.5.

Jesus was not identical with the God of the all-embracing decrees, or (c) Jesus was sinning by not rejoicing in the Will of God for those for whom he wept.

(4) God is dark—inscrutable.

(5) God is hatred, not only because he has hated more people than anyone else, but because his hatred persists from the eternal past.

One must look elsewhere than the Bible to find such a view of predestination as that stated above. We have shown in the implications how irreconcilable such a conjecture is with the doctrine that God is love, the standard for all justice, and the would-be friend of his crowning creation—mankind.

Let us return to the biblically revealed God whose "fullness" is love (Eph 3:17–19). This God, out of his love for man, endowed him with the option to return his love or spurn it. On the one hand, God can command man as his creature; on the other hand, he risks leveling himself with man in the mutuality of spirits, the reciprocity of selves that occurs *whenever* love is given, received, and returned again—even in the unequal parent-child occasions of love. This freedom of God for man was expressed in his giving to man the option to accept and return his love and thereby to share his life, or to reject his love and go on through life using up his vitality in independent existence, enjoying only God's "goodness to all" regardless of their responsiveness.

If God is love, why did he hate (Mal 1:3; Rom 9:13) Esau without a cause? In a point of fact, God did not hate Esau, the man, as we use the word "hate." The Hebraism "to love one and hate the other" means in contemporary English to give priority or preference to one over the other. It does not imply animosity and malicious will against the one given second place. This use of "hate" in the words of Jesus on occasion bears out the special sense in which "hate" when used in the presence of alternatives always has a different meaning than when used with one object alone. For instance, the true disciple must love and follow the Lord and "hate" his father, mother, and wife (Matt 6:24); or the man who has two bosses must inevitably "hate" one of them (Matt 16:13).

The honored line of the Messiah could not descend through both twins, Esau and Jacob, so God chose the least promising of the two (as is his custom—1 Cor 1:27–28) in order to magnify his grace. Thus, in Malachi 1, quoted by Paul in Rom 9:13, Malachi is referring to nations, i.e. the descendents of Jacob and Esau—Israel and Edom, respectively, and that God chose the Israelites for the lineage to ultimately produce the Messiah.

Esau, in first esteeming his birthright as valueless was "immoral" in so doing, and his tears later over this decision could not change the choice that would be lifelong in effect (Heb 12:16–17). But, God did have a lesser but real "blessing" for Esau imparted to him by his father, Isaac. As far as the biblical record goes, he lived out his life in peace after the incident of his being wronged by his brother's pretending to be him.

Among other wives, Esau married Abraham's granddaughter (Ishmael's daughter), and the chronicling of his descendants is considered of sufficient importance to occupy all of Genesis 36. What is more, when Jacob sought his forgiveness and moved in on the same turf with him, he turned from his old hatred to forgiveness. They lived together, attended their father's funeral as reconciled brothers, and only split when the blessings of God upon them *both* had become so great that the land of south Canaan was not of sufficient space to accommodate their combined holdings.

If that is how God treats a man whom he "hates," there are many men who would like for God to so hate them too! It is not the same story of blessing when one considers all of Esau's descendants in Edom over the next millennium. Esau's own role in life was limited, indeed, by God's choice of his brother as a messianic progenitor, but Esau's *destiny* is another matter. Esau forgave the first time his forgiveness was asked. Esau did not retaliate though he had rights. Esau made room for his fraternal twin, and he finally "took the walk" to carve out of the red sandstone of Edom a new homeland, letting his brother, having been crippled by God's angel, remain unmoved except to absorb his old territories.

In his mature years Esau did not receive a new name as did his brother, but he did act with the ethical integrity that well befits the grandson of Abraham. "God knows those that are his," and maybe—just maybe—one of the surprises when "the sons of God are manifested" in eternity will be some locks of immortal red hair visible in a crowd of Old Testament redeemed and belonging to that one and only man that scripture says God "hated."

When God and man meet in the proclamation of the gospel on the plains of decision, both the Word and Spirit come into focus at God's end of the field and sin and spirit at man's end. God's messenger unsheathes the sword of the Spirit, the Word of God. In short, by that word man is slain, and by the Spirit he is created anew. God's call to him is a *summons* to repentance (Acts 17:30), but on the other hand, it is an *invitation* to receive grace (John 3:16; Rev 22:17). As Creator, God rightfully commands man to confess his infidelity in sin. As Savior, God graciously appeals to man to look to him and be saved. The former is judgment; the latter is grace.

Assuming the man here considered accepts in faith God's invitation and thereby receives God's grace, what is the order of the implementation of that grace in his experience? Some theologians would insist that the discernment of an order of operation in speaking of regeneration is as difficult as determining which spoke moves first when a wheel turns on its axle. With that verdict I would agree on the practical level of pastoral theology, but when it comes to matters of sequence of initiative in exposing this love affair between God and man, more can be said than merely to assert simultaneity. The initiative belongs exclusively to God. God calls man by "the word of his grace" (Acts 14:3).

The gospel, then, as objective grace, must have priority (Acts 18:27). The poor-in-spirit man turns from himself (as did the Prodigal) and believes God. His faith is the focused action of his whole spiritual being. That is, his cognitive, volitional, and emotional self actively renounces sin before God and positively holds to "the word of God's grace" extended to him. His repentance and faith are entirely shaped, then, by the word on which it is based. But he does his own repenting before God and believing. He receives the Spirit as the guarantee of abiding grace in response to faith—trusting commitment to God. The whole experience may be depicted thus with man's response surrounded by God's Word and Spirit: [Word (repentance, faith) Spirit] God initiates and consummates the experience. He calls faith forth and graciously answers faith with the Spirit delivered within.

This coming of the Spirit in *regeneration* is what is really new in the "new" covenant made in Christ's blood. God, of course, in all his dealings with man by his "word" is also "spirit." As Jesus said, his words were "spirit and life." Thus we would not say that the Spirit is not involved at the outset of man's encounter with God. He is. But the Spirit, while using the Word of God to convict man of sin and to offer grace to remove it, deals with the soul as Subject to subject, not as irresistible Will to soulless object. It is an encounter, a meeting, a hearing of evidence against the man and his Plea, an offer of divine pardon and life. It is not yet a "new birth" until man grasps the gift of grace in faith, permitting the Spirit to enter the core of his being.

Can we, then, speak of "prevenient" grace, using a theological term that has seen lots of wear? Yes, the Spirit "convicts" (John 16:8), the Father "draws" (John 6:44), and the Son "calls" nonbelievers and all these synchronous acts are merciful and loving, indeed. But as soon as God becomes operative *within* the life, we must drop all "pre's" and speak now of *saving grace* having come and abounding in spiritual presence. Saving grace is the first light of day in the "new creation." It is the first breath of life in the "new man." It is the first "new land" that appears rising out of the chaotic welter of the old creation and is the *terra firma* on which we now stand (Rom 5:2) in justification.

On the lighter side we note that grace was "prevenient" in Paul's letters, "intravenient," and "postvenient," too. He began his letters with a pronounced blessing of grace, referred to grace repeatedly throughout most of his letters (except Philemon where grace is never more forcefully implied) and he closed them with a benediction of grace. Other apostles do almost as much. To be in Christ is to be surrounded in grace (John 1:16—*charin anti charitos*).

The work of saving grace in man, that is, the coming of the Spirit as the new life in regeneration, is unique to the New Testament. Many leaders in the Old Testament era had dynamic operations of the Spirit working through them, but none—not even John the Baptist, the greatest of them all as per the word of Jesus— had what makes a man a new creation, i.e., Christ in you by the Spirit. Case in point: When Jesus's own twelve, endowed by him with spiritual *dynamis* and *exousia* to share his ministry (Luke 9:1), became separated from him in death, they had no basis for any communion with him. After his resurrection, however, they never lost spiritual contact with the ascended Lord throughout book of *Acts*.

God cannot—and to say the same thing—*will not* regenerate a heart that will not admit him. God respects the sovereignty within limitations with which he endowed man at creation. God confirmed Pharaoh in the hardheartedness he manifested toward God. He will not renew such a heart. Jesus will deliver men everywhere from the demonic spirits that bind them, but never will he "cast out" unbelief or more sinister disbelief from anyone's heart. He will speak truly, "very truly," to the Pharisee Nicodemus, but he will wait for him indefinitely to make his decision about a "new birth." It must also be remembered that the dramatic conversion of the "chief of sinners" on the road to Damascus was less the overpowering of a God-hater, than it was the enlightenment of a badly mistaken man who up to that time had thought he was serving God and was doing so "in all good conscience"!

In the Old Testament, faith preceded justification. In the New Testament faith also precedes justification. Additionally, in the New Testament with justification comes regeneration—"the spirit of life"—and sanctification—"the spirit of holiness." It does violence to the clear tenor of Scripture to reverse the order in the interest of a theological system and demand that regeneration precede faith rather than follow. That order makes faith virtually meaningless. It also would mean that justification and sanctification are separable states from regeneration. But if they all be considered simultaneous, then "faith" seems at best redundant. Does God even believe for us?

It is beautiful and true to say that salvation from sin is all of God. But it is untrue to deny the necessity for man to respond in personal faith to God, or to say that because man is "dead in trespasses and sins" that he cannot respond in faith, or in any way—absolutely. "For this reason it says: Awake, sleeper, And arise from the dead, And Christ will shine on you" (Eph 5:14). One without God sleeps in the death of his sins, but when God's call awakens him, he can respond in faith, or he can resist the Spirit and return to sleep, i.e. death.

Man, even in his sins and rebellion against God, is constantly putting his faith somewhere. It is his nature to be a believer in worldly pursuits. Not the possibility of faith, but the object of his faith, then, becomes the important consideration. Through the Gospel message and the convicting of the Holy Spirit, believing permits saving grace to be received.

One of the most common misunderstandings is that faith, including initial faith in God, is an irresistible "gift of God" or "gift of the Spirit." One would never conclude this from the great "faith" chapter of the New Testament that says: "And without faith it is impossible to please him. For whoever would draw near to God must believe that he exists and that he rewards those who seek him" (Heb 11:6). There are five passages in the New Testament that are construed by some to teach that individual faith is the immediate work of God in us—a phenomenon over which we have no control. The most well known of these and easiest to dispose of is the classic passage on soteriology in Eph 2:8–9. The text says: For by *grace* [Gr. a feminine noun] you have been saved through *faith* [another feminine noun]; and that not of yourselves, *it* [a neuter pronoun] is the gift of God. The "gift" is *salvation* as the resultant state of grace accepted through faith. The grammar will not permit "faith" to be the antecedent of "it."

The "fruit of the Spirit" is love amplified, whose varieties are listed in Gal 5:22. Virtually all the modern translations understand *pistis* there as "faithfulness," and not "faith" (as in the KJV). By the same meaning, "faithfulness," we should understand *pistis* in Rom 12:3, where the context and text itself see the individual in relationship with the whole body of believers. Faith concerns one's own relationship to God, whereas faithfulness is a whole life style in the ecclesial body of believers. God is to be credited for all faithfulness or dependability in man. But just as man has to do his own dying and choose his own *destiny* whatever his allotted *role* in life may be, so, too, it is his significance—giving responsibility to begin and continue to believe God all the days of his life: "As the outcome of your faith," Peter wrote, "you obtain the salvation of your souls" (1 Pet 1:9).

In Mark 11:22 we hear the exhortation of Jesus to the disciples saying (literally): "*Ei* (if) *echete* (you have) *pistin* (faith) *theou* (of God)." A woodenly literal translation can be made out to say, "If you have God's faith," but it is far more accurate to follow those translators who interpret *theou* as an objective genitive and translate as with the NASB, "Have faith in God." The

Bible never speaks of "God's faith," per se, unless this be the one exception. God has aseity, and faith for him would be somewhat superfluous. Since God is always presented as the proper object of faith, it would be ambiguous to speak of him as a "believer" as well. But God does trust his people to return his love.

One passage remains to be examined and this time *pistis* is clearly a *charisma* of the Spirit (1 Cor 12:9), being one of nine "gifts" listed there and in v 10. Three observations are crucial:

(1) The context would indicate that the faith spoken of here is not given to make one a believer, but it is given to a believer to benefit the entire church in some manner. (2) The context also would suggest that this—to use a Latin term—is *fides miraculosa*, for doing exploits for God, and not the *fiducia* (faith as trust and commitment) that determines one's destiny in God. (3) In the exercise of this *charisma*, God gives some specific experience of assurance that enables the sharer to *see* the action or effect as a *fait accompli*. In some sense, God opens for him preternatural sensibilities that are not amenable to psychological assessment and articulation.

Changing the figure, it can be said that the receiver hears in the Spirit a divine word limited to the local, temporal situation in the worldly community or for meeting some need in the Community of the Spirit, and he participates in some way in its fulfillment. Furthermore, we conclude that: (1) Ordinary faith (*fiducia*) was made a possibility for man even during the Old Covenant (the Holy Spirit was working even then); Abraham and the Old Testament "believers" corroborate this observation. (2) The Christian faith (*fides*), the content of the gospel, may rightfully be considered a gift from God and the result of the new creation that began with Jesus's resurrection. (3) It is proper to consider objective faith, that is, the Christian faith (*fides*), as a gift from God; and it is improper to consider subjective faith, that is, personal reception and retention of the gospel, as an irresistible "gift from God." It does not glorify the grace of God to predicate to it more than the biblical revelation itself claims. Such ambiguity ultimately undermines the whole divine-human encounter.[3]

Let us be clear about this matter. What is the threefold "gift of God"? Answer: "Jesus" as the *object* of faith historically given, the "Spirit," drawing people and convicting the world of sin (John 6:44; 16:8), and the Spirit indwelling as the *result* of faith. We can speak generally, then, of the gospel of Jesus Christ as the gift, of the grace of God as the gift, of the life of the

---

3. However, subjective faith is *influenced* by the Gospel message: "So faith comes from hearing, and hearing by the word of Christ." (Rom 10:17); and by the Father through the Holy Spirit: "*No one* can come to me unless the Father who sent me draws him" (John 6:44).

Spirit as the gift, of the fruit of the Spirit as the gift, but we must respect the preposition that sets "faith" off as personal response *(dia pisteos)*. We do not magnify God if we say that God gives a gift that only he can receive, that he extends his gift from one position and then turns 180 degrees to receive it from man also, because—so the reasoning goes—man, being "dead in sins," is *absolutely* dead, metaphysically as well as morally.[4]

He who comes to God must come believingly, diligently, and ready to receive the promised "Spirit of grace." "In spirit" he receives "the Spirit"; through *(dia)* faith he receives the saving grace of God. The giving is totally God's to do, and the receiving in faith is the wisest, most commendable, and most integrative (of one's whole psyche) decision that man ever makes. At this point I can hear someone crying, "foul," by saying, "You are making faith into a meritorious work." Never. It is a response *to God,* not something done *before God;* a "work" must be independent if it is to provide grounds for a man's own boasting.

But the remarkable thing about faith is that while it is no oasis for man's boasting before God, it is *the basis for God's boasting in men!* Case in point: the hall of faith in Hebrews 11, including such suffering men of faith of whom "the world was not worthy." God is pleased by faith and honors it—even though it is only a *response* to him. The faith-response is not passive, as though we were only spectators. John glimpsed a beautiful scene in the revelation of Jesus and inquired as to the identity of the white-robed people who surrounded and served the Lamb on the throne of God. The answer underscores the *active* character of faith: "These are they who . . . have washed their robes and made them white in the blood of the Lamb." *They* washed them!

III. THE HOLINESS AND VULNERABILITY OF "THE SPIRIT OF GRACE"

The contact of Holy Spirit and human spirit must be taken into consideration with all seriousness. There is no place for the wicked man to hide from God except in his own evil heart. God is not to be accused of spiritual assault or breaking and entering. God respects man's identity as a person, even if men do not always respect each other as such. The entrance of the divine Spirit into one's life is a stupendous and unforgettable event deemed worthy of celestial celebration—a party given by the angels—and is as traumatic

---

4. Arminian theologians commonly say that "dead" here means separated from God and that the convicting and drawing work of the Spirit plays a key role in leading us to cooperation with the Gospel message.

as being born! Moreover it is a holy experience for the man, for the Spirit is holy and sanctification is the predictable result of the Spirit's presence in one's life.

The "image of God" remains in fallen man (Gen 9:6; 1 Cor 11:7). He can do relative good—morally, socially, and culturally—even if he is lost and cannot find his way back to God. He can still copy God in certain remembered ways, even though he cannot commune with the *holy* God, toward whom he is "dead" in his sins. Holiness is the personal presence of God being what he is. That is a circular definition, and it only points to the indefinable grandeur of the presence that can be known only when experienced within one's life. To predicate to the Spirit daily and ceaseless operations within man, however, while denying the "holy" character of the Spirit's presence, belittles the Spirit beyond biblical recognition. The more accurate word than "belittles" is "depersonalizes," for the Spirit of God is thereby reduced to a function, a *deus ex machina,* needed to enforce decrees and explain that which runs counter to a system of supposed divine totalitarianism.

God *has* set a moral censor in man to restrain the evil and encourage the good, but the biblical term for this guard of morality is "conscience" and not the Holy Spirit. God has given man as man the capacity to create culture, to produce that which will outlast his temporal mortality. He has the potential of being a creator and only he among the creatures of earth has this ability. It is his not by a special infusion of the Holy Spirit, but by virtue of the fact that his life was originally shaped "in the image of God," the Creator.

We must return to the thesis, therefore, that whenever the Spirit of God enters a person's life it means:

(1) that God comes as the holy One, whose holiness purifies the heart to which he comes and that God the Spirit cannot divest himself of his pervading holiness when he comes in;

(2) that God does not invade a person's privacy, but enters only where he is welcomed;

(3) that such entries of the Spirit of Jesus Christ into individuals is missing in the Old Testament (though a miniscule number of chosen individuals were "charismatized" to perform feats and services for Israel in the power of God's Holy Spirit). John the Baptist was the greatest of the prophets, yet the least person in the kingdom of God has the Spirit of grace in a manner John did not have;

(4) that such an entry of the Spirit into one's inner man is the identifying characteristic of the post-resurrection-of-Jesus faith of the New Testament, and that, ontologically, a New Testament new creature is one who has received the Spirit of Christ;

(5) that the one New Testament word best describing the New Testament coming of the Spirit into a life is "grace," and that to speak of any activity of God as "grace" that does not include the overcoming of sin by the life of the Spirit within, is to obfuscate "grace" beyond biblical recognition.

God is so great in his moral excellence, so absolute in his goodness, so full in his love, that he can expose himself to the agony of rejected love without bitterness or change. He can compress his grandeur into a One-to-one meeting with man with all the risks for him that such an encounter involves. He does not have to play it safe and meet a man reduced to zero in a One-to-it (a "dead" abstraction) relationship. On the contrary, in Jesus, where all God's nature was gloriously displayed, we see him loving his own until the end of his mortal life (John 13:1) and we see him forgiving without their intercession those who were attempting to rob him of his life by nailing him to a cross. He gave his life, making it impossible for him to be robbed of it.

The doctrine of the deity of Christ will not let us think of "God" as being expressed elsewhere than in Jesus as to his corporeality. Scripture teaches that he is the image of the invisible God (Col 1:15; Heb 1:3). We are only, then, paraphrasing Scripture when we say that man has slapped and punched God in his mortal face, that man has spit upon the deity—and that Jesus did not spit back! It is heartbreaking to hold that scene even momentarily in mental view. But it was true. God is like that. He can be hurt by his creatures, and we must conclude from biblical history as well as all history up to the present that we are not speaking of an isolated *modus operandi* of God in the first century. God has always been secure in himself, yet relationally vulnerable.

This relational vulnerability, this *personal* openness to frustration— to use the theological term—this *possibility of God* over against his creation is the enormous cost he is willing to bear that his grace may be freely offered and freely received. God's grace, to use a tautology, is no more and no less resistible than God himself. To treat God's grace as if it were irresistible will asserting itself robs grace of all its glory. The glory of "predestination" is its Christocentricity. Grace is glorious as God's supreme expression of himself in man precisely because it is uncompelled. It is as magnificent and tender as Jesus was in his dealings with people. It is grounded in God's love ("God so loved the world. . ." John 3:16) and calls man to return God's love ("My son, give me your heart" (Prov 23:26). Grounding grace in intransigent will and hidden decrees would caricature God as a monolithic monster, would make grace as faceless as law (but see 2 Cor 4:6), and would exchange the openness of the future under the living God for fatalism. What is even worse, as the most elementary logic would demand, we would have to insist that God alone was culpable for having opened the polluted watergate of sin in the world. But biblical revelation says: ". . . sin came into the world through one man . . ." (Rom 5:12).

Culpability in God would be lethal for theology. Vulnerability in God, on the other hand, is not offensive to a true theology. God's vulnerability is not grounded in finitude but in the personal shape and perfection of God's being. It is his glory to reveal himself under the conditions of vulnerability. If we deny this, then we have no grounds upon which to accept the fact of the incarnation. In a sense, Jesus may have suffered as much or more when the rich and legally righteous young ruler came to him as he suffered in Pilate's hall. Jesus "loved" *(agapao*—Mark 10:21) that upright leader of men who retreated from him and went away despondently. I wonder if Jesus may have mused: "Alas, we put him on the enemies list by eternal decree; I must bring my emotions into line with divine will." Never! His love was not a masked hate; that would have been out of character for Jesus. His love was real and the tragedy of that man's momentous decision is matched in pathos by the Lord's own vulnerability on that occasion.

Having dealt at length with the nature of "the Spirit of grace" (Heb 10:29) and the vulnerability of that Spirit in the concourse of God-man relationships, it becomes unnecessary here to explicate in detail all the ways in which man rejects God to his own detriment and damnation. The Spirit can be slandered—that is, blasphemed (Matt 12:32; Mark 3:28–29)—resisted resolutely (Acts 7:51), insulted by apostasy (Heb 6:4–6; 10:26–31), put out like fire (1 Thess 5:19), refused (Heb 12:25), and grieved (Eph 4:30). Grace can be frustrated (Gal 2:21), emptied of effect (2 Cor 6:1), and no longer the ground under one who turns to another means of justification (Gal 5:4). To turn to the positive possibility, we see men of faith interacting with God and being taken seriously by God. Moses, for instance, pled with God for mercy for the rebellious Israelites after the golden calf incident, and "The Lord," he said, "hearkened to me that time also" (Deut 9:19).

When we move to the New Testament scene man stands in faith, not before relentless Will, nor inscrutable decrees fixed forever beyond him, but he stands before "the throne of grace" (Heb 4:16). It is God's willingness to give that makes his throne (i.e., rulership or decisive administration) such a wonderful place. What God gives there, whatever its full extent, always includes himself in the gift. God's Spirit is given and that experience is properly called grace, because the primary transaction at "the throne of grace" is to dispense Jesus's fullness (John 1:17) by "the Spirit of grace."

When all this age is past and time has run out for all who would construct their lives without God, there will be, nevertheless, myriads of grace-made people. When the elements disappear under them and the sky dissolves over them, they will stand secure in grace under the rainbow of love, as the spectacle of the new creation unfolds before them. God will have a people who joyously return his love. They will radiate forever the love of Christ, a love the limitless dimensions of which, wrote the Apostle Paul, are truly *inscrutable* (Eph 3:19).

7

Predestination in the Old Testament

David A. Clines

When we turn to the Bible with our questions about predestination, we are running the risk of committing two errors. First, we may fail to see the whole range of the biblical revelation on the subject because *we* have chosen the categories and terms that are going to count as answers to our questions.

Secondly, we may mistake the relative importance of the biblical teaching on the subject because *we* are focusing on that subject. Perhaps the Bible does *not* focus on that subject, but only sees it in relationship to something else. But we may give the doctrine, biblical though it is, not its truly biblical significance, but the significance it has come to have for us in our particular stream of theological tradition.

The errors that can be made are, then, errors about the *form* and the *role* of predestinarian thought in the Bible. The best way to minimize such errors is to look at the biblical teaching as a whole. But since that is not only difficult but also affords plentiful opportunities for our own conceptions of what is important to enter in, perhaps the most practical method is to begin with considering the Bible's parts individually. Certainly the method to be avoided is to build isolated verses from all parts of the Bible into a logical system, without regard for the larger contexts in which they occur or the overall thrust of the Bible's major parts.[1]

---

1. The type of approach I am rejecting is exemplified in Loraine Boettner, *The Reformed Doctrine of Predestination* (Grand Rapids: Eerdmans, 1941), 26–29, 81f., etc.

The method we adopt in this essay, therefore, is to examine books of the Old Testament, from the historical, wisdom, and prophetic literature, with a view to discovering the form and role of predestinarian ideas in them.

I. THE HISTORICAL LITERATURE

A. Genesis: The Patriarchal Histories

Let us begin with the patriarchal histories (Genesis 12—50). The theme of these narratives, most simply stated, is the survival and growth of Abraham's family. The dramatic unity of the stories, however, lies in the tension between the threats to the survival of the family and the divine promise that they will live and multiply (Gen 12:2). The threats to survival follow in rapid succession: famine in the land of promise (12:10); Sarai, the wife through whom the promise is to be fulfilled, is taken into the Pharaoh's harem (12:11–20); Abraham's nephew Lot, his male heir, leaves the patriarchal family (chap. 13); Sarai is barren (chap. 16); Sarah falls prey to Abimelech (chap. 20); Ishmael, Abraham's son, is cast out from the family (chap. 21); Isaac, now his only heir, is offered as a sacrifice (chap. 22); Rebekah is barren (25:21); Rebekah and Isaac run the danger of death in Gerar (chap. 26); Esau plots to kill Jacob (27:42); Rachel is barren (30:1); famine drives Jacob and his family out of the promised land and into dangers in Egypt (42:1–4).

Here the *form* that predestination takes is the promise. God has long-term intentions for the Abrahamic family, which he alone will bring about—no word is spoken in Gen 12:1–3 of conditions Abraham must fulfill.[2] That is surely a predestination. But the specific form that predestination takes is a Promise of descendants, a land, divine blessing, and blessing to the Gentiles. That is, the predestining does not point Abraham's attention to immutable decrees established in eternity past, but to a future in which the destiny will progressively be realized. God's predestination is thus not a possession Abraham and his descendants can count their own, but an announcement of what God will make of the patriarchal family. Abraham's response to the announcement will not be thanksgiving that everything has been settled long ago in the counsels of eternity, but *faith* in God that he will bring that destiny into being.

2. The imperative of v. 1 "does not . . . have any kind of conditional undertone, as if the promise of Yahweh were dependent on the obedience of Abraham. Rather, it sounds like a summons to receive the repeatedly promised gift" (Hans Walter Wolff, "Kerygma of the Yawhist," *Interpretation* 20:2 [April 1966]: 138).

The promise (predestination) is for the sake of the Abrahamic family
and of the Gentile nations. The text of Gen 12:1–3 does not enable us to
establish where the emphasis lies: Is it first and foremost on the blessing to
Abraham, or climactically on the blessing to the nations? It is not important
to decide the priority, but the dual direction of the Promise *is* significant.
The predestination is not for the sake exclusively of those who are predestined, but for the sake of world blessing; but neither does it relegate them to
a secondary role just because they are only part of God's larger intentions.
Many traditional studies of predestination have erred in neglecting God's
wider intentions that reach beyond his chosen people (Jews or Christians).
But it is unnecessary to over-react to this misplaced emphasis with a hesita-
tion to speak of God's predestination of the chosen people.

What now is the *role* of predestination in the patriarchal stories? It
might be thought that since the divine promise precedes all that happens,
there can be no real crises that call the promise into question but only an
outworking of the divine intentions, recognized by the actors in the story as
inevitable. But that is plainly not the mood of the patriarchal narratives. The
story is focused, as we have seen earlier, on the hazards the promise faces
just as much as it is on the promise itself. It is from the tension between the
promise and the realities of life that the story gains its momentum. So the
predestination is not the absolutely determinative factor in what happens.
The story is as much about what happens *against* the promise as about how
the promise is fulfilled.

That is not to deny that in one way or another everything that happens
advances the fulfillment of the promise, or even, perhaps, that in retrospect,
God's predestination can be seen also in some happenings that were apparently against the promise. Thus Joseph can say that his bondage in Egypt,
though plotted by the brothers, was equally intended by God (Gen 45:5;
50:20); and perhaps the same thing could be said truly enough of other re-
verses in the patriarchal fortunes. But that is precisely what these narratives
do *not* keep on saying, and it would be wrong to insist that the narrator
intends us to extrapolate Joseph's remarks to every detail of the histories.

Whether or not it is true that God has planned *everything* in advance,
all that the patriarchal stories show is the promise beset by hazards but moving towards fulfillment nevertheless. That is what Genesis 12—50 means by
predestination.

B. Genesis: The Primeval History

The primeval history (Genesis 1—11) is, unlike the patriarchal history, a history without a promise. It is, in fact, a history in which predestination in general is conspicuous by its absence. We cannot here speak (with one or two exceptions) of the form or role that predestinarian ideas have, but only of what takes their place. The movement of the primeval history is largely initiated by men; God's action is positive or negative response to the decisions of men. If Adam decides to become an independent being, determining for himself what is good and evil, God's response is to turn him loose from the garden and—make him independent. If Cain defiles the tilled ground with spilled blood, God responds by driving him away from the tilled ground that will no longer yield its strength to him.

If man's wickedness spreads so drastically that the earth is "filled with violence" (6:11), God responds by being sorry that he has made man, and by determining to destroy mankind. If the men of Babel say, "Come, let us build a tower with its top in the heavens," God responds, even to the extent of imitating their speech, with: "Come, let us go down and destroy their tower" (11:4, 7). Yet also, when Adam and Eve sense their nakedness before God and prepare makeshift clothes, God responds to this appropriate sense of shame and provides proper clothes for them. When Cain shouts that his punishment, to be driven from the society of men *and* from the presence of Yahweh, is greater than he can bear, God responds even to the murderer and sets a mark on him to protect him from his fellows.

And where is the predestination in all this? To suppose that any of this catches God by surprise, or even that all of these human decisions are merely human decisions which God has to make the best of now that they have happened would doubtless be contrary to the spirit of the Old Testament. But the story does not stop to point to decrees established in the dark counsels of eternity. What is important in the story of mankind, Genesis 1—11 might well be saying, is not what God has already decided to do, but with what freedom he can respond, in mercy or judgment, to man's decisions,[3] creating good from evil and swallowing up wrath with mercy. Though this is the major thrust of the primeval history, as I see it, there are some secondary elements that belong to the realm of predestination. First, the creation story of Genesis 1 plainly envisages God creating everything

---

3. Cf. the view of Georg Fohrer, that the Old Testament is not so much a history of salvation *(Heilsgeschichte)* as a history of decisions, in which man decides for or against God. George Fohrer, "Action of God and Decision of Man," *Biblical Essays. Proceedings of the Ninth Meeting of Die Ou-Testamentiese Werkgemeenskap in Suid-Afrika* [1966], 31–39.

with a *purpose*. The sun is created in order to rule the day, to distinguish day from night, to act as a marker of time. Man is created in order to rule on earth as God's vice regent.

All living things are created according to their kind, that is, what they are and can be is a determinate part of the created order. God has not created an aimless, formless, indeterminate world, but a world of beautiful order where everything has a destiny: to be what God made it to be. Predestination in this sense, then, is an aspect of the doctrine of creation. Needless to say, this is not a predestination to salvation or damnation, but an affirmation of God's purposive in creation.

Secondly, there is a predestinarian type of idea in God's selection of Noah and his family to be saved from the flood. The story of Noah fits the pattern of the other narratives of the primeval history in that after the judgment upon man's sin is announced, grace intervenes and mitigates the punishment. But the Noah story is unlike the preceding narratives in that God's act of grace toward sinful humanity does not extend to all those who have sinned. It is only given to a chosen family, in whose salvation the human race will be kept alive.

But why does God choose Noah to survive? It is not that Noah is the one righteous man on earth, to whose righteousness God can respond with salvation. For it is significant that God's favor rests on Noah (6:8) *before* any word is spoken of Noah's righteousness (6:9).[4] Here the form predestination takes is unmerited election.

Thirdly, from the perspective of Genesis 12, it becomes clear that a predestined goal was shaping the course of the primeval history. What would otherwise be a collection of unconnected episodes in Genesis 1—11 is seen from the standpoint of Genesis 12, to be a *sequence* that leads to Abraham. The primeval history itself has had no interest in stressing God's control of history, for its interest has been in God's freedom to respond to human decision. But in its setting in the book of Genesis, the primeval history takes on a new significance. It is but the prelude to the story of the promise.

II. THE WISDOM LITERATURE

A.Proverbs

The heart of the theology of Proverbs is that good or bad deeds bring appropriate reward or punishment from God.

---

4. See W. Malcolm Clark, "The Righteousness of Noah," *Vetus Testamentum* 21 (1971), 261–280.

A perverse man will be filled with the fruit of his ways and a
good man with the fruit of his deeds. (14:14)

The righteous is delivered from trouble, and the wicked gets into
it instead. (11:8)

He who is steadfast in righteousness will live, but he who pur-
sues evil will die. (11:19)

That is, the destiny of men is determined by their own behavior. The
form predestination takes, then, in Proverbs' theology of reward is human
self-determination. It is not God who decides whether a man shall be counted among the righteous and the wicked; it is his own actions that determine
that. Thus Proverbs contains not only predictive proverbs, of the kind I have
quoted, but also descriptive proverbs about what constitutes wickedness,
folly, wisdom, sloth, prudence, generosity, deceit, so that a man may recognize himself and know his destiny.

Predestination in Proverbs is not contradictory to or incompatible
with predestination as we have seen it in Genesis, but the emphasis is very
different. Proverbs is not denying the promise to Abraham and his seed, but
neither does it find it necessary to affirm it. When it is a matter of how a
man should live his life, Proverbs is saying, *divine* predestination is not the
point; what counts is how a man is destining his own future. No doubt there
are ways in which divine predestination could be relevant to ethics: another
Israelite teacher might well have exhorted his hearers to "walk worthy of
the vocation with which you are called" (Eph 4:1). But Proverbs does not
choose that route. Proverbs of course does not claim to be the whole of
Scripture, and it would be a mistake to regard the theology of Proverbs as
the only valid way of looking at the question of ethics. But it is a legitimate
position, and as such receives confirmation in the New Testament (see Rom
2:6–10), even by Paul, whom most would regard as the New Testament's
chief apostle of divine predestination.

Already something has been said about the *role* of predestination
in Proverbs: in the sense of human self-predestination, it is central to the
teaching of the book. But the role such predestination plays in the theology
of Proverbs can be more carefully evaluated if we consider how God is related to this scheme of deed and retribution. In the first place, it is clear that
God is the one who brings reward or punishment. Yet it is noticeable that
God's activity in this respect is not often explicit in Proverbs (10:29 is about
the nearest Proverbs comes to saying it). More frequently good or bad seems
to bring its own reward automatically: "The work of a man's hand comes

back to him" (12:14).[5] It is not of course denied that this is God's doing, but the emphasis does not lie there.

Secondly, and more important, God's relation to men's destiny is that he creates the path of life, which is wisdom, and summons men to follow that path. If a man is righteous, that is, in the terminology of Proverbs, if he has wisdom, it is not because he inherently has a good streak in him. It is because he has been amenable to the teaching of the wisdom that is a gift from God. "Folly is bound up in the heart of a child, but the rod of discipline drives it far from him" (22:15). That "discipline" or "instruction" is ultimately "the Lord's discipline" (3:11), and the wisdom the maturing child develops is regarded as "given" by God (2:6). So while growth in wisdom and goodness is a matter of effort and discipline, Proverbs' concept of wisdom as essentially God's creature (cf. 8:22–31) makes it impossible for a righteous man to regard his wisdom as his own achievement. In a word, a man prepares his own destiny, but if his destiny is life, he has God to thank, and not himself. But if a man is headed for destruction, he has only himself to thank for that.

Finally, having observed where the emphasis lies in Proverbs' teaching about predestination, we are perhaps in a better position to understand some sentences which apparently set forth a rigorous divine predestination:

> The LORD has made everything for its own purpose, even the wicked for the day of evil. (16:4)

Some might see a presupposition here of "double predestination," but what is really involved is the usual teaching of Proverbs about appropriate retribution. The Hebrew word translated "purpose" also means "answer," which is "according to God's plan. The wicked suffer the evil they have plotted (Ps 49:5; Jer 17:18; Rom 9:21ff.). Sinning and suffering answer to each other and are ultimately and indissolubly united."[6] The TEV translation is compelling here: "Everything the Lord has made has its own destiny; and the destiny of the wicked is destruction."

That is, the wicked man is on his way to his appropriate fate. However, this does not mean that his destiny is fixed and irreversible; iniquity *can* be atoned for (16:6), thus he need not remain wicked. Again, when we find:

5. For an exposition of the "act—consequence relationship," see Gerhard von Rad, *Wisdom in Israel* (London: SCM-Canterbury, 1972), 128–133.

6. J. D. Douglas, James K. Hoffmeier, Ted A. Hildebrandt, Mark R. Norton, eds., *New Commentary on the Whole Bible Old Testament Volume* (Wheaton, Ill.: Tyndale House, 1990), 830.

> The king's heart is a stream of water in the hand of the LORD; he
> turns it wherever he will (21:1),

we do not have some doctrinaire assertion that a king never makes
any decisions of his own and is only a puppet in God's hand. That would be
contrary to the general outlook of Proverbs, though the proverb in isola-
tion could doubtless mean that. Rather, what is taught here is that God, the
world's governor, cannot be thwarted even by kings, who are accustomed to
having their own way. It is a variation on the theme of 21:30: No wisdom,
no understanding, no counsel, can avail against the LORD. Similar proverbs
are:

> A man's mind plans his way, but the LORD directs his steps.
> (16:9)

> The plans of the mind belong to man, but the answer of the
> tongue is from the LORD. (16:1)

> The horse is made ready for the day of battle, but victory rests
> with the LORD. (21:31)

Our English equivalent is: "Man proposes, God disposes." Anyone who believes that God rules the world is bound to say as much. But the author did
not mean God always sets aside human plans or that it is only divine decisions that matter. Let's look at these verses further. For 16:9, there is God's
side and there is the human side, expressed in 3: 5–6: "Trust the Lord with
all your heart and lean not on your own understanding; in all your ways
acknowledge him, and he will make your paths straight." This also applies to
16:1. Trust the Lord and he will give you the proper words at the right time.
As for 21:31 and the matter of battle, man may prepare with warhorses and
chariots, but victory comes from the Lord.

B. Ecclesiastes

Ecclesiastes is surely the leading Old Testament exponent of predestination.
Life is essentially for the author (thought to be Solomon) a matter of God's
"allotment" or "gift" (3:13; 5:18; 6:2; cf. 7:13). Everything in life happens
according to its allotted occasion (3:17); so he says in his most famous lines:

> There is an appointed time for everything. And there is
> a time for every event under heaven—
> a time to give birth and a time to die;
> a time to plant and a time to uproot what is planted.
> a time to kill and a time to heal. (3:1–3a, NASB)

That does not mean that there is an appropriate time for every human activity, which a man must recognize and fall in with. This is not an ethical precept, but a global statement about the nature of human existence, that the variegated experiences of life do not occur by human design but when their "time" arrives.[7]

Once again, however, it is valuable to consider the form and role of Ecclesiastes' idea of predestination. As for its *form*, we can observe first that Ecclesiastes is not thinking about differentiated destinies for man after death. For the author, good and bad alike meet the same ultimate destiny—death. If there is any hereafter, Ecclesiastes does not reckon with it; it simply asks, "Who knows whether the spirit of man goes upward and the spirit of the beast goes down to the earth?" (3:21). The horizon is the span of a human life. Secondly, Ecclesiastes is not thinking about a predestination to good or evil deeds. The author believes that there is a distinction between the righteous and the wicked (e.g. 8:14),[8] and that men ought to be righteous, fear God, and keep his commandments (12:13). The book is not arguing that the righteous and the wicked are so because of any predestination.

Yet, thirdly, there is something predestined for every man—that is, his death. Death is undeniable "in the hand of God": "the time to die" (3:2) is appointed by God as the conclusion of these "days of life which God gives" man under the sun (8:15), when man's "spirit returns to God who gave it" (12:7).

Ecclesiastes is not viewing death as a punishment, or as a tragedy, but as a most significant factor in the created order. Men are mortal; it is God who has made them so; the time when they succumb to their mortality is likewise of his making. Now, fourthly, God's sovereign freedom over death becomes for Ecclesiastes the paradigm example of God's freedom over all reality: "I know that whatever God does endures forever; nothing can be added to it, or anything taken from it" (3:14). He is not speaking of God's initial creation, but of the multifarious activities which go on upon earth (3:1–8), all upon the occasion appointed for them (3:17). To put it rather crudely: all that life adds up to is death, so if death is destined by God, all that life is, is equally destined by God.

Death is plainly a nodal point in Ecclesiastes' theology. Probably the author is an old man himself, who, as he faces the prospect of death, asks what "profit" there has been in life. Death negates all the values that men strive for in life; pleasure, fame, success, possessions, even wisdom and

---

7. Cf. O. S. Rankin, "The Book of Ecclesiastes. Introduction and Exegesis," *The Interpreter's Bible* (New York: Abingdon, 1956), V:41ff.; von Rad, *Wisdom in Israel*, 263f.

8. Though he realizes that it is not an absolute distinction (7:20).

righteousness, are empty in the face of death (cf. 2:1; 9:11; 4:7f.; 6:1–2; 2:12–17; 8:14). This realization brings the author into conflict with the ideals of wisdom teaching, as they are to be seen especially in Proverbs. Wisdom offers life, but what about when life itself is no longer desirable (12:1), or when life has been overcome by death?

The fact of death is a constituent element of the created order; it is part of *God's* world, God has made things like this. Then he too has created the relationship between the values of life and the fact of death. It is God who has created a world in which all values add to zero and what is crooked cannot be made straight (7:13; 1:15). Weeping, laughter, seeking, losing, silence and speech, war and peace (3:1–8) are real, but each has its time, and one is superseded by the other without any discernible progress or any measurable profit. So the catalogue of the "times" concludes: "[But] what gain has the worker from his toil?," or better, "What does the doer [of these] add by his effort?"[9] And that is the world God has made; that is his destined order of things, so argues Ecclesiastes.

Fifthly, we may note that predestination for Ecclesiastes does not mean that the particular acts of individuals are fixed in advance by God. Rather, the possibilities open to man and the value of human activities are settled in advance by the framework of God's created order, which terminates everything human with death. When we come to enquire about the *role* that these ideas of predestination, so difficult to nuance correctly, play in Ecclesiastes' book, we may be surprised that Ecclesiastes is not impelled by this view of life to advocate suicide or despair. Ecclesiastes is, however, far from pessimistic; its message is life-affirming to a remarkable degree: "There is nothing better for a man than that he should eat and drink, and find enjoyment in his toil. This also, I saw, is from the hand of God" (2:24).

There are two reasons for Ecclesiastes' positive attitude. First, Ecclesiastes does not doubt that God knows what he is doing. "It is an unhappy business that God has given to the sons of men to be busy with" (1:13), when looked at from a human perspective. Yet God has "made everything beautiful in its time" (3:11), it says, echoing the repeated phrase of Genesis 1: "And *God* saw that it was good." It is simply that God's purpose is inaccessible to man; he has so made man that he "cannot find out what God has done from the beginning to the end" (3:11). That is, he cannot understand the totality of God's purposes nor how the individual event is related to the totality. "As you do not know how the spirit comes to the bones in the womb of a woman with child, so you do not know the work of God who makes everything" (11:4; cf. & 16f.; 9:1; Prov 30:3). God is inscrutable.

9. R. B. Y. Scott, *Proverbs Ecclesiastes* (Garden City, N.Y.: Doubleday, 1965), 220.

In so saying, Ecclesiastes holds up a needful warning sign before the teachers of wisdom who claimed they could know how and when God would act, ever faithful to the principle of retribution.[10] Job knows well that retribution is only a general rule, not an infallible one: the righteous may suffer. The Psalmists too experience the prosperity of the wicked and the victimization of the innocent, quite contrary to the principle of retribution. So also Ecclesiastes; its extremism, neglectful of God's actual revelation of himself to Israel, is because the book is working stolidly from a theology of creation. To Ecclesiastes, God is essentially Creator (cf. 12:1); and a creator must be wise, he must know what he is about, even if we can know nothing of his purpose. This is a world away from a belief in a blind fate or a capricious Deity.

Secondly, as a theologian of creation Ecclesiastes' author must accept that what *is* is "from the hand of God." And part of what *is* is happiness, work, wisdom, righteousness, and the commandments. Since they exist, they were created, and to deny them would be to deny, or "forget," one's Creator. Whatever else the world is for, it is given to man for his enjoyment (2:24; 5:18f.); therefore let a man busy himself with his work and his pleasure (3:12f.; 8:15; 9:9; 11:9). Precisely because these "goods" have been created, they are approved by God (9:7). Whatever one's hand finds to do (9:10) is what one is intended to do.

What we find, then, in Ecclesiastes, is a radical awareness of a divine predestination which encompasses the whole of human activity but which, just because it is inscrutable, imposes no constraints on men, nor weakens their self-determination. It rather points them from the mystery of their existence to the mystery of the Creator God.

III. THE PROPHETIC LITERATURE

In the prophets, predestinarian ideas take on two major forms: the concept of God's election of Israel, and the concept of divine purposes in history.

The first major *form* predestination takes on is that the people of Israel have been *chosen* by God to be his people. That is a predestination because it is not just an act of grace or salvation but an act which establishes Israel's future destiny, and an act that defines what it will mean to be Israel. The occasion of this election is not for the prophets an eternal decree but a

10. "Ecclesiastes is the frontier-guard, who forbids wisdom to cross the frontier towards a comprehensive art of life" (Walther Zimmerli, "The Place and Limit of the Wisdom in the Framework of the Old Testament Theology," *Scottish Journal of Theology* 17 [1964], 158).

historical act: the election took place at the exodus from Egypt (Ezek 20:5f.). It was then that Israel was "chosen," "formed" (Isa 43:20f.), "called" (Hos 11:1), "wooed" (Hos 2:14f.), and "known" (Amos 3:1f.). All these terms belong to the election vocabulary, for they all point to the divine action which constituted Israel.

The nature of this election is expressed by many images of Israel found in prophetic poetry.[11] Israel is God's vineyard, planted and tended by him (Isa 5:1–7); God's bride, whom he took to himself in Egypt (Jer 31:32), led through the wilderness (2:2), and lavished gifts upon (Hos 2:7f.); God's servant, whom he has chosen (Isa 41:8f.; 43:10; 44:1f.) and "formed" (44:21) and destined to glorify him (49:3); and God's adopted son, called by him from Egypt (Hos 11:1).

We should also enquire about the *role* of the idea of election in the prophets, that is, why should the election of Israel be mentioned at all by the prophets? The major emphasis of the pre-exilic prophets is the announcement of imminent judgment upon Israel. Sometimes it is said that repentance is still possible, and the doom can be averted (e.g. Hos 14:2). At other times it appears that it is too late for repentance (e.g. Amos 8:2), but in either case the focus is upon the heralded doom. The role of election in such a context is to highlight the contrast between God's grace and Israel's sin. Election in the prophets is no guarantee of eternal security. Amos is characteristic of prophetic theology when he proclaims this word from God:

> You only have I known of all the families of the earth;
> therefore I will punish you for all your iniquities. (3:2)

God's "knowledge" of Israel here is clearly identified with his election of them in Egypt. The word is spoken "against the whole family whom I brought up out of the land of Egypt" (3:1).[12] And it is precisely because of the prophet's belief in election that he can be sure that Israel's iniquities will not be overlooked by God. Elsewhere this same connection is apparent: the picture of Israel as God's vineyard is introduced in order to denounce Israel's sin:

> For the vineyard of the LORD of hosts is the house of
> Israel, and the men of Judah are his pleasant planting; and
> he looked for justice, but behold, bloodshed; for righteousness,
> but behold, a cry! (Isa 5:7)

11. See George A. F. Knight, *A Christian Theology of the Old Testament* (London: SCM-Canterbury, 1959), chap. 15.

12. "'To know' approaches the sense of 'to choose' (cf. Gen 18:19; 2 Sam. 7:20; Jer 1:5; Hos 13:5)" (Erling H. Hammershaimb, *The Book of Amos: A Commentary* [Oxford, U.K.: Basil Blackwell, 1970], 56f.).

and to announce its destruction:

> And now I will tell you what I will do to my vineyard.
> I will remove its hedge, and it shall be devoured; I will break
> down its wall, and it shall be trampled down. (5:6)

Likewise in Jer 2:2, Israel's marriage to the Lord is the backcloth to the Lord's current controversy with his people, and in Hos 11:1 Israel's call to sonship is but the preface to the irony of election: "The more I called them, the more they went from me." It is noteworthy also how often in Isaiah, Israel is referred to as God's people in the context of its disobedience or its impending destruction (e.g., Isa 1:3; 2:6; 5:13, 25). The role of election theology, then, is to heighten the gravity of Israel's sin and to guarantee that there is no escape from the consequences of their guilt. However, the doom of Israel, though the major preoccupation of the pre-exilic prophets, is not their only concern. They, together with the prophets of the exile and beyond, also deliver prophecies of hope. In this setting, the role of election is different.

Here election takes on the character of promise, assurance that Israel will become what she was called into being to become. Israel must respond to the prophetic reminders about election with courage, faith, work. Thus we find:

> But you, Israel, my servant, Jacob, whom I have chosen, the offspring of Abraham, my friend; you whom I took From the ends of the earth, and called from its farthest corners, saying to you, "You are my servant, I have chosen you and not cast you off"; fear not, for I am with you, be not dismayed, for I am your God. (Isa 41:8ff.) (Cf. also Isa 43:1f.; 44:1ff., 21f.; Hos 2:14ff.; Hag 2:4f.)

The other major *form* prophetic predestination takes on is the idea that events of world history are planned by God.[13] A clear example is Isa 14:24–27:

> The LORD of hosts has sworn: "As I have planned, so shall it be, And as I have purposed, so shall it stand, that I will break the Assyrian in my land, and upon my mountains trample him under foot. . ." This is the purpose that is purposed concerning the whole earth; and this is the hand that is stretched out over all the nations. For the LORD of hosts has purposed, and who will annul it? His hand is stretched out, and who will turn it back?

13. Most helpful on this subject is "The Divine Plan in History" Albrektson, *History and the Gods*, chap. 5

Other references to God's "purposes" or "plans" or "thoughts" occur in Isa 25:1; 46:10; Mic 4:12; Jer 23:20; 29:11; 49:20; 50:45; 51:11. And of course the whole rationale of prophetic prediction is that God has plans or intentions, whether of judgment or salvation, which are so sure of fulfillment that they may be announced in advance.

Almost all of the specific references to God's plans have in view a particular event or a limited series of events, for example, "his purposes against the land of the Chaldeans" (Jer 50:45). Furthermore, it is not a matter of a *single* divine plan; various passages speak of various intentions, and some references are in fact to God's plans in the plural. So it cannot be shown that the prophets believed in a fixed divine plan that extended from the beginning to the end of world history.

When they spoke of God's plan they referred to the obvious truth that God is purposive in his actions. As for the prophetic statements of what God is going to do, it can be freely acknowledged that they are extremely varied in their scope, comprehensiveness, and time range. But they do not amount to a claim that all the events of history move towards a divine goal. They are rather an assertion that within history God is working his purposes out.[14]

The *role* of this form of predestination must be defined in terms of the main foci of the prophetic message. Characteristically the announcement of God's "plan" is an announcement of doom, whether against foreign nations (Isa 14:26; Mic 4:12; Jer 49:20; 50:45; 51:11, 29) or against Israel itself (Jer 23:20—30:24; cf. Isa. 5:19). On one occasion, it is a promise of the future welfare of Israel (Jer 29:11). That is, the predestinarian element functions as an assurance that the prophetic message will take effect. It is not an expression of a broad philosophy of history so much as an affirmation of the inescapability of God's wrath or the certainty of God's blessing. The same is true of the predictive or predestinarian aspect of prophetic oracles of judgment or hope, even when terms for God's "plan" are not used.

IV. OTHER OLD TESTAMENT LITERATURE

We can here only glance at some of the other Old Testament writings. The so-called "*Court History*" of David (2 Sam. 9 to 1 Kings 2), is a complex narrative of events in both the personal and national spheres. Throughout, the story moves on the level of human intrigue, ambition, lust, revenge, vacillation, magnanimity. The narrator does not pause to indicate where God's

---

14. "In so far as it is at all possible to speak of a divine plan it concerns a definite chain of events and a limited goal" (Albrektson, *History and the Gods*, 87). Similarly, Georg Fohrer, *History of Israelite Religion* (London: SPCK, 1973), 275.

hand may be in this *melee* of incidents. However, the frame within which
the story is set leaves us in no doubt that this is not a purely human story,
but a story of God's doing. Before the narrative begins, 2 Samuel 7 recounts
God's assurance through Nathan that David is his chosen king (7:8), and
God's promise that David's son will succeed to the throne and will build
the temple (7:12f.). And after the court history has concluded, 1 Kings 3
records Solomon's acknowledgment that his succession is due to God (3:7),
and 1 Kings 5 records Solomon's intention to build the temple (5:5). How
the history can be both human and divine the story itself does not divulge.

A similar outlook is held by the *Chronicler* of the post-exilic era. To
mention only one example, at the completion of the rebuilding of the temple, the Chronicler observes that what has come about is the doing both of
God and of the Persian emperors: "They finished the building by command
of the God of Israel and by decree of Cyrus and Darius and Artaxerxes king
of Persia" (Ezra 6:14). The divine and human are artlessly conjoined. *How*
God's purpose becomes also the emperor's purpose the Chronicler does not
precisely say; he only knows that somehow "the LORD . . . had turned the
heart of the king of Assyria to them" (6:22), or that he had "stirred up the
spirit of Cyrus" (1:1).

In *Deuteronomy* we have an important exposition of the truth that
Israel is God's *chosen* people.[15] In this book the focus is on the relation between God and Israel as a whole, and in that context the question is raised:
Why should there be any relation at all between God and Israel? The reason
for God's choice cannot be that Israel was more numerous than other nations (7:7), any more than the reason why Israel is given the land can be
that they were more righteous than its former inhabitants (9:4ff.). The only
possible reason is that "the LORD loves you, and is keeping the oath which
he swore to your fathers" (7:8). That is, there is no cause for Israel's election
outside God himself. Here the *form* predestination takes is the unmerited
election of the people. Its *role* is to establish the ground of the relationship
which the book is setting forth.

In *Daniel* we find the nearest approach the Old Testament makes to the
idea of a fixed divine plan that determines the course of history. The scheme
of successive world empires (Daniel 7—12), whose fortunes demonstrate
the truth of the programmatic utterance, "The Most High rules the kingdom of men and gives it to whom he will" (4:32), would seem to go beyond
the prophetic conception of particular divine goals in history. Yet it would
be mistaken to see in Daniel some of the more dogmatic predestinarian

15. Ronald E. Clements, *God's Chosen People: A Theological Interpretation of the Book of Deuteronomy* (London: SCM-Canterbury, 1968), 45–49.

teaching developed by later apocalyptic literature,[16] and it is noteworthy how much of Daniel's visions merely predict what human rulers will do (e.g. Daniel 11), while God's determination of events is restricted to those which impinge most closely on the people of God (e.g.7:25ff.).

SUMMARY

Though it does the rich and varied teaching of the Old Testament on predestination an injustice to attempt to summarize it within a few propositions, we will make the attempt nevertheless.

(1) The Old Testament knows nothing of a divine predestination that determines in advance the particular acts of an individual.

(2) Nor does it affirm a predetermined destiny for individuals in an afterlife.

(3) When it speaks of God's purposes, they are usually specific and comparatively short-range. There is no thought of a detailed blueprint for history.

(4) There are, however, long-range promises whose fulfillment God sees to.

(5) Besides divine predestination, the Old Testament wants to affirm a human predestination (Proverbs).

(6) Predestination in whatever form usually plays a role subsidiary to that of the full and (to all intents and purposes) undetermined relationship of God and man.

And as far as our method goes in approaching the Old Testament's teaching, we may summarize:

(1) Our method cannot be via the accumulation of proof texts drawn indiscriminately from the whole Old Testament. Rather, we should move via the appreciation of the total message of each part of the Old Testament to the particular *form* predestinarian ideas take on there.

(2) Even more important than deciding what is *true* in this subject is to decide how *important* various truths are. No doubt there are many reasonable inferences that may be made from biblical statements about predestination. But to be faithful to the Bible means in part to follow the Bible's emphases and not erect mere inferences into essential

---

16. Leon Morris, *Apocalyptic* (Grand Rapids: Eerdmans, 1972), 48f, 76–81.

biblical doctrine. This is an appeal for sensitivity to the *role* predestinarian ideas play in the Old Testament writings.

8

Predestination in the New Testament

I. Howard Marshall

Our first task in this essay will be to set out the New Testament evidence relating to predestination (I). We shall then examine how this sort of language is used on a human level (II) as a prelude to observing the difficulties that arise when it is applied to God (III). This will lead to a consideration of the causes of these difficulties (IV) what predestination language is meant to do and what it cannot do (V) and conclusions (VI).

I. THE NEW TESTAMENT EVIDENCE

The verb "to predestinate" occurs in the KJV (AV) four times as the translation of the Greek verb *proorizō* (Rom 8:29, 30; Eph 1:5, 11). The same Greek word also occurs in Acts 4:28 (translated "to determine before") and 1 Cor 2:7 ("to ordain"). In accordance with its policy of always translating any Greek word by the same English word if possible; the ASV (RV) has "to foreordain" in all six passages. Later translations adopt a variety of renderings. The NASB has "predestined" in Rom 8:29, 30; the NIV uses the same translation in these two verses and in Eph 1:5, 11.

This Greek word is thus comparatively rare in the New Testament,[1] but of course the *idea* is much more widespread, and a larger word field

---

1. It is not found in the LXX.

demands investigation. "*Pre*-destination" in English, as in Greek, refers to an act of decision prior to a later action; one decides beforehand what one is later going to do. This means that all *pro*-verbs that refer to God purposing or choosing in advance must come into our field of interest. Such verbs can of course be used of human purposing. Thus Paul speaks of the Corinthians making their gifts based for each "what he has decided in his heart to give" (*proaireomai*, 2 Cor 9:7), and of course there are many such verbs that simply indicate that one action preceded another. Prophets can *fore-see* what is going to happen, i.e., see it before it happens, and *fore*-tell it or "*fore*-write" it (e.g., Acts 2:31; Gal 3:8; Acts 1:16; Rom 9:29; Heb 4:7; 2 Pet 3:2; Jude 4). In the same way, God (who was of course the inspirer of the prophets) can have foreknowledge of what is going to happen (Acts 2:23) or of particular people (Rom 8:29; 11:2; 1 Pet 1:2). A special case is where Jesus and his career are said to be foreknown by God (Acts 2:23; 1 Pet 1:20).

But God also prepares things beforehand for his people (Heb 11:40), and chooses people beforehand for various tasks (Acts 10:41; 22:14; 26:16; cf. 3:20 with reference to the Messiah). The verb *protithēmi* can be used in this way with the meaning "to propose" or "to plan beforehand." In Rom 1:13, it refers to a purpose of Paul which had been thwarted, and in Eph 1:9 it is used of God's purpose of salvation.[2] The corresponding noun *prothesis* ("purpose, plan") is more frequent, and refers to God's purpose in Rom 8:28; 9:11; Eph 1:11; 3:11; 2 Tim 1:9. Finally, we may note that the preposition *pro* ("before") can be used to refer to things God planned, promised or did before the creation of the world (John 17:5; 1 Cor 2:7; Eph 1:4; 2 Tim 1:9; Tit 1:2; 1 Pet 1:20; Jude 25).

In many of the above texts the use of *pro-* is strictly unnecessary, since it is obvious that willing and purposing *must by their very nature precede* the action willed and purposed. (We may perhaps compare the increasing use of "pre-" in such phrases as "pre-packaged vegetables"; which are identical with packaged vegetables when they reach the shopper's table.[3]) But this means that all texts in which God is described as willing, planning and purposing must also come within our survey, since here too we are concerned with acts of predestination. So we must note the use of *thelō*, "to will" and of *thelēma*, "will." This verb can be used to express what God *desires* (Matt 9:13; 12:7; Heb 10:5, 8) and what God actually *wills* to happen (1 Cor 12:18; 15:38; Col 1:27); sometimes the dividing line between these two is not absolutely clear (cf. John 5:21; Rom 9:18, 22; 1 Tim 2:4).

2. The meaning in Rom 3:25 is different: "to display publicly."

3. The difference is presumably that "pre-packaged" vegetables are packed *before* they reach the shelves in the retailer's shop, while others are packed (if at all) at the time of purchase.

What God thus desires or purposes can stand in opposition to the desires of people and even of his Son (Mark 14:36; cf. Matt 26:42 and Luke 22:42). What people purpose stands, therefore, under the condition "if the Lord wills it" (Acts 18:21; 21:14; 1 Cor 4:19; James 4:15; 1 Pet 3:17). The noun can stand for what God wishes that people should do (Matt 7:21; 12:50; cf. 21:31); so Jesus did the will of the Father and not his own will (John 4:34; 5:30; 6:38–40). God's plan of salvation can be spoken of as his "will" (Acts 22:14; Eph 1:5, 9; Col. 1:9), as can his plan in creation (Eph 1:11; Rev 4:11). The life of the church in detail—the choice of apostles and the actions they perform—follows the purpose of God (e.g., Rom 1:10; 15:32; 1 Cor 1:1); and his purpose for humanity is that they should obey his will in ethical action and holiness (e.g., Rom 2:18; 12:2; 1 Thess 4:3; 5:18).

A very similar picture is presented when we look at the synonymous verb *boulomai*, "to wish"; and the noun *boule*, "plan." The former is used of God's will that can stand over against man's (Luke 22:42), and of his plan of salvation, whether only intended (2 Pet 3:9) or actually carried out (James 1:18; cf. Heb 6:17). It is also used of the way in which the Son reveals the Father to those whom he wishes (Matt 11:27; cf. Luke 10:22). As for the noun, it can be used in general terms of God's plan that he wants people to follow for their lives (Luke 7:30), of his plan of salvation (Acts 20:27), and of his purpose which is accomplished in the death of Jesus and the lives of other people (Acts 2:23; 4:28; cf. 13:36). God is the one who accomplishes all things according to the purpose of his will, says Paul as he piles up the expressions for rhetorical effect (Eph 1:11).

Other words are also used for what God appoints to happen. Thus *horizōn* has a similar meaning to *prooorizō*. The life of Jesus and his future activities were appointed by God (Luke 22:22; Acts 2:23; 10:42; 17:31; cf. Rom 1:4). God appoints the times at which things happen in the world (Acts 17:26), and the day of salvation (Heb 4:7). Similarly, *prooorizō* is used of Herod and Pilate acting in accordance with God's plan in the condemnation of Jesus (Acts 4:28). God made a plan before the ages for our glory (1 Cor 2:7). He foreordained certain people to be like his Son (Rom 8:29, 30), and indeed to become his adopted children (Eph 1:5) and his portion (Eph 1:11). Again, the verb *tassō*, "to appoint," can be used of rulers (Rom 13:1), those appointed to eternal life (Acts 13:48)[4], and the details of an apostle's career (Acts 22:10).

---

4. It is not unusual for commentators to interpret "tassō" here as meaning "those who were disposed" to eternal life, or "those who marshaled themselves." See Richard B. Rackham, *Acts of the Apostles: An Exposition* (London: Methuen, 1953), 221; J. Vernon Bartlet, Walter F. Adeney, *The New Century Bible: The Acts* (London: Henry Frowde, 1929); and Robert Shank, *Elect in the Son* (Minneapolis: Bethany House,

Finally in this catalog, we have the verb *eudokeō*, "to be pleased," and the noun *eudokia*, "pleasure, will," which often bring out the element of God's pleasure in doing certain things or choosing certain people. He delights in his Servant, Jesus (Matt 3:17; 12:18; 17:5; cf. Col 1:19). He delights to save believers by the preaching of the word (1 Cor 1:21), to reveal himself to Paul (Gal 1:15), and to bestow the kingdom on the disciples (Luke 12:32). It is his pleasure to reveal himself by the Son (Matt 11:26; Luke 10:21); salvation is for those on whom his favor rests (Luke 2:14), and the carrying out of his plan expresses his favor to them (Eph 1:5, 9).[5]

II . THE LANGUAGE OF PREDESTINATION—AS APPLIED TO HUMAN AGENTS

This summary of the terms used to express predestination in the New Testament may have been tedious, but it is necessary. It is not complete, for it has omitted words referring to calling and election, discussed elsewhere in this symposium. But it is comprehensive in that an attempt has been made to cover the whole vocabulary of predestination and to indicate in broad terms how it is used. The concept of God's plan as it affects his Son, the creation of the world, the redemption of mankind, and the individuals who compose the church, is clearly present in the New Testament. It is no part of our purpose to obscure this fact by hiding any of the evidence; our task in this volume is to be true to Scripture.

But it is one thing to *state* what Scripture says; it is another to *understand* it and to bring it into relation with the rest of what Scripture says. Here there are real difficulties, and we must now try to deal with them. We hope that we shall not be criticized for turning to theology and philosophy in order to perform our exegesis better.

When we use the language of predestination and speak of God as willing and purposing, we are using human language to describe God in personal terms. If God is a person, we must use personal language to describe him—which is what the Scriptures do. That he wills and purposes is one aspect of the fact that he is a person. (We may recall that one argument for the personality of the Holy Spirit is that he wills certain things: 1 Cor 12:11).

1989), 183–188.

5. Most of these words are discussed in Gerhard Kittel and Gerhard Friedrich, eds., *Theological Dictionary of the New Testament* (Grand Rapids: Eerdmans, 1977): 2: 629–637 (G. Schrenk); 2:738–751 (G. Schrenk); 3:44–62 (G. Schrenk); 5:452–456 (K. L. Schmidt); 8:164–167 (C. Maurer). See further the discussions of calling (3: 487–496, K. L. Schmidt) and election (4:144–192, G. Quell and G. Schrenk).

But the Scripture is using a human analogy when it describes God in this way, and we have to be very careful when using analogical language. We have to find out how the language is used when applied to people, and what similarities and differences must be noted when it is applied to God.

(1) We observe first that willing and purposing are essential attributes of persons. They can make plans, form intentions, and then act to carry them out; if they could not do so, they would fall short of being real persons.

(2) We can distinguish between the elements of "*desire*" and "*resolve*." The former is the wish to do something without necessarily being able to carry it out or even intending to carry it out (for example, because we prefer to follow some other wish). The latter is the actual decision to do something, and entails at least attempting to put it into effect. For example, there is a difference between my present *desire* to read a novel instead of typing this essay, and my *resolve* to remain at my desk.

(3) It is of the essence of both human desires and resolves that *they may not be fulfilled.* Paul wished to visit Rome in a particular way, but was not able to do so (Rom. 1:13). Circumstances prevent us doing all that we want to do, and these circumstances may include our own mental and physical limitations.

(4) More important, there may be *a clash between* the *wills* of two or more people, so that one of them does not achieve her desire or resolve. While I may not be tempted from my desk by the lure of my unfinished novel, I may be forced away by a persistent knocking at the door and the need to obey somebody else's command.

(5) A particularly tricky situation arises when we ask whether it is possible for somebody to *predict* infallibly and in detail what I shall will and do. I am writing these words on the eve of a British election. It is possible for people who know me well to make a good prediction of how I shall vote in the light of my general character, statements that I have made, and so on. They might even know the physical state of my brain and all the factors that will influence it over the next few hours, so that they can predict confidently what I will do. (The practical impossibility of anybody possessing such knowledge is of course overwhelming.)

Does this mean that my behavior is predetermined, so that I am not able to choose freely? There is one case at least where this is not so. If somebody says to me, "I predict that you will vote for X," I know that I am free to falsify this prediction by voting for Y. For if I am told the prediction, this changes the situation on which the prediction is based and thereby makes it invalid.[6] It would seem to follow that I may be acting equally freely even when somebody makes such a prediction without telling me about it.

There are, of course, situations in which I am not free, and my behavior is predetermined. The most obvious is that of a post-hypnotic suggestion. Here a person is hypnotized and told to perform a certain act at a given time. She is then released from hypnosis, and the experimenter can know confidently that she will perform the act (assuming that it is not physically impossible or morally repulsive). But such subjects think that they are performing the act freely, although it is in fact in response to hypnosis. If they think that they are free, are they "really" free?

(6) If an outside observer cannot predict my behavior infallibly *and* inform me of the prediction, it follows that it is impossible for me to predict infallibly my own activity. For even if I can assemble all the information about myself, I can never dissociate my roles as observer and acting subject, and hence can always falsify my own predictions, if I want to do so. In principle I cannot predetermine my own future states of mind. The attempt is *logically inconceivable*, quite apart from its practical impossibility.

(7) Even more difficult to imagine is the possibility of my *predetermining a course of action involving myself and another subject*: "First I will say A to her, then she will say B to me, then I will reply with C, and she will respond with D. . . ." Naturally, this can be done to some extent: there have been games of chess in which one player has been able to force a predetermined sequence of moves on the opponent, leading to checkmate. But this assumes that the opponent is playing according to the rules of the game (which lay down a finite set of possibilities) and will respond intelligently to each situation. However, on the level of free agents it is impossible. For in the chess illustration, the moves of the opponent are not "free" in fact or in his subjective consciousness. Moreover, we reach the situation that the "moves" of the person doing the predetermination also cease to be free. Having decided what he are going to do at each particular state (if, for the sake of argument, this is possible), he is then bound to that course of action and cannot change it, for if he does, then he must replan the other subject's responses.

---

6. See especially Donald M. MacKay, "The Sovereignty of God in the Natural World," *Scottish Journal of Theology*, 21 (1968), 13–26; *The Clockwork Image: A Christian Perspective on Science* (London: Methuen, 1974).

(8) An interesting point arises if we consider the situation of *the author of a play* who invents characters and has them perform the parts "in character," but so that the ultimate goal for the action of the play is achieved. We can then speak of the various characters acting "freely," but with the result that in their freedom they advance the action to the desired point, since the author has been able to foresee where their freedom would lead and to account for it in framing his plot.[7] But when applied to real life this analogy breaks down at two points. One point is when the author walks on stage and becomes a participant. What happens then? MacKay admits that it lies beyond our conception. For then the drama becomes free and extempore, and the actors do not know what to say. The lines they learned do not take account of such untoward events, unless the appearance of the author as player is built into the original dialogue, in which case, as we have seen, the author has no freedom. But the other point is perhaps more important. We have spoken in terms of the *characters,* but the characters are played by actors, and the *actors* are bound by the characters assigned to them and the lines that they have learned.

There is no question of the "character" saying "I am free what to say"; this is an unreal question. She simply says what is in the script. But the actor too knows that she is bound by her lines, and her freedom lies simply in the way in which she says them; if she varies them, she ceases to be the character she is meant to be. A better possibility might be provided by a jazz band in which the various instrumentalists provide their own extempore harmony and counterpoint, yet in such a way that the piece does eventually come to a conclusion and has some sort of unity. But in this case the players collectively know roughly where they are going and their musical sense enables them to recognize where the music as a whole is going, and even to cope with changes in direction (if, say, the composer is playing the melody line and chooses to vary it). It is not so certain that sinful human beings are willing to cooperate with God in the same way.

The purpose of the above eight points has been to show something of what is involved in using the language of "willing" in respect of free human agents. It has particularly brought out the problems inherent in talking about predicting the free decisions of another person or of myself or of both of us interacting with each other. It emerges that it is doubtful whether I can predict the willing of another free person; that it is impossible for me

7. Dorothy L. Sayers, *The Mind of the Maker* (London: Methuen, 1941), appears to be a major modern influence on the use of this analogy.

in principle to predict my own willing; and that (consequently) it is impossible for me to predict the pattern of an interaction involving myself. (Note: "predict" here means "predict infallibly.") Naturally, there are situations in which I can predict in broad terms what I am going to do, and what other people will do. A lover can reach the stage where he can determine that when he meets his beloved tomorrow he will make a proposal of marriage and predict with reasonable certainty that she will respond favorably. The same thing happens in a host of other situations, but this is not the same thing as the strict determination that is at issue here.

III. THE LANGUAGE OF PREDESTINATION—AS APPLIED TO GOD

A. Factors in the Situation

So now the question arises of what happens when we use this kind of personal language in order to talk about God. Let us first ask what exactly the Bible is using this language to express. We may list the following ideas:

(1) God is *personal*. He can will and purpose what he wants to do, and has freedom to do so.

(2) God is *sovereign*. Ultimately his purpose for the universe will be achieved, so that "God is all in all."

(3) God is *gracious*. The salvation of sinful humans depends entirely upon his gracious initiative; nobody can come to Jesus unless the Father draws them. It would not be too difficult for the theologian to construct a scheme in which these three elements are preserved.

But the problem is sharpened by the existence of three other equally real factors which stand over against the three points we want to preserve:

(1) *People are personal* and have wills of their own. We face the problem of possible opposition to the will of God, and the difficulty of balancing human freedom over against divine predetermination.

(2) *Evil exists* as a factor that is contrary to the will of God, and of which God is not the author. We have the difficulty of fitting it into God's plan.

(3) *Some people are not saved.* The implication is that grace was not shown to them, and we then have the difficulty that grace has been bestowed arbitrarily.

B. The Calvinist Solution

The typical Calvinist approach in face of these factors admits the ultimate mystery of the problem with which we are dealing, but nevertheless attempts to come to terms with it. It plays down the fact of human freedom in two ways. On the one hand, it argues that divine predestination and prediction of human willing and acting and the subjective experience of human freedom are not incompatible, even if we find it impossible to explain how they can be compatible. (The important essay by MacKay is a major attempt to find a way of stating how they can be compatible.) On the other hand, so far as the limited area of faith in God is concerned, it asserts plainly that humanity has no freedom, not even to respond to the grace of God. Unbelievers are dead in sins and must be given the capacity to believe by God (who gives this to the elect).

Second, the Calvinist allows that somehow even evil acts are included in the all-embracing purpose of God; he tolerates or decrees (Calvinists vary on this point) evil in his system so that good may come out of it. But while he allows people to commit evil, it is they who are responsible and bear the guilt for what they freely do, while God himself bears no blame.[8]

Third, the Calvinist insists that God is not under obligation to show grace to any guilty sinner, and therefore he does no injustice in merely showing grace to some; indeed (if many Calvinists are to be believed) such grace may extend to most sinners.[9] Moreover, no sinner need feel excluded from grace, because any person who looks for grace does so only because God has appointed her to do so; it is not possible that a person should seek for grace and yet find that she is not one of the elect. In this way, the Calvinist insists that justice is done to the antinomies found in Scripture. Moreover, justice is being done to the complete sovereignty of God and the apparent freedom of man. One difficulty that remains is that caused by statements implying that God wishes all people to do what is right and to be saved. But this is solved by a distinction between the preceptive will of God and the *decretive* will of God. The former expresses what God wants people to do, while the latter (secret) will expresses what he in fact resolves will happen.

8. The danger of this type of argument should be noted. The late atheist Antony G.N. Flew argued (orally) that if God is omnipotent, and can create beings who, while free, will do what he intends and predicts (as in the analogy of posthypnotic suggestion), then he could have created them so that they would freely choose good instead of evil, and thus would have avoided all the pointless suffering in the world; but since there is suffering, it follows that God is not omnipotent—or not good—or simply does not exist. Flew favored the last possibility. However, near the end of his life, he professed a belief in God. See Antony Flew, *There is a God* (New York: HarperCollins, 2007).

9. B. B. Warfield, *Biblical Foundations* (London: Tyndale, 1958), 246–309.

C. Difficulties in the Calvinist Solution

This package solution, however, is exposed to considerable objections.

(1) In the previous section we have explored the difficulties that arise when we try to think of a person foreordaining the course of a relationship with another person. *This concept is logically self-contradictory,* like the medieval concept of a God who can do anything, and therefore can create a stone so big that he himself cannot lift it. The difficulty arises, as we have seen, as soon as the creator of the universe is himself a participant in it. This produces a self-contradictory situation. It can be argued that God is above logic, and that the rules of logic do not apply, just as in mathematics the normal rules for finite quantities do not apply in the realm of trans-finite numbers.[10] But this objection misses the point: we are not concerned with what God can do, but whether we can use our language of predestination to describe him without the language breaking down. And the point is that when this language is applied to divine-human relationships, it *does* break down.

It is worth reflecting that, by applying the scriptural language of human generation to the relation between Father and Son, the Arians (and others of their ilk) ran into difficulties and tried to solve them by the solution that Jesus had a beginning in time. Origen rightly saw that this false solution arose because language was being misused, and introduced the necessary qualification by speaking of the "eternal generation" of the Son. Here is a perpetual reminder that human language cannot be applied to God without qualification. It leads to results incompatible with other statements (as in the Arian controversy) or to self-contradiction. The Calvinist is using human language without observing that it breaks down when applied to God.

(2) *The problem of evil* also causes difficulties. The Calvinist view that God can cause evil and suffering through "free" human agents without himself being responsible is untenable. I am responsible for what my agent does.[11] One may, therefore, seek refuge in a modified sense of the word

---

10. A similar point has been made by statistician Paul D. Sampson (in a letter dated Nov. 19, 1974) in which he points out how a circle can be defined as a conic section which passes through two points on the line at infinity. These points are both "real" and "imaginary" (in the nonmathematical sense of these terms). The rules of logic do not apply in the normal way when we are dealing with the infinite, and here we must recognize that logic has limitations when applied to the relations between man and God.

11. Admittedly, the Jews argued that if a principal ordered an agent to do something illegal, it is the agent who carries the sin on his own shoulders. In this situation, there is no "agency." But this ruling was designed to prevent agents hiding behind their superior

"cause," so that people are not the agents of God, following out his will when they commit evil. But this is another way of admitting that the model of thought we are using, in which God foreordains all things, is breaking down and will not bear the weight that we are putting on it.

(3) To say that God shows mercy to one sinner and not to the next, i.e., to adopt a doctrine of double predestination (as is done in orthodox Calvinism), is to land in *a moral difficulty*. In this case, divine mercy is not being understood in terms of divine justice. I cannot see how it can be just arbitrarily to save one guilty sinner and not another. And there can be no doubt that any human judge (for it is the pattern of the judge which provides the model) who behaved in this way, and *a fortiori* any human father who treated his sons in this way, would be regarded as falling below the standards of Christian justice. To this the reply may be made that we cannot understand the secret working of the mind of God, that he has freedom to show mercy or to harden, as he chooses, and that we must be prepared to trust the inscrutable will of God as being ultimately just, even if we cannot see it from our limited point of view. But again this objection misses the point which is that the use of the language has broken down; it does not explain, but leaves a mystery.

Now there can of course be situations of this kind. There is the case of Job who does not know why he is suffering; the point of the suffering (from God and Satan's angle) would disappear if Job knew why it was happening. For God's aim is to show to Satan: Here is a person whom I allow to suffer very grievously, and yet will not curse me. The point of the experiment is lost if Job sees that he has no need to question the ultimate goodness of God. Similarly, Paul endured his "thorn in the flesh" when it wasn't God's will to remove it, and then learned to experience the grace of God in a situation of human weakness. But it is one thing to attempt to reconcile experience with faith and another to have a faith which cannot reconcile an apparent contradiction in God himself.

(4) The contrast between the preceptive and decretive wills of God does not really help the situation. We should note that in these two phrases we are really talking about two different things, for *the word "will" is being used in two different senses*. God's preceptive will is his desire that people should do certain things and that all should be saved by responding to the gospel. It is God *commanding* people to do certain

---

authority if they acted wrongfully. John D. M. Derrett, *Law in the New Testament* (London: Darton, Longman and Todd, 1970), 52f.

things. "This do, and you shall live." (For the Christian, "this do" means of course "believe in Jesus," John 6:28f.) But God's decretive will is the expression of his resolve that he will accomplish certain things by whatever form of *causation* leads people to act in accordance with it.

The problems that arise here are great. First, God's preceptive will is *not* always obeyed, and therefore his sovereignty is not fully obeyed. What he desires is not accomplished. So, second, we have to fall back on his decretive will. But this means that his preceptive will and his decretive will stand in contradiction to each other on many occasions. In the Calvinist view, he gives a person the precept "believe in Jesus," and at the same time by his decretive will he resolves that this person is not one of the elect and therefore cannot obey his preceptive will. But such a self-contradiction is intolerable.

The reason why the two wills do not coincide in their effects is of course because of human sin. But in the Calvinist view, the decretive will of God embraces human sin and the ultimate reason why some sinners are saved, and others not saved, rests in the secret will of God. If we say that it is God's will that not all will be saved, this stands in plain contradiction with his expressed desire that all people should repent and come to a knowledge of the truth. (The Calvinist way out of this difficulty is to deny that God does wish *all* to be saved by reading an unlikely meaning into the verses and erecting a doctrine of sovereign election only for those God has chosen.)[12] So the sovereignty of God is not preserved by this distinction.

Worse still perhaps is the fact that it makes God out to be hypocritical, offering freely to all a salvation that he does not intend them all to receive. Certainly, on the human level, all who wish to respond to the gospel can respond; nobody who wants to respond is excluded. But on the divine level, when we look "behind the scenes" at what God is doing, he is doing one thing with his right hand and another with his left. From these considerations it becomes clear that the Calvinist attempt to use the language of predestination with respect to God lands in great difficulties, both logical and moral.

IV. THE CAUSES OF THE DIFFICULTIES

(1) The basic difficulty is that of attempting to explain the nature of *the relationship between an infinite God and finite creatures*. Our temptation

---

12. See the essay by Vernon Grounds in this volume.

is to think of divine causation in much the same way as human causation, and this produces difficulties as soon as we try to relate divine causation and human freedom. It is beyond our ability to explain how God can cause us to do certain things (or to cause the universe to come into being and to behave as it does). Predestinarian language must not be pressed so as to become a doctrine of "mechanical" causation.

(2) A second difficulty is *the fact of evil.* The Bible is clear that God is not the author of evil. Its origin is and perhaps *must* be a mystery. Its evilness lies in its lack of good purpose, and thus in its irrationality and opposition to the purpose of God. How it can have come to exist in a universe created by God is unknowable. We must be content to leave the question unresolved. The Calvinist falls into error when he ascribes the reason why some people are not saved to the decretive will of God; in effect, he is trying to *explain* evil. It is wiser to locate the reason why some people are not saved in the sheer mystery of evil. Admittedly, this way of looking at things also has its dangers; the Calvinist suspects that it conceals an ultimate and intolerable dualism, which Christian theology has in general rejected as a false option. Biblical faith, however, insists that in the sovereignty of God evil will be brought to an end.

(3) A third difficulty is due to the existence of more than one type of language to describe God in the New Testament, or perhaps rather to *the existence of different types of relationship between God and his creatures.* The Calvinist approach regards all God's dealings with people as being expressed ultimately in terms of his decretive will, which means that his relationship to people is that of a dramatist to his characters. Basically, what God does is to predetermine everything that people think, will and do. But this approach has the effect of denying the validity of the other type of language used to describe God. Here God is regarded as standing over against the wills of people. He can give commands to them which they may obey or disobey (his preceptive will). He expresses desires.

He speaks of his love for them, demonstrates it in action, and looks for answering love. He can place his will over against their wills, as when he threatens that those who disobey his will shall endure his wrath. *This language is as real in the Bible as the predestinarian language, and it cannot be reduced to the latter or expressed completely in terms of it.* This should be obvious from the analogy of the dramatist which, as we have already seen, breaks down when applied to God. A dramatist may indeed say that he has come to love his characters (Sir Arthur Conon Doyle, it is said, came to hate Sherlock Holmes!), but it is obvious that this is a special use of the term "love." It does not include the possibility of the characters loving the dramatist, and, even if the dramatist makes them say "I love my creator" in the drama, this is not mutual love in the real sense. So too it makes nonsense of God's joy over the repentance of the sinner (Luke 15:10) if the whole thing, joy and all, has been predestined by God. What the Calvinist approach does is to reduce all this language of interpersonal relationships to the expression of the decretive will of God; and to do this is to turn the story of creation and redemption into sheer farce.

The reason why Calvinists do this is because they want to insist that God is sovereign over all things and that his will is always done; they think that this can be done only by claiming that God predetermines *all* that happens. This solution does not work, because it creates a clash between what God desires (in his so-called prescriptive will) and what actually happens. It is not true that everything that happens is what God desires. But further this solution arises because the Calvinist cannot see any possibility of God's will being done other than by predetermination of all that happens. There is, however, another way in which God's will can be sovereign, and that is by reason of its superior power, so that God can place his will over against ours, and say, "You may want to do X, but you shall do Y." And this is how the Bible portrays the ultimate victory of God. He will be all in all when all creatures bow down before his will and obey it, willingly or unwillingly (not because their wills have been predetermined to obey it, but because they have to bow to his superior power). A solution to the problem of predestination must do justice to the way in which the Bible speaks of God as one who places his will over against ours and acts like another person, rather than as a being who does not enter into real relationships with his creatures but simply treats them as the unconscious objects of his secret will.

This does not mean, however, that we can do away with predestinarian language. We may illustrate this point by referring to prayer. The Bible commands us to pray that God's will may be done, as if this was dependent on our prayers. Prayer influences God. (We can, of course, say that we pray because God wills that he should be moved to act in response to the prayers which he himself has moved us to make. But this reply reduces God to the level of the dramatist.)

But prayer also influences people, in that (for example) the work of preaching the gospel effectively depends upon the intercession of the people of God. The wills of people can thus be affected by prayer—or else we would not pray for them. *To believe in prayer is thus to believe in some kind of limitation of human freedom, and in some kind of incomprehensible influence upon the wills of people.* (This raises a problem of a different kind: does A have a better chance of salvation than B because X prays for A and not for

B? But this is part of the general problem of theodicy, e.g., that a person in Birmingham or Boston has a better chance of hearing the gospel than one in Borneo or Bangladesh.) We must freely admit that there is an element of mystery here, and not try to tone down either aspect of the language of the Bible.

V. THE PURPOSE AND LIMITS OF PREDESTINARIAN LANGUAGE

(1) The New Testament clearly teaches that God has desires and acts to put them into effect. He is God, and he is free to do what he likes, choosing one person for a particular task rather than another. He is sovereign in that he is supreme. But we do not yet see all things under the feet of Jesus or the Father. The language of predestination voices the assurance that in the end God's sovereignty will be entire and complete, all opposition having been quelled and his plan of salvation having been accomplished.

(2) Predestinarian language safeguards the truth that *in every case it is God who takes the initiative in salvation* and calls people to him, and works in their hearts by his Spirit. Salvation is never the result of human merit, nor can anybody be saved without first being called by God. People cannot in any sense save themselves. It must be declared quite emphatically that *the non-Calvinist affirms this as heartily as the Calvinist* and repudiates entirely the Pelagianism which is often (but wrongly) thought to be inherent in this position.

When a person becomes a Christian, she cannot do anything else but own that it is all of grace—and even see that she has been affected by the prayers of other people. But whether we can go on to speak of an "effectual" calling of those who are saved is dubious. The terminology is not scriptural, and is due to an attempt to find the explanation why some respond to the call of God and others do not respond in the nature of the call itself. Rather, the effect of the call of God is to place people in a position where they can say "Yes" or "No" (which they could not do before God called them; till then they were in a continuous attitude of "No").

(3) Predestinarian language roots salvation in past eternity, "before the creation of the world." This leads to the temptation to think of God acting in terms of a blueprint prepared in eternity past. But this is to misinterpret the language and leads to illogical consequences. It destroys

the freedom of God who can, for instance, be grieved that he has created sinful humans, and then decide what he is going to do next. *The Bible has the picture of a God deciding fresh measures in history and interacting with the wills of people alongside the picture of a God planning things in eternity past,* and both pictures are equally valid. Neither is to be subordinated to the other. Our difficulties in appreciating this arise from our inability to cope with the concept of eternity and its relation to time. The predestinarian language is meant to affirm that God's plan has all along been one of salvation, and that he created the universe in order to have fellowship with humanity.

(4) Predestinarian language expresses the fact that *God can foretell what is going to happen,* and can act to bring about his will. Somehow this truth has to be safeguarded despite the difficulties which attach to the idea of prediction. The answer may lie in the fact that in general, individuals do not know about the existence of predictions relating to their willing and behavior and hence do not have the possibility of refusing to obey them. Nor is the language of God predicting what certain individuals will do confused with the language of God himself entering into personal relationships with them; nor, or course, is the language of prophecy entirely unconditional. But many prophecies are conditional on the obedience or disobedience of the people concerned; nor again is all prophecy concerned with the predetermining in detail of how certain people are going to act.

(5) But now we must assert that *predestinarian language must not be used to make God responsible for evil.* Certainly he is able to make evil subserve his purposes, but this is not the same thing as being responsible for it. It follows that predestinarian language must not be used to assert that everything that happens is what God wants to happen. His perceptive will, i.e. his desires, are not always fulfilled in this present world, although the New Testament promises that one day his complete sovereignty will be revealed. At the same time the Christian confesses that in all things God works for the good of those who love him (Rom 8:28), and can rest in the goodness of God.

(6) Predestinarian language must not be pressed to express *praedestinatio in malam partem,* the reprobation of certain individuals by the will of God. God wants the wicked person to turn from wickedness and live. He has no delight in the death of the sinner, and that is his last word on the matter. We have no right to go beyond Scripture and assert that he determines otherwise in the secret counsel of his heart. He is not willing that any should perish but that all should come to a knowledge

of the truth and be saved (1 Tim 2:4). "Let the one who wishes take the water of life without cost" (Rev. 22:17b). That is God's *final* word on the matter.[13]

VI. CONCLUSION

It will be clear that the writer of this essay believes in predestination; he cannot do anything else and remain faithful to the testimony of Scripture. Our purpose, therefore, has been to *explain* the meaning of the phrase, to point out the logical difficulties and moral dangers involved in its use, to place alongside it other types of language that are equally valid and important in understanding the biblical doctrine of God, and so to see how the phrase may legitimately be used. In the end, however, we have seen that we are confronted by mysteries which cannot be solved by the theologians. It is here that they must confess their faith that, although they cannot solve the problems rationally, what they know of the power and goodness of God revealed in Christ means that there are answers.

---

13. It should not be necessary to point out that the writers of this symposium would emphatically reject universalism in the sense that all humanity will be saved. The offer of the gospel is indeed for *all* people, but not all accept that offer.

9

Jacobus Arminius: Reformed and Always Reforming

J. Matthew Pinson

Jacobus Arminius has been the object of much criticism and much praise during the past four centuries. Arminians have usually poured praise on him as the progenitor of their theological tradition, while non-Arminians, specifically those within the Reformed-Calvinistic tradition, have heaped criticism on him for departing from the Reformed faith. Both praise and criticism, however, have most of the time proceeded from partisan biases and rest on misinterpretations of Arminius's theology. Most Reformed critics have portrayed him as a semi-Pelagian and a defector from Reformed theology, while most Arminians—Wesleyans and Remonstrants—have cast him in Wesleyan or Remonstrant terms, failing to take seriously his theology itself and the context in which it was spawned.[1]

Both Reformed and Arminian scholars have traditionally portrayed Arminius's thought as a departure from Reformed theology, or, as Richard A. Muller has described it, "a full-scale alternative to Reformed theology."[2]

1. The best, most accessible source for becoming acquainted with Arminius's soteriology in the context of the Arminian Calvinist debate is Robert E. Picirilli, *Grace, Faith, Free Will: Contrasting Views of Salvation—Calvinism and Arminianism* (Nashville: Randall House, 2002).

2. Richard Muller, *God, Creation, and Providence in the Thought of Jacob Arminius* (Grand Rapids: Baker, 1991), 281.

Many Reformed thinkers have portrayed Arminius as "a clever dissembler who secretly taught doctrines different from his published writings."[3] Most writers commit the *post hoc ergo propter hoc* fallacy by attributing to Arminius theological movements that came after him. Roger Nicole, for example, described Arminius as the originator of a slippery slope that started with Episcopius and Limborch (who were "infiltrated by Socinianism") and ended with Unitarianism, Universalism, and the philosophy of E. S. Brightman.[4] Reformed writers traditionally described Arminius as a semi-Pelagian, an appellation that persists to this day. Several Reformed authors have recently characterized Arminius's thought as "semi-Pelagian"[5] or even "similar to Pelagianism."[6] These comments are remarkable given Arminius's often stated aim to maintain "the greatest possible distance from Pelagianism."[7]

Most Arminians, while praising Arminius, have viewed him in the light of either Remonstrant or Wesleyan theology, thus describing him in more synergistic or semi-Pelagian terms. The tendency of most Arminians is to give a brief biographical sketch of Arminius, with the customary discussion of "Arminius as the Father of Arminianism," and then to offer an exposition of the five points of the Remonstrants. Or, as Carl Bangs says, the biographical sketch is many times followed by "copious references to Arminius's successor, Simon Episcopius, who, although in many ways a faithful disciple of Arminius, is not Arminius."[8]

3. Bangs, "Arminius and the Reformation," *Church History* 30 (1961), 156. Muller resurrects this specter, seeming to leave Arminius's honesty open to question; see his "Arminius and the Reformed Tradition," *Westminster Theological Journal* 70 (2008), 41. Cf. Stephen M. Ashby, "Notes on Arminius" (unpublished notes).

4. Roger Nicole, "The Debate over Divine Election," *Christianity Today*, October 21, 1959, 6.

5. Carl Trueman, "Post-Reformation Developments in the Doctrine of the Atonement," in Richard D. Phillips, ed., *The Precious Atoning Work of Christ* (Wheaton: Crossway, 2009), 184; Trueman, *John Owen: Reformed Catholic, Renaissance Man* (Burlington, Vt.: Ashgate, 2007), 26; David Dockery, *Southern Baptist Consensus and Renewal* (Nashville: B&H, 2008), 67; Alan F. Johnson and Robert Webber, *What Christians Believe* (Grand Rapids: Zondervan, 1993), 223–224; W. Robert Godfrey, review of *Jacob Arminius: Theologian of Grace* at Reformation21.com (*http://www.reformation21.org/shelf-life/jacob-arminius-theologian-of-grace.php*).

6. Paul Enns, *The Moody Handbook of Theology* (Chicago: Moody, 2008), 323–324. Ralph Keen, in *The Christian Tradition* (Lanham, Md.: Rowman and Littlefield, 2008), says that Arminius believed "the human will is capable of doing good" and "the believer cooperated with grace" (234). See Olson, *Arminian Theology*, for more examples.

7. Jacobus Arminius, *The Works of James Arminius*, 3 vols., James Nichols and William Nichols, trans., (Nashville: Randall House, 2007), 1:764, "Apology against Thirty-One Defamatory Articles" (this edition of Arminius's *Works* is hereafter cited as "Arminius, *Works*").

8. Carl Bangs, "Arminius and Reformed Theology," Ph.D. diss., University of

None of these things, however, is true of Arminius, and only when one brings certain assumptions to his writings will one interpret him in these ways. Bangs summarizes this problem well:

> It is evident that such accounts of Arminius assume a defini-
> tion of Arminianism which cannot be derived from Arminius
> himself. It means that the writers begin with a preconception of
> what Arminius should be expected to say, then look in his pub-
> lished works, and do not find exactly what they are looking for.
> They show impatience and disappointment with his Calvinism,
> and shift the inquiry into some later period when Arminianism
> turns out to be what they are looking for—a non-Calvinistic,
> synergistic, and perhaps semi-Pelagian system.[9]

Those who bring presumptions into the study of Arminius by reading later Arminian themes into his thought fail to realize perhaps the most impor-tant thing about his theology: that it is distinctively Reformed, and that it is a *further development* of Reformed theology rather than a *departure* from it. By focusing on Arminius's doctrine of predestination and its dif-ferences with both Calvin and post-Dort Calvinism, people have tended to emphasize Arminius's differences with Calvin and the Reformed tradition rather than his similarities with them. Both Arminians and Calvinists have thought of Arminius's theology as essentially a reaction against Reformed theology rather than the self-consciously Reformed theology that it is.[10]

Chicago, 1958, 23. The best comparison and contrast of Arminius and the later Remon-strants (and one of the best treatments of Arminius I recommend) is Hicks, "Theology of Grace in the Thought of Jacobus Arminius and Philip Van Limborch: A Study in the Development of Seventeenth-Century Dutch Arminianism," PhD. diss., Westminster Theological Seminary, 1985. This dissertation may be downloaded free from *http://evangelicalarminians.org/wp-content/uploads/2013/07/Hicks.-The-Theology-of-Grace-in-the-Thought-of-Arminius-and-Limborch.pdf*; see Hicks's briefer article "The Righ-teousness of Saving Faith: Arminian versus Remonstrant Grace," *Evangelical Journal* 9 (1991) 27–39. See also Mark A. Ellis, *Simon Episcopius' Doctrine of Original Sin* (New York: Peter Lang, 2006); and Sarah Mortimer, *Reason and Religion in the English Revo-lution* (Cambridge: Cambridge University Press, 2010); Mortimer is correct in saying that the Remonstrants "did not feel themselves bound to preserve Arminius's system in its entirety, and from the start they began to alter and reshape it" (26). In her important book, she ties Henry Hammond's Anglican Arminianism more to the Grotian strand of Remonstrantism and to Socinus, and not to Arminius, arguing that early Remonstrants Hugo Grotius and Simon Episcopius diverged radically from Arminius. See 25–26, 119–125.

9. Bangs, "Arminius and Reformed Theology," 14.

10. Recent scholars have taken one of two broad positions on the soteriology of Jacobus Arminius. One group holds that his theology was a *development* of the Dutch Reformed theology of his day, while the other says that it was a radical *departure* from Reformed categories. Following Carl Bangs, scholars such as Hicks, Picirilli, Roger E.

William den Boer is correct when, discussing Arminius in his Reformed context, he favorably cites Willem J. Van Asselt's comment that there were "different trajectories" in sixteenth-century Reformed theology, and that it was "not monolithic." Thus, den Boer places Arminius's thought in the "spectrum" of sixteenth-century Reformed theology—a "movement" that was "multi-faceted, dynamic, and ever-developing." He thus rightly criticizes the view that there was "*the* Reformed theology."[11]

Those who see predestination as the essential core of Reformed theology find it easy to say that, since Arminius did not articulate predestination in the same way Calvin did, he is a semi-Pelagian. Then they transfer this alleged semi-Pelagianism to all of his theology. Generations of theological students have received this picture of Arminius. But this approach fails to take his theology seriously. The best way to understand Arminius, and thus to benefit from his unique and substantial contribution to Protestant theology, is to understand his theological context, his stated view of Reformed theology (specifically that of Calvin), his confessional beliefs, and his published writings. If one believes Arminius to be an honest man, rather than

---

Olson, F. Stuart Clarke, William G. Witt, William den Boer, G. J. Hoerdendaal, Ellis, and Mortimer fall into the first category. Richard Muller, Keith Stanglin, and Thomas McCall fall into the second. See Bangs, *Arminius: A Study in the Dutch Reformation* (Nashville: Abingdon, 1971); Bangs, "Arminius and the Reformation"; Bangs, "Arminius and Reformed Theology"; Hicks, "The Theology of Grace"; Picirilli, *Grace, Faith, Free Will*; Picirilli, "Arminius and the Deity of Christ," *Evangelical Quarterly* 70 (1998), 51–59; Roger E. Olson, *Arminian Theology: Myths and Realities* (Downers Grove, Ill.: InterVarsity, 2006); William G. Witt, "Creation, Redemption, and Grace in the Theology of Jacobus Arminius," Ph.D. diss., University of Notre Dame, 1993; William den Boer, *God's Twofold Love: The Theology of Jacob Arminius (1559–1609)* (Gottingen: Vandenhoeck and Ruprecht, 2010); G. J. Hoerdendaal, "The Debate about Arminius outside the Netherlands," in *Leiden University in the 17th Century* (Leiden: Brill, 1975), 137–159; Mark A. Ellis, *Simon Episcopius*; Mortimer, *Reason and Religion in the English Revolution*; Muller, *God, Creation, and Providence*; Keith D. Stanglin, *Arminius and the Assurance of Salvation* (Leiden: Brill, 2007); Keith D. Stanglin and Thomas H. McCall, *Jacob Arminius: Theologian of Grace* (New York: Oxford University Press, 2012).

11. *God's Twofold Love*, 43–44. Den Boer's perspective has much to commend itself over against the tendencies of Muller and colleagues to see Reformed theology as more of a monolith. Cf. Den Boer, "'Cum delectu': Jacob Arminius's Praise for and Critique of Calvin and His Theology," *Church History and Religious Culture* 91 (2011), 73–86. Cf. Wilhelm Pauck, who described Arminius's theology as an outgrowth of Reformed theology: "Indeed, there are many Calvinist theological traditions. The Reformed theologies of the Swiss, the German, the French, the Dutch, the Scotch, etc., are not so uniform as the theologies of the various Lutheran bodies are. The Arminians belong as definitely to the Calvinistic tradition as the defenders of the decisions of the Synod of Dort" (*The Heritage of the Reformation* [Boston: Beacon Press, 1950], 272. Quoted in Bangs, "Arminius and Reformed Theology," 25).

a treacherous one, one will see a picture of him emerge that is radically different from the one(s) above.[12]

ARMINIUS'S LIFE

Before discussing the theological milieu in which Arminius taught and wrote, it will be helpful to give a brief sketch of his life.[13] Arminius, born in 1559 and named Jacob Harmenszoon, grew up in Oudewater, Holland, and later studied at the newly established University of Leiden. After graduation from Leiden in 1581, he was brought to Geneva to study under Theodore Beza, Calvin's successor and son-in-law. He left there to study at Basel for a year but returned and studied at Geneva until 1586. Arminius's second stint at Geneva went smoothly. Beza gave a glowing report to the Amsterdam burgomasters, who were inquiring if Arminius was fitting in well.

In 1587 Arminius was assigned a pastorate in Amsterdam and was ordained in 1588. Before assuming his pastorate, Arminius traveled with his friend Adrian Junius to Italy and studied philosophy for seven months with James Zabarella at the University of Padua. Arminius took this journey without the permission of the Amsterdam burgomasters. Though he said that the experience made the Roman Church appear to him "more foul,

---

12. Richard Muller and his students (e.g., Stanglin, McCall, and Raymond Blacketer), place more emphasis on Arminius's differences with Reformed orthodoxy than most scholars do. I disagree with them on this, yet in most respects they avoid the conventional stereotypes of Arminius characterized above. They are astute interpreters of Arminius and are more attentive to his historical and theological context than most scholars (e.g., Stanglin's setting of Arminius's thought in the context of that of his academic colleagues at Leiden). In particular, students of Arminius should be grateful to Muller (*God, Creation, and Providence*) for correcting the notion that Arminius was a humanist rather than a scholastic thinker. Arminius can be properly interpreted only in the context of the Reformed scholastic theology of his day. Muller has argued that Arminius's view of creation and providence and his intellectualism vs. voluntarism differ somewhat from Reformed Scholasticism. This is perhaps responsible for his divergent view of predestination. This observation, however, does not obscure the fact that there was no consensus on predestination, free will, etc., in the Dutch Reformed Church of Arminius's time. Nor does it detract from Arminius's inherently Reformed views on original sin, total depravity, human inability, the penal-satisfaction nature of the atonement, or the imputative nature of justification. (See also Raymond Blacketer, "Arminius' Concept of Covenant in Its Historical Context," *Nederlands archief voor kerkgeschiedenis*, 80 [2000], 193–220.)

13. This brief summary information relies on Carl Bangs, *Arminius*. For two valuable shorter introductions to Arminius's life, but longer than this sketch, see Stephen M. Ashby, "Introduction" to *The Works of James Arminius* (Nashville; Randall House, 2007) and Picirilli, "Arminius and the Calvinists," *Dimension* (Spring 1985), 7–15.

ugly, and detestable" than he could have imagined,[14] some of his later enemies used the trip to suggest that he had sympathies with Rome, "that he
had kissed the pope's shoe, become acquainted with the Jesuits, and cher-
ished a familiar intimacy with Cardinal Bellarmine."[15]

In 1590 Arminius married Lijset Reael, a daughter of a member of the
city council. About this time he became involved in theological controversy.
Arminius was asked to refute the teachings of Dirk Coornhert, a humanist
who had criticized Calvinism, and two ministers at Delft who had written
an anti-Calvinist pamphlet. The traditional view was that Arminius, in his
attempt to refute these anti-Calvinist teachings, converted from Calvinism
to anti-Calvinism. Yet Bangs has shown that there is no evidence that he
ever held strict Calvinist views. At any rate, he became involved in controversy over the doctrines of the strong Calvinists. In 1591, he preached on
Romans 7, arguing against the Calvinists' view that the person described in
vv. 14–24 was regenerate. A minister named Petrus Plancius led the charge
against Arminius. Plancius labeled Arminius a Pelagian, alleging that he
had moved away from the Belgic Confession of Faith and the Heidelberg
Catechism, advocating non-Reformed views on predestination and perfectionism. Arminius insisted that his theology was in line with that of the
Reformed Church and its Confession and Catechism, and the Amsterdam
burgomasters sided with him. About a year later, after a sermon on Romans
9, Plancius again led the charge against Arminius. The latter insisted that
his teachings were in line with Article 16 of the Belgic Confession, and the
consistory accepted Arminius's explanation, urging peace until the matter
could be decided by a general synod.

For the next ten years, Arminius enjoyed a relatively peaceful pastorate and avoided theological controversy. During this decade, he wrote a
great deal on theology (things that were never published in his lifetime),
including extensive works on Romans 7 and 9 as well as a long correspondence with the Leiden Calvinist Francis Junius. In 1602, after Leiden professor Lucas Trelcatius the elder died from the plague, there was a move on
to get Arminius appointed to his position, but there was also opposition
to Arminius's appointment, led by Leiden professor Franciscus Gomarus.
Despite this opposition, the Leiden burgomasters appointed Arminius as
professor of theology in May 1603. Soon he was awarded a doctorate in
theology.

14. Arminius, *Works*, 1:26.

15. Caspar Brandt, *The Life of James Arminius, D.D.*, trans. John Guthrie (London:
Ward and Company, 1854), 28.

Arminius would spend the last six years of his life at Leiden, struggling with tuberculosis but always in a firestorm of theological controversy. The primary source of the controversy was predestination, and this is what Arminius and the movement that was named after him became known for. Another issue of dispute was the convening of a national synod. Arminius's side wanted a national synod convened with power to revise the Confession and Catechism, while the strict Calvinists relied more on local synods. In 1607 the States General brought together a conference to prepare for a national synod. Arminius recommended the revision of the confessional documents but was voted down. He continued to be accused of heresy and false teaching, which resulted in his petitioning the States General to inquire into his case. Eventually, Arminius and Gomarus appeared before the High Court in 1608 to make their respective cases. This was the occasion for Arminius's famous *Declaration of Sentiments*.[16]

In his *Declaration of Sentiments*, Arminius forthrightly argued against the Calvinist view of unconditional election.[17] He concluded his declaration by asking again for a national synod with hopes for a revision of the Confession. Gomarus appeared before the States General and accused Arminius of errors on not only original sin, divine foreknowledge, predestination, regeneration, good works, and the possibility of apostasy, but also the Trinity

---

16. The references to the *Declaration of Sentiments* in this chapter are from the recent translation from the Dutch: W. Stephen Gunter, *Arminius and His Declaration of Sentiments: An Annotated Translation with Introduction and Theological Commentary* (Waco: Baylor University Press, 2012).

17. He also was cautious in his statement regarding perseverance, insisting that he "never taught that a true believer either totally or finally falls away from the faith and perishes; but I do not deny that there are passages of Scripture that seem to indicate such." (Gunter, *Declaration of Sentiments*, Kindle locations 3292–3294; cf. Arminius, 1:667; lit. "Ingenue tamen affirmo, nunquam me docuisse, quod vere credens aut *totaliter* aut finaliter a *fide deficiat, sicque pereat*," in Iacobi Arminii, *Opera Theologica* [Leiden: Godefridus Basson, 1629], 123). It is difficult, if not impossible, to decipher where Arminius comes down on perseverance. Scholars such as Picirilli, Olson, and Clarke seem to think Arminius was agnostic on the possibility of apostasy, while Stanglin thinks Arminius believed one could apostatize by committing sin and then regain salvation through penitence (see Stanglin, *Arminius and the Assurance of Salvation*, 133–139). Stephen M. Ashby and I have emphasized Arminius's statement that only when one declines from belief (and thus union with Christ) can one decline from salvation (see Pinson, "Introduction" and Ashby, "Reformed Arminianism," in Pinson, ed. *Four Views on Eternal Security* [Grand Rapids: Zondervan, 2002], 15, 137, 187). Arminius is so ambiguous on the subject that Reformed Arminians (who emphasize irremediable apostasy only by renouncing Christ through unbelief), conventional Arminians (who emphasize apostasy through sinning and regaining salvation through repentance), and once-saved, always-saved advocates all claim him as their own. I have almost given up on the possibility of ascertaining Arminius's position.

and biblical authority. While the States General did not support Gomarus, the controversy became more heated.

In August of 1609, the States General invited Arminius and Gomarus back for a conference. They were each to bring four other colleagues. Arminius's illness, which had been worsening, made it impossible for him to continue the conference, which was dismissed. The States General asked the two men to submit their views in writing within two weeks. Arminius never completed his, owing to his illness, and he died on October 19, 1609.

ARMINIUS'S THEOLOGICAL CONTEXT

An awareness of the theological situation in the Dutch Reformed Church before and during Arminius's lifetime enhances one's understanding of his theology. Most of the interpretations of Arminius's theology have been based on misconceptions about his situation.[18] Bangs mentions six misunderstandings that are common among interpreters of Arminius:[19] (1) that Arminius was reared and educated amidst Calvinism in a Calvinist country; (2) that his education at the Universities of Leiden and Basel confirmed his acceptance of Genevan Calvinism; (3) that as a student of Theodore Beza he accepted supralapsarianism; (4) that, while a pastor in Amsterdam, he was commissioned to write a refutation of the humanist Dirck Coornhert, who "attacked predestination, and who had declared that the doctrine of original sin is not in the Bible;"[20] (5) that while preparing his refutation, he changed his mind and went over to Coornhert's humanism[21] and (6) that thus his theology was a polemic against Reformed theology. None of these six points, as Bangs has shown, are true.[22]

Arminius was not predisposed to a supralapsarian view of predestination. He rather shared the views of numerous Reformed theologians and pastors before him. He was not reared in a "Calvinist country." A brief look at the Reformed Church in the sixteenth century will reveal this. The origins of the Reformed Church were diverse, both historically and theologically. When Calvin came out with his views on predestination in the 1540s, there was a strong reaction from many within the Reformed Church. When

18. The historical information in this section relies on Bangs, "Arminius and the Reformation," 155–160.

19. These misconceptions arise from the Peter Bertius's funeral oration for Arminius and Caspar Brandt's *Life of James Arminius.*

20. Ibid., 156.

21. Ibid.

22. See Bangs, *Arminius,* 141–142.

Sabastien Castellio exhibited disagreement with Calvin's view of predestination, he was banished from Geneva but was given asylum by the Reformed
in Basel and soon offered a professorship there. It was said that, in Basel, "if
one wishes to scold another, he calls him a Calvinist."[23] Another Reformed
theologian who reacted negatively to Calvin's doctrine of predestination
was Jerome Bolsec, who settled in Geneva in 1550. When Calvin and Beza
sent a list of Bolsec's errors to the Swiss churches, they were disappointed
with the response. The Church of Basel urged that Calvin and Bolsec try to
emphasize their similarities rather than their differences. The ministers of
Bern reminded Calvin of the many biblical texts that refer to God's universal grace. Even Bullinger disagreed with Calvin, though he later changed
his mind. Bangs notes that "the most consistent resistance to [Calvin's]
predestination theory came from the German-speaking cantons,"[24] but that
even in Geneva there was a fair amount of resistance. This is evidenced by
the presence of the liberal Calvinist Charles Perrot on the faculty of the
University of Geneva, even during Beza's lifetime.

"From the very beginnings of the introduction of Reformed religion
in the Low Countries," says Bangs, "the milder views of the Swiss cantons
were in evidence."[25] Because of Roman Catholic persecution, the first Dutch
Reformed synod was held at the Reformed church in Emden, where Albert
Hardenberg was pastor. Hardenberg, who was closer to Melanchthon than
to Calvin on predestination, exerted great influence on the early leaders in
the Dutch Reformed Church—most notably Clement Martenson and John
Isbrandtson, who "publicly resisted the introduction of Genevan theology
into the Low Countries."[26] At the Synod of Emden, the Heidelberg Catechism and the Belgic Confession of Faith were adopted. Both these documents allowed room for disagreement on the doctrine of predestination,
but some ministers who had been educated in Geneva began attempts to
enforce a supralapsarian interpretation of these documents.

Soon there arose two parties in the Dutch Reformed Church. Those
who were less inclined to a Calvinistic view of predestination were more
inclined toward a form of Erastianism and toleration toward Lutherans
and Anabaptists, while the Genevan elements wanted strict adherence to
Calvinism and Presbyterian church government. The lay magistrates and
lay people tended toward the former, while more clergy tended toward the
latter. However, a significant number of clergy clung to the non-Calvinistic

23. Bangs, "Arminius and the Reformation," 157.

24. Ibid., 158.

25. Ibid.

26. Ibid., 159.

view of predestination. As late as 1581, Jasper Koolhaes, a Reformed pastor in Leiden, after being declared a heretic by the provincial Synod of Dort because of his non-Calvinistic interpretation of predestination, was supported by the magistrates at Leiden.[27] The provincial Synod of Haarlem of 1582 excommunicated him, and this action was opposed by the magistrates and some ministers of Leiden, the Hague, Dort, and Gouda. The Synod also attempted to force the Dutch churches to accept a rigid doctrine of predestination but did not succeed. As Bangs says, "Koolhaes continued to write, with the support of the States of Holland and the magistrates of Leiden. A compromise reconciliation between the two factions was attempted, but it was not successful. This indicates something of a mixed situaton in the Reformed churches of Holland at the time that Arminius was emerging as a theologian."[28] Thus there was no consensus on the doctrine of predestination in the Dutch Reformed Church of Arminius's time.

ARMINIUS, THE CONFESSIONS AND CALVIN

It is within this historical context that Arminius worked out his Reformed theology. As a devout Dutch Reformed theologian, Arminius was loyal to the symbols of his Church: The Heidelberg Catechism and the Belgic Confession of Faith. He reaffirmed on numerous occasions his faithfulness to these documents. Responding to the consistory in Amsterdam in 1593, Arminius felt it necessary to affirm his loyalty to the Catechism and Confession. He repeatedly reiterated this loyalty, as in 1605, when he responded to deputies of the Synods of North and South Holland.[29] In 1607, at the meeting of the Preparatory Convention for the National Synod, Arminius and some other delegates, emphasizing the priority of the Word of God as the church's rule of faith and practice, argued that the Confession and Catechism should be open to revision by the Synod, to clarify certain doctrines (e.g., the use of the plural when discussing original sin in the Catechism). This did not mean, however, that Arminius disagreed with anything the documents said. Arminius made this clear in a letter to the Palatine Ambassador, Hippolytus à Collibus, in 1608: "I confidently declare that I have never taught anything, either in the church or in the university, which contravenes the sacred writ-

27. Koolhaes taught at the University of Leiden while Arminius was a student there. The first rigid predestinarian did not teach at the University until the arrival of Lambert Daneau.

28. Bangs, "Arminius and the Reformation," 160.

29. Carl Bangs, "Arminius as a Reformed Theologian," in *The Heritage of John Calvin,* John H. Bratt, ed. (Grand Rapids: Eerdmans, 1973), 216.

ings that ought to be with us the sole rule of thinking and of speaking, or which is opposed to the Dutch [Belgic] Confession or to the Heidelberg Catechism, that are our stricter formularies of consent."[30]

In his *Declaration of Sentiments* that same year, he challenged any-one to prove that he had ever made doctrinal pronouncements that were "contrary to God's Word or to the Confession and Catechism of the Belgic Churches."[31] Arminius lived and died with complete loyalty to the Heidel-berg Catechism and the Belgic Confession of Faith. It is hard to believe that one could consistently lie both in public statements and in published writ-ing after published writing (when it would have been much easier to do as Koolhaes did and enter some other occupation that was less psychically strenuous). If Arminius was not a dishonest, surreptitious, treacherous man, it may be confidently believed that he was a loyal defender of the symbols of his church to his dying day.

In light of the fact that most interpreters have cast Arminius as a foe of Calvin, Arminius's statements on Calvin are most interesting. Arminius made explicit references to Calvin throughout his writings—most of the time favorable ones. He had a high regard for Calvin as an exegete and theo-logian. His only important disagreement with Calvin was on the particulars of the doctrines of predestination and the resistibility of grace. Arminius did not, however, think predestination was the essential core of either Re-formed theology or Calvin's theology. He expressed his high esteem for Calvin in a letter to the Amsterdam Burgomaster Sebastian Egbertszoon in May of 1607. The occasion of the letter was a rumor that Arminius had been recommending the works of the Jesuits and of Coornert to his students. Arminius said: "So far from this, after reading the Scripture . . . I recom-mend the *Commentaries of Calvin* be read. . . . In the interpretation of the Scriptures Calvin is incomparable, and . . . his *Commentaries* are more to be valued than anything that is handed down to us in the writings of the Fathers. . . . His *Institutes* . . . I give out to be read after the [Heidelberg] Catechism. But here I add—with discrimination, as the writings of all men ought to be read."[32]

In his *Declaration of Sentiments*, Arminius, setting forth his doctrine of justification, says, in essence, that if he is wrong, then Calvin too must be wrong: "Whatever one might say about this, no one among us accuses Calvin or considers him heterodox on this point, and my position is not

---

30. Arminius, *Works*, 2:690. "Letter to Hippolytus à Collibus."

31. Gunter, *Declaration of Sentiments*, Kindle locations 2324–2325; cf. Arminius, *Works*, 1:600.

32. Quoted in Bangs, "Arminius as a Reformed Theologian," 216.

so different from his as to prevent my signing my name to the positions he takes in Book III of his *Institutes*. To these opinions, I am prepared to state my full approval at any time."[33] Arminius's opinion of Calvin in these passages does not sound like that of an antagonist, but rather like one who has great respect for Calvin and is in agreement with him on most things. It is a mistake to exaggerate the importance of the doctrine of predestination to the point that it is the only doctrine that matters. Though Arminius differed with Calvin on predestination, Arminius was, and believed he was, consistently Reformed.

Though an examination of Arminius's historical and theological context, his confessional loyalties, and his opinion of Calvin do a great deal to establish his theological position, the final court of appeal are his writings. An analysis of them will show that he was in essential agreement with the Augustinian, Calvinistic, and Reformed expressions of the Faith with regard to original sin, the radical depravity and inability of humanity, the nature of atonement, and justification. Arminius differed from the strong Calvinists on *how one comes to be* in a state of grace, but not on *what it means to be* in a state of grace. A study of his writings shows that Arminius should not be described as semi-Pelagian or synergistic, but rather articulated the reality of original sin and total depravity and the necessity of divine grace in salvation just as strongly as any Calvinist.

ARMINIUS AND PREDESTINATION

Before undertaking that discussion, however, it will be instructive to summarize the primary doctrinal difference between Arminius and his strict Calvinist interlocuters: how one comes to be in a state of grace or not, that is, the doctrine of predestination.

Predestination as Conditional, Christocentric, and According to Foreknowledge

Robert E. Picirilli encapsulates Arminius's view of predestination when he says that, for Arminius, "the unconditionality of God's sovereign 'decisions' (plan, purpose) does not necessarily mean that all the ends God

---

33. Gunter, *Declaration of Sentiments*, Kindle locations 3437–3440; cf. Arminius, *Works*, 1:700. Arminius's doctrine of justification will be dealt with later in this essay.

has purposed are achieved unconditionally or necessarily."[34] God *uncondi-tionally* decrees that election and reprobation are *conditioned* on belief or unbelief.

F. Stuart Clarke and William den Boer are correct when they argue that Christ's satisfaction of divine justice is the driving force behind Armin-ius's doctrine of predestination, not free will.[35] As den Boer says, Arminius's view of freedom of the will "flows from" his doctrine of divine justice "as a consequence."[36] For Arminius, the primary problem with the strong Calvin-ist views on predestination, whether supralapsarian or infralapsarian,[37] was that they did not root predestination in the mediatorial work of Christ. It was as though Christ and his work were an afterthought. In both supra-lapsarianism and infralapsarianism, God decreed first which individuals would be elected and which would be reprobated. Only then did he decree to appoint Christ as mediator for the salvation of the elect. This is backward, Arminius argued. It "inverts the order of the gospel."[38] Instead, predestina-tion must be grounded in Christ and "with respect to" his mediatorial work and the believer's union with him. In his *Examination of Perkins's Pamphlet*, Arminius argued that "God acknowledges no one for His own in Christ and on account of Christ, unless that same person be in Christ." Yet he argued that, in Calvinism, election is "without respect to Christ" and his mediato-rial work. On the contrary, he said, Scripture "puts Christ as the foundation, not of the execution only, but also of the making of election itself."[39]

In his discussion of predestination in his *Declaration of Sentiments*, Arminius began by responding to the Calvinist doctrine that God has nec-essarily decreed certain people to eternal life and other people to eternal destruction "whom he was not viewing as already created or even as fallen," without reference to their belief or unbelief.[40] Arminius objected to (1) the view that God unconditionally decreed the Fall, and (2) the view that God

34. Picirilli, *Grace, Faith, Free Will*, 45.

35. The Christocentricity of election is the theme of Clarke's book, *The Ground of Election*, while the centrality of divine justice is the theme of den Boer's book, which is entitled *God's Twofold Love*, with reference to, first, God's love for his justice, and second, God's love for people.

36. Den Boer, *God's Twofold Love*, 120.

37. Supralapsarians said that God had decreed the fall ("lapse"), while infralapsar-ians said that he had not. But both held that God had unconditionally decreed the election of individuals without regard to their status as believers.

38. Gunter, *Declaration of Sentiments*, Kindle location 2908; cf. Arminius, *Works*, 1:632.

39. Arminius, *Works*, "Examination of Perkins's Pamphlet." 3:296, 303.

40. Gunter, *Declaration of Sentiments*, Kindle location 2537; cf. Arminius, *Works*, 1:614.

unconditionally decreed that certain people would be saved without regard to their belief and that he unconditionally decreed that the rest would be damned without regard to their sin or unbelief. Arminius disagreed with supralapsarian Calvinism because he believed that it makes God the author of sin because God decrees that the fall of man must necessarily occur. He disagreed with both supralapsarian and infralapsarian Calvinism because he believed they remove election from its grounding in Christ's satisfaction of divine justice.[41]

In his *Declaration of Sentiments*, Arminius advanced an alternative schema of the divine decrees that upholds God's justice and righteousness and places Christ and the gospel at the center of predestination. First, Arminius argued, God decrees unconditionally to appoint Jesus Christ as "Mediator, Redeemer, Savior, Priest and King," who by his obedience and death obtains salvation. Second, God unconditionally decrees to save those who repent and believe in Christ but to leave impenitent unbelievers in sin and thus under divine wrath. Third, God unconditionally decrees to administer the means of salvation according to his wisdom and justice. Fourth, God unconditionally decrees "to save and to damn certain particular persons" according to his foreknowledge "through which God has known from all eternity those individuals who through the established means of his prevenient grace would come to faith and believe, and through his subsequent sustaining grace would persevere in the faith. Likewise, in divine foreknowledge, God knew those who would not believe and persevere."[42]

Thus Arminius taught *conditional, individual election* and *conditional, individual reprobation.* Those individuals whom God lovingly foreknew as believers, he elected as his own.[43] Those individuals whom he foreknew to be unbelievers, he reprobated.

Predestination, Foreknowledge, and Free Will

Arminius's views on predestination comport with a libertarian free will perspective on divine sovereignty and human freedom. Key to his approach was his distinction between necessity, contingency, and certainty. In his "Apology Against Thirty-One Defamatory Articles," he explained, "No contingent thing,—that is, nothing which is done or has been done contingently,—can be said to be or to have been done necessarily *with regard to the*

---

41. Cf. Arminius, *Works*, "Letter to Hippolytus à Collibus" 2:698–700.

42. Ibid., Kindle locations 3168–3170; cf. Arminius, *Works*, 1:653–654.

43. For more on Arminius's view of God's foreknowledge of the elect, not only as prescience but as intimate foreknowledge, see Picirilli, *Grace, Faith, Free Will*, 56.

Divine decree.[44] Contingent things are things that did not have to turn out the way they in fact did. Necessary things are things that did have to turn out the way they in fact did. In God's universe, Arminius believes, there are necessities and contingencies, and for an act to be truly free, it has to be a contingency—it has to have been able to go one of two or more ways.[45]

Thus Arminius agreed with the idea that is now known (somewhat redundantly) as "libertarian freedom."[46] This is freedom, not from the power of sin or depravity, but from necessity. God has created his universe in such a way as to maintain creaturely freedom. Therefore, Arminius taught that the fall of man was contingent and not necessary. That is, God did not decree that Adam and Eve would fall by necessity. They fell as a result of their free choice to disobey God.

Arminius also distinguishes between events that are necessary and those that are "certain" or "infallible." While contingent events cannot be necessary, they can be certain. Arminius says,

> Because God, in virtue of His boundless knowledge, saw from eternity that man would fall at a certain time, hence the fall happened infallibly, in respect only of that foreknowledge, not in respect of any act of God's will, either affirmative or negative. For whatever happened infallibly in respect of God's will, the same happened also necessarily. . . . Hence it may be allowed to note briefly the difference between what comes to pass *infallibly*, and what *necessarily*: for the former is from the infinity of God's knowledge, the latter from the act of God's will: the former respects God's knowledge alone, to which it appertains to know contingencies infallibly and certainly: the latter belongs to the very existence of the things: the necessity for which arose from God's will.[47]

44. Arminius, *Works*, "Apology against Thirty-One Defamatory Articles," 1:755.

45. Ibid., 750–760.

46. The reason for the redundancy of the phrase "libertarian freedom" is probably to distinguish it from the soft-deterministic notion called "compatibilism." Compatibilism holds that divine determinism and human freedom are compatible. Yet, libertarians insist, the only way compatibilists can make divine determinism and human freedom compatible is to redefine free will to mean, not *the ability to have chosen otherwise*, but rather *the ability to do what one wants to do*. In other words, Arminians believe that freedom is, by definition, the ability to have done something other than what one did in fact do. Compatibilists do not believe individuals have such freedom. So they have to redefine freedom as the quality of not being coerced (or at least, the Arminian would respond, not *feeling as though* one has been coerced)—the ability to do what one wants to do. So compatibilists simply believe that God, through regeneration prior to faith, determines that the will of the elect will *want* to desire God.

47. Arminius, *Works*, "Friendly Conference with Francis Junius" 3:179–180.

Thus, Arminius believed that an action can be both contingent and certain, but not both contingent and necessary.[48] For the Calvinistic determinists of his day, God's foreknowledge was causal. Arminius replied that God foreknows all things that will come to pass; thus it is certain that they will come to pass. But this does not mean that God made it so that they must necessarily come to pass: "For a thing does not come to pass because it has been foreknown or foretold; but it is foreknown and foretold because it is yet (*futura*) to come to pass."[49] Some events have to be the way they are, because God foreordained them. Other events fall out a certain way but could have been another way. If free human actions had occurred in an alternative way because of free human choice, then God would have had foreknowledge of them instead.

Arminius would have disagreed with what has come to be known as "open theism," the idea that God does not have exhaustive foreknowledge of future free contingencies. The reason he would have opposed this notion is that he did not believe, like both open theists and classical Calvinists, that God's foreknowledge of future free contingencies causes them or makes them necessary.

Arminius's views also militate against a Molinist account of predestination, as presented, for example by recent scholars such as William Lane Craig and Kenneth Keathley.[50] While Arminius showed awareness of Luis de Molina's concept of middle knowledge, he did not utilize it in his doctrine of predestination. Arminius nowhere intimates that, in eternity past, God, knowing what everyone would do given certain circumstances, selected the possible world, from among all possible worlds, in which exactly what he desires to occur will occur, while at the same time human beings retain freedom. Instead, Arminius argued that God knew the future infallibly and certainly. Thus, he knew what everyone was freely going to do in the actual (not possible) world. This includes their union with Christ through faith or their rejection of him through impenitence and unbelief.[51]

---

48. For more on this, see Picirilli, *Grace, Faith, Free Will*, 35–63; and Picirilli, "Foreknowledge, Freedom, and the Future," *Journal of the Evangelical Theological Society* 43 (2000), 259–271.

49. Arminius, *Works*, Private Disputation 18, "On the Providence of God." 2:368.

50. See, e.g., Craig, *The Only Wise God: The Compatibility of Divine Foreknowledge and Human Freedom* (Eugene, Ore.: Wipf and Stock, 2000) and Kenneth Keathley, *Salvation and Sovereignty: A Molinist Approach* (Nashville: B&H Academic, 2010).

51. Scholars such as Picirilli, Olson, Clarke, Witt, and more recently Hendrik Frandsen properly interpret Arminius on this point, while scholars such as Eef Dekker, Muller, Stanglin, and (to a lesser degree) den Boer read too much Molinism into Arminius. The most that can be said is that Arminius toyed with the concept of middle knowledge but was ambiguous on it and did not actually articulate a Molinist

It is crucial to emphasize, as will be further discussed later, that Arminius believed human free will was freedom from necessity, not freedom from the bondage of sin. He said that, if left to themselves, without divine grace, human beings will be completely sinful: "The will, indeed, is free, but not in respect of that act which cannot be either performed or omitted without supernatural grace."[52]

Predestination and Romans 9

Arminius responded to Calvinist exegetical arguments with his own *Analysis of the Ninth Chapter of St. Paul's Epistle to the Romans*. He taught there that Paul's intent in Romans 9 was to show that believers are justified by faith alone, not to teach unconditional election and reprobation. Stephen M. Ashby is correct when he notes that "Arminius felt constrained by the text to address the redemptive-historical dilemma facing the Apostle Paul, rather than merely attaching himself to the commonly held interpretation of the Reformed divines."[53] Paul had been preaching that salvation comes through faith in Christ alone. This entailed that most Jews were not part of the covenant. Thus the Jewish response that Paul anticipates was that if God had rejected most of the Jews, God's word or covenant with Abraham was of no effect. According to Arminius, Paul's burden is to show that God's word still stands even if Jews who do not have faith in Christ are excluded, just as some descendants of Abraham have always been excluded.

For Arminius, the question of the text is not whether people are elected unconditionally but whether God's Word fails if Jews who seek righteousness by the law instead of by faith are excluded from the covenant. This is Paul's real question in Romans 9.[54] Arminius argued that Paul's point is that

---

doctrine of predestination. See Dekker, "Was Arminius a Molinist?" *Sixteenth Century Journal* 27 (1996), 337–352; Hendrik Frandsen, *Hemmingius in the Same World as Perkinsius and Arminius* (Praestoe, Denmark: Grafik Werk, 2013), cited by Olson, (*http://www.patheos.com/blogs/rogereolson/2014/05/something-for-arminius-geeks/ #ixzz32q65yuR6*). Cf. Olson's insightful comments in his blog post, "Are Arminianism and Middle Knowledge Compatible?" (*http://www.patheos.com/blogs/ rogereolson/2013/09/are-arminian-theology-and-middle-knowledge-compatible/*).

52. Arminius, *Works*, 3:178. "Friendly Conference with Francis Junius."

53. Ashby, "Introduction" to Arminius's *Works*, xix.

54. Ashby, "Introduction," xix–xx. For a contemporary Arminian treatment of Romans 9 that builds and improves on Arminius, see F. Leroy Forlines, *Classical Arminianism: A Theology of Salvation* (Nashville: Randall House, 2011), chapter 3. It should also be noted that since Arminius's era, additional schools of thought have developed within Arminianism on this issue. See in this volume, "God's Promise and Universal History: The Theology of Romans 9" by James Strauss and John D. Wagner.

God's Word has not failed simply because some Jews have been excluded from the covenant, because Paul argues in verses 6 through 8 that not everyone who is physically an Israelite or child of Abraham is spiritually an Israelite or child of Abraham, (vv. 6b-8).

Thus Arminius interpreted Ishmael and Isaac, and Esau and Jacob, as types—the former in each pair represent children of the flesh, the latter children of the promise. Arminius quotes Galatians 4:21–31 to show that Paul himself sees these pairs as types or allegories: "the primary sense which God wished to signify . . . is not literal, but allegorical."[55] In that passage, Paul had contrasted Hagar and Sara and Ishmael and Isaac, and then expressly stated that they were symbolic or allegorical (v. 24), and specified, "Now we, brethren, as Isaac was, are children of promise" (v. 28, NKJV). So Arminius concludes: "Isaac is reckoned in the seed: Isaac is the type of all the children of the promise: Therefore, all the children of the promise are reckoned in the seed. . . . Ishmael is not reckoned in the seed: Ishmael is the type of all the children of the flesh: Therefore none of the children of the flesh are reckoned in the seed."[56]

Ashby correctly states that, according to Arminius, "when man had failed in performing the demands of the Creation covenant, and indeed had 'by the fall incurred inability to perform it,' God transferred the condition of this covenant to faith in Christ."[57] God was, Arminius averred, "at liberty to fix in that [subsequent] covenant whatever conditions He might have thought fit. . . . It is free to Him to make a decree according to election, by which He may ordain to have mercy on the children of promise, but to harden and punish the children of the flesh.'"[58] Arminius was simply saying that God has mercy on the children of the promise (believers who seek righteousness through faith) and hardens and punishes the children of the flesh (unbelievers who seek righteousness by the works of the law) (vv. 31–32).

How did Arminius interpret the "vessels of wrath" and "vessels of mercy" in Romans 9? He said that God determined to make people vessels of mercy "who should perform the condition [of the covenant]" and vessels of wrath "those who should transgress it, and should not desist from transgressing." In essence, Arminius remarked, "God makes man a vessel: man makes himself a bad vessel, or sinner: God decrees to make man, according to conditions pleasing to Himself, a vessel of wrath or of mercy; which

---

55. Arminius, *Works*, "Analysis of the Ninth Chapter of St. Paul's Epistle to the Romans" 3:490.

56. Ibid., 3:491.

57. Ashby, xxi, quoting Arminius, *Works*, 3:497.

58. Arminius, *Works*, 3:502.

in fact He does, when the condition has been either fulfilled, or wilfully neglected."[59]

> God has the power of making men out of shapeless matter, and of enacting a decree about them, by the mere judgment and pleasure of His will, ratified by certain conditions, according to which He makes some men vessels to dishonor, others vessels to honor: and that therefore man has no just ground of expostulation with God because He has made him to be hardened by His irresistible will; since obstinacy in sins intervenes between the determination of His will and the hardening itself; on account of which God wills, according to the same pleasure of His will, to harden man by His irresistible will. If any simply say that God has the power of making man a vessel to dishonor and wrath, he will do the greatest injustice to God, and will contradict clear Scripture.[60]

In other words, whom does God will to harden? Arminius believed God wills to harden those whom he foreknows will not meet the faith-condition of the covenant: the children of the flesh. On whom does God will to have mercy? Those whom he foreknows will meet the faith-condition of the covenant: the children of the promise.

Arminians and Calvinists alike have been fairly clear on Arminius's teaching on *how one comes to be* in a state of grace; Arminians agree, and Calvinists disagree. The primary misconceptions regarding Arminius have traditionally surrounded his understanding of *what it means to be* a sinner and *what it means to be* in a state of grace. An examination of Arminius's doctrines of original sin, human depravity and inability, and of the nature of atonement and justification reveal an agreement, not only with the Reformed confessions and catechisms, but also with the mainstream of Reformed thought in his day.

ARMINIUS AND ORIGINAL SIN

Arminius has usually been associated with semi-Pelagianism, and sometimes with outright Pelagianism. Most writers, both Arminian and Calvinist, have tended to dissociate Arminius's theology with that of Augustine. An investigation of Arminius's theological writings, however, reveals that he held to an Augustinian view of original sin that was within the bounds of Reformed confessional theology.

59. Ibid., 3:513.
60. Ibid., 3:514.

Before examining Arminius's writings, it will be beneficial to investigate his confessional beliefs. A look at the Heidelberg Catechism will reveal the Reformed hamartiology that characterized his theology. Questions seven, eight, and ten of the Catechism read thusly:

Q. 7. *Where, then, does this corruption of human nature come from?*

A. From the fall and disobedience of our first parents, Adam and Eve, in the Garden of Eden; whereby our human life is so poisoned that we are all conceived and born in the state of sin.

Q. 8. *But are we so perverted that we are altogether unable to do good and prone to do evil?*

A. Yes, unless we are born again through the Spirit of God.

Q. 10. *Will God let man get by with such disobedience and defection?*

A. Certainly not, for the wrath of God is revealed from heaven, both against our in-born sinfulness and our actual sins, and he will punish them accordingly in his righteous judgment in time and eternity, as he has declared: "Cursed be everyone who does not abide by all things written in the book of the Law, and do them."[61]

The Belgic Confession of Faith, in Article 15, *The Doctrine of Original Sin,* says: "We believe that by the disobedience of Adam original sin has been spread through the whole human race. It is a corruption of all nature—an inherited depravity which even infects small infants in their mother's womb. . . . Therefore we reject the error of the Pelagians who say that this sin is nothing else than a matter of imitation."[62]

Thus, if Arminius was telling the truth when he stated his agreement with the confessional documents of his Church, the doctrines of the Heidelberg Catechism and the Belgic Confession of Faith may rightly be said to have been Arminius's doctrine. These confessional statements provide the backdrop of his writings on the doctrine of original sin.

In his *Apology Against Thirty-One Theological Articles,* Arminius was arguing against teachings that certain individuals had ascribed to him or his colleagues, but which neither he nor they had ever taught. In the essays on Articles 13–14, Arminius was arguing against the condemnation of infants based on original sin; however, he stopped far short of a disavowal of original sin itself, but rather attempted to defend his position on Reformed grounds. Arminius began the essay with a saying that had been attributed

61. *The Constitution of the Presbyterian Church (U.S.A.), Part I: Book of Confessions* (New York: The General Assembly of the Presbyterian Church [U.S.A.], 1983), 4.005-.012.

62. *Ecumenical Creeds and Reformed Confessions* (Grand Rapids: CRC, 1987), 91.

to Borrius, but which, Arminius argued, Borrius never said: "Original sin will condemn no man. In every nation, all infants who die without [having committed] actual sins, are saved."[63] Arminius proceeded to say that Borrius denied ever having taught either statement.[64] Arminius's primary aim here was to deny infant damnation. The doctrine of original sin and its imputation to the race was tangential to his argument. Yet he discussed the doctrine of original sin, and, while disagreeing with Augustine on infant damnation, he is thoroughly Augustinian on the doctrine of original sin, saying with Borrius that all infants "existed in Adam, and were by his will involved in sin and guilt."[65] Arminius argued that Francis Junius had said the same thing that Borrius had said, that the infants of unbelievers may be saved only by "Christ and his intervention."[66]

Arminius discussed his views on original sin in a more systematic manner in his *Public Disputations*, explaining his doctrine of original sin in the passage entitled "The Effects of This Sin." It is clear here that Arminius was Augustinian. He said that the violation of the divine law results in two punishments: *reatus*, two deaths—one physical and one spiritual; and *privatio*, the withdrawal of man's primitive righteousness.[67] Arminius believed that Adam's sin caused physical death for the entire race and spiritual death for those who are not in Christ. His position on the effect of Adam's sin on the race was that "the whole of this sin . . . is not peculiar to our first parents, but is common to the entire race and to all their posterity, who, at the time when this sin was committed, were in their loins, and who have since descended from them by the natural mode of propogation."[68] According to Arminius, all sin in Adam and are guilty in Adam, apart from their own actual sins.

In the *Private Disputations*, Arminius echoed the sentiments of his *Public Disputations*. In disputation thirty-one, he stated that "all men who were to be propagated from [Adam and Eve] in a natural way, became

---

63. Arminius, *Works*, 2:10.

64. Ibid., 2:11.

65. Ibid., 2:12.

66. Ibid., 2:14.

67. Ibid., Public Disputation 7, "On the First Sin of the First Man" 2:156.

68. Ibid. It may be inferred from this statement that Arminius would accept (in the terminology of later Protestant Scholastic theology) a "natural headship" view of the transmission of sin, rather than a "federal headship" view. Rather than Adam being "federally" appointed as head of the race, he was naturally the head of the race, and individuals are sinful as a natural consequence of their being "in Adam" or in the race.

obnoxious to death temporal and death eternal, and (*vacui*) devoid of this gift of the Holy Spirit or original righteousness."[69]

Statements such as these make it impossible to understand why so many interpreters have believed, like James W. Meeuwsen, that Arminius's view of original sin "shatters Adamic unity" and "implies that original sin is nothing more than a habit which was eventually acquired by man."[70] How can Arminius's clear affirmations cited above be reconciled with such statements? Arminius makes it clear that human beings deserve the punishment of God (eternal death) because of original sin and original guilt, not merely their own actual sin and their own actual guilt.[71] Meeuwsen went on to say that Arminius denied that humanity is guilty on account of Adam's sin.[72] But Arminius made it clear that he did not. When asked the question, "Is the guilt of original sin taken away from all and every one by the benefits of Christ?" Arminius said that the question is "very easily answered by the distinction of the *soliciting, obtaining,* and the *application* of the benefits of Christ. For as the participation of Christ's benefits consists in faith alone, it follows that, if among these benefits 'deliverance from this guilt' be one, believers only are delivered from it, since they are those upon whom the wrath of God does not abide."[73] Furthermore, Arminius said to Francis Junius that God "imput[ed] the guilt of the first sin to all Adam's posterity, no less than to Adam himself and Eve, because they also had sinned in Adam."[74]

Arminius's treatment of original sin and guilt was clearly Reformed. Meeuwsen and other scholars too often read later theology into Arminius's thought, mistaking later Arminian theology for Arminius's. Only when this is done can Arminius be labeled as semi-Pelagian or Pelagian in his doctrine

---

69. Ibid., 2:375. Private Disputation 31, "On the Effects of the Sin of Our First Parents."

70. See James W. Meeuwsen, "Original Arminianism and Methodistic Arminianism Compared," *Reformed Review* 14 (1960), 22. Meeuwsen relied heavily on Presbyterian theologian William G. T. Shedd (*A History of Christian Doctrine* [New York: Scribner's, 1867]), who wrongly read Arminius through the lense of the works of Episcopius and other Remonstrant theologians whose theology differed significantly from that of Arminius. At one point, Meeuwsen said: "Arminius and his followers held that the imputation of actual guilt was entirely contrary to the justice and equity of God. Shedd fully agreed with such an interpretation when he paraphrased their beliefs in this way: 'Imputation is contrary to divine benevolence, right reason, in fact it is absurd and cruel'" (23). Meeuwsen then went on to quote Episcopius for about half a page.

71. Arminius, *Works*, Private Disputation 31, "On the Effects of the Sin of Our First Parents," 2:374.

72. Meeuwsen, 23.

73. Arminius, *Works*, "Nine Questions" 2:65.

74. Ibid., "Friendly Conference with Junius" 3:224.

of sin. An objective examination of either Arminius's confessional beliefs or his writings shows that such allegations cannot be sustained.

ARMINIUS: SOLA GRATIA AND SOLA FIDE

With Arminius cleared from the charge of semi-Pelagianism with regard to original sin, it will be beneficial to examine what he believed about human inability in salvation and how he believed people may be rescued from this state. On the subjects of grace and faith, again Arminius has been charged with holding semi-Pelagian and synergistic views that make God's foreknowledge of a person's merit the basis of redemption or that view individuals as sharing with God in their salvation. A brief look at Arminius's perspectives on grace, free will, and human inability, followed by an examination of Arminius's doctrine of justification, will reveal Arminius's loyalty to Reformed categories.

Human Inability

Arminius believed that people have no ability to seek God or turn to him unless they are radically affected by his grace. It is commonly assumed that Arminius held a doctrine of free will that makes individuals totally able to choose God. However, Arminius's view of human freedom does not mean freedom to do anything good in the sight of God or to choose God on one's own. For Arminius, the basic freedom that characterizes the human will is freedom from necessity. Indeed, "it is the very essence of the will. Without it, the will would not be the will."[75] This has sounded to some like semi-Pelagianism. Yet, though Arminius averred that the human will is free from necessity, he stated unequivocally that the will is not free from sin and its dominion: "The free will of man towards the true good is not only wounded, maimed, infirm, bent, and (*attenuatum*) weakened; but it is also (*captivatum*) imprisoned, destroyed, and lost: And its powers are not only debilitated and useless unless they be assisted by grace, but it has no powers whatever except such are excited by divine grace."[76]

Fallen humanity has no ability or power to reach out to God on its own. Arminius details "the utter weakness of all the powers to perform that

---

75. Bangs, *Arminius*, 341.

76. Arminius, *Works*, Public Disputation 11, "On the Free Will of Man and Its Powers" 2:192.

which is truly good, and to omit the perpetration of that which is evil."[77] He argued at length that the whole person—mind, affections, and will—is completely sinful. One would be hard-pressed to find a more thorough definition of total depravity than what Arminius articulated. He stated that the human mind "is dark, destitute, of the saving knowledge of God, and, according to the Apostle, incapable of those things which belong to the Spirit of God," having no perception of the things of God.[78] The affections and the heart are perverse, with a hatred and aversion to the true good and to what pleases God, and with a love for evil and the pursuit of it. In their deceitful, perverse, uncircumcised, hard, and stony hearts, unregenerate people have set themselves up as enemies of God.[79] The will has no power to perform the true good or keep from committing evil, because the unregenerate are slaves to the devil and under his power.[80] The entire life—mind, heart, and will—is submerged under sin and dead in sin.[81] These views led Moses Stuart to aver that "the most thorough advocate of total depravity will scarcely venture to go farther in regard to man in his unregenerate state, than . . . Arminius goes."[82]

Divine grace is the only power that can bring persons out of this state. Arminius was not a synergist; he did not believe that individuals share with God in their salvation.[83] Human beings are saved by grace alone through

77. Ibid., 2:193.

78. Ibid., 2:192.

79. Ibid., 2:193.

80. Ibid., 2:193–194.

81. Ibid., 2:194. Cf. "Letter to Hippolytus à Collibus" 2:700,

82. Moses Stuart, "The Creed of Arminius," *Biblical Repository* 1 (1831), 271. Stuart said Arminius went even further than most of the "orthodox" theologians of Stuart's own day. Cf. Hicks, "Theology of Grace," 22. Charles Hodge said similar things; see *Systematic Theology* (New York: Charles Scribner's Sons, 1888), 3:187.

83. Bangs boldly states, "Arminius was a monergist" ("Arminius and Reformed Theology," 166). Some scholars, such as Stanglin, McCall, and Olson prefer to think of Arminius as a synergist, whereas scholars such as Bangs, Picirilli, den Boer, Ellis, and Arthur Skevington Wood do not. I agree with the latter approach. Arminius would not have been comfortable with the term synergist or the idea of humans cooperating or working together with God in any way in their salvation. I would say of Arminius what Gregory Graybill says of Martin Luther's associate Phillip Melanchthon in his recent monograph, *Evangelical Free Will* (Oxford, U.K.: Oxford University Press, 2010). Conversion for Melanchthon, Graybill insists, "was a passive *reception* of merit rather than an active cooperative work that earned merit. It was not synergism!" (Ibid., 297) Graybill distinguishes Melanchthon's view from that of Peter Lombard, which "required God and the human working together in synergism." (Ibid.) Just as it is unfair for Lutheran theologians to attribute a term to Melanchthon that was readily associated with his later followers, it is unfair to saddle Arminius with a term that he did not employ and which was foreign to his theological context. This perspective concurs with

faith alone. This excludes human merit of any kind. The faith that is the instrument of justification (not the meritorious cause or ground) could not be had without the grace of God. The grace of God alone gives individuals the power to come to Him.[84] Grace for Arminius was necessary and essential to salvation from start to finish. However, Arminius differed from Calvin and many Reformed theologians of his day by stating that this grace of God "which has appeared to all men" can be resisted. Arminius denied the distinction between a universal call and a special call. He insisted that the divine call is universal. However, the grace of God through this call can be and is resisted by individuals. He said that "the whole of the controversy reduces itself to this question, 'Is the grace of God a certain irresistible force?'" Arminius answered, "I believe that many persons resist the Holy Spirit and reject the grace that is offered."[85] Rather than an "irresistible force," grace, from Arminius's perspective, is a "gentle and sweet persuasion . . . not by almighty action or motion, which they neither will nor can resist, nor can will to resist."[86]

Key to Arminius's understanding of divine grace in salvation is that God desires the salvation of all people and provides atonement for every individual, not just for the elect. Arminius maintained against Perkins that "Christ stood in the stead of all men universally . . . and not in the stead of the elect only."[87] Arminius charged Perkins with confusing the obtaining of redemption with its application. Believers "were not redeemed" at the time Christ died, but "by those actions redemption was obtained, and then applied to them by faith, and so at length they were redeemed."[88] Arminius emphasized the importance of distinguishing "between redemption

---

what Muller said in an earlier work: "It is difficult to label [Arminius's approach] synergism" (Muller, "The Priority of the Intellect in the Soteriology of Jacobus Arminius," *Westminster Theological Journal* 55 [1993], 70. In a more recent article, however, Muller characterizes Arminius as a synergist: "Arminius and the Reformed Tradition," 29). See Stanglin and McCall, *Jacob Arminius*, 152; Olson, "Was Arminius an Arminian?" (*http://www.patheos.com/blogs/rogereolson/2013/11/was-arminius-an-arminian-report-on-a-vigorous-discussion/*); Picirilli, *Grace, Faith, Free Will*; den Boer, *God's Twofold Love* (191), and den Boer, "Cum delectu," 83–84; Ellis, *Simon Episcopius*, 84; Wood, "The Declaration of Sentiments: The Theological Testament of Arminius," *Evangelical Quarterly* 65 (1993), 111–129.

84. Arminius, *Works*, Public Disputation 11, "On the Free Will of Man and Its Powers" 2:194–195.

85. Quoted in Bangs, *Arminius: A Study in the Dutch Reformation*, 343.

86. Arminius, *Works*, "Examination of Perkins's Pamphlet" 3:443. Cf. F. Leroy Forlines's juxtaposition of "influence and response" and "cause and effect" in *Classical Arminianism*, 49–61.

87. Arminius, *Works*, "Examination of Perkins's Pamphlet" 3:332.

88. Ibid., 3:333.

obtained and *applied*; and I affirm that it was *obtained* for all the world, and for all and every man; but *applied* to believers and the elect alone."[89]

Arminius's main argument for that assertion was that, unless God obtains redemption for all people, he cannot require faith in Christ from all people, nor can he blame people for "refusing the offer of redemption. For he refuses what cannot be his."[90] Thus, "if Christ has not obtained redemption for all, He cannot be the Judge of all."[91] For Arminius, this was the only way to explain the New Testament passages that seem to indicate God's desire for all to be saved and come to the knowledge of the truth (1 Tim 2:4). Arminius spends several pages responding to Perkins's explanation of the meaning of "all" in New Testament passages that teach God's desire for all to be saved. Arminius believed this is the clear teaching of Scripture, and he wondered how those who believe Christ died only for the elect can explain Scripture passages like 1 John 2:2; John 1:29; John 6:1; Rom 14:15; and 2 Pet 2:1, 3.[92]

Though Arminius differed from Calvin and the mainstream of Reformed theology on the particulars of grace, he still maintained that salvation is *sola gratia*. Arminius cannot be considered a semi-Pelagian or a synergist.[93] This fact is further attested in Arminius's doctrine of justification.

Justification by the Imputed Righteousness of Christ

Justification is another doctrine on which Arminius has been grossly misunderstood. As with the doctrines of original sin and grace, Arminius's doctrine of justification is usually interpreted through the lens of later Arminian theology.[94] Many Reformed writers have harshly criticized Arminian

89. Ibid., 3:425.

90. Ibid.

91. Ibid., 3:426.

92. Ibid., 2:9–10. "Apology against Thirty-One Defamatory Articles."

93. Rather than being a synergist, Arminius would have been more in line with recent theologians who prefer terms like "conditional monergism" (Forlines) or "monergism with resistible grace" (e.g., Keathley, Jeremy Evans, and Richard Cross). See F. Leroy Forlines, *Classical Arminianism*, 264, 297; Cross, "Anti-Pelagianism and the Resistibility of Grace," *Faith and Philosophy* 22 (2005), 199–210; Keathley, 88, 103–108; Evans, "Reflections on Determinism and Human Freedom," in *Whosoever Will: A Biblical-Theological Critique of Five-Point Calvinism* (Nashville: B&H Academic, 2010), 253–274; cf. Kevin Timpe, "Grace and Controlling What We Do Not Cause," *Faith and Philosophy* 24 (2007), 284–299.

94. See, e.g., Meeuwsen, 27–28. The best treatments of this and the general graciousness of Arminius's theology (and two of the works I most highly recommend be read about Arminius's theology) are John Mark Hicks's dissertation, "Theology of

soteriology because, by and large, it has rested on the Governmental theory of atonement as articulated by the Remonstrant theologian Hugo Grotius.[95] However, to read Arminius in light of Grotius is to misread Arminius.[96]

Arminius agreed with the Belgic Confession statement on justification. Article 22, after stating that justification is "by faith alone, or faith without works," says that "we do not mean that faith itself justifies us, for it is only an instrument with which we embrace Christ our Righteousness. But Jesus Christ, imputing to us all his merits, and so many holy works, which he hath done for us and in our stead, is our Righteousness."[97]

The Heidelberg Catechism states that "God wills that his righteousness be satisfied; therefore payment in full must be made to his righteousness, either by ourselves or by another." However, individuals cannot make this payment themselves. Only Jesus Christ, God incarnate, can make the payment for them. Thus, he pays the "debt of sin" and satisfies God's righteous requirements. Through saving faith, believers are "incorporated into [Christ] and accept all his benefits." They are in union with Christ, which means Christ bears their sins and they have the benefit of his righteousness.[98] The Catechism goes on to say, in question sixty, that "God, without any merit of my own, out of pure grace, grants me the benefits of the perfect expiation of Christ, imputing to me his righteousness and holiness as if I had never committed a single sin or had ever been sinful, having fulfilled myself all the obedience which Christ has carried out for me, if only I accept such favor with a trusting heart." Question sixty-one reads: "Why do you say that you are righteous by faith alone?" The answer is: "Not because I please God by virtue of the worthiness of my faith, but because the satisfaction, righteousness, and holiness of Christ alone are my righteousness before God, and because I can accept it and make it mine in no other way than by faith alone."[99] This is the same conception as that in the Belgic Confession. Arminius claimed to agree with both these documents, and, as will be seen, his writings are fully consonant with them.

Arminius's view of justification is summarized in his *Public Disputations*. There he said that justification is that act by which one, "being placed before the throne of grace which is erected in Christ Jesus the Propitiation,

---

Grace" and article "Righteousness of Saving Faith."

95. Ibid.

96. See the above-cited works by Hicks and Ellis.

97. Arthur C. Cochrane, ed., *Reformed Confessions of the Sixteenth Century* (Philadelphia: Westminster, 1966), 204.

98. Ibid., 307–308, 311–312.

99. Ibid., 315.

is accounted and pronounced by God, the just and merciful Judge, righteous and worthy of the reward of righteousness, not in himself but in Christ, of grace, according to the Gospel, to the praise of the righteousness and grace of God, and to the salvation of the justified person himself."[100]

Justification for Arminius was forensic or imputative in nature. Arminius stated: "In his obedience and righteousness, Christ is also the Material Cause of our justification, so far as God bestows Christ on us for righteousness, and imputes his righteousness and obedience to us."[101] Arminius went as far as to say in his letter to Hippolytus à Collibus that God "reckons" Christ's righteousness "to have been performed for us."[102] In his *Declaration of Sentiments*, he averred: "I believe that sinners are accounted righteous solely by the obedience of Christ, and that the obedience and righteousness of Christ constitute the only meritorious cause through which God pardons the sins of believers and accounts them as righteous, as if they had perfectly fulfilled the law."[103]

Like the Reformed, Arminius believed that God must punish sin with eternal death unless one meets the requirement of total righteousness before him. So he portrayed God as a judge who must sentence individuals to eternal death if they do not meet His requirements. In typical Reformed fashion, Arminius employed the analogy of "a judge making an estimate in his own mind of the deed and of the author of it, and according to that estimate forming a judgment and pronouncing sentence."[104] The sentence pronounced on the sinner who cannot meet the requirements of God's justice is eternal death. Yet, since no one has this righteousness, it must come from someone else. It can come only from Christ, who pays the penalty for sin on the cross—"the price of redemption for sins by suffering the punishment due to them."[105] When an individual exhibits saving faith, Arminius maintained, he comes into union with Christ; this union results in his being

---

100. Arminius, *Works*, Public Disputation 19, "On the Justification of Man before God" 2:256.

101. Ibid., "Private Disputation 48," "On Justification" 2:406.

102. Ibid., "Letter to Hippolytus à Collibus" 2:702.

103. Gunter, *Declaration of Sentiments*, Kindle location 3433–3435; cf. Arminius, *Works*, 1:700.

104. Arminius, *Works*, Public Disputation 19, "On the Justification of Man Before God" 2:253.

105. Ibid., Oration IV, "The Priesthood of Christ." 1:419. For more on Arminius's doctrine of the nature of atonement, see J. Matthew Pinson, "The Nature of Atonement in the Theology of Jacobus Arminius," *Journal of the Evangelical Theological Society* 53 (2010): 173–185.

identified with Christ in his death and righteousness.[106] Hence, justification takes place when God as judge pronounces believers just or righteous because they have been imputed this righteousness of Christ, which is theirs through faith alone.

For Arminius, this emphasis on justice does not militate against God's mercy, as some later Arminians held. God never had to offer Christ for the redemption of humanity in the first place. If God had not made a way of satisfaction for his justice (through mercy), *then*, Arminius said, is when humanity would have truly been judged according to God's "severe and rigid estimation." Those who are under the law, according to Arminius, are judged in this severe and rigid way; those who are under grace, through faith, are graciously imputed the righteousness of Christ, which in turn justifies them before God the Judge.[107]

106. Arminius, *Works*, Private Disputation 41, "On the Communion of Believers with Christ, and Particularly with His Death" 2:403–404.

107. Ibid., Public Disputation 19, "On the Justification of Man before God," 2:256–257, and Private Disputation 48, "On Justification" 2:406, A few scholars have attempted to make the case that Arminius's doctrine of imputation focused exclusively on the passive obedience of Christ. This is an overstatement. The reality is that the doctrine of the imputation of the active and passive obedience of Christ did not become the consensus of the Reformed community until long after Arminius's death. Arminius never denied the doctrine of the imputation of the active obedience of Christ, which is implied by other statements he made. The seventeenth-century English General Baptist Thomas Grantham (like later Free Will Baptist scholars such as Forlines and Picirilli) was unequivocal in his confession of the imputation of the active obedience of Christ. Calvinists and Reformed Arminians alike might wish there was more of a consensus among the early Reformed divines on the imputation of the active obedience of Christ. But, alas, there was not. Though Arminius believed that Christ's fulfillment of the law in his life of obedience is one of the benefits received by the believer via union with Christ, he wanted to stay out of the controversy in the French Reformed Church surrounding Piscator, who denied outright the active obedience of Christ. Arminius said, "I never durst mingle myself with the dispute, or undertake to decide it; for I thought it possible for the Professors of the same religion to hold different opinions on this point from others of their brethren, without any breach of Christian peace or the unity of faith." This is essentially the same position taken by the Westminster Assembly and the Synod of Dort, as well as the framers of the Belgic Confession, Heidelberg Catechism, and Thirty-Nine Articles of the Church of England. All these people and confessional documents did not "undertake to decide" this controversy, because so many early Reformers did not articulate the imputation of the active obedience of Christ with the clarity of the later Reformed consensus. See Alex F. Mitchell, *The Westminster Assembly: Its History and Standards* (London: James Nisbet & Co., 1883); William Barker, *Puritan Profiles: 54 Contemporaries at the Westminster Assembly* (Ross-shire, Scotland: Christian Focus, 2000); R. W. Landis, "What Were the Views Entertained by the Early Reformers, on the Doctrines of Justification, Faith, and the Active Obedience of Christ?" *The American Biblical Repository* 11 (1838): 31:179–197, 32:420–457; and Robert A. Letham, *The Westminster Assembly: Reading Its Theology in Historical Context* (Phillipsburg, NJ: P&R, 2009). Interestingly, the Reformed theologian J. V. Fesko argues that Arminius's

Arminius's enemies had charged him with teaching that we are not justified by the imputation of Christ's righteousness which is ours through faith, but that it is our faith itself that justifies us. In the *Apology Against Thirty-One Defamatory Articles,* Arminius dealt with the statement his enemies had attributed to him: "The righteousness of Christ is not imputed to us for righteousness; but to believe (or the act of believing) justifies us."[108] Arminius's reply was that he never said that the act of faith justifies a person. Arminius held that Christ's righteousness is imputed to the believer by gracious imputation *and* that our faith is imputed for righteousness. The reason he held both of these was because he believed they were both taught by St. Paul.

> I say that I acknowledge, "The righteousness of Christ is imputed to us;" because I think the same thing is contained in the following words of the Apostle, "God hath made Christ to be sin for us, that we might be made the righteousness of God in him."
> . . . It is said in the third verse [of Romans 4], "Abraham believed God, and it was imputed unto him for righteousness;" that is, *his believing* was thus imputed. Our brethren therefore do not reprehend me, but the apostle. . . .[109]

Arminius thought his foes were wrong to place the two concepts in opposition to one another, since Holy Scripture did not. He argued that faith is not the meritorious cause, the ground or basis, of justification, but rather the instrument *through which* one is imputed the merits of Christ.[110] Faith is necessary for Christ's righteousness to be imputed, and Arminius did not see a necessary opposition between the phrases "the righteousness of Christ imputed to us" and "faith imputed for righteousness."

Arminius's view of justification by grace through faith and the imputed righteousness of Christ is thoroughly Reformed, and bears no influence of semi-Pelagianism or synergism. In another place, to clear himself of any misunderstanding, Arminius states his full agreement with what Calvin said with regard to justification in his *Institutes*. Calvin wrote: "We are justified before God solely by the intercession of Christ's righteousness. This is equivalent to saying that man is not righteous in himself but because the righteousness of Christ is communicated to him by imputation. . .

---

theology entails the imputation of both the active and passive obedience of Christ; see his *Beyond Calvin: Union with Christ and Justification in Early Modern Reformed Theology (1517–1700)* (Göttingen: Vandenhoek and Ruprecht, 2012), 277, 282.

108. Arminius, *Works,* "Nine Articles" 2:42.

109. Ibid., 2:43–45.

110. Ibid., 2:49–51.

. You see that our righteousness is not in us but in Christ, that we possess it only because we are partakers in Christ; indeed, with him we possess all its riches."[111] This phrase is almost identical to many of Arminius's statements on justification in the *Public Disputations*.

CONCLUSION

An examination of Arminius's writings shows that his theology must be cleared of the charge of semi-Pelagianism, Pelagianism, and synergism. For Arminius, humanity is dead in trespasses and sin, guilty before God, and can be saved only by grace alone, by the imputed righteousness of Christ alone, through faith alone.

This examination of Arminius's historical and theological context in the Reformed Church of his day, his loyalty to the Belgic Confession of Faith and the Heidelberg Catechism, his stated views of Calvin, and most importantly his writings has shown that Arminius's understanding of the nature of sin and salvation, rather than semi-Pelagian and synergistic, was broadly Reformed. Most interpreters of Arminius have viewed him in light of later Arminianism, most of which has tended toward a denial of the Reformed view of original sin and total depravity, and toward an espousal of synergism in the plan of salvation, the governmental view of atonement, and perfectionism.[112] It has been shown that it is irresponsible simply to read these later Arminian themes back into Arminius simply because his name is attached to the Arminian theological systems. A thorough analysis of Arminius's theology itself reveals that it was more a nuanced development of Reformed theology than a radical departure from it.[113]

---

111. *Institutes,* 3.11.23.

112. With regard to perfectionism, Arminius said in his *Declaration of Sentiments* that he "never actually stated that a believer could perfectly keep the precepts of Christ in this life." Nor did he deny it. He left it as an open question, contenting himself with the sentiments of Augustine. In short, Arminius believed that, through grace, perfection was a logical possibility but that an individual who had attained it had never yet been found! (Gunter, *Declaration of Sentiments,* Kindle locations 3313–3314; cf. Arminius, *Works,* 1:677–678).

113. I am grateful to the editors of *Integrity: A Journal of Christian Thought* for their permission to adapt for this chapter portions of a previous article entitled "Will The Real Arminius Please Stand Up? A Study of the Theology of Jacobus Arminius in Light of His Interpreters," *Integrity: A Journal of Christian Thought* 2 (2003), 121–139.

10

John Wesley's Doctrines on the Theology of Grace

Vic Reasoner

In 1958, Zondervan Publishing House reprinted the fourteen-volume edition of *The Works of John Wesley*, edited by Thomas Jackson. This reprint made available the bulk of Wesley's writings for the first time in nearly a century. However, Mark Quanstrom wrote that Wesley's writings "were not entirely consistent with the holiness writings that the Church of the Nazarene had recommended."[1]

At a grassroots level, Elmer Long and A.J. Smith had been trying to make this point since 1948.[2] Rob Staples wrote that in the early 1960s when he first became aware of a shift from Wesley's view to the equation of entire sanctification with Pentecost.[3]

Samuel Powell wrote about the "back to Wesley" movement, which began in the 1960s. This was primarily the discovery that Wesley's understanding of holiness differed in significant respects from that of the holiness movement, whose adherents claimed Wesley as their founder and

1. Mark Quanstrom, *A Century of Holiness Theology* (Kansas City, Mo.: Beacon Hill, 2004), 129

2. Vic Reasoner, *A Wesleyan Theology of Holy Living for the 21st Century* (Evansville, Ind.: Fundamental Wesleyan, 2012), 2:623–626.

3. Rob Staples, "The Current Debate on the Baptism with the Holy Spirit," unpublished mss (March 1979), 2.

theologian.[4] Thus, questions were continuing and scholars saw a need for clarification in multiple areas of Wesley's theology.

In 1961, Albert Outler called for a reevaluation of Wesley as a theologian. He gave the Presidential Address to the American Theological Society and his paper was titled, "Towards a Re-Appraisal of John Wesley as a Theologian." Outler argued that Wesley was a major theologian, that his methodology and motifs were still significant for contemporary theology, and that he has rarely been fairly and fully read, due in part to the lack of a critical edition of his works.

However, Outler concluded that Wesley was a "folk theologian." He observed that for half a century Wesley was involved in one controversy after another and all of them were theological. Wesley's chief concern was a theology for the laity. Outler said that Wesley's agenda was to rise above classic disjunctions between Roman and Protestant extremes.

> He believed in faith *and* good works, Scripture *and* tradition, revelation *and* reason, sovereign grace *and* human freedom, particularism *and* universal redemption, the witness of the Spirit *and* an ordered polity, repentance *and* the expectation of perfection, the priesthood of all believers *and* an authorized representative ministry.[5]

At the academic level, a board of directors was established in 1960 to produce the first critical edition of Wesley's works. The first volume was produced in 1980. By 1987, Albert Outler had completed the four-volume set of Wesley's sermons.[6]

Since the "back to Wesley" movement began, there have been several major attempts to interpret Wesley.

In his book *Responsible Grace,* Randy Maddox wrote that "without God's grace we *cannot* be saved; while without our (grace-empowered, but uncoerced) participation, God's grace *will not* save."[7] Yet Kenneth Collins expressed concern that this emphasis on synergism and process focused

---

4. Samuel M. Powell, "The Theological Significance of the Holiness Movement," *Quarterly Review* 25:2 (Summer 2005) 134–135, 137.

5. Albert Outler, "Towards a Re-Appraisal of John Wesley as a Theologian," in *The Wesleyan Theological Heritage,* Thomas C. Oden and Leicester R. Longden, eds. (Grand Rapids: Zondervan, 1991), 39–54.

6. Nineteen volumes of a projected 35-volume set, the *Bicentennial Edition,* are currently available.

7. Randy Maddox, *Responsible Grace: John Wesley's Practical Theology* (Nashville: Kingswood, 1994), 19.

on the *possibility* of attainment rather than on the realization of God's full grace.[8]

In 1995, John B. Cobb Jr. published *Grace and Responsibility: A Wesleyan Theology for Today*. In the preface, Cobb said his initial fear was that a "back to Wesley" movement would ignore the theological and scientific changes of the past two hundred years. But eventually Cobb felt it was time to reappraise Wesley. He conceded that United Methodism had lost its way theologically.[9] The result he claimed, incredibly, was a Wesley who was very open to the process theology of John Cobb.[10]

In 2002 Laurence Wood published *The Meaning of Pentecost in Early Methodism*. Wood attempted to connect Spirit baptism with entire sanctification and salvage the old holiness theology. This project tried to establish Wesley's theology through a reinterpretation of John Fletcher.[11]

In 2007 Kenneth Collins published *The Theology of John Wesley*. Collins was especially troubled with the suggestion by Cobb that believers remain under the power or dominion of sin.[12] Collins advocated a conjunctive reading of Wesley which emphasized holy love *and* grace.

Then in 2012, Thomas Oden published three volumes of *John Wesley's Teachings*. He claimed "nothing like this text-by-text review of the content of Wesley's teaching exists in Wesley studies." Essentially, Oden quadrupled the material of his 1994 work, *John Wesley's Scriptural Christianity*. Oden's purpose was to demonstrate that Wesley was a systematic theologian.[13] Oden works from the primary sources, arranging Wesley's writings in systematic order. Thus, he demonstrates an internal consistency across sixty years. He acknowledged Outler as his mentor.

The first attempt at such an arrangement was *Wesleyana*, first published in 1825. It was basically a cut-and-paste arrangement of Wesley's sermons.

8. Kenneth J. Collins, "The State of Wesley Studies in North America: A Theological Journey," *Wesleyan Theological Journal* 44:2 (Fall 2009), 18–20.

9. John B. Cobb, Jr., *Grace and Responsibility: A Wesleyan Theology for Today* (Nashville: Abingdon, 1995), 7–9.

10. Bryan Stone and Thomas Oord claimed *Grace and Responsibility* by Cobb was the most important published interpretation of Wesley's theology in light of process thought. (Brian Stone and Thomas Oord, *Thy Nature and Thy Name is Love: Process and Wesleyan Theologies in Dialogue* [Nashville: Kingswood Books, 2001], 12).

11. Laurence W. Wood, *The Meaning of Pentecost in Early Methodism: Rediscovering John Fletcher as John Wesley's Vindicator and Designated Successor* (Lanham, Md.: Scarecrow, 2002).

12. Kenneth J. Collins, *The Theology of John Wesley: Holy Love and the Shape of Grace* (Nashville: Abingdon, 2007), 220–221.

13. Thomas C. Oden, *John Wesley's Teachings: Volume 1 God and Providence* (Grand Rapids: Zondervan, 2012), 23, 8–29.

The second attempt was *A Compend of Wesley's Theology*, edited by Robert W. Burtner and Robert E. Chiles in 1954. It drew from all of Wesley's major writings.

With volume 4 of *John Wesley's Teachings*, published in February 2014[14], this set may be the culmination of a renewed interest in Wesley's theology that has mushroomed over the last fifty years.

WESLEY'S GRACE ENCOUNTER

Although Wesley was reared in an orthodox environment, he did not encounter God's saving grace until his conversion at Aldersgate.[15] Wesley frequently referred to events in his journal in terms of *anno meae conversionis*, dating them from 24 May 1738.[16] He later explained that he had the form of godliness many years, but not the fruits of the Spirit.[17] Baker wrote, "At that time God's law meant more to Wesley than his grace."[18]

A year after his conversion Wesley conceded that for ten years he had preached faith and works. But in 1739 he declared that he preached no meritorious cause of our justification but the death and righteousness of Christ; no conditional or instrumental cause but faith.[19]

Wesley developed an order of salvation based on his theology of grace. He declared,

> All the blessings which God hath bestowed upon man are of his mere grace, bounty, or favour: his free, undeserved favour, favour altogether undeserved, man having no claim to the least of his mercies. It was free grace that "formed man of the dust of the ground, and breathed into him a living soul," and stamped on that soul the image of God, and "put all things under his feet."

---

14. Thomas C. Oden, *John Wesley's Teachings: Volume 4 Ethics and Society* (Grand Rapids: Zondervan, 2014).

15. While Wesley's Aldersgate experience has been subject to reinterpretation, and debated by Kenneth Collins and Randy Maddox, I survey the basic literature and argue that it was his new birth experience in Reasoner, *Holy Living*, 1:114.

16. George Croft Cell, *The Rediscovery of John Wesley* (New York: Henry Holt, 1935), 185.

17. *The Bicentennial Edition of the Works of John Wesley* [*BE Works*], W. Reginald Ward, ed. (Nashville: Abingdon, 1990), 19:29–30. *Journal*, 4 January 1739.

18. Frank Baker, ed. *The Heart of True Spirituality* (Grand Rapids: Francis Asbury, 1985), 1:13.

19. Wesley, *BE Works*, 19:89. *Journal*, 27 August, 1739.

The same free grace continues to us, at this day, life, and breath, and all things.[20]

Oden concluded that Wesley's doctrine of grace is in most ways Augustinian.

> It sees God's favor at work throughout the whole narrative of salvation. (1) Common grace is present in the whole of nature and history, preceding all acts of human decision. (2) Saving grace is given in Jesus Christ and received by faith alone. (3) Completing grace is given through the Holy Spirit to nurture the life of faith toward holy living.[21]

GOD'S SOVEREIGNTY AND GRACE

While God is not abusive or capricious, he does rule, in Wesley's view. Wesley affirms the sovereignty of God, but always in tension with his other attributes. "For the Scripture nowhere speaks of this single attribute, as separate from the rest."[22]

Might does not make right. Righteousness flows from the character of God. Wesleyan-Arminians affirm God's sovereignty, but believe that God has the prerogative of not always exercising total sovereignty. Thus, we have true libertarian freedom. Yet God never surrenders the consequences of our free choices to us. He always has the last word. God is so sovereign he can allow human rebellion, yet that rebellion does not thwart his ultimate purpose.

In his essay "Thoughts Upon God's Sovereignty," Wesley wrote of God as creator and as governor. As creator, God has acted in all things according to his own sovereign will. But when God acts as governor, he no longer acts as a mere Sovereign, but as an impartial judge. Rather than acting by fiat decree, God allows humanity moral freedom and responsibility. God does not reproach anyone "for doing anything which he could not possibly avoid" or for "omitting anything which he could not possibly do."[23]

---

20. Wesley, *BE Works*, Albert C. Outler, ed. (Nashville: Abingdon, 1984), 1:117–118. "Salvation by Faith," Sermon #1, ¶1.

21. Oden, *John Wesley's Teachings*, 2:137.

22. John Wesley, *The Works of John Wesley*, Thomas Jackson, ed., 3rd ed. 1872. Rpt. (Grand Rapids: Baker Books, 1979), 10:220.

23. Wesley, *Works*, 10:361–363.

Wesley rejected the view that

> The greater part of mankind God hath ordained to death. . . .
> Them God hateth; and therefore, before they were born, de-
> creed they should die eternally. And this he absolutely decreed;
> because so was his good pleasure; because it was his sovereign
> will. Accordingly, they are born for this: to be destroyed body
> and soul in hell. And they grow up under the irrevocable curse
> of God, without any possibility of redemption; for what grace
> God gives, he gives only for this, to increase, not prevent their
> damnation.[24]

In *Predestination Calmly Considered*, he wrote,

> If this were true, we must give up all the Scriptures together; nor
> would the infidels allow the Bible so honourable a title as that of
> a "cunningly devised fable." But it is not true. It has no colour of
> truth. It is absolutely, notoriously false. To tear up the very roots
> of reprobation, and of all doctrines that have a necessary con-
> nexion therewith, God declares in his word these three things,
> and that explicitly in so many terms: (1) "Christ died for all" (2
> Cor 5:14), namely, all that were dead in sin, as the words imme-
> diately following fix the sense. Here is the fact affirmed. (2) "He
> is the propitiation for the sins of the whole world" (1 John 2:2),
> even of all those for whom he died. Here is the consequence
> of his dying for all. And, (3) "He died for all, that they should
> not live unto themselves, but unto him which died for them" (2
> Cor 5:15), that they might be saved from their sins. Here is the
> design, the end of his dying for them.[25]

Wesley added:

> God, as sovereign Lord and Proprietor of all, dispenses His gifts
> or favours to his creatures with perfect wisdom, but by no rules
> or methods of proceding that we are acquaintted with. . . . But
> God's methods of dealing with us, as our Governor and Judge,
> are clearly revealed and perfectly known; namely, that he will fi-
> nally reward every man according to his works: *he that believeth
> shalt be saved, and he that believeth not shall be damned.*[26]

---

24. Wesley, *BE Works*, 3:545. "Free Grace," Sermon #110, ¶ 4.

25. Wesley, *Works.* 10:225.

26. John Wesley, *Explanatory Notes Upon the New Testament.* 1754. Rpt. (Salem, Ohio: Schmul, 1976), 389–390.

THE TOTAL INABILITY OF MANKIND

Wesley wrote that people who denied original sin are but heathens still. He claimed this as "the first grand distinguishing point between heathenism and Christianity."[27] Collins argued that "a weak doctrine of original sin could only result in an equally weak doctrine of the new birth. For it the extensiveness of the problem was relinquished or soft-pedaled, the radical nature of the solution would be lost as well."[28]

Harald Lindström wrote that Wesley's evangelical sermons were based on three main assumptions:

- natural man is totally corrupt
- this corruption is the result of original sin
- man can be justified only through God's grace in Christ.[29] Lindström explained what "original sin" meant for Wesley:

> The Fall, he believed, had deprived man of his original perfection and occasioned total corruption of human nature. Consequently, Adam's descendents are spiritually dead at birth and utterly devoid of any righteousness and holiness in which he himself was created. Sometimes original sin is described as an inclination to evil, or a condition in which all the faculties of man, understanding, and will and affections, have been perverted. But he can use stronger language, defining it as total corruption of the whole human nature.[30]

The Methodist Articles of Religion state, "Original sin standeth not in the following of Adam (as the Pelagians do vainly talk) but it is the corruption of the nature of every man, that naturally is engendered of the offspring of Adam, whereby man is very far gone from original righteousness, and of his own nature inclined to evil, and that continually."

And Wesley elaborated as follows about the natural man's condition:

> His spiritual senses are not awake; they discern neither spiritual good nor evil. The eyes of his understanding are closed; they are sealed together, and see not . . . Hence, having no inlets for the

---

27. Wesley, *BE Works*, 2:183. "Original Sin," Sermon #44, 3.1.

28. Kenneth J. Collins, *Wesley on Salvation* (Grand Rapids: Francis Asbury, 1989), 22.

29. Harald Lindström, *Wesley and Sanctification* (Grand Rapids: Zondervan, 1980), 21.

30. Ibid. 27.

knowledge of spiritual things, all the avenues of his soul being shut up, he is in gross, stupid ignorance of whatever he is most concerned to know. He is utterly ignorant of God, knowing nothing concerning him as he ought to know. He is totally a stranger to the law of God, as to its true, inward, spiritual meaning. He has no conception of that evangelical holiness, without which no man shall see the Lord; nor of the happiness which they only find whose "life is hid with Christ in God."[31]

Semi-Pelagianism holds that we are fallen, but retain free will and the ability to seek God apart from any special grace. Wesley was neither Pelagian nor semi-Pelagian. Oden declared,

When Wesley is mistakenly portrayed today as a Pelagian or semi-Pelagian, the portrayer owes it to fairness to read *The Doctrine of Original Sin*. When Wesley is portrayed as a cheery humanistic type of Arminian who supposedly stressed the natural abilities of man, the critic reveals ignorance of the defining Doctrinal Minutes of August 1745 instructing all preachers in Wesley's connection.[32]

William Abraham wrote, "Wesleyan Arminanism is monergistic to the degree that all saving grace is acknowledged as coming from God, and that even man's free cooperation is made possible by prevenient grace."[33] Thus, God must make the first move.

Oden explained,

One could not cooperate with God had not the power and possibility of cooperating come from God. So it is no offense to grace to say that grace enables human freedom to cooperate with grace. The right use of freedom, far from detracting from the glory of God, enhances God's glory.

By cooperation Wesley was not implying that fallen freedom retains a natural capacity to reach out and take the initiative and establish a restored relation with God. Rather, by cooperating grace he means that human freedom by grace is being enabled to cooperate interactively with God's saving plan.[34]

---

31. Wesley, *BE Works*, 1:251, "The Spirit of Bondage and Adoption," Sermon #9, 1.1.

32. Oden, *John Wesley's Teachings*, 2:158.

33. William Abraham, "Monergism," Richard S. Taylor, ed., *Beacon Dictionary of Theology*, (Kansas City, Mo.: Beacon Hill, 1983), 344.

34. Oden, *John Wesley's Teachings*, 2:180–181.

Recent Nazarene theologians have reinforced the doctrine of total inability. Kenneth Grider explained, "Original sin refers to a state of sin in us due to that original act of sin on Adam's part."[35] Ray Dunning concluded, "Humanity is wrong, all wrong, before God and therefore everything that is done is wrong. It is in this way that actual sin is always an expression of original sin."[36] Samuel Powell wrote that original sin is more than the first sin. "*Original* means *universal*."[37]

A consequence of Adam's sin was not only death for Adam, but for all his descendents. Oden concluded, "A high doctrine of original sin is the premise and companion of a high doctrine of grace. Since the whole of humanity is involved in sin and punishment, having no possibility of self-salvation, we do well to cast ourselves solely on the grace offered in Jesus."[38]

WESLEY'S THEOLOGY OF GRACE

1. Preliminary grace

Since Wesleyan-Arminian theology affirms total depravity, early Methodism emphasized free grace, not free will. Thus, Wesley said that Methodism came to the very edge of Calvinism in ascribing all good to the free grace of God, in denying all natural free-will and all power antecedent to grace and in excluding all merit from man, even for what he has or does by the grace of God.[39]

Wesley used the word "prevenient" to describe the grace which comes before salvation. *Prevenient* comes from two a Latin words, *prae*—before and *venire*—to come. Prevenient grace is the grace of God which precedes or comes before human action, enabling the sinner to repent and believe. Thus, Greathouse declared that "sanctification begins with prevenient grace."[40]

Oden wrote that freedom grows through stages. "Preparatory (or prevenient) grace is the lowest gear in the drive train of grace that enables one to move from inertia so that one may gradually be brought up to speed."

35. J. Kenneth Grider, *A Wesleyan-Holiness Theology* (Kansas City, Mo.: Beacon Hill, 1994), 277.

36. H. Ray Dunning, *Grace, Faith, and Holiness* (Kansas City, Mo: Beacon Hill, 1988), 301.

37. Samuel M. Powell, *Discovering Our Christian Faith* (Kansas City, Mo: Beacon Hill, 2008), 134.

38. Oden, *John Wesley's Teachings*, 2:215.

39. Wesley, *Works*, 8:285.

40. William M. Greathouse, *Wholeness in Christ* (Kansas City, Mo.: Beacon Hill, 1998), 129.

Oden emphasized that no one is saved by preparatory grace. The sinner is free to resist this grace, but not to initiate it.[41]

Thus, Collins argues that prevenient grace is irresistible grace. "Irresistibility in this context pertains not to the call or overtures made to these faculties (that can be resisted) but to the reestablishment of these faculties that constitute responsible personhood and accountability."[42] Thus, preliminary grace restores the capacity of every person to accept salvation.

However, preliminary grace is not justifying grace. Diane Leclerc writes, "Since prevenient grace is given to all, humanity 'without God' is a 'logical abstraction.'"[43] But Eph 2:12 describes the state of those who are without God. Wesley entreated all who were without God in the world:

> You do not see the Sun of righteousness. You have not fellowship with the Father, nor with his Son, Jesus Christ. You never heard the voice that raiseth the death. Ye know not the voice of your Shepherd. Ye have not received the Holy Ghost. Ye have no spiritual senses . . . . O cry to God that he may rend the veil which is still upon your hearts! . . . O that you may this day hear his *voice*.[44]

Everyone may be under common grace, but preliminary grace may be resisted. Some Wesleyan theologians have taken prevenient grace further than Wesley did. The result is that Wesley's teaching has been misappropriated to support a kind of universalism.

Wesley described prevenient grace as a temporary condition, not a permanent one. Wesley said that "preventing grace" included "all the 'drawings' of 'the Father,' the desires after God, which, if we yield to them, increase more and more." But Wesley also observed that while the Holy Spirit produces conviction from time to time in every child of man, "the generality of men stifle them as soon as possible, and after a while forget, or at least deny, that ever they had them at all."[45] Thus, Collins insists that a distinction must be made between preliminary grace and justification.[46]

In describing the awakened sinner struggling to keep the law, Wesley wrote, "Such is the freedom of his will — free only to evil."[47] Wesley stated

41. Oden, *John Wesley's Teachings*, 2:138.

42. Collins, *Theology of John Wesley*, 80–81.

43. Diane Leclerc, *Discovering Christian Holiness* (Kansas City, Mo.: Beacon Hill, 2010), 158.

44. Wesley, *BE Works*, 4:175–176. "On Living without God," Sermon #130, ¶ 16.

45. Wesley, *BE Works*, 2:157. "The Scripture Way of Salvation," Sermon #43, 1.2.

46. Collins, "State of Wesley Studies in North America," 23–24.

47. Wesley, *BE Works*, 1:258. "The Spirit of Bondage and of Adoption," Sermon #9, 2.7–8.

that he and John Fletcher "absolutely deny natural free will. We both steadily assert that the will of man is by nature free only to evil. Yet we both believe that every man has a measure of free will restored to him by grace."[48] Wesley preached "the grace or love of God whence cometh our salvation, is free in all, and free for all."[49] "Free in all" describes prevenient grace. "Free for all" declares that the atonement is universal in scope.

Chiles observed that "Human goodness was Wesley's goal, not his starting point."[50] Oden observed that preparatory grace is sometimes misunderstood in a Pelagian sense as natural human ability. Reformed critics who have not studied Wesley's *Doctrine of Original Sin*, his longest treatise, might worry that he was secretly speaking of some universal natural capacity to do good.[51]

In fact, Millard Erickson declared, "The problem is that there is no clear and adequate basis in Scripture for this concept of a universal enablement. The theory, appealing though it is in many ways, simply is not taught explicitly in the Bible."[52]

Yet Oden asserts, "Calvin's doctrine of common grace forms the background of Wesley's teaching of preparatory grace that precedes saving grace."[53] In one of his books on this issue, Oden devotes an entire chapter, entitled "Preparing and Cooperating Grace," to discuss the scriptural *and* the consensual teachings of the first five centuries of Church doctrine regarding prevenient grace.[54] Actually, the dogmatic category which cannot be substantiated biblically is what Calvinists term "effectual grace." Daniel Whedon wrote,

> The distinction made in predestinarian theology between God's common call and his "effectual call" upon sinners to repent, implies that God does not truly mean his common call to be effectual, and so imputes insincerity to God. The true distinction lies not in the intrinsic nature of God's call itself, but in the different acceptance by man. There is truly a *rejected calling*

48. Wesley, *Works*, 10:466.

49. Wesley, *BE Works*, 3:544. "Free Grace," Sermon #110, ¶ 2.

50. Robert E. Chiles, *Theological Transition in American Methodism: 1790—1935* (New York: Abingdon, 1965), 143. See Chapter 5, "From Free Grace to Free Will," 144–183.

51. Oden, *John Wesley's Teachings*, 2:151–152; 158.

52. Millard Erickson, *Christian Theology*, One-Volume Edition (Grand Rapids: Baker, 1986), 925.

53. Oden, *John Wesley's Teachings*, 2:149.

54. Thomas C. Oden, *The Transforming Power of Grace* (Nashville: Abingdon, 1993), 25, 47–59.

and an *obeyed calling*, and those who obey God's call become permanently *the called*.[55]

However, the real question is not whether there is preliminary grace, since salvation is all of grace from beginning to end, but whether that grace is irresistible and election is unconditional. Wesley held that if salvation is by absolute decree, it is not by works, but neither is it by faith, "for unconditional decree excludes faith as well as works."[56]

Wesley used several phrases to differentiate between the preliminary grace and justifying grace. He referred to the awakened state, the almost Christian, the legal state, and the faith of a servant.[57]

In Wesleyan-Arminian exegesis, Romans 7 is the classic passage which describes the awakened sinner under preliminary—and not justifying—grace. Romans 7 makes no mention of enabling grace. It describes one who sins compulsively. This is the classic struggle between conscience and will. The Holy Spirit is conspicuous by his absence in this chapter. Wesley warned that we should never fancy ourselves "a believer in Christ, till Christ is revealed in you, and till His Spirit witnesses with your spirit that you are a child of God."[58] In Romans 8, the Holy Spirit is named twenty times.

In Romans 7, the personal pronoun "I" is used 32 times and the emphatic Greek form *ego* is used eight times. The climax in v. 25 employs the double pronoun "I myself" for emphasis. Although vv. 14–25 recall this struggle in the historical present tense, in which a past event is viewed with the vividness of a present occurrence, no major Wesleyan-Arminian interpreter has understood this passage to be a description of justifying grace.[59]

Charles Hodge declared, "There is no believer, however advanced in holiness, who cannot adopt the language used here [v. 14] by the apostle."[60]

55. Daniel D.Whedon, *Commentary on the New Testament*, (Salem, Ohio: Schmul, [1871] 1977), 3:293.

56. Wesley, "Thoughts on Salvation by Faith, *Works*, 11:494.

57. See Wesley, *BE Works*, 1:142–158, "The Almost Christian," Sermon #2; *BE Works*, 2:155–169, "The Scripture Way of Salvation," Sermon #43; *BE Works*, 3:199–209, "On Working Out Your Own Salvation," Sermon #85; and the analysis by C. Leslie Mitton, *A Clue to Wesley's Sermons* (London: Epworth, 1951), 44 pages; Oden, *Transforming Power of Grace*, 38–51, 108–124.

58. Wesley, *BE Works*, 2:59. "The Nature of Enthusiasm," Sermon #37, ¶ 35.

59. See the major treatise of James Arminius, "Dissertation on the True and Genuine Sense of the Seventh Chapter of the Epistle to the Romans," *The Works of James Arminius: The London Edition* [Hereinafter called *Works*], James Nichols, transl. 1828 Rpt. (Grand Rapids: Baker, 1996) 3:471–683; Vic Reasoner, *A Fundamental Wesleyan Commentary on Romans* (Evansville, Ind.: Fundamental Wesleyan, 2002), 275–303.

60. Charles Hodge, *Commentary on the Epistles to the Romans*, 1886; Rpt. (Grand Rapids: Eerdmans, 1950), 229.

In recent years, however, several Calvinistic commentators have broken ranks and conceded that Romans 7 does not describe Christians, who are "miserable sinners still."[61] The list includes Herman N. Ridderbos (1959), Martyn Lloyd-Jones (1973), Anthony A. Hoekema (1987), Thomas R. Schreiner (1998), Douglas Moo (1991), and R. J. Rushdoony (1994).[62]

2. Justifying grace

Wesley rejected unconditional election "not only because I cannot find it in Scripture, but also (to wave all other considerations) because it necessarily implies unconditional reprobation."[63] Wesley declared, "Unconditional election cannot appear without the cloven foot of reprobation."[64] In Scripture the idea of reprobation is never explicitly contrasted with election.[65] Yet F. Leroy Forlines has estimated that 80 percent of the commentaries covering Romans 9 advocate unconditional election.[66]

Wesley taught that election was conditional and that God's eternal decree was stated in Mark 16:16. In *Predestination Calmly Considered*, he cites twenty two passages emphasizing human responsibility, and thirteen passages promising that God is willing to save all men, and eleven passages proclaiming that Christ died for all men.[67]

Nor is justifying grace irresistible grace. Oden wrote, "The ordinary work of the spirit is not coercive. That the Spirit can be resisted is evident from Acts 7:51 on stiff-necked people."[68]

In this context, when Wesley argues for free will, he is arguing for libertarian choice. Oden writes,

> Wesley held to the freewill defense that God Creates freedom, and freedom chooses evil in its own struggle against God, who is the author not of sin but of freedom, which is created good

---

61. This is the language of B. B. Warfield, *Perfectionism*, 1931; Rpt. (Grand Rapids: Baker, 1981), 1:113–132.

62. Reasoner, *Romans*, 300–302.

63. Wesley, *Works*, 10:210–211.

64. Ibid., 10:209.

65. Gottlob Schrenk, *Theological Dictionary of the New Testament*, Gerhard Kittel, ed. (Grand Rapids: Eerdmans, 1967), 4:175.

66. F. Leroy Forlines, *Classical Arminianism* (Nashville: Randall House, 2011), 97–98.

67. Wesley, *Works*, 10:204–259. For a comprehensive statement on election, see Wesley's *Journal*, 24 August 1743.

68. Oden, *John Wesley's Teachings*, 2:172.

even if prone to fall. . . . Take away freedom and you take away
the greatest expression of God's glory in creation. . . . Wesley
took special delight in quoting back to Reformed advocates the
language of the Westminster Assembly, which allowed that "god
hath endued the will of man with that natural liberty that is neither forced, nor by an absolute necessity of nature, determined
to do good or evil."[69]

Wesley rejected unconditional election and irresistible grace, because
he rejected the broader concept of double predestination. Oden documents
that Wesley built on a strong Calvinistic heritage. He concluded that Wesley's theology retained most other standard features of Reformed exegesis.
Yet Wesley taught

Double predestination makes the devil's work unnecessary.
If true, God would be worse than the devil. Scripture teaches
that God's sovereignty is directed by his love and views love as
God's foremost attribute. Absolute predestination disorders the
primacy of God's love among the divine attributes.[70]

There are at least four key issues in which the Wesleyan-Arminian
understanding of justification differs from the Calvinistic understanding:

- Is faith a condition of salvation or a consequence of salvation?

- Does justification by faith involve the non-imputation of all past, present, and future sins?

- Should imputed righteousness and imparted righteousness be separated or kept together?

- Does God impute our faith in the atoning work of Christ to us as righteousness or is the obedience of Christ transferred to us in lieu of future personal righteousness?

The popular teaching today is that we are legally declared to be just
and holy, but we do not live righteous lives. Instead the obedience of Christ
is reckoned to us while we continue to live in disobedience. But Scripture
never teaches that the *obedience* of Christ is credited to us.

Robert Gundry reviewed every text where *logizomai eis* occurs and
concluded that the interpretation that makes faith the instrument by which
righteousness is received does not make good contextual sense. The lack of
any reference in Galatians 3 and Romans 4 to Christ's righteousness confirmed Gundry's observation that the counting of faith as righteousness is

69. Ibid., 2:180.
70. Ibid., 2:167.

not Paul's shorthand expression in which faith is the instrument by which Christ's righteousness is received. Rather, this phrase "counted as" is used to describe an identification of what is counted, with what it is counted as. Gundry concluded that Paul wants to emphasize the obedient life of righteousness that we are supposed to live and indeed will live if we are true believers.[71]

Michael Bird concluded,

> Romans 4 does not assert that one is justified because of the imputed righteousness of Christ or that God reckons faith as covenantal conformity. Instead, God regards faith as the condition of justification (reckons faith as righteousness) and justifies believers (credits righteousness) because of their union with Christ (raised for our justification).[72]

Wesley objected to a distortion of the doctrine of imputation which results in God being deceived regarding those whom he justifies, "that he thinks them to be what in fact they are not, that he accounts them to be otherwise than they are. . . . He can no more in this manner confound me with Christ than with David or Abraham."[73]

Rather our *faith* is credited to us as righteousness. We are both declared to be righteous and made righteous. John Fletcher explained that we are made righteous, not by a speculative imputation of the works of Christ, but by being made partakers of the divine nature, begotten of God, and clothed with righteousness and true holiness.[74]

Wesley stood with the Protestant Reformers regarding the *nature* of justification as a forensic declaration by God by which he graciously forgives and accepts sinners. With the Reformers, Wesley held that the *basis* of justification is faith alone. Collins pronounced Wesley's sermon "Justification by Faith" as "typical of the Continental Reformation, especially the later Lutheran tradition, but one that gains maintains the graciousness of the gospel by viewing justification as a forensic act by the most High."[75]

71. Robert Gundry, "The Nonimputation of Christ's Righteousness," in Mark Husbands and Daniel J. Treier, eds., *Justification: What's at Stake in the Current Debates?* (Downers Grove, Ill.: InterVarsity, 2004), 17–45. See also Michael F. Bird, *The Saving Righteousness of God* (Colorado Springs: Paternoster, 2006), 2.

72. Michael Bird, "Incorporated Righteousness: A Response to Recent Evangelical Discussion Concerning the Imputation of Christ's Righteousness in Justification," *Journal of the Evangelical Theological Society* 47:2 (June 2004), 264; 267.

73. Wesley, *BE Works*, 1:188. "Justification by Faith," Sermon #5, 2.4

74. Fletcher, *Works*, 1:308.

75. Kenneth Collins, "The Doctrine of Justification: Historic Wesleyan and Contemporary Understandings," in Husbands and Treier, *Justification*, 184.

However, Wesley broke with them concerning the *results* of justification. He rejected the view that the Christian is at once just and yet a sinner. Nowhere in the New Testament is the Christian termed a "sinner."[76] While Wesley saw himself within the Protestant tradition, he disagreed with Luther's conclusion that the Christian is at the same time just and yet sinful (*simul justus est et peccat*).

Wesley declared, "I believe God *implants* righteousness in every one to whom he has *imputed* it."[77] Wesley maintained a connection between justification, regeneration, the indwelling of the Holy Spirit, and initial sanctification. Wesley maintains that regeneration is concomitant with justification. "And at the same moment that we are justified, yea, in that very moment, *sanctification* begins. In that instant we are 'born again,' 'born from above,' 'born of the Spirit.' There is a *real* as well as a *relative* change."[78] Wesley declared "at the same time a man is justified sanctification properly begins."[79]

Thus, Romans 8:1 deals with the nonimputation of sin. But according to vv. 1–4 the result of this justification is not merely forensic, it is transformational. The justified believer no longer walks according to the sinful nature. Thus, imputed and imparted righteousness are connected.

3. Perfecting grace

Philip Watson summarized the Wesleyan message with this simple formula:

All men need to be saved.
All men can be saved.
All men can know they are saved.
All men can be saved to the uttermost.[80]

Wesley preached a free salvation for all men and a full salvation from all sin. The atonement is universal in scope and the cure for sin is as radical

---

76. In thirty-eight New Testament passages where Christians are described, they are called believers, saints, disciples, and brethren. However, the New Testament never identifies a Christian as a sinner. The only exception which might be cited is found in 1 Tim 1:15–16 where Paul described himself twice as a sinner. But the question is whether that was his present state or his previous identify. Verse 13 seems to settle the question. "Chief of sinners" is his *before* and not his *after* picture.

77. Wesley, *BE Works*, 1:458–359. "The Lord Our Righteousness," Sermon #20, 2.12.

78. Ibid., 2:158. "The Scripture Way of Salvation," Sermon #43, 1.4.

79. Ibid., 3:506. "On God's Vineyard," Sermon #107, 1.6.

80. Philip S. Watson, *Message of the Wesleys: A Reader of Instruction and Devotion*, 1964 Rpt. (Grand Rapids: Zondervan, 1984), 35.

as the disease. The progressive work of sanctification is the work of the Spirit beginning with prevenient grace and continuing until final glorification.

Wesleyan theology is pessimistic about the sinful nature of mankind, but optimistic about the power of God's grace. His grace can enable us to love him with our whole heart and to love our neighbor as ourselves. But this condition, which by definition displaces everything contrary to the love of God, must be maintained by appropriating all the means of grace.

This is a responsible grace. Randy Maddox wrote, "Without God's grace we *cannot* be saved; while without our (grace—empowered, but un-coerced) participation, God's grace *will not* save."[81] Wesley insisted, "God works; therefore you *can* work. . . . God works; therefore you *must* work." Wesley ended his sermon by quoting Augustine, "He that made us without ourselves, will not save us without ourselves."[82]

We must avail ourselves of the means of grace or else we may fall from grace. Keith Stanglin and Thomas McCall explain that for Arminius, "the claim that grace is resistible means that God's gift of salvation is never ir-revocable in this life."[83]

We must not stop. The Christian walk does not end with acceptance of new life in Christ. Wesley liked the phrase *moi progressus ad infini-tum*, my progress is without end.[84] Even J. I. Packer commended Wesley "and his refusal to set limits to the transforming power of God's Spirit in us here and now."[85] Oden stated it thus, "God works, therefore you must work." He explained, "Every subsequent act of cooperating with grace is premised on God's preceding grace, which elicits and requires free human responsiveness."[86]

In his *Plain Account of Christian Perfection* Wesley argued that God will save us from all sin because of his promises, his commands, scriptural examples, and scriptural prayers. Yet Wesley's doctrine of Christian Per-fection is misunderstood. Albert Outler pointed out that the Latin word *perfectus* means unimprovable. The Latin understanding of perfection was static. But Wesley defined perfection with the understanding of the Greek

---

81. Maddox, *Responsible Grace*, 19.

82. Wesley, *BE Works*, 3:206; 208. "On Working Out Our Own Salvation," Sermon #85, 3.2; 3.7.

83. Keith D. Stanglin and Thomas H. McCall, *Jacob Arminius: Theologian of Grace* (New York: Oxford University Press, 2012), 24.

84. Robert G. Tuttle, *Mysticism in the Wesleyan Tradition* (Grand Rapids: Francis Asbury, 1989), 156.

85. J. I. Packer, *Keeping in Step with the Spirit* (Old Tappan, N.J.: Revell, 1984), 137.

86. Oden, *John Wesley's Teachings*, 2:142.

word *teleios*—i.e. maturity or completeness.[87] It does not connote a static attainment, but rather an ongoing life of wholeness.[88] Oden wrote, "He never meant by perfection a static condition."[89]

> Wesley himself was working constantly out of the Greek text, not the Latin Vulgate or the King James Version in his daily meditations on Scripture. Therefore, when we say "perfect" in our modern vocabulary, our Latinized English language yields to us a static notion of perfection. Wesley's references to "perfection" instead assumed the Greek notion of a perfecting (not perfected) grace.[90]

Particularly important, Wesley explained:

> Everyone may *mistake* as long as he lives. . . the most perfect have continual need of the merits of Christ, even for their actual transgressions, and may well say, for themselves as well as their brethren, "Forgive us our trespasses."[91]

> By "perfection" I mean having "perfect love" of the loving God with all our heart, so as to rejoice evermore, to pray without ceasing, and in everything to give thanks. I am convinced every believer may attain this, yet I do not say, he is in a state of damnation, or under the curse of God till he does attain.[92]

Oden further noted:

> Wesley disputed the fantasy of a sinless perfection that would imagine itself exempt from all future struggle with temptation, and all conflict between flesh and spirit. Resisting the phrase "sinless perfection," Wesley preferred to speak of "perfect love."[93]

While the believer is progressively sanctified, being conformed more and more into Christlikeness, he may be brought by the Spirit to a point of deeper revelation of himself, led by the Spirit to a deeper and more intelligent surrender of himself, and to a confession of a deeper need. He is then

---

87. Albert Outler, *John Wesley* (New York: Oxford University Press, 1964), 30–33.

88. Gerhard Delling, τέλειος, Gerhard Friedrich, ed., Geoffrey W. Bromiley, trans., *Theological Dictionary of the New Testament*, (Grand Rapids: Eerdmans, 1972) , 8:77.

89. Oden, *John Wesley's Teachings*, 2:241.

90. Ibid., 2:249.

91. Wesley, BE *Works*, 10:284-285.

92. Wesley, *Works*, Jackson ed., 12:227. Letter to Elizabeth Hardy, 5 April 1758.

93. Oden, *John Wesley's Teachings*, 2:272.

cleansed to the level of that consciousness. This perfecting grace is received and maintained by a moment-by-moment faith.

God's grace can enable us to love him with our whole heart and to love our neighbor as ourselves. But this condition, which by definition displaces everything contrary to the love of God, must be maintained by appropriating all the means of grace.

Wesley advised those who were entirely sanctified to watch and pray continually against pride and fanaticism, to be zealous of good works and to avoid the thinking that because I am filled with love, I need not pray always and I need not set aside time for self-examination. Beware of desiring anything but God, beware of division. Be an example in all things. None of this comes automatically. We must constantly pursue holiness.[94]

But this pursuit is not a futile attempt to grasp the wind through an endless regimen of good works. Wesley said, "I believe this perfection is always wrought in the soul by a simple act of faith."[95] He explained,

> Exactly as we are justified by faith, so are we sanctified by faith. Faith is the condition, and the only condition of sanctification, exactly as it is of justification. It is the condition: none is sanctified but he that believes; without faith no man is sanctified. And it is the only condition: this alone is sufficient for sanctification.[96]

Wesley explained that there is not a formula or set pattern. God's relationship with us is personal and yet sovereign:

> There is likewise great variety in the manner and time of God's bestowing his *sanctifying grace*, whereby he enables his children to give him their whole heart, which we can in no wise account for. We know not why he bestows this on some even before they ask for it (some unquestionable instances of which we have seen); on some after they have sought it but a few days; and yet permits other believers to wait for it perhaps twenty, thirty, or forty years; nay, and others till a few hours or even minutes before their spirits return to him. . . .God undoubtedly has reasons; but those reasons are generally hid from the children of men.[97]

---

94. Wesley, *Works*, 11:427–441. This paragraph is a summary of Wesley's pastoral advice in *A Plain Account of Christian Perfection* to those who had experienced it.

95. Ibid., 11:446.

96. Ibid., 2:163. "Scripture Way of Salvation," Sermon #43, 3.3.

97. Ibid., 2:584. "The Imperfection of Human Knowledge," Sermon #69, 3.5.

Wesley felt that this message of heart holiness was the grand depositum of Methodists[98] and that God had providentially raised them up to spread scriptural holiness over the land.[99] But Wesley's theology cannot be reduced to one doctrine. Oden warned, "One does an injustice to Wesley by viewing all his teaching in the light of this single point, yet those who disregard it miss something crucial in Wesley."[100]

Wesley saw salvation from beginning until end as a work of God's grace. He ascribed all good to the free grace of God and excluded all merit from man.[101]

98. Wesley, *Letter* to Robert Carr Brackenbury, 15 September 1790.

99. Wesley, *BE Works*, 10: 845.

100. Oden, *John Wesley's Teachings*, 2:237.

101. Wesley, *BE Works*, 10:153.

11

Exegetical Notes on Calvinist Texts

Grant R. Osborne

Many of the difficulties between Arminianism and Calvinism would disappear if scholars were to abandon the common practice of "proof texting." The problem is that in the past, systematic theology has by and large taken passages out of context, grouped them together in a logical order, and in many cases made them say things not intended by the original authors.

This error is common to both sides in the debate. The answer is to be found in the methods of biblical theology, whereby we take every passage in its own context and interpret it in light of the author's intended meaning. We do not place a verse from John next to a verse from Hebrews and interpret one by the other; rather we allow John to speak for himself and the writer to the Hebrews to speak for himself.

For this reason, we are not going to arrange the discussion according to theological categories (i.e., according to the so called "five points") but rather according to book, and we hope to shed new light on the subject in this way. For those who are interested in the "five points," however, we will provide a "key" to the passages below, arranging the verses systematically:

Total depravity—John 6:44, 65; 8:44; Rom 3:9–12; 1 Cor 2:14; Eph 2:1–3; 4:17–19.

Unconditional election—John 6:35–40, 15:16; Rom 8:28–30, 33[1]; Eph 1:3–12; 1 Pet 1:1, 2; 2:8.9; Phil 2:12,13.

1. Romans 9—11 is discussed in a separate chapter of this symposium and so will

Limited atonement—John 6:35–40; 10:14–18, 24–29; 17:1–11; Rom 5:32–34.

Irresistible grace—Matt 11:25–27, 13:10–16; John 6:44–45, 64–65; Acts 13:48; Eph 2:8, 9; Rom 8:30.

Perseverance (final) of the saints—John 10:27–30; Rom 8; Phil 1:6 (1 Cor. 1:7–9); Eph 4:30; 1 Pet 1:3–5.

I. THE SYNOPTIC GOSPELS

Here, of course, we will be considering the *Logia Jesu*[2] as these shed light on the relationship between sovereignty and responsibility in salvation. At the outset, we would note that Jesus reacted against the Jewish stress on responsibility and so emphasized the divine activity in salvation. However, this must be interpreted in light of his eschatology, which contained both elements. The future aspects of the kingdom called for responsibility and perseverance (Matt 6:33, 24:13; Luke 18:29f.), and the present aspects were grounds for security (Matt 11:25f.; 13:10f.). The answer is then to be found in this tension between the present possession and the future hope regarding salvation, which reflects the eschatological tension between the already and the not yet throughout Jesus's teaching and the New Testament as a whole. As Marshall says, "As far as the outlook of Jesus is concerned, entry to the kingdom of God is something which takes place in the future, although men can participate in the blessings of the kingdom."[3] It is in this light that we must interpret the evidence.

Matt 11:25–27— This passage, paralleled by Luke 10:21–22, is used by many Calvinists to teach a combined doctrine of election and irresistible grace. Here it is said that "God makes known to His chosen ones the secrets

---

not be covered here.

2. Meaning the Sayings of Jesus. Of course, we are not going to get into the involved debate regarding the authenticity of these sayings. We will assume the conservative conclusions of scholars like C.H. Dodd, Oscar Cullmann and C.F.D. Moule, that they are basically trustworthy and will follow evangelicals like I. Howard Marshall, George Eldon Ladd and Clark Pinnock who argue that they are indeed authentic. However, we would note that the question itself is unnecessary, since we are studying the church's theology itself. Cf. I. Howard Marshall, *Kept by the Power of God* (Minneapolis: Bethany, 1975), 34, and E. M. B. Green, *The Meaning of Salvation* (Philadelphia: Westminster, 1965), 96f.

3. Marshall, *Kept by the Power of God,* 36. In fact, it could be said that salvation is equated with the kingdom of Christ (Mark 10:17–25) and the early church (Acts 8:12, 19:8, 28:23f.). That is, they contain both present (the kingdom blessings) and future (final salvation) aspects.

of the kingdom through the inward personal revelation given by the Spirit,"[4] and that therefore this revelation has the divine seal. Those to whom "the Son chooses to reveal" (11:27) the Father are given a special inward call which they cannot resist. This passage is indeed important for an understanding of Jesus's unique sonship[5] and parallels the many statements in the Johannine corpus that the only true revelation of the Father comes through the Son. The election motif is an important element in the theology of Jesus and transforms the corporate identity of Israel's view to the individual thrust of Jesus's view (note the "anyone" of v. 27).

Nevertheless, we must ask exactly what this doctrine entailed. Does it mean that God irresistibly draws to himself those he chooses and guarantees their salvation? This is certainly not the emphasis here, for Jesus centers on the revelation aspect, not the election aspect, of salvation. The latter doctrine is used by Jesus to stress the redemptive activity of God, and the place of the Son as the means of the effective outworking of that divine plan. Therefore, election is taught in this passage, but irresistible grace is not.

Matt 24:24—The Olivet Discourse is the only place in the Gospels where "elect" is used of Jesus's followers (cf. Mark 13:20, 22, 27; Luke 18:7; also Matt 24:22, 31), and so it is important to understand Jesus's use of the title here. In the Old Testament, the title is used to designate the people of God (Ps 105:6, 43; Isa 65:9f.), and many scholars have noted that in the Old Testament as well as the New Testament, election "is conditional upon (one's) desire to retain it,"[6] i.e., that God's choice of a person does not occur irrespective of his will and does not guarantee that he will never deny God's gift of salvation. This certainly seems to be indicated here, where Christ warns that the deception of the Antichrist will be so severe that "if possible, even the elect" will apostatize.

The interpretation hinges on the meaning of "if possible," which many say teaches the impossibility of leading the elect astray. However, this need not be true; in fact, the force of Mark 13:13 and Matt 24:13 proves the *crux*

---

4. David N. Steele and Curtis C. Thomas, *The Five Points of Calvinism* (Philadelphia: Presbyterian & Reformed, 1963), 52.

5. George E. Ladd, *A Theology of the New Testament* (Grand Rapids: Eerdmans, 1974), 165, calls it "the most important passage for the study of synoptic Christology." This, however, is probably overstated, since the theology of this passage is more closely related to the Johannine emphases. The synoptics stress more the messianic tension of Jesus's ministry, reserving the sonship motif for critical points in the narrative (cf. Mark 1:11; 9:7; 15:39) or to indicate his power over the forces of evil (cf. Mark 3:11; 5:7).

6. Cf. Marshall, *Kept by the Power of God*, 52, who quotes H. H. Rowley on this point.

interpretum for the passage, indicating that some will fail to "endure to the end," i.e., be "led astray."[7]

It is difficult to make a case that the context of Mark 13:13 does not indicate true believers, since Christ was talking to the disciples. Dispensational Calvinists[8] argue that the passage speaks about Israel in the tribulation period and so cannot be applied to believers now. However, this fails to consider the constant emphasis throughout the New Testament on the church as New Israel. It would be difficult to show that all Jesus's teachings to the disciples applied only to Israel, not the church. While this passage does apply to the specific conditions of the final tribulation, it applies to general problems believers have faced in every general "tribulation" and must teach a genuine danger for the believer. Mark 13:13, then, takes "salvation" in the same sense as the writer to the Hebrews, as expressing the final gift of salvation rather than the present possession of eternal life (see the chapter on Hebrews in this compendium). It is interesting here to note the other synoptic parallel to Mark 13:13—Luke 21:18, 36—which stresses security in the midst of endurance. The danger is real, but Christ here promises God's protection; yet that protection can only be realized *via* prayer and perseverance. The security makes the danger slight, but it is nevertheless a real warning.[9]

II. THE JOHANNINE CORPUS

The theme of all these writings is redemptive history, with the Gospel representing (from John's viewpoint) the past basis, the Epistles the present application, and the Apocalypse the future hope. The Gospel, even more than Paul, stresses divine sovereignty in salvation. Here Jesus is seen, even more

---

7. Ibid., 54, Marshall believes the "if possible" clause expresses the mind of the deceivers ("Let us lead them astray if we can") rather than the comment of Jesus. The use of the first-class condition (*ei*) which normally assumes reality or valid possibility, would favor this interpretation.

8. See Lewis Sperry Chafer, *Systematic Theology*, 8 vols. (Dallas: Dallas Seminary, 1947–1948), 3:292.

9. Other synoptic passages which provide warnings of apostasy would be the parable of the sower (Mark 4:3–9, 14–20 & par., especially vv. 5–6, 16–17), where it says they "believed for a time"; the parable of the tares (Mark 4:26–29, elaborated in Matt 13:24–30, 36–43), which shows the church contains both good and bad elements; the parable of the talents (Matt 25:14–30), which seems to indicate that Christians who fail to show fruit will be "cast into utter darkness"; and Jesus's saying about "salt which has lost its taste" in Matt 5:13, which relates to judgment. See the discussions of these in Marshall, *Kept by the Power of God*, and Robert Shank, *Life in the Son* (Springfield, Mo.: Westcott, 1960).

than in the synoptics, to be the sovereign over history, and God's salvation plan is assured. Numerous passages in John stress this crucial element in salvation, stating that men come only when drawn to Christ by him. These provide the strongest New Testament evidence for the Calvinist claim that God's salvation is final, achieved by his sovereign choice, and so is ultimately guaranteed to the elect.

Boettner, for instance, believes that there is a dualism of mankind into two separate classes, the elect and the nonbelievers, and that there can be no cross-over between those two distinct divisions, i.e., the unconverted cannot become elect.[10] However, this is certainly not true for John. One of the major characteristics which distinguishes John from the synoptics lies in his dualism; in the synoptics it is horizontal (i.e., this age vs. the age to come), but in John it is vertical (heavenly vs. earthly).[11] Thus there is no true ground for Boettner's horizontal view in John. This is best seen in a study of *kosmos*, the fourth Gospel. The "world" is pictured as mankind in general (7:4, 12:19, etc.) and is seen in a twofold relation to Christ. Primarily it denotes those who have rebelled against God (17:25) and have followed their "ruler," Satan (12: 31; 14:30; 16:11); as such it is dominated by wickedness (7:7) and has rejected Jesus (1:10) and his disciples (15:18, 17:14).

On the other hand, however, it is still the object of God's love (3:16) and salvation (3:17; 12:41), and Jesus came to provide life for it (1:29; 6:33). The disciples are to continue Jesus's salvific mission to the world (17:17–19). Therefore, the dualism that Boettner theorizes is simply not true. There is a dynamic relation between the world and the believer, and it is possible to move from one to the other. Let us look at the key passages for Johannine soteriology.

John 6:35–40, 44–45, 64–65—The question here is not whether this passage teaches divine sovereignty in the salvific decision but rather what this means. In this passage three Calvinist doctrines are discovered—predestination, irresistible grace, and eternal security. Murray sees in this passage a progressive development—they will not be cast out, they were given, they will not be lost, they will be raised up at the last day—and asserts that election is the basis for the believer's final perseverance.[12]

---

10. Loraine Boettner, *The Reformed Doctrine of Predestination* (Grand Rapids: Eerdmans, 1958), 109f., 291f. His style is typical systematic prooftexting, but much of his argument is taken from John.

11. See Ladd, *Theology of the New Testament*, 223; and Raymond E. Brown, *The Gospel According to John, I—XII (Anchor Bible)* (Garden City, N.Y.: Doubleday, 1966), CXV—CXVI.

12. John Murray, *Redemption—Accomplished and Applied* (Grand Rapids: Eerdmans, 1955), 196–197. Robert Gromacki, *Salvation is Forever* (Chicago: Moody, 1973),

The theme of God "drawing" the elect to Jesus in v. 44 and their "coming" to Jesus in v. 45 seems to reenforce this by stressing the sovereign power
behind that "inevitable decision." Morris points out that the verb *helkuo*
here implies resistance to the drawing power, but that there is no instance in
the New Testament where that resistance is successful. "Always the drawing
power is triumphant, as here."[13] The same thought is expressed in vv. 64, 65,
which say no one comes unless the Father gives him the ability to do so; "left
to himself the sinner prefers his sin."[14]

However, the above statements for the most part neglect John's other
emphasis, man's responsibility. In each of the above passages, that is forcefully brought out.

Verses 37-40 are based upon v. 35, where we see that eternal life is
dependent on coming and believing. Moreover, the present tenses of the
participles indicate it does not speak about a crisis faith-decision but rather
about persevering in those two states. As Brown says, "The stress in v. 37
that God destines men to come to Jesus does not in the least attenuate the
guilt in v. 36 of those who do not believe . . . with all John's insistence on
man's choosing between light and darkness, it would be nonsense to ask if
the evangelist believed in human responsibility."[15]

This is not to denigrate the strong emphasis on the sovereign will in
this passage; it is rather to point out that the sovereign force considers human responsibility before moving. There are four major words in these three
sections of John 6, organized into two sets of synonymous pairs: drawing =
giving and coming = believing. They illustrate the two sides of the salvific
act, God's part in drawing, man's part in coming. Here we must ask if God's

---

84, says, "Since every believer is a gift from the Father to the Son, everyone of these will
come to Christ."

13. Leon Morris, *Commentary on the Gospel of John* (Grand Rapids: Eerdmans,
1971), 371n. On the other hand, Yeager writes: "It [helkuo] does not necessarily involve coercion, though it does involve persuasion and motivation—John 6:44;
12:32. . . .[Helkuo] does not imply coercion in the two places where it is applied to the
elect [the two just-mentioned verses]. Swords, fish nets and political prisoners (John
18:10; 21:6, 11: Acts 16:19) may resist, but the element of resistance is not implicit in
the word itself. . . ." (Randolph O. Yeager, *The Renaissance New Testament* [Gretna, La.:
Pelican Publishing, 1980], 483–484).

14. Morris, *Commentary on the Gospel of John*, 387. Steel and Thomas, *The Five
Points of Calvinism*, 29, say, "Men left in their dead state are unable of themselves to repent, to believe the gospel, or to come to Christ. They have no power within themselves
to change their natures or to prepare themselves for salvation." The classic work on this,
of course, is Martin Luther's *The Bondage of the Will*.

15. Brown, *Gospel of John*, 276. He adds, "It would be just as much nonsense to
doubt that, like the other biblical authors, he saw God's sovereign choice being worked
out in those who came to Jesus."

drawing determines man's coming and if man's coming thereby is an act apart from the decision of his will. In 6:44 this verse must be taken seriously in light of John's entire "draws" theology, which stresses the attraction itself, not the certainty of it. In 12:32, Jesus says that as a result of his death,[16] he will "draw all men" to himself. In itself, then, it does not teach irresistible grace but rather God's universal salvific love.

Moreover, the context of those verses presupposes responsibility, for v. 45 says that only those who have "heard and learned" will "come" to Christ.[17] As Marshall concludes:

> The purpose of the predestinarian language in John is not to express the exclusion of certain men from salvation because they were not chosen by the Father. . . but to emphasize that from start to finish eternal life is the gift of God and does not lie under the control of men. A person who tries to gain eternal life on his own terms will find himself unable to come to Jesus because it has not been granted to him by the Father (John 6:65); he has in fact been resisting the leading of the Father.[18]

10:14, 14–18, 27–30—Verses 11, and 14–18 are used along with Mark 10:45 as primary texts for the Calvinist doctrine of limited atonement. Many assert that Christ died for "many" not all[19] and for "the sheep" not those who are wolves, etc. This is especially seen in comparison with passages like "you are not my sheep" and "you are from your father, the devil."

However, this is to misunderstand Jesus's teaching here. The primary principle for interpreting any parabolic saying is that one must not go beyond the central teaching (see Jeremias's or Dodd's studies of the parable); especially, one must not base doctrines on what it does *not* say. Here Jesus

---

16. "Lifted up" is a Johannine term which speaks of Christ's passion as being "lifted up" on the cross (it results in being "lifted up" in glory). It is a strong salvific term looking back to Moses' "lifting up" the serpent in the wilderness (3:14–15; cf. 8:28). In conclusion, this verse would deny Morris' contention that "resistance is never successful." In fact, his discussion of this verse is particularly clumsy, for he still tries to interpret this word as teaching final salvation and so must wrestle with the question of universalism, i.e., the belief that all will be saved.

17. Note the parallel to 12:32 in this verse, "It is written in the prophets. 'And they shall all be taught by God,'" which is a free translation from Isa 54:13 LXX. The drawing power is entirely God's, and that is universally applied; but the act of coming proceeds only when one "hears" and "learns."

18. Marshall, *Kept by the Power of God*, 177. Robert Shank, *Elect in the Son* (Springfield, Mo.: Westcott, 1970), 176–177, argues that God's drawing is "compelling" but not "coercive," i.e., it is the call of salvation rather than the guarantee of salvation.

19. But note 1 Tim 2:5, 6, which says Jesus gave his life a "ransom for all" in a clear paraphrase of Jesus's statement here.

is teaching about his death, not the efficacy of it; in this context he could hardly have said he laid down his life for all the animals! This must be interpreted in light of the other Johannine passages which connect Jesus's death with "all" or with the "world" (1:12, 29; 3:16–17; 12:32). In short, Jesus here teaches that he shows his love for his sheep by dying for them but nowhere limits his death to them alone.[20] To use his imagery, he died so that "all" may become "sheep." Calvinists who argue it is sufficient for all but efficient only for some are correct, but the criterion for the latter group is not a rigid predestination, as we have just argued, but rather the faith decision of the individual. This, in fact, is the central theme of the fourth Gospel. Verses 27–30 are the major proof text for eternal security, since it in a sense promises the double protection of the believer by both Christ and the Father. As Boettner argues, this grounds security in God's omnipotence and in effect removes the believer from ultimate spiritual peril.[21] Calvinists base their interpretation on three points here: the presence of eternal life (cf. 5:24), the phrase "shall never perish" (with the emphatic ou me), and the promise of God's omnipotent protection (cf. Col 3:3). The result is that nothing can remove the believer from his elect position.[22]

To understand the thrust here we must identify the theological meaning given to "eternal life" in the fourth Gospel. John stresses the realized aspect and makes it a present possession secured under the power of God. The verses herein are a part of that present thrust. Nonetheless, there is a future aspect to the gift of salvation, and it must be secured by perseverance. This has been noted in 6:35, 45 and is seen in the present tense verbs of v. 27, "hearing," "knowing," and "following." To be sure, these are not conditions for salvation in this context (contra Shank), but they are conditions in light of John's total theology. This is especially seen in the vine and branches mashal of 15:1–7. There we are told that those branches which stop abiding in the vine and cease bearing fruit will wither, be stripped from the vine, and be thrown aside for burning. In spite of all attempts to assert otherwise,[23]

20. The same is true regarding the picture of 12:40, where we have the picture of God "blinding the eyes" and "hardening the heart" of those who have disbelieved (v. 39). Some take this in a double predestinarian sense, but neither in Isa 68:10 nor here has God moved in a vacuum. Rather, he has finalized the consequences of their own rejection. See Morris, Gospel of John, 604.

21. Boettner, Reformed Doctrine of Predestination, 198.

22. See Gromacki, Salvation is Forever, 76f.; J.F. Strombeck, Shall Never Perish (Chicago: Moody, 1966), 2–3. Both declare that "they follow me" is a statement of fact rather than a condition and expresses a guaranteed aspect of the salvation process.

23. There are three Calvinist approaches: 1) Murray, Redemption—Accomplished and Applied, 190–191, and John Calvin, Commentary on the Gospel According to John, 2 vols. (Grand Rapids: Eerdmans, 1949), 2:108, assert that this refers only to professing

this gives a valid warning to the believer regarding the consequences of failure to "abide" in him. So we can conclude that while eternal life is a present possession, it is not a future certainty. One must add perseverance to the security before one can be certain of that future attainment.

Marshall in this respect notes the Johannine themes of discipleship and faith.[24] John stresses two types of disciples and two aspects of faith, one continuing to abide and having a dynamic inward relationship to Christ, the other having a superficial relationship to Christ and only a partial faith. However, we must note that John nowhere denies that this partial faith is real. In fact, the close connection between partial faith and John's signs theology (cf. 2:23–25: 10:38; 14:11) shows there is validity in it. Jesus's works are insufficient in themselves to produce faith but can become a valid first step to an understanding of Jesus's person. The best example of this is Judas. While many have noted that he is called a "betrayer" in 6:64 long before his actual act of betrayal,[25] we may note that this is an editorial aside which looked ahead to what Judas would become (not what he was then). The significant phrase is found in 17:12, which says, "I kept them in your name, whom you gave me; I have guarded them, and none of them is lost but the son of perdition." Here we have some of the major terms of security—"given," "kept," "guarded"—used with relation to Judas, who was "lost."

Chapter 17—Christ's intercessory prayer here (and his present intercession mentioned in Heb 7:24, 25) is said to be evidence for the final perseverance of the elect. Jesus's prayer here is justly labeled his "high priestly prayer," for he both consecrates his coming sacrifice and intercedes on behalf of the people. It may be divided into three sections: (1) prayer for glory, vv. 1–8; (2) prayer for the disciples, vv. 9–19; and (3) prayer for future believers, vv. 20–26. Chafer notes two themes as indicative of security—the intensity

---

believers who have the external resemblance but not the internal life; however, we must agree with B.F. Westcott, *The Gospel According to St. John* (London: John Murray, 1882), 216–217, that the branches are definitely "in Christ" and are receiving nourishment from him. 2) Chafer, *Systematic Theology* 3: 289–298, believes that what it teaches is that the Christian can lose his communion (fellowship) with Christ but not his union, i.e., it is their testimony, not their soul, that is lost; however, this does not fit the imagery of the passage, which hardly speaks of a testimony—it is the branch itself, not just the bark, etc., which is burned. 3) William N. Clarke, *An Outline of Christian Theology* (New York: Scribner's Sons, 1911), 421–422, takes this as a hypothetical possibility, i.e., God uses these very real warnings as the means of ensuring the final perseverance of his saints. Against this approach, see the discussion on "Soteriology in Hebrews" in this symposium (especially on 6:4f.).

24. Marshall, *Kept by the Power of God*, 279–281.

25. See Chafer, *Systematic Theology*, 3: 286; Morris, *Gospel of John*, 386. On this point Marshall, *Kept by the Power of God*, 179, is in agreement on the grounds that this was John's belief.

of Christ's love and his dependence on the Father's protective power.[26] Gromacki finds the presence of security in the stress on Christians as (1) gifts to the Son, vv. 2, 6, 9, 11, 12, 24; (2) possessions of the union between Father and Son, vv. 9c-10a; (3) possessing eternal life, v. 2; and (4) objects of Christ's prayer for their preservation, v. 11, and eternal dwelling, v. 24.[27]

However, again we must ask what this is really saying. Certainly Christ's prayer is given entirely with the disciples in mind. Even the prayer for glory (vv. 1–5) is given not for his own sake but that his followers may have life (v. 2). Security is indeed the teaching; the divine name is pledged as the basis of the disciples' protection (v. 12a). Nevertheless, we must continue to remember that security does not mean an absolute guarantee. In the same context with the promise of protection (v. 12), we have the example of danger. In itself, of course, we dare not make too much of Judas, for some have called him "the exception which proves the rule." However, the conclusion here fits the data noted above.

In conclusion, John's major emphasis is definitely upon sovereignty and security. However, this does not contradict the doctrine of perseverance; rather it strengthens it by adding the aspect of God's promises and aid in accomplishing it. It is certainly "not by might, nor by power, but by his Spirit," but this is the promise side of the perseverance, not the totality of perseverance.

1 John 5:11–13—As might be expected, 1 John continues the same themes as the Gospel, especially the possession of eternal life (5:13) and abiding (2:24–25). At the same time, however, John stresses perseverance in sinlessness (3:6f.; 5:16f.) and in prayer (1:8–10). Of course, in the first instance, it is not freedom from individual acts of sin but rather the absence of persistent sinning which is commanded. Christ in 2:1 is called the "advocate" (*paraclete*) for those who do sin, and security is again seen to be the major concomitant of perseverance. Indeed, the two cannot be separated and are interdependent.

III. THE BOOK OF ACTS

Several passages in Acts seem to teach the doctrine of unconditional election and indicate to many that Luke had a predestinarian theology. Acts, like John, defines the basic message of Christ and the church as one of salvation. The basic events all relate to the soteriological message of the church, as the followers of Jesus fulfilled his commands and promises relating to mission.

26. Chafer, *Systematic Theology*, 3:332.
27. Gromacki, *Salvation is Forever*, 49–50.

In relating this, Luke in Acts is careful to show that all was accomplished under divine impetus and occurred as part of his redemptive plan. It is God who at each critical node intervenes directly to guide the church in its salvific purpose (cf. 1:8, 24f.; 5:19f.; 8:26f.; 9:3f.; 10:10f.; 13:2f.; 15:7f.; 16:9f., 25f.). So God is the prime mover in salvation for man, and this leads to those verses which seem to extend this to a predestinarian salvation:

11:18—This verse culminates the Cornelius episode (ch. 10) and Peter's report to the "apostles and brethren" (11: 1–17); they concluded, "Then to the Gentiles also God has granted repentance unto life." Here, God is the principal actor in redemption (cf. 5:31), but we must ask whether this is an unconditional choice on his part, and whether man's volition plays a part. The passage, of course, does not say, but there is some evidence that the latter is more probable. Cornelius was a "God-fearer" (10:2), a Gentile who worshipped God but had not taken the final step of circumcision.[28] As such he was a "devout man" and was open to God's call.

13:48—Here is the major election passage in Acts; Luke here says of the Gentiles in Antioch of Pisidia, "As many as were ordained to eternal life believed." Calvinist theologians[29] say the force of "ordained" here dare not be toned down; election must precede man's faith and form the basis for it. However, while we agree that the basic thrust is divine election,[30] this does not negate the presence of human volition, as seen in the context. The preceding passage, especially v. 46, notes the responsibility inherent in salvation. There, the unbelieving Jews were rejected on the basis of their personal decision: by their action they "judged themselves unworthy" in the presence of God. The best thrust for the perfect passive "have been ordained" is that combination of divine election and human volition which has already been noted in John, with stress on the former aspect here.

This is especially seen when one notes the passages on perseverance and the danger of apostasy in Acts. In 20:30 it says false teachers will arise who will seek "to draw away the disciples after them." This does not mean backsliding but apostasy, as seen in the term "draw away." The warning was real and involved heresy and apostasy. Also, we have examples of apostasy,

28. F. F. Bruce, *The Epistle of Paul to the Romans (Tyndale New Testament Commentaries)* (Grand Rapids: Eerdmans, 1963), 216, says, "it was such God-fearers who formed the nucleus of the Christian community in one city after another in the course of Paul's missionary activity."

29. Ibid., 283n; and Boettner, *Reformed Doctrine of Predestination*, 102.

30. It is interesting that two other scholars take opposite sides from their normal positions, with Marshall, *Kept by the Power of God,* 84, agreeing with Bruce on linguistic grounds, while James O. Buswell, *A Systematic Theology of the Christian Religion,* 2 vols. (Grand Rapids: Zondervan, 1962), 152–153, agrees with Alford that it should be translated "as many as were disposed to eternal life."

possibly Ananias and Sapphira[31] but probably Simon Magus. He "believed and was baptized" (8:13) but later tried to buy his way into a miraculous ministry. As a result Peter tells him he no longer has a part in the kingdom. Here again the key is the "word of grace" which edifies the believer (2:42; 4:33; 15:31f.) and the means is exhortation (11:23; 13:43; 14:22). Therefore the believer must persevere in order to inherit eternal life.

16:14; 18:10–27—These minor texts all relate to the above and are used to further state the election of the believer *via* efficacious grace. Steele and Thomas[32] declare, "Faith and repentance are divine gifts and are wrought in the soul through the regenerating work of the Holy Spirit." Acts 16:14 speaks of Lydia, saying, "The Lord opened her heart to give heed." Here, however, we must again note the context; she was a "worshipper of God" and had already been seeking the truth. Acts 18:10 says, "I have many people in this city" and 18:27 speaks of "those who through grace had believed." Once again, however, we must note that this speaks of divine election and grace but does not teach that these are final acts. Acts 18:10 speaks of future believers rather than current Christians (18:8), but this speaks of foreknowledge more than unconditional predestination.[33] The same is true of v. 27, for this does not teach irresistible grace but rather the basis of salvation in general, God's grace. There is no hint of a rigid application to a select few only. In conclusion, Luke in Acts stresses the divine activity behind salvation but does not identify this with a rigid predestinarian call.

IV. THE PAULINE WRITINGS

The theologian *par excellence* of the early church is Paul. While his epistles are personal correspondence rather than treatises, and while Paul never made any real attempt to systematize Christian faith and doctrine, he nevertheless epitomizes the implications of Jesus's teaching for the church. There has been much debate regarding the central thesis of Paul's system. Since the Reformation, most have believed that justification by faith provides the key. However, apart from Romans and Galatians this is not the core of his thinking, and more recent scholars have tended to follow Schweitzer and Deissman that the "in Christ" motif is at the center.

31. This is a doubtful parallel, because one cannot know whether they knew Christ beforehand and, more importantly, because their death most probably was physical rather than spiritual.

32. Steel & Thomas, *The Five Points of Calvinism*, 53.

33. Marshall, *Kept by the Power of God*, 85.

While this is one of the major Pauline themes, however, we might question whether it is broad enough to serve as the key to Paul's thought. The best answer is seen in the recent studies of Green and Ladd,[34] who have shown that eschatological salvation best summarizes Pauline theology. It is neither justification (past) nor "in Christ" (present) nor hope (future) but the inclusion of past, present, and future in the eschatological gift of salvation, the New Age in Christ.

Rom 3:9–12; 5:12; 6:20—These passages are bulwarks of the doctrine of total depravity, defined by Steele and Thomas thusly: "The reign of sin is universal; all men are under its power. . . Men left in their dead state are unable of themselves to repent, to believe the gospel, or to come to Christ. They have no power within themselves to change their natures or to prepare themselves for salvation."[35] Rom 3:9–12 states that "all" are "under the power of sin" and concludes "none is righteous, no, not one . . .There is none who seeks for God[36] . . . no one does good, not even one. . ." This passage teaches the universality of sin and the power of sin.[37] Rom 6:20 adds to this the fact that humanity has become "slaves of sin." Calvinists use this as a basis for their theory that man cannot ever choose to accept Christ; he will always choose sin. Only when God's elective love chooses to lift individual men out of their depraved condition can anyone be saved. Before we can discuss 3:9–12, we must place it in its context.

It concludes that important section on the universal guilt and condemnation of man (1:18–3:20) and sets the scene for Paul's discussion of the path to righteousness (3:21–5:21). In this section we find the best expression of Pauline anthropology, dealing with man's bondage to sin. Sin is deliberate rebellion and transgression against the commands of God (2:23f.) and is a falling short of God's standards (3:23); man's self righteous attitude, especially for the Jew, led him to break the true law and become more guilty (2:17f.), and resulted in God's judicial wrath (cf. "God gave them up" in 1:24f.).

---

34. Green, *Meaning of Salvation*, 152–153; Ladd, *Theology of the New Testament*, 373–375.

35. Steel & Thomas, *The Five Points of Calvinism*, 28–29.

36. C. Gordon Olson offers an interesting observation about 3:11b, saying the Greek *ekzēteo*, means "no one diligently seeks God" (G. Gordon Olson, *Beyond Calvinism and Arminianism*, [Cedar Knolls, N.J.: Global Gospel, 2002], 102).

37. John Murray, *The Epistle to the Romans, (The New International Commentary on the New Testament)*; 2 vols. (Grand Rapids: Eerdmans, 1965), 104, summarizes, "To state the thought of verse 11 both negatively and positively it is that as respects well-doing, there is not one, as respects evil-doing there is no exception."

The entire section deals with the pagans (1:18–32), the moral Jew (2:1–16), Jewish guilt (2:13—3:8) and concludes by bringing together both Jew and Gentile under one roof—universal guilt. Therefore we must conclude that the universality here deals with the quantity (all people) rather than quality (total sin) regarding depravity. There is no hint that depravity means man cannot accept Christ.[38] This is especially true when we remember that the Holy Spirit is convicting the world of sin (John 16:8), through his prevenient grace.

Chapter 8—This passage is used by Hodge exclusively to teach the doctrine of final perseverance and is indeed one of the important passages in determining Paul's view of salvation.[39] Chapter 8 in a very real sense forms the Pauline victory cry after the seeming defeatism of chapter 7 and deals with the new life of the Spirit. In an eschatological sense it deals with the life of the New Age which the Spirit produces in the life of the believer.

(1) *No condemnation, v. 1f.*—The principle of "no condemnation" is taken seriously by Calvinists as the irreversible negation of sin and guilt. The believer is given a twofold promise here—he is "in Christ" and he has "the Spirit of life." The result is "freedom from the law of sin and death." However, while we agree that there is security and promise here, we must ask whether Murray is correct when he calls the fact "complete and irreversible."[40] We must also agree with him that the passage refers to freedom from the power of sin as well as from the guilt of sin; however; this does not mean that the Christian life is guaranteed for him. Perseverance is also taught in this passage, and it is a necessity for the freedom described here. There is still the choice between a carnal and Spirit-filled mind-set (v. 6), and the believer must "walk not after the flesh but after the Spirit" (v. 4). While these are not conditions, they are valid possibilities and cannot be lightly dismissed. Calvinists love to point to v. 8 as an example of total depravity, "And those in the flesh cannot please God." But it is important to look at this in the context of the previous verses (5, 6), in which the phrase "the mind set on the flesh" is used three times (NASB). And in v. 7, "for it does not subject itself to the law of God, for it is not even able to do so." This is the natural orientation of

---

38. Here we must qualify ourselves. We do believe that man's depravity is such that he cannot come to faith-decision of his own volition. However, we also believe in the universal salvific will of God; the Spirit convicts "the world" (all men—John 16:8f.) and each man has the opportunity of yielding to the "drawing power" of Christ in the spirit. Therefore, we would basically agree with the doctrine of total depravity but stress that this does not lead to the doctrine of unconditional election and irresistible grace.

39. Charles Hodge, *Systematic Theology,* 3 vols. (Grand Rapids: Eerdmans, 1946 [originally New York: Scribner, Armstrong, 1871–1875]), 3:110–113.

40. Murray, *Epistle to the Romans,* 274. See also 275–282.

someone who willfully keeps his mind on the flesh. He cannot please God morally through the law. This also must be understood with the one thing a nonbeliever can do that pleases God: "there is rejoicing in the presence of the angels of God over one sinner who repents" (Luke 15:10).

(2) *The Principle of life, vv. 11–13*—Hodge argues that the life principle within the believer is evidence of his security. The Holy Spirit "quickens" or enlivens the believer and is himself the foundation of his security. However in vv. 11–13, this is seen to be conditional[41] upon the continual indwelling of the Spirit, and "mortification of the flesh." Both possibilities—death and life—are presented here, and the believer must choose which path to take— that of the flesh or that of the Spirit. While the victorious side is stressed here, the other side is seen as a definite danger.

(3) *Sons of God, vv. 14–17*—Sonship is a further base for security. Calvinists argue that God would not cast "sons" out of his "family." The "Abba" motif is the key to Jesus's prayer theology in connection with his sonship, and is well connected with the "adoption" theology here. "Abba" was never used in prayer by Jews because it transmitted an intimacy which was foreign to them.[42] Jesus, because of his unique relation to the Father, gave his followers a new relationship to him, and it could not be expressed better than here. Nevertheless, we note the same possibilities as in vv. 11–13, and the same need for perseverance. Verse 14 says "being led by the Spirit of God" is a prerequisite of sonship.

(4) *The purpose of God, vv. 26–30*—Here we see the juxtaposition of the Spirit's intercession (vv. 26–28) and the redemptive election by God (vv. 29–30). Both aspects are part of the Calvinist soteriology: Redemption is a gift of God and in no way an act of man. God will never fail to save those whom he has called.[43] The major question lies in the relationship between foreknowledge and election—which is prior? Murray would make election prior, saying, "The faith which God foresees is preconditioned by his decree to generate this faith in those he foresees as believing."[44] The term "foreknow," then, refers to God's elective love rather than to an actual fore-

---

41. While the particle in v. 11 is *ei*, assuming reality (perhaps equivalent to "since"), the present tense verbs of the passage and the use of in both sections of v. 13 point to an actual condition throughout the passage. We cannot be too rigid in our grammatical categories in the New Testament, since the classical distinctions were disappearing in first century Koine Greek. See also Frederic L. Godet. *The Epistle to the Romans*, A. A. Cusin, trans. (Grand Rapids: Zondervan. 1969 [originally New York: Funk & Wagnalls, 1883]), 307.

42. See the excellent discussion of this in Joachim Jeremias, *The Prayers of Jesus*, (Norwich, United Kingdom: SCM, 2012).

43. Hodge, *Systematic Theology*, 3.111.

44. Murray, *Epistle to the Romans*, 316–317.

knowledge of the believer's faith-decision. However, while we would agree that "foreknow" does contain in itself the idea of elective love,[45] we would not agree that the word itself indicates a predestinarian decree. We would state with Bruce that the two are simultaneous but separate aspects: "When God takes knowledge of people in this special way, He sets His choice upon them."[46]

There are two major approaches to the predestinarian sense of this paragraph by opponents of the Calvinist interpretation —corporate and individual. Shank believes that election is corporate and refers to the sovereign choice of the church as a whole, while individual members must come to personal decision and must persevere in the faith.[47] While this has a certain attraction, it is hardly the answer here. The phrase "conformed to the image of his Son" undoubtedly has a personal application and presupposes an individual thrust. Marshall provides a better answer; the passage itself discusses believers, and not unbelievers (cf. v. 28).[48] Therefore the election here is not unto salvation but unto conformity. We would add to this, however, that in every aspect foreknowledge and election are two aspects of divine predestination. God's sovereign choice always takes into consideration the free will of the individual.[49]

(5) *The love of God, vv. 31–39*—This passage is used by Calvinists to teach the doctrines of election (v. 33), limited atonement (vv. 32–34), and eternal security (whole passage). Calvin himself calls this "that magnificent exaltation of Paul, in defiance of life and death, of things present and future; which must necessarily have been founded in the gift of perseverance."[50] Regarding the doctrine of the atonement, Murray declares, "The succeeding context specifies just as distinctly those of whom the apostle is speaking— they are God's elect (v. 33), those on behalf of whom Christ makes interces-

---

45. Note the use of this term in 1 Pet. 1:2, where it is used as a synonym for election. The word "know" is used often for God's gracious love in the Old Testament—cf. Gen 18:19; Ex 33:12; Jer 1:5; Amos 3:3; Hos 13:5; and in the New Testament, 1 Cor 8:3; Gal 4:9.

46. Bruce, *Epistle of Paul to the Romans*, 177.

47. Shank, *Life in the Son*, 365–367.

48. Marshall, *Kept by the Power of God*, 93.

49. Ibid., 93. Marshall notes about Wesley's comment here that the passage never says the same number are called, justified, and glorified. It simply describes the salvation process. Nothing said removes the necessity for perseverance or makes faith a God—given commodity only for the elect.

50. John Calvin, *Institutes of the Christian Religion*, (Grand Rapids: Eerdmans, 1957), 3:xxiv, 10; G. C. Berkouwer, *Faith and Perseverance* tr. K. D. Knudson (Grand Rapids: Eerdmans, 1958), 9–10, speaks of the timelessness of the doctrine of final perseverance, founded on "the richness and abidingness of salvation."

sion (v. 34), those who can never be separated from the love of Christ (vv. 35, 39). The sustained identification of the persons in these terms shows that this passage offers no support to the notion of universal atonement."[51]

At the outset we must note the optimism of Paul which runs throughout this passage. Towards man he is pessimistic, but when he considers the Father and the Son his rapture knows no bounds. Man may fail, but God will never fail, and the love of Christ is not dependent on the vicissitudes of man. Here we might note the arguments of Arminius and Wesley.[52] This passage does not relate to perseverance but simply speaks of the believer's encouragement in the faith. Paul here states his confidence in God's part but elsewhere notes his own responsibility and danger (1 Cor 9:27). Outside pressures can't separate us from God's love, but inward apostasy can. It is God's love rather than his divine decree which is discussed here.

We might add that the context provides the solution. Again Paul is speaking to believers, and the "elect" must be interpreted in light of vv. 28–30 (see above).[53] It states the same truth as seen in John 10: 28–29, that no outward force can separate us from God. The emphasis is on this, but other contexts provide the basis for the further thought (not discussed here), "Can we ourselves fail to use this promise?" We might conclude by saying that even the apostate—apart from those who have committed the unpardonable sin(s) of Mark 3:28f. and parallels, Heb 6:4f., and 1 John 5:16b—is still loved and sought by God.[54]

1 Cor 2:14—This is a key verse in the Calvinist doctrine of total depravity. The "natural man," when confronted with "the things of God," can neither "receive" them nor "know" them; to him they merely seem "foolishness." Therefore, Hodge concludes, only when man's inward state is changed by the Holy Spirit can he begin to comprehend spiritual truth. "If our gospel is hid, it is hid to those who are lost."[55] However, this is to misunderstand

---

51. Murray, *Epistle to the Romans*, 325.

52. James Arminius, *The Works of James Arminius,* 3 vols. (Grand Rapids: Baker , 1956 [originally Auburn, N.Y.: Derby and Miller, 1853]), 3:314–315; John Wesley. *The Works of John Wesley,* 14 vols. (Grand Rapids: Zondervan, 1958–1959), 10:291.

53. This also provides the answer to Murray's thesis that limited atonement is taught here. "Us" does refer to the "elect," but these are believers, and the nonelect have no part in the discussion. This must be balanced by the other Pauline statements regarding the universal salvific will—Rom 5:18; 11:15; 1 Cor 15:22; 2 Cor 5:19; Col 1:20; 1 Tim 2:4, 6; 4:10—and the two aspects are found in Pauline theology in the same way as already noted in Johannine theology.

54. Shank, *Life in the Son,* 309–329. While he is wrong in saying the apostasy of Heb 6:4f. is redeemable (see the chapter on Hebrews in this symposium), he is correct regarding apostasy in general.

55. Charles Hodge, *An Exposition of the First Epistle to the Corinthians* (New York:

the Pauline doctrine of faith. He is not contrasting free will and sovereignty here but the natural man and the spiritual man. Man's depravity is such that left to himself he could find nothing about God. However, he is not left alone, but is given the Spirit to aid him. Ladd notes "the gnostic-sounding language that sets forth a very ungnostic theology."[56] He is referring to the context in this chapter of the Holy Spirit unveiling God's hidden wisdom (2:6–13) in the historical act of the cross (1:18, 2:2).[57] This can be understood only when the Spirit reveals it; but there is no hint here that the Spirit works only among the elite, i.e., the elect. Rather, his convicting work (John 16:8) is universal, but man must yield to it before they can "discern" spiritual truth.

Eph 1:3–12—This important passage relates both to unconditional election and final perseverance. Next to Romans 9—11, this is the most important passage for the Pauline doctrine of predestination. Here we are told that "before the foundation of the world" God "chose us in him," "destined us in love to be his sons," and "appointed [us] to live for the praise of his glory." Boettner uses this passage to refute the Arminian doctrine of foreknowledge, since this "makes faith and holiness to be the consequents, and not the antecedents, of election (Eph 1:4, John 15:16; Titus 3:5)."[58] The phrase "before the foundation of the world" is a Hebraism for "from eternity" and refers to God's eternal decree of redemption. That decree is eternal and immutable.[59] Yet there are striking similarities to Rom 8:29–30. In both passages Paul is speaking to believers, and the "we-you" terminology in both is paralleled by the election itself, which is not to eternal life but to "holy and blameless" lives (v. 4), to sonship (v. 5, note the parallel to "conformed to the image of his son," Rom 8:29), and to living "for the praise of his glory" (v.

Robert Carter & Brothers, 1860), 44.

56. Ladd, *Theology of the New Testament*, 490.

57. Olson notes: "Here Paul is speaking about the whole process of revelation and inspiration by which the Holy Spirit communicated even the 'deep things of God' through the apostles, which were ultimately written down in Scripture. It [the natural man] is in obvious contrast to the 'spiritual man' who appraises all these deep truths. Thus he was not speaking of the inability of the unregenerate to understand and believe the simple gospel message as proclaimed by the apostles. The fact is that we were all 'natural' men once, but we did come to understand the simple demands of the gospel" (Olson, *Beyond Calvinism and Arminianism*, 109–110).

58. Boettner, *Reformed Doctrine of Predestination*, 98. See also Chafer, *Systematic Theology*, 3:174: "men are not first holy and then elect; but they are first elect and that election is unto holiness."

59. Buswell, *Systematic Theology*, 2:145, says in this regard, "If God has unconditionally elected to save a people, and if He has provided atonement which makes their salvation certain, it follows by inevitable logic that those whom God has elected to eternal salvation will go on to eternal salvation."

12). While redemption and forgiveness are a central part of this passage (v. 7), the election itself looks at believers only and does not consider election out of unbelief, i.e., election here looks at the benefits of the salvation act, not at the act itself.[60]

A further point is noted by Dibelius, who sees a twofold contrast here: 1) between the part in accomplishing salvation and the human part in hearing and believing; and 2) between "we" or the church and "you" or the one-time pagan readers of Paul's epistle.[61] In both contrasts the benefits are seen on both sides. Election in this respect is not a guarantee given to the privileged few and does not relate to the faith-response as provided only by the overwhelming call of the Spirit. Rather, it refers to God's gracious providence and purpose for those whom he chooses and who respond to the gospel. It relates to privilege as well as status.

Eph 1:13–14; 4:30—Both these passages (see also 2 Cor 1:18–22) relate to the "seal" placed upon the believer by the Spirit. Calvin defines the "earnest" of v. 14 as a security or promise of the remainder "which, therefore, is not taken back, but kept till the residue is paid to complete the whole sum."[62] The Holy Spirit, then, is the "guarantee" of the believer's future inheritance. Strombeck notes three aspects to the seal here—sealed as to position (eternal salvation), as to ownership (purchased by his blood), as to future (eternal life).[63] Therefore, Calvinists argue, the seal of the Spirit does not rest on the continuance of man's faith; belief is the antecedent but not the grounds of the sealing.

The "seal" as such does indeed denote authentication, possession and protection, and the "earnest" refers to the first installment which guarantees full payment later (cf. 2 Cor 1:22; 5:5). There is a very real security in this passage. However, we must ask if this is an unconditional, final security. Personal responsibility parallels divine protection in 4:30, where the Christian is warned not to "grieve" the Spirit (cf. 1 Thess 4:8). Ladd relates this to Pauline eschatology, noting that "the presence of the Holy Spirit in the

---

60. Arminius, *Works*, 3:490, argues that in Ephesians 1 faith is presupposed as the basis of predestination (cf. John 1:12).

61. Martin Dibelius, *An die Kolosser, Epheser; an Philemon* (Tubingen, Germany: Mohr, 1953), 62f., as cited in Marshall, *Kept by the Power of God*, 106, concludes, "Nothing is said which would deny that certain people heard the Gospel and did not believe, and it is not suggested that such people did not believe because they were not predestined to believe. All that we are told is that God foreordains those who believe to become holy and to be His sons."

62. Calvin, *Commentaries on the Epistles of Paul to the Ephesians and Galatians* (Grand Rapids: Eerdmans, 1949), 209. See also Berkouwer, *Faith and Perseverance*, 212.

63. Strombeck, *Shall Never Perish*, 58f.

church is itself an eschatological event."[64] This is certainly true, for Pentecost in the early church was viewed as an eschatological event (note the Joel
prophecy) which became the presence of the New Age in the believer. Paul,
like the other writers we have noted, interpreted salvation in terms of the
tension between the "already" and the "not yet," and the present possession
of security is held in tension with the need for future perseverance. The "day
of redemption" is secured here, and God's protection is promised, but the
believer dare not assume he plays no part. The danger of apostasy is real,
and he dare not "grieve" the Spirit.[65]

Eph 2:1–3; 4:17–19—These two passages contrast the ignorant, rebellious course of the heathen to the enlightened walk of the true follower of
Christ. The pagans are "children of wrath" who are "darkened in their understanding" and "alienated from the life of God" "due to their hardness of
heart." They are "dead in their trespasses and sin." Many think that these
powerful passages, growing out of the death-to-life metaphor of 2:1, teach
the impossibility of human response; God must override man's propensity
to evil as he sovereignly chooses, thereby bringing the "dead" to "life" *via*
elective love. Yet we must ask if this is really what Paul is trying to say. He is
not denying man's faith response to the salvific call; it is in every way the response of individual volition to God's love and the Spirit's convicting work.
Being "dead" in sin means "man is separated from God, dead in relationship
to God."[66]

Eph 2:8, 9—Closely connected to this is the important passage which
provides the Pauline definition of the salvific act: "For by grace you have
been saved through faith; and this is not your own doing, it is the gift of
God— not because of works, lest any man should boast."

This has long been a major Calvinist proof text against the "error" of
Wesleyan-Arminianism. The latter, they say, teach a salvation by "works"
and thereby deny the "grace" of God in redemption. Hendricksen, for instance, believes that *touto* in v. 8 refers not to "grace" or to "saved" but to
"faith," saying that anything else would amount to needless repetition.[67] In

64. Ladd, *Theology of the New Testament*, 484.

65. "Grieving" the Spirit is probably taken from Isa 63:10, which speaks of Israel's
rebellion against God, who "turned to be their enemy" as a result. William Hendricksen, *Exposition of Ephesians* (Grand Rapids: Baker, 1967), 222, calls this the first step on
the downward path to resistance (Acts 7:51) and then to quenching the Spirit (1 Thess
5:19). We would go further and note this as a definite warning to a church which would
later foster apostates (i.e., the false teachers noted in the epistles to Timothy).

66. F. Leroy Forlines, *Classical Arminianism* (Nashville: Randall House, 2011), 23.

67. Hendricksen, *Exposition of Ephesians*, 121–123. He argues against Robertson
who relates it to grace, i.e., God's grace and man's faith; and against Grosheide (with
whom we agree), who says it relates to the whole phrase. In the latter sense, however,

this respect, then, the believer's faith does not come from within him but itself is an external gift from God. If faith decision were an act of human volition, it would become works and lead to self-boasting.

There is another approach to the passage, one which does greater justice to the context and to the neuter force of *touto*. That is to take the latter term as referring to the whole previous phrase rather than to any particular part within it. Salvation is the cover term which has two aspects—God's grace and man's faith. All come within the category of "gift." This is not to say that man's faith is not really man's but originates from the activity of the Spirit; rather, it is a volitional yielding to the activity of the Spirit within. The gift is not forced upon man but must be received on the part of man "by faith." It is not "works" because it is from God; man is the passive recipient because he yields to the Spirit in faith-decision.[68] So *touto* refers to salvation, which is by grace, through faith.

Phil 1:6; 2:13—Berkhof takes these two verses with John 6:37–40 as illustrating the "covenant of redemption" which finalizes the gift of salvation; it is both final and eternal.[69] Phil 1:6 relates the apostle's confidence that God would safeguard his "good work" among them and "bring it to completion at the day of Jesus Christ," and 2:13 says God works within his follower "both to will and to work for his good pleasure." The first verse also relates to 1 Cor 1:7–9, which says God will "sustain you to the very end." In both cases, Paul is speaking to the church as a whole in his customary "thanksgiving" section, and the context favors a corporate rather than individual interpretation, i.e., the church will be sustained. But individuals will be protected only so long as they remain in the church. However, we would agree that this dare not be taken too far (as, for instance, Shank tends to do), as an answer to the predestination problem.

Paul does intend that the promise extend to the individual. He will be kept by God with a view to the final salvation,[70] but this does not obviate the

---

Hendricksen's arguments are directed more against the application to "saved."

68. The rigid external interpretation of many Calvinists is exactly the reason many modern scholars have objected to the doctrine of "substitutionary" atonement (e.g., Vincent Taylor, *The Atonement in New Testament Teaching* [London: Epworth, 1963], 60, as noted in Ladd, *Theology of the New Testament*, 426–427), namely, because they make it entirely outside of and apart from man's decision so that man can do nothing. However, there is both an objective (Christ's substitution) and subjective (man's response) side to salvation.

69. Louis Berkhof, *Systematic Theology* (Grand Rapids: Eerdmans, 1956), 547.

70. Again we see the concept of eschatological salvation. Paul placed his greatest emphasis on the present aspects of salvation, i.e., justification and sanctification. However, the future aspect was still noted, and while Paul was confident he nevertheless stressed the necessity for perseverance (see below).

need for perseverance. That necessity is noticeable in 2:12, 13. The promise of v. 13 is related to the command of v. 12, that each person must "work out [his] own salvation with fear and trembling." Once again we have that combination of corporate and individual thrust, with probably a stronger hint of individual application due to the presence of "your own salvation" here.[71] Verse 13, then, is not a promise that the perseverance of v. 12 will be assured. Phil 2:16 states the possibility of failure; they could negate his activity among them by failing to "hold fast the word of life."

In conclusion, Paul stresses security and election in his writings, but this never removes human responsibility and the place of perseverance in one's life. Election is related to those who have believed and promises God's strength in bringing them to a life of holiness and to final salvation. At the same time Paul realizes the personal responsibility involved in perseverance. While the Christian is promised God's power, he still must continue to avail himself of that strength. Paul alludes to the danger of apostasy in Rom 8:12–14; 1 Cor 9:27; 15:1–2; Col 1:21–23; 1 Tim 1:18–20; 4:1, 16 (on these passages, see the short discussion at the close of the article on "Soteriology in Hebrews"). This was a very real danger, and the only antidote was perseverance; while the Christian is promised God's help and protection, he is not given a guarantee.

V. I PETER

The stress in this epistle is upon joy and hope in the midst of persecution. As such, it gives good coverage to both aspects of salvation, i.e., promise and responsibility. The opening tone catches this spirit, speaking of the readers as "sojourners and aliens" who are "elect . . . according to the foreknowledge of God" (1:1–2). Their "living hope" consists of an "inheritance" which is "kept in heaven" for them, and they are "guarded" by God "unto salvation" (1:3–5). The stone imagery (2:4–10) especially emphasizes their chosen position, likening them to the "elect cornerstone," Jesus, and calling them a "chosen race." The Christian life in this epistle is eschatological, lived in present stress but looking forward to the fulfillment of the hope at the manifestation of Christ in glory; to that end God is strengthening and helping them (1:5–9; 2:12; 4:13.17f.; 5:10).

---

71. Marshall, *Kept by the Power of God*, 113, gives a cogent argument (*contra* Ralph P. Martin, *The Epistle of Paul to the Philippians (Tyndale New Testament Commentaries)* [Grand Rapids: Eerdmans, 1959], 110–111) for an individual rather than corporate interpretation here. While salvation can mean corporate "health" (Acts 27:34), it is always used in Paul in a spiritual sense.

At the same time Peter is aware of the dangers to faith which persecution brings. It is interesting that just as in Hebrews "salvation" in Peter is eschatological, looking forward more to the final reward than the present experience (1:4, 5, 13; cf. 4:13f.; 5:1, 40), although the present aspect is seen proleptically (1:9–10) on the basis of Jesus's bringing in "the end of times" (1:20). For this reason the readers were called upon to persevere in their faith-belief (1:5, "through faith") and to strengthen their hope *via* sober thinking (1:13). They must stop living according to sinful man's standards (2:1, 11f.; 3:11; 4:1) and start seeking a pure and holy life (1:15; 2:12, 21; 4:2). A special word in Peter is "do good," found in his epistle four times as opposed to none in Paul (cf. 2:15, 20; 3:6, 17); this aspect of the Christian life was not just "good works" but persistence in righteous conduct, following Christ's example (2:21) in the face of pagan persecution (3:13f.) and involved submission to all aspects of authority, whether the state, the slave-master relationship, or the home. Satan is active and seeks to lead believers astray (5:8), and so the follower of Christ must persist in his walk (5:6f.) and be steadfast in God's grace (5:12c). As in Paul we note the beautiful blend of optimism and exhortation. Election is not a guarantee but rather an encouraging promise.

CONCLUSION

It is the conclusion here that the New Testament writers each stress differing nuances of the salvation-truth. John and Paul stress the sovereignty side while Hebrews stresses the aspect of responsibility. Yet all are in agreement that there is both sovereignty and responsibility, both security and perseverance. The time of eschatological salvation had begun, and the church was indeed the chosen people of God. Yet at the same time this was a proleptic gift, looking forward to the final salvation which would be secured at the eschaton. There was security in the sovereign bestowal of eternal life in the present and yet responsibility in the human need for perseverance with regard to the future. With this in mind we will attempt a reinterpretation of the fine points at the Synod of Dort.

(1) Man is totally depraved, i.e., he can do no good in himself and cannot choose Christ over sin. However, this does not mean he has no volition, for the Spirit convicts all men equally and enables them to come to faith-decision, i.e., to the point of yielding to the Spirit's convicting power.

(2) Believers are elect or predestined to a life of holiness and conformity to the Son. This salvific choice is concomitant with foreknowledge and

does not amount to an ineffable call to a chosen few but rather is the accompanying force with man's faith-decision.

(3) The atonement is universal, i.e., for all men, and is limited only by man's failure to respond.

(4) The call of God's grace is not irresistible and limited to the elect: rather the "drawing" power of God is universally applied but effective only for those who accept it by faith. God's grace and man's faith are separate aspects of the same salvific act.

(5) Perseverance is a necessity rather than a guaranteed, final promise. It relates to man's need rather than God's protection. Security is the other side of that need, for God does promise his protecting power. However, the believer must avail himself of that strength, lest he slip away and apostatize from the faith.

12

God's Promise and Universal History
The Theology of Romans 9

James D. Strauss and John D. Wagner

2 Cor 1:20—All promises are yes in Christ.

2 Pet 1:4—He has granted to us his precious and very great promises.

Ours is an age that would have sent the Greeks to their oracles. Cultural fragmentation in the form of paralyzing pluralistic pragmatism causes many in the twenty-first century to despair of God's presence in any dimension of reality except "the depth of being" and this only begrudgingly, if at all. Here he is privately locked out of the physical, biological, social, and historical processes of the universe. God's transcendence over the universe has been seriously challenged since the seventeenth century astronomical revolution.[1] This challenge to God's providential guidance of the universe was later intensified by the Hegelian dialectical view of all reality which claimed to answer the question: What is the total purpose of the world? This is especially relevant at this juncture in human history, when postmodernism and no absolute truths are the order of the day.

1. A. Rupert Hall, *From Galileo to Newton* (New York: Harper & Row, 1963); Alexandre Koyre, *The Astronomical Revolution* (Ithaca, N.Y.: Cornell University Press, 1974).

The first time the gospel according to Romans was heard, the world
was in a cauldron of misery. Life was intolerable and death unbearable, men
turned to demons, astral deities, Zeus, fate (contra grace and freedom),
Caesar (god manifest), Apollo, stoicism, gnostics, hermeticists, aesthetism,
neoplatonism (mysticism). (Seneca's note of despair-"Where will you find
him whom we have been seeking so many ages?") Venerable systems col-
lapsed; customs and conventions were caught in a flood of change. It was
a bewildering new age, before the rising of the "Son" with healing in his
wings. Men were seeking deliverance from the Republican wars and 191
civil wars, devastating earthquakes, frequent famines, gradual extermina-
tion of the middle class, universal misery, atrocious tax systems, political
crises, barbarian invasions, world weariness and pessimism.

The then the glory of God appeared in the night of the mind, the night of
morals and the night of Greco-Roman culture (Rom 1:18f.). God appeared
in the night to take away man's "darkness at noon." This light prevailed for
a millennium and a half, then crises severed Europe's nerve. This third
great failure of nerve within Western Christian civilization set the stage
for a secular revolution, Instead, God's Word created the greatest spiritual
revolution since the day of Pentecost. Europe was saved from a moral and
cultural plague by the power of the gospel according to Romans. Now that
we have plummeted into the twenty-first century, the voice of God has been
stilled in many areas of the West, at least, by the voices of prevalent secular-
ists and of post-modern futurologists who are busy planning our future by
choosing "the best of all possible worlds" out of countless possibilities. From
Parmenides to Moltmann and beyond, the watchword is: We shall choose
a world out of the infinite number of ontological possibilities; then we shall
rise up and build it. This attitude would be more than difficult to harmonize
with the theology of universal history in Romans, under the sovereign control of the creator-redeemer of the fallen universe.

Historically, the theology of sin in Romans 5 from the Protestant perspective often suggested a view of sin which made any conditional element
in the receiving of the saving grace of God impossible. Though this is not
our concern in this essay, our theological judgment concerning the nature
of sin and whether or not the saving grace of God has any contingency, we
believe the Scriptures suggest, in both Old and New Testaments and especially in Romans 9, 10, and 11, that men are responsible for their sinful
violations of the will of God. We also believe that it pleased him to make
faith and obedience contingencies of his saving grace.[2]

2. Mauritius Flick, *De gratia Christi* (Rome: Gregorian, 1962); Juan Alfaro, *Fides spes
caritas: adnotationes in tractatum de virtutibus theologicis* (Rome: Pontificia Universitas
Gregoriana, 1964); Paul Marston and Roger Forster, *God's Strategy in Human History*

In order better to hear God's word from Romans 9, we propose a brief sketch of three "contexts" in which we find this profound chapter: (1) God's Total Eschatological Promise; (2) The Obedience of Faith: Missionary Framework of Romans; (3) The Cosmic Purpose of God in Romans 9—11; then from these three perspectives a study of the theological claims of Romans 9. Our concern is—What does Romans 9 say, not whether it fits some preconceived theological notions about the nature of sin, faith, grace, God's sovereignty, etc. In this way, we might reduce the dangerous possibilities entailed in isolating any verse or pericope of Scripture from its larger context.[3]

(Eugene, Ore.: Wipf and Stock, 2000); Henri Rondet, *The Grace of Christ* (Westminster, Md.: Newman , 1967); Samuel J. Mikolaski, *The Grace of God* (Grand Rapids: Eerdmans, 1966); James Moffatt, *Grace in the New Testament* (New York: R. Long and R. R. Smith Inc., 1932); and Robert Shank, *Life in the Son* (Minneapolis: Bethany House, 1989). *Old Testament Vocabulary for Sin:* Early vocabulary-*hattah,* miss the mark (Judges 26:16); *awon,* iniquity, crookedness (Gen 4:13; 15:16); *ra,* evil (earliest root) (Gen 2:9). Physical calamity or violent breaking of God's orders; Patriarchial Period: two new words—*resha,* wickedness, (Gen 18:23, root, loose, ill-regulated); *pesha,* transgression (Gen 50: 17, root rebel), 1 Kings 12:19, deliberate and premeditated-Job 34:37 speaks of adding *pesha* to *hattah.* Moses' Period-two new terms: *ma-al,* trespass (Lev 5:15; Num. 5:12), marital faithlessness, root, treachery, or faithlessness to covenant (1 Chron 9:1); and *awel* (or *awal),* perversity (Lev 19:15) root, to deviate, man's deviation from right course. Moses-David. *Awen,* wickedness, root, to be tried. *New Testament Vocabulary for Sin:* Sin in the New Testament is regarded as missing of the mark or aim *(hamartia* or *hamartema);* the overpassing or transgressing of a line *(parabasis*); the inattentiveness or disobedience to a voice *(parakoe);* the falling alongside where one should have stood upright *(paraptoma);* the doing through ignorance of something wrong which one should have known about *(agnoema);* the coming short of one's duty *(hettema);* and the non-observance of a law *(anomia); (adikia),* unrighteousness.

3. For theological structure of Romans see: Jules Cambier, *L' JEvangile de Dieu Selon l'Epitre aux Romains. L'Evangile de la Justice et de La Grace, (*Bruges: Desclée De Brouwer, 1967); Ulrich Luz, *Das eschichtsverstandnis des Paulus (*München: C. Kaiser, 1968); P. Eduard Pfaff, *Die Bekehrung des H. Paulus in des Exegeses des 20 Jahrhunderts* (Rome: Pontificae Universitatis Gregorianae, 1942); Hans Werner Bartsch, "Die Historische Situation des Römerbriefes," *Communio Viatorum,* 8 (Winter 1965); Xavier Leon-Dufour. "Juif et Gentil dans l'Epitre aux Romains," *Studiorum Paulinorum Congressus* (Rome: Pontificio Istituto Biblico, 1969), 309–315; Albert Descamps, "La structure de Rom 1—11," in Studiorum Paulinorum Congressus (Rome: Pontificio Istituto Biblico, 1963); *Analecta Biblica* 17 (Rome: 1963); Andre Feuillet, "Le plan salvifique de Dieu d'apres l'epitre aux Romains. Essai sur la structure litteraire de l'epitre et sa signification Theologique," *Revue Biblique* 57 (Jerusalem, 1950); Stanislas Lyonnet, "Note sur Ie plan de l'epitre aux Romains," *Recherches de Science Religieuse* (Paris: 1951–1952). Jacque Dupont, "Le probleme de la structure litteraire de l'epitre aux Romains," *Revue Biblique* 62 (Jerusalem, 1955); Hermann Strack and Paul Billerbeck, *Kommentar zum Neuen Testament aus Talmud und Midrasch* (München: C.H. Beck, 1926), 3:258–294; For Paul's hermeneutical use of the Old Testament in Romans, especially Chapter 9, see Joseph Bonsirven, *Exegese Rabbinique et exegese Paulinienne* (Paris: Institut Catholique de Paris, 1939), 324—"His typological method is what distinguishes him most deeply from the preachers of the synagogue. His Christian faith alone revealed to him the

As we examine these three contexts and Paul's argument, especially in Romans 9, we will test three operating assumptions: (1) The creator-redeemer is sovereign and has a plan for humanity through the Son; (2) man, even in a fallen state, has a range of freedom, thus responsibility; and (3) no man can be saved apart from God's grace, conditioned on man's obedient faithfulness to God's will as revealed in Christ and the Scriptures.

I. GOD'S ESCHATOLOGICAL PROMISE

God created and ordered the universe; then man rebelled against God's order and the disorganizing power of sin required the intervention of the creator-redeemer, the Lord of nature-history. The first glimmer of God's glory appears in Gen 3:15, in which God says to the serpent, "And I will put enmity between you and the woman, And between your seed and her seed; He shall bruise you on the head, And you shall bruise him on the heel." Here, with the *protoevangelium*, we are given both the positive and negative dimensions of God's promise. The promise next comes to Abraham (Gen 12:1ff.). In particular, we read, "In your seed, all the nations of the earth shall be blessed" (Gen 22:18, NKJV).

The seed is promised to Abraham, Sarah, Isaac, and Jacob (Gen 13:14ff.; 15; 17:6–7; 26:3–4; 28:3–4; 35:11–12; 48:3–4). The promise is later renewed to Israel and David (Israel—Exod 6:7; Deut 29: 12–13; House of David— 2 Sam 7:1; 1 Chron 22:9). The promise of David parallels that to the patriarchs and Israel of the Exodus. In God's great mercy he extends the promise through the prophets and Psalms (Ps 89; Isa 55: 1–3; Zech 14:16–21) to all who believe in Yahweh's purpose. What or who is the "seed"? Gal 3:16 answers this question: "Now the promises were spoken to Abraham and to his seed. He does not say, 'And to seeds,' as referring to many, but rather to one, 'and to your seed' that is, Christ."

Then ultimately, the promised Messiah comes as a light to the nations. He is the kingdom bearer—the bearer of "the last days" and calls all to repentance—Jew and Gentile alike.

---

whole profound significance of the O.T. and its symbolic meaning."; Barnabus Lindars, *New Testament Apologetics* (Philadelphia: Westminster, 1961), 238ff; E. Earle Ellis, *Paul's Use of the Old Testament* (Grand Rapids: Eerdmans, 1957), esp. 114ff.

II. THE OBEDIENCE OF FAITH

The concept of Israel,[4] as a people of God made up of true believers, was fundamental to Jewish proselytism. The Hebrew word for a foreigner who had been accepted in Israel was *(gēr)—Abraham* was called a *gēr*. This phenomena must be understood before a clear evaluation of Paul's theology of Israel in Romans and Galatians can be made.[5]

It is of inestimable value to keep in mind that Romans is Paul's declaration of the nature of the gospel and he is its bearer. Paul is an evangelist establishing the "body of Christ," primarily beyond the context of his ancient heritage. He is on the way to Jerusalem, then to Spain. He has been called ". . . to bring about the obedience of faith among all the Gentiles, for His name's sake" (Rom 1:5). After showing us the glory of God through our need for redemption and its availability in Christ, he then reveals his broken heart over his disobedient kinsmen (Romans 9—11).

III. COSMIC PURPOSE OF GOD: ROMANS 9—11

The fundamental problem about which Paul bears both the heartbeat of God's cosmic purpose and his own broken heart results from the unbelief of his brothers according to the flesh. Next, he defends God's purpose in the course of human history (9:6–18). Israel's unbelief is not proof that God's word of promise has failed. God's faithfulness, first, is to the patriarchs whom he elected, as a lineage to the Messiah (9:6–13). God's choice of Moses and Pharaoh is proof of his justice. God's justice is personal and not necessarily legal. As Paul continues his close argumentation, he responds to an objector to God's ways with man (9:19–24). The objector misunderstands the entire nature of God's sovereign power; God does not treat man merely as an object to be manipulated for his ultimate purpose. Paul magnificently makes this point by presenting God's choice of the nation as an act of grace which does not preclude a remnant in Israel (9:25–29). Throughout his defense of

---

4. Yves Congar, *The Mystery of the Temple* (Westminster, Md: Newman, 1962); Walter Gutbrad, "Israel," Gerhard Kittel and Gerhard Friedrich, eds., *Theological Dictionary of the New Testament* (Grand Rapids: Eerdmans, 1977) 3:356–391; Peter Richardson, *Israel in the Apostolic Church* (Cambridge: Cambridge University Press, 1969).

5. See the following works on proselytism: Frederick Milton Derwacter, *Preparing the Way for Paul: The Proselyte Movement in Later Judaism* (New York: MacMillan, 1930); Bernard J. Bamberger, *Proselytism in the Talmudic Period* (Cincinnati: Hebrew Union College Press, 1939); Peter Dalbert, *Die Theologie der hellenistisch-jüdischen Missionsliteratur unter Ausschluss von Philo und Josephus* (Hamburg-Volksdorf: H. Reich, 1954)

God's sovereign grace, freedom, and mercy, Paul is heartbroken because of Israel's unbelief (9:2–3, 30–33; 10:1–2).

Israel's unbelief is not grounded in genuine knowledge of God's purpose (10:2–3). Surely Israel has heard that faith comes by hearing (10:14–18). But the historic tragedy is now before us. Israel did not accept the ultimate promise of God, Jesus Christ (10:19–21). Does this present rejection frustrate the effectiveness of God's promises? God's apostle-prophet now declares that Israel's disobedience is partial (11:2–10) and not permanent and is for the everlasting benefits of the Gentiles (11:11–24). The ultimate solution for Israel's present unbelief is now affirmed to lie in our coming to understand the mystery of God's gracious mercy, and his creative and saving word that will work good out of Israel's present disobedience (11:25–32). What more can Paul now do as he stands in awe before his sovereign Lord than conclude these theological claims with a praise to the ever-healing help of God's wisdom? (11:33–36).[6]

IV. GOD'S UNIVERSAL PURPOSE AND ISRAEL'S UNBELIEF

Paul is deeply involved in Israel's present unbelief (vv. 1–5). His feelings and conscience *(sunedesis,* literally to see together where integration or wholeness is attained)[7] are vividly "aware before God" of the scandalous disobedience of the nation of Israel, even within the historically visible "light of the world." Yet, he stands in God's presence as a believing seed of Abraham under excruciating agony for his people, like Moses (Exod 32:32). If Paul believed that God's arbitrariness or "secret will" sovereignly chooses some to life and others to condemnation, his emotional state here would be quite baffling, even as their biologico-historico kinsman.[8]

In resolving this crisis of faith, Paul will seek to penetrate the mystery of God's saving activity as creator-redeemer of the universe. Neither

---

6. Andre Feuillet, *Le Christ, Sagesse de Dieu d'apres les Epitres Pauliniennes* (Paris: J. Gabalda, 1966).

7. Christian Maurer, "Suneidesis," Kittel and Friedrich, *Theological Dictionary of the New Testament,* 7: 898–919, esp. 914ff; Jacques Dupont, "Syneidesis. Aux origines de la notion Chretienne de conscience Morale," *Studia Hellenistica,* 5, (Leuven, Belgium: 1948), 119–153; C. A. Pierce, *Conscience in the New Testament* (Naperville, Ill.: Alec R. Allenson, 1955).

8. A second example of this is Rom 10:1, in which Paul says, "Brethren, my heart's desire and prayer to God for Israel is that they may be saved." If Romans 9 is about God's sovereign election of only certain Jews from eternity past, why would Paul pray such a contrary request for the larger Israel?

problem nor the solution is given providential perspective. Rather, we are brought face to face with the purpose and promise of our sovereign Lord who is working out his will within the space/time categories of human history during the biblical era, and universal human history.[9]

How can Israel's historic defection be harmonized with the gift of God's gracious election? How can Israel disregard all her privileges which include "sonship," God's presence (Hebrew *kobad; doxa*—LXX and New Testament), the covenants, and the word of God given to Abraham, Moses, and David, which spells out the will of God for the fallen creation, Israel and nations? All of Israel's history is set out for microscopic observation by Paul in 9:5, ". . .whose are the fathers, and *from whom* is the Christ according to the flesh, who is over all, God blessed forever, Amen."

V. THE PROMISE: NEITHER FRUSTRATED NOR FAILED

Paul's doxology (v. 5) is his firm basis for the following theological consideration of the dialectical tension between fulfillment/nonfulfillment of the promise of God. First, Paul emphatically denies that God's Word has failed or that his gracious manifestation of justice can be impugned. Paul next reasons from historic illustrations of how God has worked in Israel's past to bring to fruition his efficacious promise. No man can lay claim to the promise on his own. God's promise becomes visible in history where his justice is observable in the lives of his obedient children (Rom 3:21–25). God's purpose is salvific. His election is based beyond human standards of moral achievement (vv. 9–13), and the Exodus deliverance (vv. 14–18). Human responsibility for the covenant relation with God is clearly revealed throughout Israel's history (note the basis of denial in v. 21). In Paul's overall perspective, God's "call" is ordered to his final glory. (Compare God's presence in the tabernacle, temple, and God's departure from the temple because of Israel's unbelief. Compare Ezek 48:35, "Yahweh shall be there," and Revelation 21). Paul's perspective is from God's acts in salvation history, not from all eternity "prior" to the creation of heaven and earth. In man's *de facto* condition, he cannot become righteous; only God's righteousness graciously extended through Christ can reconcile man to God.

---

9. Henrik Ljungman, *Pistis. A Study of Its Presuppositions and Its Meaning in Pauline Use* (Lund, Sweden: C.W.K. Gleerup, 1964); Ulrich Luz, *Das Geschichtsverstandnis des Paulus,* (Munich: Christian Kaider Verlag, 1968); Herbert Butterfield, *Christianity and History* (London: Fontana, 1957); Arend Theodoor van Leeuwen, *Christianity in World History* (New York: Charles Scribner's Sons, 1964).

Paul's consideration of Jacob, Esau, Moses, and Pharaoh is not occupied with their ultimate personal salvation, but rather with their role in the historic working out of the promised blessing. Paul is only concerned with the details in each person's life which radically effect the historic fulfillment of the salvific promise of God. Paul's major emphasis in Romans 9 is the understanding of God's word and justice as achieved through men but neither have been realized because of men's actions. The true people of God, in a salvation context, are not as such biologico-historico Israel, but rather are those who believe the promise of God and that he will ultimately fulfill what he has promised. Paul next explains the relationship of God's sovereign promise, justice and mercy by examining a series of events centering around persons involved in vital periods of Israel's history.

VI. GOD'S ULTIMATE CONCERN

Paul sets forth the doctrine of the remnant[10] (v. 6), i.e. the Israel of faith, which obviates the charge that the promise of God has failed. ". . .it is not as though the Word of God has failed" *(ekpeptoken*—perf. tense, ind. voice— not permanently failed). For Israel[11]—why hasn't the word permanently

10. See Donald M. Warne, "The Origin, Development and Significance of the Remnant in the Old Testament" (PhD Dissertation: University of Edinburgh, 1958); Gerhard F. Hasel, *The Remnant* (Berrien Springs, Mich.: Andrews University Press, 1972), 216–403; Reiji Hoshizaki, "Isaiah's Concept of the Remnant" (MTh Thesis, Southern Baptist Theological Seminary, 1955); Ben F. Meyer, "Jesus and the Remnant of Israel," *Journal of Biblical Literature,* 84 (1965), 123–130; Valentin Weber, *Kritische Geschichte Der Exegese Des 9 Kapitels, Resp. Der Verse* 14–23, *Des Romerbriefes Bis Auf Chrysostomus und Augustinus Einschliesslich,* (Wurzburg: Becker's Universitats Buchdruckerei, 1889); Wilhelm Visches, "Das Geheimnis Israels, Eine Erklaruug der Kapitel 9–11 des Romerbriefs," *Judaica,* (1950), 6: 81–132.

11. Our brief exposition of Romans 9 precludes a technical encounter with a major alternative interpretation to the one presented in this essay, but see Hilton C. Oswald, ed., *Luther's Works,* (St. Louis: Concordia, 1972), 25: 371–403; David W. Torrance and Thomas. F. Torrance, eds., *The Epistles of Paul the Apostle to the Romans and to the Thessalonians.* (Grand Rapids: Eerdmans, 1960), 190–261; and John Murray, *The Epistle to the Romans* (London: Marshall, Morgan and Scott, 1970). (Two volumes in one—part 2 of new edition, 1–103.) As is widely known, the central problem with respect to the theological content of Romans 9—11, etc., is how are we to relate the sovereign power of our Creator-Redeemer God and a range of human freedom even in view of the Fall. To the grassroots reader it seems an insurmountable problem to intelligently relate the determining power of God and the possibility of free responsible human decision. The real issue is not is Calvinism logically coherent as a theological system, but is it biblical? In the milieu of the Old and New Testament world deterministic world views were set forth. Some examples of such systems are: (1) Democratian physics, that is, classical Greek physics. (2) Several species of Gnosticism. (3) The Dead Sea Scrolls,

failed? Because in the first place, "For they are not all Israel [i.e. the Israel of faith] who are descended from Israel [i.e. Jacob]" (verse *6-ou gar pantes hoi ex Israel, houtoi* Israel). This means there is national Israel and the Israel of faith within it.

Paul then goes back multiple generations to explain the start of God's chosen genealogical lineage leading to ethnic/national Israel: "Nor are they all children because (causal *hoti)* they are Abraham's descendants, but (contrastive *all)* through Isaac your descendants will be named" *(en Isaak klethesetai*—fut. ind., passive—*soi sperma),* v. 7. Paul here declares that not all of Abraham's descendents are called. Abraham in fact had eight children through Sarah, Hagar and Keturah, but only those descending from Isaac were the chosen lineage.[12] This election was a sovereign choice of God. The

---

especially the *Thanksgiving Hodayot* (see 1QH, 1Q35 and 4Q427–432). Rabbi Akiba states, "Everything is foreseen, but freedom is still left." In the traditions of Judaism, the Pharisees defended human liberty, but in a context in which the idea of predestination of everything, both good and bad, for individuals and nations alike was maintained. The Essenes maintained fatalism, and the Sadducees completely rejected fatalism. (4) *The Koran* teaches a strict predestination and man's possibility of free decision. In all classical forms of astrology we encounter complete determinism. This is also true in the modern forms. (5) We encounter the same deterministic perspective in much contemporary physical theory, psychological theory (Skinner), bio-chemical determinism, especially as a result of the work of Greek and Monad on the gene code; in social theory respecting environmental determinism. Skinner calls us to beyond freedom and dignity, but in this instance is somehow freed from the determining factors of the gene code and the environment, in order to direct us toward the brave new world.

For sources that examine from a non-Calvinist perspective the issues and texts used to defend the five points of Calvinism, see Samuel Fisk, *Election & Predestination* (Eugene, Ore.: Wipf and Stock, 1997), and Robert Picirilli, *Grace Faith Free Will* (Nashville: Randall House, 2002) For more on election, see Karl Barth, *Church Dogmatics* (Edinburgh: T. T. Clark, 1957), II.2.3–506, "The Election of God"; John Calvin, *Calvin's Calvinism: Treatises on the Eternal Predestination of God & the Secret Providence of God* (Grand Rapids: Reformed Free, n.d.); Erich Dinkler, "Pradestination bei Paulus-Exegetische Bemer—Kungen zum Romerbrief " *Signum Crucis Aufsatzezum Neuen Testament Undzur Christlichen Archgologie* (Tubingen: J.C.B. Mohr, 1957); J. I. Packer, *Evangelism and Sovereignty of God,*(Downers Grove, Ill.: InterVarsity, 1961). Concerning the five points of Calvinism, see John Calvin, *Institutes of the Christian Religion* (Peabody, Mass.: Hendrickson, 2007); The Westminster Confession; B. B. Warfield, *Predestination in the Reformed Confessions* (Philadelphia: MacCalla, 1901). The five points refer only to the fact that there were five Arminian points for the Synod of Dort to "answer," with: (A) Total Depravity, (B) Unconditional Election (Augustine's *DeLibro Arbitrio),* (C) Limited Atonement (also called Definite or Particular Atonement), (D) Efficacious Call or Irresistible Grace, and (E) Perseverance of the Saints.

12. Calvinists would claim that the choice of Isaac over Ishmael would mean Isaac was chosen by God for salvation and Ishmael was not. However, we should note that in Gen 16: 20, God says about Ishmael, "I will surely bless him. . ." In Gen 21:17–19, God saved the lives of Hagar and Ishmael in the desert. God tells Hagar "I will make him (Ishmael) into a great nation" (v. 18) and we read "God was with the boy as he grew

ultimate purpose of this free choice of God was that "all the nations of the earth shall be blessed" because of God's promise to Abraham (Gen 12:1ff.). The mere fact of being a child in the historic family of Abraham does not make one a child of the promise *(alla ta tekna tes epangelias logizetai EIS sperma)*—here Paul uses *logizetai,* meaning "considered to be, counted on, looked upon as," the chosen lineage (v.8).[13]

The emphatic word in this verse is "promise" *(epangelias),* v. 9. God's purpose becomes more visible in this promise to Sarah (Gen 18:10–4). Only God could enable a woman of Sarah's advanced age to have the son of promise. God alone could know that it would be a son, the very son which would be received back as from the dead (Heb 11:17–19). Abraham's response to Isaac on Mt. Moriah reveals the sovereign activity of God in history. Abraham answers Isaac, "Yahweh will provide himself"; the Hebrew text contains a reflexive form. The Hebrew grammar entails the great sacrificial activity of Yahweh. Yahweh shall provide himself—Jesus Christ—on the cross. Finally, the purpose of the blessing of the nations will be accomplished.

Paul's examples of Jacob and Esau enables him to illustrate that their moral statures as well as their biological potential are not the determining factors in God's choice of the younger over the older as the instrument for further realizing this promised blessing. Also, the example completely inverts the cultural behavioral pattern of the Near East, i.e. that the younger always serves the older. Paul quotes from Mal 1:2–3, which is a discussion of the prospective nations—not the individuals, Jacob and Esau. The context from which Paul draws his pointed example states: "The oracle of the word of the Lord to Israel through Malachi. 'I have loved you,' says the Lord. But you say, 'How have you loved us?' 'Was not Esau Jacob's brother?' declares the Lord. 'Yet I have loved Jacob; but I have hated Esau and I have made his mountains a desolation and appointed his inheritance for the jackals of the wilderness.' . . . 'The Lord be magnified beyond the border of Israel!'"

Hosea also mentions Jacob in a corporate sense, not as an individual, in Hos 12:2ff., "The Lord has an indictment against Judah, and will punish Jacob according to his ways, and requite him according to his deeds." If Paul had wished to discuss Jacob and Esau as elected individuals, one to salvation and the other to condemnation, it is strange that he chose a passage of Scripture in Malachi, which reveals the exact opposite as his Old Testament proof of God's sovereign act.

---

up." We conclude that God loved Ishmael and cannot rule out that Ishmael became a believer from the level of revelation available at the time.

13. Jack Cottrell, *The College Press NIV Commentary Romans* (Joplin, Mo.: College, 1998), 2:75.

This is also true concerning Rom 9:10–12, referring to Rebecca's pregnancy of Jacob and Esau and afterward. Here, Paul is referring to Gen 25:23: "The Lord said to her, 'Two nations are in your womb; And two peoples will be separated from your body; And one people shall be stronger than the other; And the older shall serve the younger.'"

But historically, the individual Esau never did serve the individual Jacob; only the Edomites as a nation served Israel as a nation.

The phrase in 9:13, "Just as it is written, Jacob I loved, but Esau I hated" refers not to Genesis but to Malachi at a time in Israel's history when the nation as a whole was under consideration. The phrase is a Semitic idiom of sharp contrasts; it does not reveal God's personal disposition, only in the sense of the function each group played in the realization of the promise. Paul then, anticipating an objection, asks: "There is no injustice with (*para*—with respect to) God, is there? Absolutely not." What does all of this have to do with Israel's present unbelief? How can God's promise to Israel be harmonized with their disobedience?

God had an ultimate historical purpose for the Israelites, i.e. the corporate Jacob. This was (as noted in 9:5) to physically produce the "seed," Christ in the flesh,[14] i.e. the Messiah (Gal 3:16)[15] as well as the Israel of faith, the seed that are in Christ (Gal 3:29). However, the true Israel has been and still is only that latter group— those who obey the covenant responsibility to God. The example speaks strongly against the covenant people as possessing the "irresistible gift of faith." There is a consistent use of the adultery metaphor for Israel's unbelief in the Old Testament (Exod 32:12ff.; Lev 20:5–6; Judg 2:17; Ps 73:27). Three of the greatest prophets in the Old Testament condemn Israel for her unfaithfulness to Yahweh by charging them with spiritual adultery.

In Isa 1:21 he asks, "How is the faithful city become a prostitute!" Jeremiah denounces Israel with these biting words, ". . . you have played the prostitute with many lovers; yet return again to me, says the Lord" (Jer 3:1). The great co-laborer of Isaiah, Hosea, movingly pleads with Israel declaring that ". . . the spirit of whoredom has caused them to err, and they have gone a whoring from under their God," and ". . . your daughters shall commit whoredom, and your wives shall commit adultery" (Hos 4:12–13; 9:1ff.). Yahweh speaks to uprooted exiles saying, "I am broken with their whorish heart" (Ezek 6:9; also Ezek 16:30ff.; and 23:1ff.). Clearly from these brief

14. Christ's ancestry certainly did not include just those from the Israel of faith. Looking at his legal kingly lineage, we see that it included on one hand, Abraham, David and Hezekiah. But it also included at least five evil kings: Jehoram, Ahaz, Mannaseh, Amon and Jehoiachin. (Matt 1:8–11)

15. However, nonbelieving Israel would not benefit from producing Christ.

references to Israel's past history of disobedience, Paul's generation is not the first to reject the promises of God.

Paul moves to show that God's justice is one with his mercy. The first example Paul employs comes from Exod 33:19, "I will have mercy on whom I have mercy, and I will have compassion on whom I have compassion." The theme of the Exodus passage is the presence of God. This presence has been denied to rebellious Israel, but given to Joshua and Moses at the tent of meeting. As always, only a remnant of true believers has access to the presence of God. Moses then seeks a guarantee of God's presence for the people of Israel. God then promises Moses his presence and Israel ultimate rest in Canaan. (Exod 34:9–10) Moses also asks for a vision of God (33:17–23). He prays to see the glory of God.

His revelation is his name proclaimed in terms of his acts to man. God's nature is defined as goodness and grace, v. 19.[16] The object of God's goodness is disloyal disobedient Israel, "I will be gracious to whom I will be gracious." This Hebrew phrase can in no way imply any abrupt arbitrariness of God's act toward Israel. Though the English translation might imply this connotation, the Augustinian understanding of v. 19 as it is quoted in Rom 9:15 cannot be sustained from either the Exodus context, or its place in Romans 9. God's promise entails only mercy, never injustice.

Similarly, Paul says in 9:16: "So then, it does not depend on the man who wills or the man who runs, but on God who has mercy." This is another Calvinist favorite, in which their exegesis claims this supports God's sovereign individual election to salvation, with man having no say in the matter.[17] The verse in fact starts with "it,"—referring back to mercy, with no specific mention of salvation.[18] Looking at this in the context of vv. 12–15 makes clear this is another verse indicating God's decisions to choose individuals or nations—Moses, Jacob, or disobedient Israel as examples— for historical destiny, which has the ultimate originating source in God's sovereign purpose and His historical salvation plan.

---

16. For discussion of the Hebrew *tub*, "goodness," see James Philip Hyatt, *Exodus (New Century Bible Commentary)* (Philadelphia: Eerdmans, 1980)

17. R.C. Sproul has called this verse "the coup de grace against Arminianism and all other non-Reformed views of predestination" and adds "This one verse is absolutely fatal to Arminianism" (*Chosen by God* [Wheaton, Ill.: Tyndale House, 1986], 151). This is not the least bit true.

18. The term "mercy" is used in more than one way in Scripture. As Jack Cottrell notes: "God's mercy (grace, favor) is sometimes the grace of forgiveness and salvation for individuals (Ps 51:1), but more often it refers to some temporal blessing (Gen 33:4, 11; 2 Sam 12:22). The nation of Israel as such is often the recipient of such temporary mercy (favor, grace)" (Cottrell, *College Press NIV Commentary Romans*, 2:93).

VII. SOVEREIGNTY, FREEDOM, AND RESPONSIBILITY

Paul's second example of God's merciful justice is Pharaoh. Paul quotes from the LXX rather than the Hebrew text in the quotation in v. 17. "For this very purpose I raised you up, to demonstrate my power in you, and that my name might be proclaimed throughout the whole earth." In Exod 9:16 the Hebrew *he emadhtikha* literally means "caused you to stand"; rendered "maintained you alive."[19] A major theological point in the context of Exodus 9 is God's merciful patience, despite the plagues. God gave Pharaoh multiple chances and could have destroyed Egypt during the plagues, but did not.[20] This, too, is Paul's point about Pharaoh in Rom 9:17 and 18:b. God did not treat Pharaoh as a cosmic marionette.

God also could have destroyed the Israelites during their troubled journey to the Promised Land, but he had elected them to participate in his purpose of redemption (Rom 9:15, 16, 18a). It is very important to remember the cosmic perspective of three consecutive verses in Exod 9: 14, 15, 16, "in all the earth," "from the earth," and (again) "in all the earth," and how the universal implications of God's sovereign power fits the contexts of Rom 9:17–18. The LXX version of Exodus 9 quoted by Paul in Romans 9 has been used to suggest God's arbitrary fiat against Pharaoh. The passage in Exodus does not mean that God created or "raised up" Pharaoh to show his superior might with Pharaoh having no choice. The hardening of Pharaoh's heart in no way is to be taken to mean that God arbitrarily closed Pharaoh's heart against God's people.[21] Pharaoh was by his own decision a wicked tyrannical ruler and "the hardening" was a *judicial hardening*—the further hardening or strengthening of an already stubborn heart. Also, several times during the plagues, the account tells us Pharaoh hardened his own heart.

19. Umberto Cassuto, *A Commentary on the Book of Exodus* (Jerusalem: Hebrew University Magnus Press, 1967), 116; and Hyatt, *Exodus,* on this verse.

20. H.L. Ellison writes: "Egypt would not be eliminated, for God's purpose was to show his power in deliverance, not in destruction" (*Exodus* [Louisville: Westminster John Knox, 1982], 53).

21. Three Hebrew words describe Pharaoh's condition: (1) The first word is *kabed* which means "to be heavy, insensible or dull." (See Exod 7:14; 8:15, 32; 9:7, 34. Francis Brown, S.R. Driver, and Charles A. Briggs, *A Hebrew and English Lexicon of the Old Testament* [Oxford, U.K.: Clarendon Press, 1952], 457].) (2) The second word is *qasah* and carries the significance of "being hard, severe, or fierce." In the Hif'il stem it means "making hard or difficult." *(ibid.,* 904; appears in Exod 7:3; 13:15.) (3) The third term is *hazaq* and means "to be or grow firm, strong." (ibid., 304. See Exod. 7:13, 14, 22; 8:15, 19, 32; 9:7, 34–35; 13:15) The same term is also employed in Josh 11:20 which relates that God ". . . hardened their (inhabitants of Canaan) hearts that they should come against Israel in battle, that he might destroy them completely. . . . "

Pharaoh refuses to free the children of Israel. God pleads with him through Moses and Aaron, but he only becomes more obdurate and vengeful to the Semitic slaves. God's mercy and justice are made available to both Israel and Pharaoh. But the former accepts his mercy (while in Egypt), and the latter refuses and experiences justice. Paul advances his argument by responding to an objector (v. 19) who supposes that the apostle regards God's act in hardening Pharaoh's heart as an unjust and overwhelming brute force which no one has resisted or can resist. Now Paul uses imagery from different periods of the history of Israel's unbelief, i.e. apostasy from covenant responsibility—Isa 45:9–11; 64:8; 29:16; and Jer 18:8. The English text of Rom 9:20–22 might suggest a mechanically arbitrary relationship between the potter and the clay, which none of the Old Testament references to this image will support.

Jeremiah 18 follows a powerful appeal to rebellious Israel to repent. Trust in the Lord and return to Israel. ". . . Israel will know my power and my might, and they shall know that my name is the Lord" (Jer 16:21). Further, God tells Jeremiah to go stand in the Benjamin Gate and commands him to speak to the kings of Judah. "Take heed for the sake of your lives . . . Yet they did not listen or incline their ear, but stiffened their neck, that they might not hear and receive instruction" (Jer 17:21–23). If you do not heed the prophet's warnings, then you will be destroyed. These are the ringing words of the weeping prophet. Then comes the great chapter which contains the imagery employed by Paul, the potter and the clay. God has appealed to Israel, and now they respond to him, " . . . we will follow our own plans, and will everyone act according to the stubbornness of his evil heart" (Jer 18:12).

Now we present the blow to a Calvinistic interpretation of Paul's example in Rom 9:20–21. God asked Jeremiah to go down to the potter's house. We read in Jer 18: 6–10 the conditionality of God as the potter: "Can I not, O house of Israel, deal with you as this potter does?" declares the Lord. "Behold, like the clay in the potter's hand, so are you in my hand, O house of Israel. At one moment I might speak concerning a nation or concerning a kingdom to uproot, to pull down, or to destroy it; but *if that nation against which I have spoken turns from its evil*, I will relent concerning the calamity I planned to bring on it. Or at another moment I might speak concerning a nation or concerning a kingdom to build up or plant it. *If it does evil in my site* by not obeying my voice, then I will think better of the good with which I had promised to bless it."

God warns his chosen nation: "Oh turn back, each of you from his evil way, and reform your ways and your deeds" (18:11). Because they will not respond to God's gracious call, judgment is inevitable. "I will show them my back, not my face, in the day of their calamity" (18:17). Apostasy is the condition of Israel. They refuse God's gracious warning. They are committing spiritual adultery by worshipping false gods (19:1ff.). Jeremiah prophesies in the court of the Lord's house, "Behold, I am bringing upon the city and upon all its towns all the evil that I have pronounced against it, because they have stiffened their neck, refusing to hear my words" (Jer 19:15). The same themes are present in the other Scriptures where this imagery appears. Isaiah says that Israel ". . . draws near with their mouth . . . while their hearts are far from me" (Isa 29:13). In Isa 45:9–11, the context is of captivity and God's sovereign employment of Cyrus as liberator of imprisoned unfaithful Israelites. This great passage again affirms that men are morally responsible for their behavior; they can repent, but if they will not, then God's merciful justice will prevail in spite of their self-destructive refusal.

In the great eschatological section of Isaiah 60—66, we note again the potter-clay imagery. We hear a prayer for mercy, "Yet O Lord, you are our Father. We are the clay, you are the potter; we are all the work of your hand" (Isa 64:8). In every passage in which the above imagery appears, God is calling his rebellious people to repentance. If they cannot repent, then what is the moral significance of asking them to do something which God knows they cannot do? It is most important to note that Paul implies human responsibility as he goes on to speak of God's patient endurance toward "vessels of wrath prepared for destruction" (v. 22).

Many vessels of wrath, both Jews and Gentiles, repented and thus became vessels moving toward mercy (*eis*-preposition meaning motion in the direction of, used of both mercy and absence of mercy in v. 21). The standard English translation "vessels of mercy" and "vessels of wrath" are not precisely what the Greek text declares because the grammar uses the preposition *eis* plus accusative case, and not the genitive case from which we might derive the translations "of mercy," "of wrath." The Greek word for this later translation is not *orge* but an alpha privative on the root word "mercy." The word literally means the absence of mercy. This is true because God's mercy (salvific in v. 23) is available only to the faithful and obedient individual, Jew or Gentile.

The doctrine of the irresistible gift of faith is not taught in this passage, or for that matter elsewhere in Scriptures. Often Eph 2:8 is given as a proof text that faith is a gift. However, the gender of the Greek form of the pronoun "that" is neuter and has as its antecedent salvation by grace, through faith as a whole and not just faith (which is a feminine noun) because the antecedents must agree in gender.

The phrase "vessels of wrath prepared for destruction," translates *skeue orges katertismena eis apoleian*. The English translation generally implies— or so it appears— that some individuals were prepared by a sovereign act of

God for destruction. At least since Augustine and Calvin this viewpoint has been widely held. But the form of *katertismena* is a perfect passive or middle participle. In the perfect tense the passive and middle have the same form, only the context will determine which way the word should be translated. The context of this term is Paul's argument, which immediately stems from the three questions asked in vv. 20–21.

The larger context has been the entire structure of Romans 9. Every example Paul has shown stresses personal responsibility on man's part, and justice and mercy on God's part. The whole of Romans 9 is concerned with Israel's unbelief, and it is central to Paul's total argument that Israel is responsible for its rebellious attitude toward God's promise. God always judges unbelief; this is his justice. It is always possible to repent and return to the presence of God; this is his mercy. In this context, I see no justification for translating the word under consideration as passive, i.e., the subject is acted upon; rather, the translation should be in a middle voice as "fitted themselves" for destruction. From 1:18 we learn that God's "wrath" is continually being revealed *(apokaluptetai,* pres. ind. passive—presently and not at some further event of judgment) from heaven against all ungodliness and unrighteousness of men, who suppressed the truth in unrighteousness. Paul's kinsmen according to the flesh were experiencing the wrath of God outside of God's righteousness in Christ. Rebellion against God's promised purpose has always brought his wrath, but only after calling to repentance and restoration.

There are vessels of mercy and vessels of wrath among both Jews and Gentiles. The purpose of God's patience (v. 22) was to give those who prepare themselves by unbelief for God's destruction a time to repent. "The Lord is not slow about his promise as some count slowness, but is forbearing toward you, not wishing that any should perish, but that all should reach repentance" (2 Pet 3:9). The glory of God is his presence among his people. Paul has already set forth that Christ is our righteousness, the object of our faith, and the source of the distinction between "vessels of mercy" and "vessels of wrath" (compare Rom 8:28–30 and 9:23–24). We must be most careful in the manner in which we complete the conditional clause in vv. 22–23. This is all the more imperative because Paul's sentence dissolves into an *anacoluthon* or an erratic sentence, though the context points us to what God has actually done without discriminating between Jews and Gentiles.

God has mercifully deferred his wrath from those who prepare themselves for destruction, by showing his patience. Thus, God's power, even with regard to those on whom he could wish (v. 22, *thelon*—participle) to reveal his wrath, has been exercised with limits and not annihilation (e.g., Pharaoh and Egypt during the plagues and Israel during her many periods of unbelief). More in accord with Paul's entire development would be the conclusion (though it is not provided in Paul's Greek text as we are here dealing with a grammatical anacolution) ". . .how can you, mere man, suppose that God exercises his will in an arbitrary and capricious manner, as though it were brute force?" God's sovereign freedom does not mean that he will disregard the limited freedom of his creatures; and so we must recognize the qualitative aspects of God's power even where the rebellious unbeliever is concerned (Rom 2:3–4).

The objector is rebuked for his insolent assumption that he has a right to challenge the power of God, especially by supposing that God's power is not graciously exercised. God's word has truly not failed, because it is his word that must be understood as a promise realized on the basis of God's free choice (9:6–13). God commits no injustice in the realization of his promise (9:14–18). God's free act is ordered to the salvation of humanity (not universalism). Even in the case of those who fitted themselves for God's wrath (they are responsible, Rom 2:3–5), God's freedom has been mercifully exercised.

Paul next spells out God's historically manifested mercy for Jews as well as Gentiles (9:25–33). Paul appeals to God's word through Hos 1:10. (This quotation is not from the New Testament, nor the LXX of any known version, though it contains the awkward LXX translation in essence.) By using Hosea's great heart-rendering call to unbelieving Israel, Paul describes God's merciful call to the Gentiles. The original text contains God's appeal to Israel to repent after she had continually committed spiritual adultery. After Israel's adulterous affair with Baal, God says that she ceased to be his people. Hosea clearly reveals God's mercy and Israel's personal responsibility and freedom to repent and return to God.

God condemned the ten northern tribes, but he was not unjust, because they deserved his judgment. His mercy was evident in his call to repentance; his love *(hesed,* covenant love) was visible in Hosea's maternal situation (read chs. 1–3). The promise to restore Israel was contingent on their repentance. The theology of Hosea is crystal clear: the abandonment of God meant the loss of covenant status (no Old Testament suggestions of Eternal Security). The demand of repentance emphasized Israel's moral responsibility (freedom to act and return to God), and the "remnant" theme strongly asserts that only the faithful, i.e., believers in Yahweh's promises, will return and that corporate Israel will be destroyed, as it was historically (though Israelites remained, including in the time of Christ).

The theme taken from Hosea is present in Paul's argument. But in its Old Testament context, the word applies simply to Israel. Paul simply extends the "my people" to include Gentile believers, expressing the point that all true believers are God's people not just those from biologico-historico Israel. The universal scope of Hosea's message as applied to Gentile believers is appropriated as proof of the actual fulfillment of the intention of God's word. The "not my people" are now called "sons of the living God." God's call of Israel must be understood as the call of a remnant in the days, ". . . but also from among Gentiles" (v. 24).

VIII. GOD'S PROMISE AND THE BELIEVING REMNANT

God's promise is being fulfilled; the fulfillment deals with a believing remnant as well as the coming of the Messiah—both through Israel. Paul concludes this particular defense of the efficacy of the Lord's word of promise by pointing out that its apparent failure is really the failure of some to understand God's promise. God's word has not failed (9:6, *ekpeptoken*, fallen down); rather, unbelieving Israel has stumbled over it. Paul denies that God's word has failed even in a most remote detail. From Abraham forward, God's promised material and spiritual blessings entails *only believers*.[22] Israel's failure is evidenced by their false striving after righteousness according to the law. Paul quotes from Isaiah in order to emphasize both the remnant theme and the punishment of faithless Israel. In v. 27, Isa 10:22—23 (modified LXX) is used to support the remnant motif. This remnant pericope contains the dual polarity (10:20-21; 10:22-23), "For though your people, O Israel, were like the sand of the sea, a remnant would return from them. Destruction is decreed, overflowing with righteousness" (Isa 10:22). The remnant will be a community of faith.

There is an unquestionable correlation between the leaning on Yahweh in truth and the demand for faith. The reference to the "house of Jacob" (v. 20) seems to call to remembrance that those from the nation who trust in God can count upon the saving action of God and will be the inheritors of the election promises connected with the patriarch Jacob. The name of Isaiah's oldest son, Shear-jashub, is introduced in the form of a sentence that provides a commentary on it. The idea of remnant serves to provoke hope and, at the same time, is a summons to repentance. The remnant will be the recipients and fulfillment of the election promises made to the founding father of Israel. The fulfillment is through them being "in Him [Christ]" (Eph 1:4, 7) and therefore part of the promised "seed" (Gal 3:29).

It is most important that we take note of the fact that the absolute election promises of salvation and blessing to Israel are conditional. The election promises are placed in direct correlation with the faithfulness of the

---

22. The plan for the lineage leading to the Messiah is broader, as we have seen.

elected ones. This is precisely Paul's claim in Rom 9:27. Both Isaiah and Paul juxtapose *salvation* and *judgment,* in order to prevent any misunderstanding of God's promise, whereby the remnant could claim to be a privileged group. The ominous tone of Isa 10:20 seems obvious. God's promise to make Israel as the sand of sea (Gen 22:17; 32:13) will not prevent him from bringing about a decisive end to Israel's national existence. This is the second time Isaiah refers to the Abrahamic promise in connection with the negative aspects of the remnant motif (Isa 1:9—which Paul quotes in Rom 9:29). In both passages the *promise* has been made *conditional.* Only true believers will inherit the promise, because the multitude is unwilling to repent and return to God.

The principal emphasis in both Isaiah and Paul is for the express purpose of confuting a false reliance upon the election promise given originally to Abraham (Gen 22: 17) and repeated to Jacob (Gen 32:13). The mere fact of a physical, patriarchal ancestry will not spare unbelievers in the future judgment. This is precisely Paul's thought in Rom 9:27. Faith, which was always so intricately connected with the remnant motif, now has an explicit object.

In Isaiah it is faith in Yahweh's promise; and in Paul it is faith in Jesus Christ— the righteousness of God and the fulfiller of God's promise who comes through Israel. In v. 29 Paul refers to another reference in Isa 1:9 (LXX). Isaiah declares that only because of God's grace and mercy "a few survivors" (The Hebrew word carries connotation of *fleeing*) were left. Had it not been for the power of "Yahweh of hosts" and especially his mercy, the entire nation would have been wiped off the face of the earth as Sodom and Gomorrah had been in the time of Abraham (Genesis 18—19; note also that there is the remnant motif "mercy" and call to repentance in the narrative of the cities of the Plain.) Isaiah compares the city of Jerusalem with Sodom and Gomorrah because both narratives reflect on the actual historical situation.

The comparison is not between the "means" but the "totality" of destruction. There was no remnant from Sodom and Gomorrah; but repentance and faithfulness to the covenant would enable even a "few survivors" to continue the historic unfolding of the promise. Israel's rebelliousness brings God's punishment for their breach of his most holy covenant (Isa 1:4), which is God's "alien work" (Isa 28:21). In referring to Israel's unbelief, Isaiah raises the question, will Israel understand that the time given her is but a time of probation? God extends his grace in order to give the "few survivors" another chance to return to him in faith. God preserves the seed-promise through "a few survivors."

With splendid urgency Paul suggests that this same situation hovers over his kinsmen according to flesh. Paul, as did Isaiah, clearly assumes the freedom to return to God and that individuals are responsible for their own actions. God has shown patience and mercy toward those who are "fitting themselves" for God's condemnation; the overriding perspective for understanding God's action, however, is that he prepares men for his glory. This he has done without discriminating between Jew and Gentile (9:19–24). The actualization of God's word of promise is precisely what the Scriptures declare (9:25–30). What, then, are we to say to account for the fact of such paradoxical fulfillment which has entailed the blessing of Gentiles and disbelief of so many in Israel?

Paul responds to this question (9:30–31) by further explanation of the way in which God intends to fulfill his word of promise. God's promise to Abraham "in your seed shall all the nations of the earth be blessed" is being fulfilled in history. The conditions for participation in its fulfillment have always been the same—faith in the purpose of the one who made the covenant of promise with his people. In both the Old and New Testaments faith means obedience to covenant responsibility and thus the saving grace of God is always contingent. Biologico-historico Israel is our supreme example.

The cause of Israel's unbelief is to be found, not in God, but in Israel itself. Israel's unbelief is its freely chosen preference. As with all human choices, man possesses a limited range of freedom to choose from among alternatives, but he is not free to determine the consequences. Paul is not really intending to place praise or blame on any group. He does not say that the Gentiles did not pursue justice, but that Israel did pursue it. Nor does he say that the Gentiles have obtained justice whereas Israel has not obtained it. He does affirm in effect that one group obtained a justice from faith; and another did not obtain justice because it sought justice by human aspiration and effort. Only the perfect can pursue a law of justice.

In fact, Israel did not attain the standard set by the law itself. The defective factor was neither the law nor their striving, but as v. 32 makes clear, their nonattainment of righteousness by law stems from an improper perspective, i.e., not God's perspective of his promised intentions. God's justice is only available by faith in a person, the only one who fully explains the Father (John 1:18). Paul's gospel proclaims that in Jesus Christ alone is the goal (Rom *10:4—telos*) of the law and the fulfillment of the law (10:4).

IX. GOD'S HIGH ROCK

Paul declares that Israel stumbled over the rock of ages. The rock was laid in Zion for Israel's safety. God's gracious mercy had laid the rock. But the rock became an offense, an occasion of stumbling instead of a place of security. By way of conclusion (chap. 9) and transition (chap. 10), Paul quotes a conflated text from Isa 8:14–15 and 28:16. Christ, the living stone, serves as the basis for an edifice that will not confound the one who relies on him. Paul is the bearer of the great mystery of the divine plan of salvation. The context of Isa 28:16 (also Rom 10:11; 1 Pet 2:4–6) is a call to repent for the ". . . scoffers, who rule this people in Jerusalem" who have made a covenant with death and do not believe that justice will prevail make lies their refuge and falsehood their shelter. The command is to repent and trust the sure foundation laid in Zion because a decree of destruction has gone out from the Lord God (Isa 28:22). In Isa 8:14–15 Yahweh is once more warning rebellious Israel, but the warning is also a call to blessing.

Whether it be blessing or curse will ultimately depend on obedient faith or disobedient unfaithfulness. This, too, is Paul's point in v. 33. Those who believe will not come to grief over it. In Romans 9, God is the sovereign who has ordered all things as he pleases. He sent his Son, the "seed," through Israel (9:5) but blesses only those who accept the savior in faith. He is pleased by the gospel to save sinners (1 Cor 1:21); he is pleased by the faith of those who diligently seek him (Heb 11:6); he wills that all men be saved (1 Tim 2:4); he is willing that all come to him by repentance (2 Pet 3:9). God's promise in Christ entails universal history.

13

Saving Faith: The Act of a Moment or the Attitude of a Life?

Steve Witzki

With the title of this book being *Grace for All: The Arminian Dynamics of Salvation*, it is appropriate to talk about the Arminian understanding of saving faith that results in final salvation with God. Arminian scholars have amply demonstrated that their perspective has always taught Christians are saved by God's grace through faith from first to last.[1] One of the key Arminian scholars who argued for this was Robert Shank, author of the classic work, *Life in the Son*.[2]

Shank (1918–2006) has gone on to be with his Savior. Yet even after fifty-plus years, his book continues to be seen as one of the best biblical treatments on the security of the believer from an Arminian perspective. I would like to briefly lay out Shank's view on saving faith and address some

1. A previous version of this essay was originally published on the website of the Society of Evangelical Arminians and has been revised for inclusion in this book. See, http://evangelicalarminians.org/files/Saving%20Faith%20%28Act%20of%20a%20Moment%20or%20Attitude%20of%20a%20Life%29.pdf

See also Roger Olson *Arminian Theology: Myths and Realities* (Downers Grove, Ill.: InterVarsity, 2006). Chapter 7 is especially relevant.

2. Robert Shank, *Life in the Son: A Study in the Doctrine of Perseverance*, 2nd ed. (Minneapolis: Bethany House, 1989). This influential book was originally published in 1960 by Westcott.

of the criticisms that have been leveled against it. I believe that when the evidence is weighed, Shank's conclusions will be seen to stand firmly on the testimony of Scripture and have always been the consensual view of Classical Arminians from Arminius and Wesley to the present.

Allow me to begin with a question that Shank asked in his book which will serve as a catalyst for arriving at an answer:

> Many believe that saving faith is the act of a moment—one great moment in which the sinner humbly acknowledges his sin in repentance toward God and accepts Jesus Christ as his personal Savior. They believe that one grand and holy moment of decision ushers one into an irrevocable state of grace in which he is unconditionally secure. But others are persuaded that the moment of holy decision is but the beginning, and that the state of grace is not irrevocable in our present earthly sojourn in God's moral universe in which "the just shall live by faith." They are persuaded that saving faith is not the act of a moment, but the attitude of a life; the initial decision must be perpetually implemented throughout the life of the believer, and such is not inevitable. Who is right?[3]

Where Shank stood was made clear when he stated: "The New Testament affirms that eternal life in Christ is our present possession only on the condition of a present living faith, rather than as the irrevocable consequence of a moment's act of faith sometime in the past."[4] We need to note two things that Shank is affirming in this statement. First, eternal life is "in Christ." By "in Christ," Shank means that eternal life is possessed in a *living relationship with the living Savior, Jesus Christ*. Second, the *condition* for possessing eternal life in Christ is a *living or persevering faith*. For support, he asked his readers to consider John 1:12:

> "As many as received him [*elabon*, aorist indicative, a definite act in past time—conversion] to them gave he power to become [or, to be] children of God, those who believe [*pisteuousin*, present participle, present progressive action-perseverance in faith] in his name." John depicts both aspects—the initial act of faith at the reception of Christ, whereby the relationship is effected, and the persevering faith in Him whereby the relationship is sustained.[5]

---

3. Ibid., 51.
4. Ibid., 63.
5. Ibid., 92, brackets in original.

For Shank it necessarily follows that,

> Throughout his earthly sojourn, the relation of the individual to Christ is never a *static* relationship existing as the irrevocable consequence of a past decision, act, or experience. Rather it is a present mutual indwelling of the believer and the Savior, the sharing of a common life which emanates from Him "who is our life" (Col. 3:4). For the believer, it is a living participation proceeding upon a living faith in a living Savior.[6]

Since some teachers have objected to Shank's thesis that eternal life in Christ is conditional upon a living or persevering faith, I would like to determine if these objections are justified in light of the Scriptural evidence. But first, it would be helpful for the reader to see how Christians from different theological traditions define saving faith.

WHAT MODERATE CALVINISTS SAY ABOUT SAVING FAITH

All Calvinists believe in unconditional eternal security, but there is a distinct difference between the Reformed and Moderate versions. The Moderate Calvinist believes that *one moment of faith* secures a Christian's eternal destiny. Joseph Dillow writes:

> Even though Robert Shank would not agree, it is definitely true that saving faith is "the act of a single moment whereby all the benefits of Christ's life, death, and resurrection suddenly become the irrevocable possession of the individual, per se, despite any and all eventualities."[7]

Would "any and all eventualities" include falling away from the Christian faith and becoming an unbeliever? For the Moderate Calvinist the answer would be "Yes." Dillow says, "It is possible for a truly born-again person to fall away from the faith and cease believing."[8] "What he forfeits

---

6. Ibid., 42–43.

7. Joseph Dillow, *The Reign of the Servant Kings: A Study of Eternal Security and the Final Significance of Man* (Haysville, N.C.: Schoettle, 1992), 202. Popular author Ron Rhodes appears to agree with Dillow: "I believe that Scripture consistently teaches that once a person trusts in Christ and becomes a part of God's forever family, he or she is saved forever (Rom. 8:28–30). No matter what that child of God does after the moment of salvation, he or she is saved" (Ron Rhodes, *The Heart of Christianity* [Eugene, Ore.: Harvest House, 1996], 111).

8. Ibid., 199.

when he 'falls away' is not his eternal destiny but his opportunity to reign with Christ's *metochoi* [partners][9] in the coming kingdom."[10]

Pastor and author Charles Stanley communicates this view as well:

> The Bible clearly teaches that God's love for His people is of such magnitude that even those who walk away from the faith have not the slightest chance of slipping from His hand.[11]

> Salvation or justification or adoption—whatever you wish to call it—stands independently of [a person's] faith. Consequently, God does not require a *constant attitude* of faith in order to be saved—only an *act* of faith. . . . If I chose to have a tattoo put on my arm, that would involve a one-time act on my part. Yet the tattoo would remain with me indefinitely. I don't have to maintain an attitude of fondness for tattoos to ensure that the tattoo remains on my arm. In fact I may change my mind the minute I receive it. But that does not change the fact that I have a tattoo on my arm. My request for the tattoo and the tattoo itself are two entirely different things. I received it by asking and paying for it. But asking for my money back and changing my attitude will not undo what is done. Forgiveness/salvation is applied at the moment of faith. It is not the same thing as faith. And its permanence is not contingent upon the permanence of one's faith.[12]

9. Dillow says *the metochoi* "are those friends, partners, and companions who have endured the trials of life, were faithful to the end, who will therefore obtain the inheritance-rest" (Dillow, *Reign of the Servant Kings*, 105–106). He says this "inheritance-rest" refers to the millennial land of Canaan where faithful believers will rule with Christ during the millennium (see chapter 5).

10. Ibid., 202.

11. Charles Stanley, *Eternal Security: Can You Be Sure?* (Nashville: Oliver-Nelson, 1990), 74. Charles Ryrie says, "What grace it is that can give us not only forgiveness and eternal life through faith alone but also guarantee that the Giver will never renege on His gift! Nor can we ever give it back even if we try!" (Charles Ryrie, *So Great Salvation: What it Means to Believe in Jesus Christ* [Wheaton: Victor, 1989], 144).

12. Ibid., 80. Norman Geisler writes: "Continued belief is not a condition for keeping one's salvation. Two related questions here must be distinguished. The first one is whether continual belief throughout one's life is a necessary condition for keeping one's salvation. In distinction from Arminians, the answer is negative" (Norman Geisler, "Moderate Calvinism," J. Matthew Pinson, ed., *Four Views on Eternal Security* [Grand Rapids: Zondervan, 2002], 109). Zane Hodges says: ". . . We miss the point to insist that true saving faith must necessarily continue. Of course, our faith in Christ should continue. But the claim that it absolutely must . . . has no support at all in the Bible" (Zane Hodges, *Absolutely Free! A Biblical Reply to Lordship Salvation* [Grand Rapids: Zondervan, 1989], 63).

To say that our salvation can be taken from us for any reason, whether it be sin or disbelief, is to ignore the plain meaning of this text [Eph. 2:8–9].[13] Some people argue that the believer must maintain his *faith* in order to maintain his *salvation* . . . [I object to] those who hold that one's faith must be maintained to ensure the possession of eternal life.[14]

> *Does the Scripture actually teach that regardless of the consistency of our faith, our salvation is secure?* Yes, it does . . .
>
> If we died with Him, we shall also live with
> Him; If we endure, we shall also reign with Him;
> If we deny Him, He also will deny us;
> If we are *faithless*, He remains *faithful*,
> for He cannot deny Himself.
>
> *2 Tim 2:11–13*[15]

Dillow, Stanley and other Moderate Calvinists hold to a view of saving faith that is in stark contrast to the position held by Calvinists from the Reformed tradition.

WHAT REFORMED CALVINISTS ARE SAYING ABOUT SAVING FAITH

Heb. 3:14, says "For we have become partakers of Christ if we hold the beginning of our confidence steadfast to the end." (NKJV) Reformer John Calvin (1509–1564), commented:

> [The author] commends them for having begun well; but lest, under the pretext of the grace which they had obtained, they should indulge themselves in carnal security, he says that there was need of perseverance; for many having only tasted the Gospel, do not think of any progress as though they had reached the summit. Thus it is that they not only stop in the middle of their race, yea, nigh the starting posts, but turn another way. Plausible indeed is this objection, "What can we wish more after having found Christ?" But if he is possessed by faith, we must persevere in it, so that he may be our perpetual possession. Christ then has given

---

13. Ibid., 81.

14. Ibid., 84, 92.

15. Ibid., 93–94. Based on 2 Tim 2:11–13, Stanley holds that "the unfaithful believer," or believers who "abandon their faith" will still retain their salvation (Ibid., 94). This interpretation of 2 Tim 2:11–13 is also held by Dillow, *Reign of the Servant Kings*, 427–430; Ryrie, *So Great Salvation*, 140–142; and Geisler, "Moderate Calvinism," 111.

himself to be enjoyed by us on this condition, that by the same faith by which we have been admitted into a participation of him, we are to preserve so great a blessing even to death. Hence he says *beginning*, intimating that their faith was only begun . . . . *Steadfast* or firm; for we shall be firmly fixed and beyond the danger of vacillating, provided faith be our foundation. The sum of the whole then is, that faith whose beginnings only appear in us, is to make constant and steady progress to the end.[16]

Anthony Hoekema, longtime Professor of Calvin Theological Seminary, stated: "Peter puts it vividly: We are kept by the power of God *through faith*—a living faith, which expresses itself through love (Gal. 5:6). In other words, we may never simply rest on the comfort of God's preservation apart from the continuing exercise of faith."[17] John Murray, former Professor of Westminster Theological Seminary, agrees: "We may entertain the faith of our security in Christ only as we persevere in faith and holiness to the end."[18] Popular apologist and Reformed author James White says,

Throughout this passage [John 6:35–45] an important truth is presented that again might be missed in many English translations. When Jesus describes the one who comes to Him and who believes in Him, He uses the [Greek] present tense to describe this coming, believing, or, in other passages, hearing or seeing. The present tense refers to a *continuous, ongoing action* . . . . The wonderful promises that are provided by Christ are not for those who do not *truly* and *continually* believe. The faith that saves is a living faith, a faith that always looks to Christ as Lord and Savior. . . . Many in our world today . . . teach essentially that a person can perform an act of believing on Christ *once*, and after this, they can fall away even into total unbelief and yet still supposedly be "saved." . . . Christ does not save men in this way. The true Christian is the one *continually* coming, *always* believing in Christ. Real Christian faith is an ongoing faith, not a one-time act. If one wishes to be eternally satiated, one meal

16. John Calvin, *Commentaries on the Epistle of Paul the Apostle to the Hebrews*, John Owen, trans. and ed., obtained at Christian Classics Ethereal Library, www.ccel. org. Calvin states in his *Institutes*: "In the elect alone he implants the living root of faith, so that they persevere even to the end" (*Institutes of the Christian Religion*, 3:2.11, obtained at www.ccel.org).

17. Anthony Hoekema, *Saved by Grace* (Grand Rapids: Eerdmans, 1989), 244. He goes on to write: "As we have noted, the Bible teaches that God does not preserve us apart from our watchfulness, prayer, and persevering faith" (Ibid., 245).

18. John Murray, *Redemption—Accomplished and Applied* (Grand Rapids: Eerdmans, 1955), 193.

is not enough. If we wish to feast on the bread of heaven, we must do so all our lives. We will never hunger or thirst if we *are always coming* and *always believing* in Christ.[19]

Reformed Calvinists are essentially in agreement with what Shank has said about saving faith. Hoekema even writes,

> On this point I quite agree with Robert Shank when he says, there is no warrant in the New Testament for that strange at-ease-in-Zion definition of perseverance which assures Christians that perseverance is inevitable and relieves them of the necessity of deliberately persevering in faith, encouraging them to place confidence in some past act or experience.[20]

WHAT REFORMED ARMINIANS ARE SAYING ABOUT SAVING FAITH

While Reformed Calvinists and Arminians disagree as to whether God saves people through unconditional election and irresistible grace, they both would agree that saving faith must be a persevering faith. James Arminius (1559–1609), the theological forerunner to modern-day Reformed Arminianism,[21] succinctly wrote that God "wills that they, who believe and persevere in faith, shall be saved, but that those, who are unbelieving and impenitent, shall remain under condemnation."[22] He goes on to reiterate that God does not will "that any man shall be saved in a sense, such that salvation will, certainly and infallibly, come to him, unless he is considered as a believer, and as persevering in faith even to the end."[23]

19. James White, *Drawn by the Father* (Lindenhurst, N.Y.: Reformation, 2000), 19–20.

20. Hoekema, *Saved by Grace*, 245.

21. For more on Reformed Arminianism see Olson, *Arminian Theology: Myths and Realities*.

22. James Arminius, *The Works of James Arminius*, James and William Nichols, trans. (Grand Rapids: Baker, 1986) 3:412. In another place he writes: "God resolves to receive into favor those who repent and believe, and to save in Christ, on account of Christ, and through Christ, those who persevere, but to leave under sin and wrath those who are impenitent and unbelievers, and to condemn them as aliens from Christ" (Ibid., 2:465). He goes on to explain that God's determination to save some people and to condemn others ". . . rests or depends on the prescience and foresight of God, by which he foreknew from all eternity what men would, through such administration, believe by the aid of preventing or preceding grace, and would persevere by the aid of subsequent or following grace, and who would not believe and persevere" (Ibid., 2:466).

23. Ibid., 3:413.

Over one hundred years later, Methodist founder John Wesley (1703–1791) arrived at the same conclusions in his essay "Serious Thoughts Upon the Perseverance of the Saints." In this work, Wesley anticipates and responds to objections raised by Calvinists to his teaching that a believer may fall away from God and perish eternally. The responses reveal Wesley's firm conviction that a believer remains in a saving relationship with the Lord Jesus Christ through a continuing and enduring faith.

> "But how can this [teaching that a Christian can fall from God so as to perish everlastingly] be reconciled with the words of the Lord : 'He that believeth shall be saved'?" [Mark 16:16] Do you think these words mean, "He that believes" at this moment "shall" certainly and inevitably "be saved?" If this interpretation be good, then, by all the rules of speech, the other part of the sentence must mean, "He" that does "not believe" at this moment, "shall" certainly and inevitably "be damned." Therefore that interpretation cannot be good. The plain meaning, then, of the whole sentence is, "He that believeth," *if he continue in faith,* "shall be saved; he that believeth not," if he continue in unbelief, "shall be damned." "But does not Christ say elsewhere, 'He that believeth hath everlasting life?' (John 3:36), and 'He that believeth on Him that sent me, hath ever-lasting life and shall not come into condemnation, but is passed from death unto life?'" ([John 5:] 24). I answer, (1.) The love of God is everlasting life. It is, in substance, the life of heaven. Now, everyone that believes, loves God, and therefore, "hath everlasting life." (2.) Everyone that believes "is" therefore, "passed from death," spiritual death, "unto life;" and, (3.) "Shall not come into condemnation," *if he endureth in the faith unto the end*; according to our Lord's own words, "He that endureth unto the end shall be saved [Matt 10:22];"[24] and, "Verily I say unto you, if a man keep my sayings, he shall never see death" (John 8:51).[25]

24. Methodist Joseph Benson (1748–1821) arrives at the same conclusion as Wesley on Matt 10:22:

> But be not discouraged at the prospect of these trials, for he that *perseveres in the faith* and practice of the gospel, and who bears constantly and with invincible patience these persecutions, (which my grace is sufficient to enable you all to do,) shall be finally and eternally saved from all sin and misery, into the kingdom and glory of God. (Joseph Benson, Commentary on the New Testament: Gospel of Saint Matthew [Rio: AGES Digital Library, The Wesleyan Heritage Collection, 2002], 192, emphasis added).

25. John Wesley, *The Works of John Wesley*, third ed., complete and unabridged, 14 vols. (Grand Rapids: Baker, 2001), 10:288, emphasis added. Quotes in original.

To understand salvation as being conditional upon a faith that endures to the end inevitably raised another objection encountered by Wesley that warranted a response,

> "Nay, but are not 'all the promises, yea and amen?'" They are firm as the pillars of heavens. Perform the condition, and the promise is sure. Believe, and thou shalt be saved. "But many promises are absolute and unconditional." In many, the condition is not expressed. But this does not prove, there is none implied. . . . For example: "This is the Father's will, that of all which he hath given me I should lose nothing." [John 6:39][26] Most sure, all that God hath given him, or as it is expressed in the next verse, *"everyone that believeth on him,"* namely, to the end, "he will raise up at the last day, to reign with him forever." [John 6:40][27] "Again: 'I am the living bread:—If any man eat of this bread,' (by faith,) 'he shall live forever.' (John 6:51.)
>
> True; *if he continue to eat thereof.*"[28]

It is no surprise that Wesley admonished believers in one of his sermons to: "continue to believe in him that loved thee, and gave himself for thee; that bore all thy sins in his own body on the tree; and he saveth thee from all condemnation, by his blood continually applied. Thus it is that we continue in a justified state."[29] He went on to add,

---

26. Daniel Whedon (1808–1885): "*I should lose nothing*—There will be no erratic self-will in Christ, darting off from the divine plan; no remissness, no oversight, no failure. All who perseveringly believe in him, he will as faithfully and powerfully save . . ." (Daniel Whedon, *Commentary on the New Testament: John* [Rio: AGES Digital Library, *The Wesleyan Heritage Collection*, 2002], 325).

27. Wesley, *Works*, 10:290–291, emphasis added. Joseph Benson wrote: "It is the fixed determination of the Father, to bestow everlasting life on all who persevere in this faith; and therefore, in execution of my Father's will; *I will raise* all such *up at the last day*" (Joseph Benson, *Commentary on the New Testament: The Gospel of Saint John* [Rio: AGES Digital Library, *The Wesleyan Heritage Collection*, 2002], 103). Whedon says:

> So long as he performs the condition, so long is he heir of the salvation. When he ceases to be a believer he loses all claim to the divine promise, and all interest *in eternal life.* That he has once believed no longer secures him heaven, any more than the fact that he has once disbelieved secures eternal death. (Whedon, *Commentary on the New Testament: John*, 325)

28. Wesley, *Works*, 10:290–291, emphasis added. Wesley simply believed that "God is the Father of them that believe, *so long as they believe.* But the devil is the father of them that believe not, whether they did once believe or no" (Ibid., 10:298, emphasis added). Quotes in original.

29. Wesley, "The Repentance of Believers," Ibid., 5:167, emphasis added.

For, by that faith in his life, death, and intercession for us, *renewed from moment to moment*, we are every whit clean, and there is not only now no condemnation for us. . . . By the same faith we feel the power of Christ every moment resting upon us . . . whereby we are enabled to continue in spiritual life. . . . *As long as we retain our faith in him, we "draw water out of the wells of salvation."* [30]

So who is right, is saving faith simply the act of a moment or must the initial decision be perpetually implemented throughout the life of the believer?

WHAT DO THE SCRIPTURES SAY ABOUT SAVING FAITH? [31]

In Him was life, and the life was the Light of all mankind. (John 1:4)

Just as Moses lifted up the snake in the wilderness, so *the Son of Man* must be lifted up, that everyone who believes may have eternal life *in him*. For God so loved the world that he gave his one and only Son, that whoever believes *in him* shall not perish but have eternal life. For God did not send his Son into the world to condemn the world, but to save the world through him. Whoever believes *in him* is not condemned, but whoever does not believe stands condemned already because they have not believed in the name of God's one and only Son. (John 3:14–18)

For as the Father has life in himself, so he has granted *the Son* also to have life in himself. (John 5:26)

You study the Scriptures diligently because you think that in them you have eternal life. These are the Scriptures that testify about me, yet you refuse to come to *me* to have life. (John 5:39–40)

---

30. Wesley, *Works*, 5:167, emphasis added. On 1 Peter 1:5, he commented: "*Who are kept*—The inheritance is reserved; the heirs are kept for it; *by the power of God*—which worketh all in all; which guards us against all our enemies; *through faith*—through which alone salvation is both received and retained" (John Wesley, *Explanatory Notes Upon the New Testament* [Salem, Ohio: Schmul, 2000], 609).

31. All Scriptures will be from the NIV 2011 version unless otherwise noted.

For my Father's will is that everyone who looks to *the Son* and believes in *him* shall have eternal life, and I will raise him up at the last day. (John 6:40)

I am the bread of life. . . . Whoever eats *my* flesh and drinks *my* blood has eternal life, and I will raise them up at the last day. . . . Whoever eats *my* flesh and drinks *my* blood remains in *me*, and I in them. (John 6:48, 54, 56)

Jesus said to her, *I am* the resurrection and the life. The one who believes in *me* will live, even though he dies; and whoever lives by believing in *me* will never die. (John 11:25–26)

But these are written that you may believe that Jesus is the Messiah, the Son of God, and that by believing you may have life *in his name*. (John 20:31)

Whoever believes in *the Son of God* accepts this testimony. Whoever does not believe God has made him out to be a liar, because they have not believed the testimony God has given about *his Son*. And this is the testimony, God has given us eternal life, and this life is *in His Son*. Whoever has *the Son* has the life; he who does not have *the Son of God* does not have the life. I write these things to you who believe in *the name of the Son of God* so that you may know that you have eternal life. (1 John 5:10–13)

The italicized words emphasize that Jesus, the Son of God, is the *source* of eternal life (cf. Heb 5:8–9),[32] but what is the *condition* for possessing the life that the eternal God has promised "in His Son?" It is time to look more closely at some of the above passages that bear directly on this issue.

Saving Faith in John 3:14–18

14 Just as Moses lifted up the snake in the desert, so the Son of Man must be lifted up, 15 that everyone who believes in him may have eternal life.(NIV 1984)

---

32. Heb 5:8–9, "Although being a Son, he learned obedience from [the things] which he suffered. And having been made perfect, he became to all the ones obeying him [the] source of eternal salvation" (Jay D. Douglas, ed., Robert K. Brown and Philip W. Comfort, trans., *The New Greek-English Interlinear New Testament* [Wheaton: Tyndale House, 1990], 767).

Evangelical commentator J. Ramsey Michaels makes an important observation about v. 15 that is obscured by the NIV 1984 and may have been missed by the average reader:

> Only here in John's gospel is the Greek preposition *en* ["in"] used with the verb *pisteuein* "to believe." Everywhere else the preposition *eis* ("into") or a dative without a preposition is used. It is therefore likely that "in" goes with the expression "to have life" rather than with "believe": "so that everyone who believes may have eternal life in him."[33]

Other commentators have reached the same conclusions,[34] and some translations make the connection of *in Him* with *having eternal life* more obvious.

> that whosoever believeth may *in him have eternal life.* (ASV)
>
> so that whoever believes will *in Him have eternal life.* (NASB)
>
> So that everyone who believes can *have eternal life in him.* (NCV)
>
> that everyone who believes *may have eternal life in him.* (NIV 2011)

Legendary Greek scholar A. T. Robertson brings up a significant insight about the verb "have" in this verse which is missed in our English translations. In the Greek *have* is a "present active subjunctive" which he translates as: "that he may keep on having eternal life."[35] So what is the *condition* for a person to keep on having eternal life "in him"—"i.e., in union or in connection with him?"[36] R.C.H. Lenski, a Lutheran scholar, says,

---

33. J. Ramsey Michaels, *New International Biblical Commentary: John* (Peabody, Mass.: Hendrickson, 1984, 1989), 61–62.

34. *So* Robertson: "*en autōi* (in him) is taken with *echēi* ['have'] rather than with *pisteuōn* ['believes']" (A. T. Robertson, *Word Pictures in the New Testament*, 6 vols. [Nashville: Broadman, 1930], 5:50). See also F. F. Bruce, *The Gospel of John* (Grand Rapids: Eerdmans, 1983), 89; D. A. Carson, *Pillar New Testament Commentary: The Gospel According to John* (Grand Rapids: Eerdmans, 1991), 202; Robert H. Mounce, *The Expositors Bible Commentary: John*, revised edition, (Grand Rapids: Zondervan, 2007), 10:398, 399. George Allen Turner and Julius R. Mantey, *The Evangelical Commentary: The Gospel According to John* (Grand Rapids: Eerdmans, 1964), 97–98.

35. Robertson, *Word Pictures in the New Testament*, 5:49. He goes on to say, "It is more than endless [life], for it is sharing in the life of God in Christ (5:26; 17:3; 1 John 5:12)" (Ibid., 5:50).

36. R.C.H. Lenski, *Commentary on the New Testament: The Interpretation of St. John's Gospel* (Peabody, Mass.: Hendrickson, 2001), 257.

> The [Greek] present tense [verb *ho pisteuōn*, "the believing"]
> describes the person by its durative [i.e., continuing] action. . . .
> The verb [*echē*, "have"] *matches* the durative [*pisteuōn*, "believ-
> ing"]. The believer has life the moment he believes and as long as
> he believes; he is not compelled to wait until he enters heaven. . .
> . Nothing dead can give itself life, least of all that life which has
> its source in the Son of God himself. . . . And this life is "eternal,"
> . . . While its nature is "eternal" and deathlessness, it may be lost
> during our stay in this sinful world, but only by a willful and
> wicked cutting of the bond "in him," a deliberate renunciation
> and destruction of faith.[37]

Reformed and Moderate Calvinists would disagree with Lenski's concluding remarks, but they naturally follow from what Jesus has said. Since
Jesus is the source of eternal life, then a person keeps on having life "in
him" as long as they *continue believing*. Of course, this believing is directed
toward an object—the Son of Man who will be lifted up on the cross. The
Gospel writer John goes on to comment:

> For God so loved the world that he gave his one and only Son,
> that whoever believes in him shall not perish but have eternal
> life. For God did not send his Son into the world to condemn
> the world, but to save the world through him. Whoever believes
> in him is not condemned, but whoever does not believe stands
> condemned already because they have not believed in the name
> of God's one and only Son. (John 3:16-18)

God gave his Son so that the world might not perish, but be saved
through him. What kind of faith placed in Christ prevents a person from
perishing or being condemned and results in them being saved and having
eternal life? Reformed Arminian Robert Picirilli says,

> We should also note the tense action of the key verbs in the pas-
> sage [John 3:16–18], especially in vv. 16, 18. In each instance,
> negative and positive, the verbs express on-going action (the
> Greek present participles and subjunctive). Everyone who *is
> believing* (v. 16) *is having* eternal life (as also in v. 15). The one
> who *is believing* (v. 18) is not being (perhaps, "is not going to
> be") condemned, while the one who *is not believing* rests un-
> der a condemnation already established. Throughout, then, the
> continuing of a given state is co-extensive with the continuing
> of faith or unbelief . . . . Surely this indicates the Scriptural ap-
> proach to the doctrine of security of the believer. Clear, on the

one hand, is the fact that faith, and faith alone, is the condition of salvation. . . . But equally clear is the fact that continuing faith is the condition of final salvation (cf. 1 Pet. 1:5; Col 1:23).[38]

Interestingly, Calvinist Alan P. Stanley agrees with Picirilli's observations:

The most well-known verse in the entire Bible is undoubtedly John 3:16 . . . . Yet while it is well-known, it may well be the least understood. Most probably think this verse is expressing the need for a simple confession of faith in Jesus to receive eternal life, that thus we believe *once* and have eternal life. Virtually all commentators on John's Gospel,[39] though, would agree that in keeping with the Greek present tense and John's theology, John 3:16 in fact means, "For God so loved the world that he gave his one and only Son, that whoever *continues to believe* in him shall not perish but have eternal life."[40]

38. Robert Picirilli, "Editor's Note: Doctrine in Jn. 3:16–18," Jack W. Stallings, *The Randall House Bible Commentary: The Gospel of John* (Nashville: Randall House, 1989), 56. See also George Allen Turner and Julius R. Mantey, *The Gospel According to John*, 99. My theology professor, Dr. Wesley Gerig, was the first person to bring to my attention the significance of the Greek present tense verb for believing in the NT when he shared with the class his own translation of John 3:16, "For so God loved the world, so that His unique Son He gave, in order that everyone who continues believing on Him may not perish but may continue having eternal life." Dr. Gerig was Professor of Bible and Theology and taught Hebrew and Greek classes at the same college for 51 years (the college underwent name changes from Fort Wayne Bible College to Summit Christian College, and finally to Taylor University Fort Wayne). He was one of the 100-plus translators used to produce the New International Version in 1978. I appreciated him taking the time to send me via e-mail (Aug 20, 2009) updated translations of several verses used in this article.

39. For example, Keener states: "Modern readers of 3:15–16 who assume that it rewards passive faith with eternal life, apart from perseverance, read these verses in accordance with a very modern theological understanding that is utterly foreign to their Johannine context" (Craig S. Keener, *The Gospel of John: A Commentary*, 2 vols. [Peabody, Mass.: Hendrickson, 2004], 1:570). *So* G. R. Beasley-Murray:

Self-evidently the hallmark of the church in the Fourth Gospel is faith in the Son of God, who was sent from God to be the Revealer and Redeemer of humankind (John 3:16). Such faith, however, goes beyond a simple profession made in the presence of others; the Gospel emphasizes the necessity of continuing in faith and adhering to the word of Christ. (G.R. Beasley-Murray, *The Gospel of Life: Theology in the Fourth Gospel* [Peabody, Mass.: Hendrickson, 1991], 107)

40. Alan P. Stanley, *Salvation Is More Complicated Than You Think: A Study on the Teachings of Jesus* (Colorado Springs: Authentic, 2007), 165–166. *So* Butler: "We must note that the promise of eternal life is to whosoever *continues* to believe in the Son. The word 'believe' is in the Greek present tense, and indicates continued action" (Paul T.

From what we have observed from various commentators/scholars on
John 3:14–18, it is evident that saving faith involves a continuing trust in
Jesus Christ.

Saving Faith in John 20:31

> But these are written that you may believe that Jesus is the
> Christ, The Son of God, and that by believing you may have life
> in (*en*) his name (John 20:31, NIV).[41]

Notice that John employs the same preposition "in" (*en*), and uses the
equivalent expression to the "in him" phrase that Jesus used in John 3:15.
Michaels notes: "The phrase . . . (lit. 'in his name') goes with the possession
of eternal life, not with the act of believing (cf. note on 3:15; what seems to
be true there is even more clearly the case in the present passage)."[42] Lenski
states, "The preposition [*en*, in] should be left in its native sense: 'in union, in
vital connection with, his Name.'"[43] Calvinist W. H. Griffith Thomas agrees:

> The sphere in which life becomes ours and is enjoyed by us is
> found in the words "in His name." . . . The name stands . . . for
> the revealed character and will of God in Christ. Thus, to have
> life in His name is to have it *in union* with what we know of Him
> and of His manifested character and revealed will. Life is thus
> "in Christ" and not outside or apart from Him.[44]

Robertson brings up another significant insight concerning the Greek
verbs for "believing" and "have" in v. 31:

Butler, *The Gospel of John: A New Commentary, Workbook, Teaching Manuel* (Joplin,
Mo.: College, 1961), 112. Williams writes: "In Greek the present tense often means
duration, thus the sense here [in John 3:16] would be 'whoever believes, and keeps on
believing'" (J. Rodman Williams, *Renewal Theology: Systematic Theology from a Char-
ismatic Perspective*, 3 volumes in one [Grand Rapids: Zondervan, 1996], 2:129 fn. 41).
Reformed commentator William Hendriksen said: "The present participle of this verb
[believe in John 3:16] with the preposition eis, in . . . = *exercising living faith in* the
person of Christ" (William Hendrickson, *New Testament Commentary: The Gospel of
John*, 2 vols. in one [Grand Rapids: Baker, 1953], 1:141 fn. 83).

41. Gerig's translation: "but these things stand written in order that you continue
believing that Jesus is the Christ, the Son of God and in order that, because you are
continuing to believe, life you may continue having in His name" (John 20:31).

42. Michaels, *New International Biblical Commentary: John*, 336.

43. Lenski, *Commentary on the New Testament*, 1398.

44. W.H. Griffith Thomas, "The Purpose of the Fourth Gospel," *Bibliotheca Sacra*
125 (July-Sept) 1968: 261–262, emphasis added.

Note the present participle *pisteuontes* (continuing to believe) and the present active subjunctive *echēte* (keep on having). "Life" (*zōēn*) is eternal life so often mentioned in this Gospel, life to be found only in the name (and power) of Jesus Christ the Son of God.[45]

Again, saving faith is a continuing or persevering faith. A person keeps on having eternal life "in him" or "in his name" as long as they are continuing to trust in Jesus Christ the Son of God. This same teaching is taught in John's first epistle.

Saving Faith in 1 John 5:10–13

"He who believes in the Son of God has the witness in himself; he who does not believe God has made Him a liar, because he has not believed the testimony that God has given of His Son. And this is the testimony: that God has given us eternal life, and this life is in His Son. He who has the Son has life; he who does not have the Son of God does not have life. These things I have written to you who believe in the name of the Son of God, that you may know that you have eternal life" (1 John 5:10–13, NKJV).

D. Edmond Hiebert nicely explains John's teaching here:

Individuals respond either positively or negatively to God's Witness. . . . Positively, "The one who believes in the Son of God has the witness in himself." The [present tense] articular participle, "the one who believes" . . . portrays the individual as exercising *a continuing faith centered on the Son of God*. The verb "believe," . . . embodies the essence of man's response to God's witness. It involves not merely an acceptance of the truthfulness of the message but also a personal trust in or committal to the One to whom witness is borne. . . . The positive and negative statements in verse 12 stress that eternal life is inseparably related to God's Son and personally obtained only *in union* with Him. Positively, "he who has the Son has the life." The present tenses mark this possession of life as a present reality. It is only through this close and *living union* between Christ and the believer that eternal life can be experienced.[46]

Hiebert finishes his comments on v. 13 in writing:

45. Robertson, *Word Pictures in the New Testament*, 5:317.
46. D. Edmond Hiebert, "An Exposition of 1 John 5:1–12," *Bibliotheca Sacra* 147 (April-June 1990): 228, 30, emphasis added.

John's stated purpose in writing is "in order that you may know that you have eternal life." . . . The content of this assured knowledge is . . . literally, "that life ye are having eternal." . . . The present tense verb asserts that the readers already are in possession of this life. The third clause, "to you who believe in the name of the Son of God" . . . characterizes the recipients of the letter. The present tense articular participle (. . . "to those believing") designates a definite group characterized by a *living faith* uniting them with the Son of God.[47]

The evidence thus far from the Scriptures is strongly in favor of understanding eternal life as a present possession experienced in *living union* with God's Son, to the ones exercising a *continuing faith* centered on the Son of God. Since the Scriptures explicitly confirm this, it would be safe to conclude that refusal to place ones faith in God's Son, or failing to persevere in a faith centered on the Son of God, would necessarily carry the same consequence—no possession of eternal life or saving relationship with Jesus Christ.[48]

Who Has or Possesses Eternal Life?

In the Gospel of John, Jesus confronts Jewish leaders who stubbornly refuse to place their faith in him who is the source of life (cf. John 5:26):

> You diligently study the Scriptures because you think that by them you *possess (echō)* eternal life. These are the Scriptures that testify about me, yet you refuse to come to me to *have (echō)* life. (5:39–40, NIV 1984).

You may have noticed that the NIV does not translate "have" as *possess* in v. 40 as it did in v. 39. In every clear instance where the Scriptures describe who is presently *having or possessing eternal life*, it is always the person *believing or trusting* in Jesus, the Son of God.[49]

---

47. Ibid., 312, emphasis added.

48. So Keener: "Faith in the Father (through his agent Jesus, 5:24; 12:44) and the Son (1:12; 3:15, 16, 18, 36; 6:35, 40, 47; 7:38–39; 8:24; 11:25–26; 12:36, 46; 16:27; 17:8; cf. 6:29) is the precondition for salvation, but in the context of the Fourth Gospel, salvation is guaranteed only if one perseveres in such faith" (Keener, *Gospel of John*, 1:327).

49. Once, in John 5:24, the person who is *possessing* eternal life is the one *believing in the Father* who sent his Son. Keener writes:

> John often speaks of "life" (5:25, 26, 29; 6:33, 57, 63; 11:26; 14:6, 19; 17:3; 20:31; cf. 4:50; 6:44) or of "eternal life" (3:15, 16, 36; 4:14, 36; 5:21, 24, 39, 40; 6:27, 40, 47, 48; 6:51, 53, 54, 58, 68; 8:12; 10:10, 28; 11:25; 12:25, 50;

Consider the essentially literal translations that I have provided of the following verses where "has, have" (*echō*) specifically appears with "life" (*zōē*) or "eternal life" (*aiōnios zōē*),[50] I have consistently translated *echō* as *possess* or *possessing*.[51]

> And just as Moses lifted up the serpent in the wilderness, so the Son of Man must be lifted up, so that everyone *believing* shall be *possessing eternal life* in Him. For God so loved the world that He gave His one and only Son, so that everyone *believing* in Him shall not perish, but shall be *possessing eternal life*. (John 3:14–16)

> The one *believing* in the Son is *possessing eternal life*; but the one disobeying the Son will not see life, but the wrath of God is remaining on him. (John 3:36)

> For this is the will of the One having sent me, that everyone looking to the Son and *believing* in Him shall be *possessing eternal life*, and I will raise him up on the last day." (John 6:40)[52]

> Truly, truly, I say to you, the one *believing* [in me] is *possessing eternal life*. (John 6:47)

17:2); although Judaism typically understood this as a future experience, John applies present tense verbs to it (3:16, 36; 5:24; 6:47, 54; cf. 14:19), connecting it with faith (3:15, 16, 36; 6:27–29, 40, 47; 11:25, 26; 20:31) and following (8:12) in the present [tense]. (Ibid., 1:385)

50. I have consulted several literal translations and evangelical commentaries in my translation.

51. The NEB translates *echō* as "possess" or "possesses" in John 3:15; 6:40, 47, 54; 20:3; 1 John 5:12. (*The New English Bible: The New Testament* [Oxford, Cambridge, U.K.: Oxford University Press, Cambridge University Press [joint project], 1970], 154, 161, 162, 190, 413). Brown, in his own translation, uses "possess" or "possesses" in 1 John 2:23 (2x); 5:10, 12 (4x); 13, 14; 2 John 9 (2x) (Raymond E. Brown, *The Anchor Bible: The Epistles of John* [Garden City, N.Y.: Doubleday, 1982]), 353–354, 600–601, 607–609, 687–689). So also Smalley: 1 John 2:23 (2x); 5:10, 12 (2x); 13; 2 John 9 (2x) (Stephen S. Smalley, *Word Biblical Commentary: 1, 2, 3 John* [Waco: Word, 1984], 115–117, 285, 288–289, 331–332). Three other joint authors give the following definition for *echō*: "bearing or possessing abstract qualities, spiritual gifts, and powers *have, possess, enjoy* (JN 3.16)" (Timothy Friberg, Barbara Friberg, Neva F. Miller, *Analytical Lexicon of the Greek New Testament* [Grand Rapids: Baker, 2000], 184).

52. Gerig's translation: "For this is the will of My Father, that everyone continuing to behold the Son and continuing to believe on Him is continuing to have eternal life and I myself shall raise him in the last day."

Then again Jesus spoke to them saying, "I am the Light of the world. The one *following* me shall by no means walk in the darkness, but shall *possess the Light of life.*" (John 8:12)[53]

But these have been written so that you shall believe that Jesus is the Christ, the Son of God, and that *believing* you shall be *possessing life* in His name. (John 20:31)

The one *believing* in the Son of God *possesses* the witness in himself, the one not believing God has made Him a liar, because he has not believed in the testimony which God has testified concerning the Son of Him. And this is the testimony, that God gave to us eternal life, and this life is in the Son of Him. The one *possessing* the Son is *possessing life*; the one not *possessing* the Son of God is not *possessing life.* These things I wrote to you that you may know that you are *possessing eternal life*, to the ones *believing* in the name of the Son of God. (1 John 5:10–13)

According to these passages, and contrary to the Moderate Calvinists' opinion, *one's faith must be maintained in Christ to ensure the possession of eternal life.*

Saving Faith in John 6:54, 56

[Jesus said] "The one eating My flesh and drinking My blood is possessing eternal life, and I will raise him up on the last day." (John 6:54, author's translation)

In this context, "eating and drinking" are metaphors for "looking and believing."[54] Comparing vv. 54 and 40 brings this out:

verse	action	object	promises
54	eating and drinking	Christ =	possessing eternal life, I will raise up on the last day
40	looking and believing	Christ =	possessing eternal life, I will raise up on the last day

53. Gerig's translation: "Again therefore Jesus spoke to them, saying, 'I myself am the light of the world; the one who continues following me will never walk in the darkness, but will have the light of life.'" Following Jesus is synonymous to trusting in Jesus.

54. Lenski says, "If the point of comparison is asked for, it is simply that eating and drinking, like believing, is a receiving of the most intimate and vital kind. As eating and drinking receive food to be assimilated in the body, so believing receives Christ with the atonement made through his sacrificial flesh and blood" (Lenski, *Commentary on the New Testament*, 494).

Since the promises are the same, "the conclusion is obvious: the former is the metaphorical way of referring to the latter."[55] According to Robertson, the verb for *eating* is a "Present active participle for *continual or habitual eating . . .*"[56] Lenski says, "We may read [*ho trōgōn kai pinōn*, the one eating and drinking] like [*ho pisteuōn*, the one believing] with regard to a quality conveyed by continuous action: eating and drinking and going on in these actions."[57] Only those who *continue* to partake of the Bread of Life by faith are possessing eternal life and can be assured of being raised up on the last day. Christ goes on to use the same metaphors in v. 56:

> The one eating My flesh and drinking My blood is abiding/remaining[58] in Me, and I in him. (My translation)

We have already seen from John 3:15; 20:31 and 1 John 5:11 that eternal life is possessed "in (*en*) the Son" (i.e., in union with him), to those continuing to exercise a faith centered on the Son of God. Here Jesus says that the one eating and drinking (believing) is "abiding in (*en*) Me, and I in (*en*) him." What does "abiding in Me" refer to? The answer becomes obvious as we compare vv. 54 and 56:

verse	action	object	promises
54	eating & drinking	Bread of Life =	is possessing eternal life, I will raise him up on the last day
56	eating & drinking	Bread of Life =	is abiding/remaining in Me, and I in him

Since *abiding in Christ* is parallel with *possessing eternal life*, and since the *condition* for each is identical, then *abiding in Christ can mean nothing less than remaining in a life-giving union or saving relationship with Jesus Christ.* Without trust there can be no union with Christ, without union there can be no possession of eternal life since life is experienced only "in him." A person

55. Carson, *Pillar New Testament Commentary*, 297. So J. Carl Laney, *The Moody Gospel Commentary: John* (Chicago: Moody, 1992), 131; Colin G. Kruse, *Tyndale New Testament Commentary: The Gospel According to John* (Grand Rapids: Eerdmans, 2003), 175. I would add that the metaphors of "eating and drinking" are equivalent to "coming" and "believing" in John 6:35, since they correspond so well with the words "hunger and thirst": "I am the bread of life. The one coming to me never hungers, and the one believing me will never thirst again" (Douglas, Brown, Comfort, *New Greek-English Interlinear*, 341–342).

56. Robertson, *Word Pictures in the New Testament*, 5:111, emphasis added.

57. Lenski, *Commentary on the New Testament*, 493.

58. "[*menei*, "abide"] pres. ind[icative] . . . Pres. indicates a continual abiding" (Cleon L. Rogers Jr. and Cleon L. Rogers III, *The New Linguistic and Exegetical Key to the Greek New Testament* [Grand Rapids: Zondervan, 1998], 198).

receives eternal life and is united with Christ the moment they partake of (or trust in) the Bread of Life. Believers remain in a life-giving relationship with Christ, and in possession of eternal life, as long as they continue eating (trusting) the Bread of Life.[59]

The figurative language of "eating and drinking" definitely suggests *dependence upon*. Just as a person's physical life is nourished and sustained by eating and drinking so, in a similar way, the believer's spiritual life is nourished and sustained by continually partaking of the Bread of Life. However, "the figure is less than the reality, for bodily eating only sustains life already present while spiritual eating or believing expels death, bestows life, and sustains that life forever. . . . Our living is conditional on our receiving Jesus . . . ."[60]

The Scriptural evidence has been decidedly in favor of Shank's thesis— eternal life in Christ is our present possession on the condition of a present living faith. In the passages surveyed, we quoted scholar who brought to the readers' attention that the Greek present tense verb for "believing," along with its metaphorical parallel "eating and drinking," expressed *continuing action*. This provided further confirmation that a person's present possession of eternal life and saving relationship with Christ is *conditional* upon a persevering or living faith in him who is the source of life.

DOESN'T JOHN 5:24 SUPPORT UNCONDITIONAL SECURITY?

Shank wrote:

> Perhaps no verse has been more cited in evidence by advocates of unconditional security than has John 5:24, "Verily, verily, I say unto you, He that heareth my word and believeth on him that

---

59. Compare my conclusions with what Calvinists J. Carl Laney and Robert H. Mounce say:

> The present tense of verbs "eat" and "drink" point to a continuing appropriation. The present tense of "remains" (*menō*) suggests a continuous relationship (cf. John 1:32–33; 14:10). The focus of this term is on the union of the believer with Christ. The relationship between Christ and the believer is depicted as a spiritual union involving a continuous, mutual indwelling. (Laney, *Moody Gospel Commentary*, 132)

> Note here that the eating and drinking is put in the present tense, which stresses its continuing quality. Those who make it a practice of eating and drinking the flesh and blood of Jesus sustain that personal relationship. (Mounce, *Expositor's Bible Commentary*, 10:450)

60. Lenski, *Commentary on the New Testament*, 494, 501.

> sent me hath everlasting life, and shall not come into condemnation, but is passed from death unto life." "Please underscore the words 'hath everlasting life,'" say the advocates of unconditional security. Indeed! But please underscore also the words "he that heareth . . . and believeth," for they denote the condition governing the promise of everlasting life and deliverance from condemnation and death. And the hearing and believing of which Jesus spoke are not the act of a moment. . . . [One must take] into account the durative [continuous] quality of the present participles *akouōn* ["hearing"] and *pisteuōn* ["believing"] . . .

Contrary to the assumption of many, John 5:24 does not present a privileged position which, once attained, is forever irrevocable. . . . Jesus declares that the happy circumstance of deliverance from present condemnation and of standing passed out of death into life is the privilege only of such as habitually hear His word and believe the Father. It is only on the basis of present hearing and believing that one shares the eternal life of God and enjoys deliverance from present condemnation and spiritual death. [Henry] Alford declares, "The *pisteuōn* ["believing"] and the *echei z[ōēn] ai[ōnion]* ["hath life everlasting"] are *commensurate*; where the faith is, the possession of eternal life is; and when the one remits, the other is forfeited."[61]

Moderate Calvinists are familiar with Shank's argument concerning the Greek present tense verb associated with believing in this context and others, but what have they offered by way of rebuttal?

CHARLES STANLEY, BELIEVING, AND THE GREEK PRESENT TENSE

> . . . Some people argue that the believer must maintain his *faith* in order to maintain his *salvation*. The primary support for this view comes from the apostle John's use of the [Greek] present tense in connection with the term *believe*, for example.

> > And as Moses lifted up the serpent in the wilderness even so Must the Son of Man be lifted up; that whoever *believes* may in Him have eternal life. For God so loved the world, that He gave His only begotten Son, that whoever *believes* in Him shall not perish, but have eternal life.

61. Shank, *Life in the Son*, 60, 61. Gerig's translation: "Truly, truly I am saying to you, that the one who continues hearing my word and continues believing on the One who sent Me continues having eternal life and into judgment is not going to come, but has passed over out of death into life."

–John 3:14–16, emphasis added; see also 3:18; 5:24; 6:29, 6:40

Those who subscribe to this argument understand the[Greek] present tense to denote continuous, uninterrupted action. In other words, they understand John 3:16 to read, "That *whoever keeps on believing* in Him should not perish, but have eternal life." The implication is that "whoever does not keep on believing will not have eternal life" or "will lose eternal life." . . .

There are several problems with this argument. The first one has to do with their understanding of the present tense. This argument restricts the meaning of the present tense. If someone were to ask me sometime this week, "Charles, what are you doing in your spare time these days," I might respond, "Well, I'm writing a book and working in my darkroom." In my response I used progressive forms of two present tense verbs, *writing* and *working.* But no one would ascertain from my answer that in my sparetime I am writing and working in my darkroom at the same time. Neither would the understanding be that I am saying, "I don't eat, sleep, talk to my wife, or answer the phone in my spare time; [because] I am continuously writing and working in my dark room."[62]

JOHN 3:16 IN THE GREEK NEW TESTAMENT

Before I respond in more detail to Stanley's comments on the Greek present tense, we should point out that a person does not have to know Greek to understand that Jesus never intended to convey that *one moment of faith* secures one's possession of eternal life forever. English-only readers can go to a local bookstore or Christian college library and pull off the shelf any one of a number of Greek-English Interlinear translations of the New Testament that translate the Greek present participial verb *pisteuō* as "believing." Consider the following evidence from the last part of John 3:16:

that everyone the believing on him not may perish but may have life eternal[63]

---

62. Stanley, *Eternal Security,* 84–85. Geisler has responded in essentially the same manner ("Moderate Calvinism," 85–87). This is not surprising since Geisler recommends his readers to see Stanley's comments on understanding the Greek present tense for believing in chapter 9 of Stanley's book on eternal security (Ibid., 85, fn. 28).

63. Stanley M. Horton, ed., *The New Testament Study Bible: John, Greek-English Interlinear* (Springfield, Mo.: The Complete Biblical Library, 1988), 70.

that everyone - believing in him may not perish but have life eternal[64]

that everyone believing into him not may perish, but may have life everlasting[65]

that every - *one* believing in Him not should perish but should have life eternal[66]

that every - *one* trusting in Him not should perish but should have life eternal[67]

One could also search the internet or find other reference works that provide a *literal translation* of the NT which yield the same results:

> that every one who is believing in him may not perish, but may have life age-during. (*Young's Literal Translation of the New Testament*, by Robert Young)[68]

> that everyone believing may not perish, but may have eternal life. (*Disciples' Literal New Testament* by Michael Magill)[69]

> so that everyone believing in him not perish but be having eternal zoe-life. (*Faithful New Testament* by William Zeitler)[70]

> so that every [one] believing [or, trusting] in Him shall not perish, but shall be having eternal life! (*Analytical-Literal Translation of the New Testament*, by Gary F. Zeolla)[71]

Without any knowledge of Greek, English readers can discover for themselves that having eternal life is *conditional* upon trusting in Christ. This being the case, what can be said about Stanley's understanding of the Greek present tense?

---

64. Douglas, Brown, Comfort, *New Greek-English Interlinear, 326.*

65. Jay P. Green Sr., ed., *Interlinear Greek-English New Testament, third edition* (Grand Rapids: Baker, 1980, 1981, 1983, 1984, 1996), 290. See also Alfred Marshall, trans., *The Interlinear NASB-NIV Parallel New Testament in Greek and English* (Grand Rapids: Zondervan, 1993), 267.

66. Arthur L. Farstad, Zane C. Hodges, C. Michael Moss, Robert E. Picirilli, William N. Pickering, trans., *The NKJV Greek-English Interlinear New Testament* (Nashville: Thomas Nelson, 1994), 334.

67. Paul R. McReynolds, ed., *The Word Study Greek-English Interlinear New Testament* (Wheaton: Tyndale House, 1999), 335.

68. See http://biblehub.com/ylt/john/3.htm. Young's translation came out in 1862 and was revised in 1887 and 1898.

69. See http://literalnewtestament.com, 2011 PDF, 443.

70. See www.faithfulbible.com, 2008 PDF, 132.

71. Published in Bloomington, Ind.: AuthorHouse, 2005, second edition, brackets are from Zeolla, 77.

First, Stanley says that to argue that the Greek present tense refers to continuous, uninterrupted action "restricts the meaning of the present tense." This simply is not the case since those who hold this position are not saying that the present tense, whenever it is used in the New Testament, *always* means continuous action. Depending on the context, the Greek present tense may be used to describe a different kind of action. But the context in which "believes" is used in our modern translations or "believing" in our literal translations, naturally refers to *continuous action*. This is confirmed by observing the following promises made to both the *believing* and the *unbelieving/disobeying* in John 3:18 and 36:

The one *believing* in Him	the one *not believing*
is not condemned	has already been condemned (v. 18)
The one *believing* in the Son	the one *disobeying* the Son
is possessing eternal life	will not see life, but the wrath of God
	is remaining on him (v. 36)[616]

Both verbs in 3:18 for *believing* are Greek present participles representing "continuous believing marking the one man, continuous non-believing the other."[73] In v. 36 *believing* and *disobeying* are present participles as well.[74] Since the grammar of the two is identical then they must be interpreted in the same way. If Stanley wants to argue, as he does, that after *one* moment of faith a person possesses eternal life *forever* even if he/she later on *becomes an unbeliever*; then he must also argue that after *one* moment of unbelief/disobedience a person is condemned *forever* to spend eternity in hell even if he/she later on *becomes a believer*. It is highly unlikely that this is what the author intended to communicate.

All 3:18, 36 mean is that the person who remains as one of the unbelieving or disobeying will inevitably share the destiny promised to them. Likewise, the person who remains as one of the believing will inevitably

72. Author's translations.

73. Lenski, *Commentary on the New Testament*, 267.

74. *So* Raymond E. Brown: "Notice the present tenses, 'believes,' 'disobeys'; John is not thinking of a single act but of a pattern of life" (Raymond E. Brown, *The Anchor Bible: The Gospel According to John*, 2 vols. [Garden City, N.Y.: Doubleday, 1970], 1:162). Frank Pack: "The words translated *believes* (*pisteuōn*) and *does not obey* (*apeithōn*) are both present participles and express the continuing pattern of one's life" (Frank Pack, *The Gospel According to John*, 2 vols. [Austin, Texas: Sweet, 1975], 1:69).

share the destiny promised to them. Since the promises of condemnation/ wrath and no eternal life to unbelievers does not mean that an unbeliever can never change his future destiny by becoming a believer, then the promises of no condemnation and possession of eternal life to a believer also does not mean that he can never change his future destiny by becoming an unbeliever.[75] Just as saving faith is not simply the act of a moment, but the attitude of a life, so condemning unbelief/disobedience is not simply the act of a moment but the attitude of a life as well.

Stanley's faulty conclusions concerning the Greek present tense are a direct result of failing to interpret in context the passages where "believing" is put in contrast to the "unbelieving/disobeying." Nevertheless, Stanley goes on to argue,

> The normal use of the [Greek] present tense does not denote continuous, uninterrupted action. Certainly it can, but it does not have to. If you were to ask me where I lived, I might say, "I live in Atlanta." In that case the present tense *live* would imply a continuous action. But even then, if you saw me somewhere other than Atlanta, you would not accuse me of lying. Why? Because that is not the way the present tense is used in real life.[76]

This argument and illustration is irrelevant since my concern is not with how the Greek present tense is used in *the English language* and thus in "real life." I am trying to determine whether a present tense verb *in the Greek language can convey continuous action.* Stanley admits that it can, but argues that this is not its "normal" usage. Unfortunately, Stanley does not provide the reader any evidence from Greek reference works to support his view?[77] Common sense would suggest that that this would be a good place to start.

---

75. In the preceding two paragraphs I am indebted to Picirilli's "Editor's Note on John 5:24: Do Promises to Believers Guarantee their Security?" 85–86. Stephen H. Travis says,

> For John, more sharply than for any other New Testament writer, people are divided into two groups with two destinies—those who are for Christ and those against him. Even so, the groups are not fixed and unchangeable. The unbeliever may still believe and cross over from death to life [John 5:24]. And—in principle at least—the believer may cease to maintain a relationship with Christ and ultimately be "thrown away" [John 15:6]. (Steven H. Travis, *Christ and the Judgment of God: The Limits of Divine Retribution in New Testament Thought* [Peabody, Mass.: Hendrickson, 2008], 274)

76. Stanley, *Eternal Security*, 85.

77. Stanley's seminary training (bachelor of divinity degree from Southwestern Theological Seminary, and his master's and doctor's degrees from Luther Rice Seminary) would have required him to study Greek, so it is surprising to find no comments

GREEK GRAMMARIANS AND
THE GREEK PRESENT TENSE

Daniel B. Wallace has produced a highly respected work.[78] He presently teaches Greek at Dallas Theological Seminary, an institution known for its belief in eternal security. Wallace is in line with what the seminary ascribes to, yet he does not hold that a person can stop trusting in Christ and still be in possession of eternal life as Stanley argues. This will become apparent as we proceed further.

Allow me to summarize the *specific uses* Wallace gives of the Greek present tense with their *definitions* and urge the reader to consult his textbook for the complete *definition, key to identification,* and Scriptural *illustrations* or examples provided.[79] Depending on the context, the Greek present tense may be used:

- to indicate that an action is completed at the *moment* of speaking—*Instantaneous Present.* It is relatively common.

- to describe a scene in progress, especially in narrative literature—*Progressive Present (or Descriptive Present).* The progressive present is common.[80]

- to describe an action which, begun in the past, continues in the present—*Extending-from-Past Present (Present of Past Action Still in Progress).* The emphasis is on the present time. Depending on how tightly one defines this category, its usage is either relatively rare or fairly common.

- to describe an event that *repeatedly* happens—*Iterative Present.* It is frequently found in the imperative mood,[81] since an action is urged to be done. The iterative present is common.[82]

---

from Greek reference works that would substantiate his views.

78. Daniel B. Wallace, *Greek Grammar Beyond the Basics: An Exegetical Syntax of the New Testament* (Grand Rapids: Zondervan, 1996.)

79. Wallace discusses the *special uses of the present tense* which have no impact on the issue at hand (Ibid., 526–529).

80. Wallace says, "The difference between this and the iterative (and customary) present is that the latter involves a *repeated* action, while the progressive present normally involves *continuous* action" (Ibid., 518).

81. Wallace: "the imperative is most often used to make a *command*" and "is commonly used to forbid an action" [for example] Rom 6:12, "Do not let sin reign in your mortal body" (Ibid., 486–487).

82. Wallace says, "This use of the [iterative] present is different from the customary present in terms of time frame and regularity. The intervals are shorter with the iterative, and less regular. However, several passages are difficult to analyze and could

- to make a statement of a general, timeless fact—*Gnomic Present*. "It does not say that something *is* happening, but that something *does* happen." The action or state continues without time limits. The verb is used "in proverbial statements or general maxims about what occurs at *all* times." This usage is common.[83]

Wallace's definition of the *Customary (Habitual or General) Present* is particularly significant for our study:

> The customary present is used to signal either an action that *regularly occurs* or an *ongoing state*. The action is usually *iterative*, or repeated, but not without interruption. This usage is quite common. The difference between the customary (proper) and the iterative present is mild. Generally, however, it can be said that the *customary* present is *broader* in its idea of the "present" time and describes an event that occurs *regularly*. . . . The two types of customary present are lexically determined: One is repeated action (habitual present [*customarily, habitually*]), while the other is ongoing state (stative present [*continually*]).[84]

Interestingly, John 3:16 is one of the clear examples that Wallace provides for the *Customary Present:*

> Everyone who [continually] *believes* in him should not perish. This could also be taken as a gnomic present, but if so it is not a proverbial statement, nor is it simply a general maxim. In this Gospel, there seems to be a qualitative distinction between the ongoing act of believing and the simple fact of believing.[85]

Wallace again uses John 3:16 as one of his biblical examples, but this time he focuses on *believes* as a "present participle." *Believes* occurs numerous times in the Gospel of John and in the rest of the New Testament as a present participle.[86] In his textbook, William D. Mounce writes: "The present participle is built on the present tense stem of the verb. It describes a continuous action. It will often be difficult to carry this 'on-going' nuance into your translation, but this must be the foremost consideration in your

---

conceivably fit in either category" (Ibid., 520).

83. Ibid., 516–525, emphasis his.

84. Ibid., 521–522, brackets are from Wallace.

85. Ibid., 522, brackets are from Wallace.

86. John 1:12; 3:15, 16, 18 (twice); 3:36; 5:24; 6:35, 40, 47, 64; 7:38; 11:25, 26; 12:44, 46; 20:31; Acts 2:44; 10:43; 13:39; Rom 1:16; 3:22; 4:5, 11, 24; 9:33; 10:4, 11; 1 Cor 1:21; 14:22 (twice); Gal 3:22; Eph 1:19; 1 Thess 1:7; 2:10, 13; 1 Pet 1:8; 2:6, 7; 1 John 5:1, 5, 10 (twice), 13.

mind."[87] Wallace brings out this "ongoing nuance" in his translation of John 3:16,

> everyone *who believes*
>
> The idea seems to be both gnomic and continual: "everyone who continually believes." This is not due to the present tense only, but to the use of the present participle of [*pisteuōn*], especially in soteriological [i.e., salvation] contexts in the NT.[88]

In his footnotes, Wallace goes on to elaborate,

> The aspectual force of the present [participle for "the believing"] seems to be in contrast with [the aorist participle for "the having believed"] . . . . The present [participle for believe] occurs six times as often (43 times) [in comparison to the aorist], most often in soteriological contexts (cf. John 1:12; 3:15, 16, 18; 3:36; 6:35, 47, 64; 7:38; 11:25; 12:46; Acts 2:44; 10:43; 13:39; Rom 1:16; 3:22; 4:11, 24; 9:33; 10:4, 11; 1 Cor 1:21; 1 Cor 14:22; Gal 3:22; Eph 1:19; 1 Thess 1:7; 2:10, 13; 1 Pet 2:6, 7; 1 John 5:1, 5, 10, 13). Thus, it seems that since the aorist participle was a live option to describe a "believer," it is unlikely that when the present was used, it was aspectually flat. The present was the tense of choice most likely because the NT writers by and large saw *continual* belief as a necessary condition of salvation. Along these lines, it seems significant that the *promise* of salvation is almost always given to ["the believing"] (cf. several of the above cited texts), almost never to ["the having believed"] (apart from Mark 16:16, John 7:39 and Heb 4:3 come the closest . . .).[89]

Wallace's comments about the Greek present tense verb *pisteuō* ("believing) in salvation contexts is consistent with what has been discovered already from the Scriptures. A person's present possession of eternal life/ salvation is *conditional* upon an ongoing trust in the source of life/salvation, Jesus Christ.[90] While it is acknowledged by Greek grammarians that "continuous action" does not monopolize the "present tense," Robertson says,

---

87. William D. Mounce, *Basics of Biblical Greek Grammar*, 2nd edition, (Grand Rapids: Zondervan, 2003), 246. So Ernest De Witt Burton, "The Present Participle most frequently denotes an action in progress, simultaneous with the action of the principal verb" (*Syntax of the Moods and Tenses in New Testament Greek*, [Chicago: The University of Chicago Press, 1900], 54).

88. *Greek Grammar Beyond the Basics:* 620–621, brackets are mine.

89. Ibid., 621, brackets are mine.

90. Daniel Steele (1824–1914), a Methodist pastor and professor of NT Greek at Boston University, arrived at parallel conclusions and wrote:

The next fact which impresses us in our investigation is the . . . *presence of the present tense whenever the conditions of final salvation are stated.* Our inference is that the conditions of ultimate salvation are continuous, extending through probation, and not completed in any one act. The great requirement is faith in Jesus Christ. A careful study of the Greek will convince the student that it is a great mistake to teach that a single act of faith furnishes a person with a paid-up, non-forfeitable policy, assuring the holder that he will inherit eternal life, or that a single energy of faith secures a through ticket to heaven . . . . The Greek tenses show that faith is a state, a habit of mind, into which the believer enters at justification. . . .

John 1:12: But as many as received (aor.) Him . . . to them gave He power to become the sons of God, even to them that are believing (present) perseveringly on His name. . .

John 3:15: That whosoever is continuously believing in Him should not perish . . . but be having everlasting life. Here, again, the present . . . participle of the verb to believe is used, as it is again in verses 16 and 36.

John 5:24: Verily, verily I say unto you, he that is always hearing My word, and constantly believing on Him that sent Me, hath eternal life, and is not coming into condemnation, but as passed over (perfect) from death unto life, and so continues. Says Alford: "So in 1 John 5:12, 13, the believing and the having eternal life are *commensurate*; where the faith is, the possession of eternal life is, and when the one remits, the other is forfeited. But here the faith is set before us as an *enduring* faith, and its effects described *in their completion.* (See Eph. 1:19, 20)." Thus this great English scholar rescues this text from its perverted use, to teach an eternal incorporation into Christ by a single act of faith, and he demonstrates the common-sense doctrine that the perseverance of the saints is grounded on persistent trust in Jesus Christ. . . .

John 6:29: . . . This is the work of God, that ye perseveringly believe [on Him whom He sent].

John 6:35: He that is perpetually coming (pres.) to Me shall not, by any means (double negative), once hunger (aor.) and he that is constantly believing in Me (emphatic) shall never, by any means, (double negative), feel one pang of thirst (aor.). . . .

John 6:54: Whoso eateth (pres., keeps eating) My flesh, and drinketh (keeps drinking) My blood, hath eternal life.

John 11:25, 26: he that believeth persistently (pres.) shall not, by any mean (double negative), die (aor.) forever.

John 20:31: That ye might believe . . . that Jesus is the Christ, the Son of God, and that, believing constantly (pres.), ye might have life through His name. . . .

In Rom. 1:16, where future and eternal salvation is spoken of, it is promised to every one that perseveringly believes (pres.). So also in Rom. 3:22; 4:24; 9:33; 10:4, 11; 1 Cor. 1:21; Eph. 1:19; 1 Thess. 1:7; 2:10, 13; 4:14. . . .

Hence we conclude from a thorough examination of the above texts, that the Spirit of inspiration has uniformly chosen the present tense in order to teach that final salvation depends on persevering faith. (Daniel Steel, *Mile-stone Papers: Doctrinal, Ethical, and Experimental on Christian Progress* [New York: Nelson and Phillips; Cincinnati: Hitchcock and Walden, 1878] 47–52, in chapter titled: "Tense Readings of the Greek New Testament") "it more frequently denotes linear [i.e. continuous] action. The verb and the context must decide."[91]

Stanley and other Moderate Calvinists have the burden of proof to demonstrate that the Greek present tense verb for "believing," in salvation contexts, does not convey *continuous action*, but some other kind of action. It was demonstrated that in salvation contexts such as John 3:18, 36, where "the believing" was contrasted with "the unbelieving/disobeying," the most natural interpretation was to see both sets of verbs as describing *continuous or ongoing actions*.[92] Furthermore, the Scriptures state that eternal life is possessed only "in Christ." A person possesses eternal life the moment they believe in Christ, and as long as they continue to trust in him they remain "in him," in a life-giving union and saving relationship with him (John 6:56; cf. John 15:1–6).

Stanley asserted that the Greek present tense does not normally convey continuous action, but failed to provide any support for his belief from Greek reference works. The evidence we have brought forth from Greek-English interlinears, literal translations, and Greek grammarians has shown Stanley's understanding of the Greek present tense, as it relates to believing and having eternal life, to be inadequate and dangerously misleading. From a pastoral perspective, it is disheartening to read Stanley telling other Christians that they can stop trusting in Christ, become unbelievers, and still be in possession of eternal life from Christ. Would it not be more pastorally responsible to tell other Christians that once they place their faith in Christ that God "irresistibly" insures that they will continue to do so till the end of their life? While I do not believe that this position can be supported from

---

91. A.T. Robertson, *A Grammar of the Greek New Testament in the Light of Historical Research* [Nashville: Broadman, 1934], 587. In the introduction to the *The NKJV Greek-English Interlinear New Testament*, it says, "The present tense often, but by no means always, has a linear, that is a continuous idea" (xvi).

92. See David Redelings excellent discussion on belief/trust in the Gospel of John in *The Epistemological Basis for Belief According to John's Gospel: Miracles and Message in Their Essentials As Non-Fictional Grounds for Knowledge of God* (Eugene, Ore.: Pickwick, 2011), 8–21. He states:

> In this gospel, several contextual factors show when the present participle of *pisteuō* is to be understood as a continuing state of belief.... The Evangelist frequently juxtaposes *believing* with the resulting state of eternal life (John 3:15, 16, 36; 5:24, 6:40, 47; 11:25, 26). At the same time, he often places it in antithesis to both *not believing* and judgment, thus requiring us to understand *believing* as a state, rather than as an action occurring at a single moment in time, which might later be reversed. The identifying characteristic of those receiving eternal life is not merely belief that happens for a moment, nor belief that continues for a time, but belief that is customary [i.e., that continues]. (Ibid., 18)

Scripture, it at least maintains that one's saving relationship with Christ rests upon a living faith in a living Savior.

SO WHO IS RIGHT?

At the beginning of this article Robert Shank asked, "Who is right?" as to whether saving faith is the act of a moment or the attitude of a life. My biblical investigation led to the same conclusions that Shank reached over 50 years ago—saving faith is the attitude of a life and "the initial decision must be perpetually implemented throughout the life of the believer."[93]

For Arminians like Shank, eternal life is not an it or a thing but a relationship with Jesus who is the source of life.[94] As long as we keep on trust-

---

93. Shank, *Life in the Son*, 51. See also Paul Trebilco's outstanding chapter on how Christians used "the believing ones" as a self-designation from a comparatively early period in, *Self-designations and Group Identity in the New Testament* (Cambridge: Cambridge University Press, 2012), 68–121. In his thorough examination of the New Testament Greek words for believe/trust, and faith/faithful, his conclusions parallel our own:

> Predominantly it is the present participle [*pisteuō*] that is used in believer-designations, with fifty occurrences out of a total of sixty-five. Given that the aorist and perfect are also used, we have quoted Wallace's comment above to the effect that the present was not "aspectually flat," but its choice reflected the fact that continual believing was regarded as vital. "Believing" was *both* an initial response to the Gospel, *and* an ongoing characteristic of Christians. This blends into the idea of "faithfulness" in the Christian life, which is clearly expressed by [*ho pistoi*, the faithful] as a designation in some books. This latter designation, used mainly in the Pastorals, but elsewhere as well, emphasizes the ongoing dimension of faithfulness and believing even more than the participle. (Ibid., 120)

94. Shank effectively answered a common objection that is raised by those who hold to unconditional eternal security: "If eternal life can be terminated, how then can it be *eternal*?" He writes,

> Such a question proceeds from a fundamental misapprehension. It rests upon the erroneous assumption that, at conversion, God somehow implants a bit of eternal life within the soul of the individual in such a way that it becomes his inalienable personal possession *ipso facto* [by the fact itself]. Certainly eternal life is *eternal*. But the Bible declares that eternal life—the very life of God Himself—can only be *shared* with men. It cannot be possessed by men apart from a living union with Christ, in and through whom that life is available to men. . . .
> There can be no question whether eternal life will endure. It cannot cease. But the point of the many solemn warnings in the New Testament is that our privilege of *participating* in that eternal life is directly dependent upon our continuing to abide in Him in whom, alone, that life is available to men. If we fail to abide in Him, the eternal life continues; but our participation in that life ceases. We share that life only as we continue to abide in Him "who is our life" (Shank, *Life in the Son*, 52, 54).

ing in Jesus we keep on receiving life from him. Shank was also right that life is *in the Son*—life is experienced in a living union with a living Savior through a living faith. Therefore, we would be wise to heed his admonishment, (which is Jesus's as well, John 15:4–5), to "continue to abide in Him 'who is our life' [Col 3:4]."[95]

95. Shank, *Life in the Son*, 54.

14

Soteriology, Perseverance and Apostasy in the Epistle to the Hebrews

Grant R. Osborne

Perhaps the most enigmatic work in the New Testament is the epistle to the Hebrews. Both authorship[1] and destination are unsolved problems, and the perspective of the book as a whole is vigorously debated. The general view is that it had a Jewish Christian provenance; in fact, the strong dualism and the figures employed (angels, Melchizedek, etc.) have led some to posit an Essenic background.[2]

---

1. Guesses, in addition to Paul (which few hold anymore), have involved Barnabas (Tertullian), Apollos (Martin Luther), Clement of Rome (Eusebius), Luke (Origen, John Calvin), Philip (William M. Ramsay), Aquilla (Henry Alford), or Priscilla (Donald Guthrie).

2. See Yigael Yadin, "The Dead Sea Scrolls and the Epistle to the Hebrews," Yigael Yadin, Chaim Rabin, eds. *Aspects of the Dead Sea Scrolls, Scripta Hierosoloymitana 4* (Jerusalem: Magnes, 1965), 36f; Jean Danielou, *The Dead Sea Scrolls and Primitive Christianity* (Baltimore: Helicon, 1958), 111f; Hans Kosmala, *Hebräer-Essener-Christen* (Leiden: E. J. Brill, 1959), passim; Philip E. Hughes, *A Commentary to the Hebrews* (Grand Rapids: Eerdmans, 1977), 12–15; and John W. Bowman, *Hebrews, James, 1 Peter, 2 Peter Layman's Bible Commentaries* (London: SCM, 1968), 13–16. F. F. Bruce, "'To the Hebrews' or 'To the Essenes'?" *New Testament Studies* 9 (1963), 217f, on the other hand, believes these are Jewish sectarians in general rather than Essenes in particular.

Others have noted an Alexandrian hermeneutic and have hypothesized a Philonic origin.[3] On the other hand, many scholars recently have argued for a Gentile destination, especially since the early church considered itself to be the New Israel, and the Old Testament was authoritative for Gentile as well as Jew.[4] In fact, parallels to gnosticism, such as the dualism throughout, the concept of the "wandering people of God," and the speculative Christology, have led some to postulate a Hellenistic provenance.[5] With regard to the present state of the question, it may be best to assume that the work was written to a mixed group of believers, possibly at Rome (13:24).[6]

The Essenic, Philonic, and Hellenistic elements are all seemingly present and may be due to the background of the author himself as well as the addresses. The danger to which the epistle speaks, then, would be a relapse into the old way of life, whether Jew of Gentile. In countering this danger, the author points to the overwhelming superiority of Christ.

Most writers believe the theology of the epistle centers on Christology, especially upon Jesus's high priesthood.[7] However, we would agree with Marxsen's statement that while "it is true that in many respects [the writer's Christology] is unusual. . . we would be interpreting the author's message wrongly, or at least in an unbalanced way, if we were to assume that he was interested in christological speculations. His approach is far more from the soteriological angle."[8]

3. See Ceslas Spicq, *L'Epitre aux Hebreux* (Paris: J. Gabalda, 1952–1953), 1:39–91 and Hugh Montefiore, *The Epistle to the Hebrews, Harper's New Testament Commentaries* (New York: Harper & Row, 1964), 8–9, who argue the author was converted from Philonism.

4. See Werner G. Kummel, *Introduction to the New Testament,* Howard Clark Kee, trans. (Nashville: Abingdon, 1975), 398–400, who argues that since in the epistle Christ is made superior to the Old Testament rather than to Judaism, the readers are probably Gentile. See also James Moffatt, *A Critical and Exegetical Commentary on the Epistle to the Hebrews* (Edinburgh: T & T Clark, 1968), xvi-xvii; and Ernest Findlay Scott, *The Epistle to the Hebrews: Its Doctrine and Significance* (Charleston, S.C.: Nabu, 2010), 30–45.

5. See Ernst Kasemann, *The Wandering People of God* (Minneapolis: Augsburg, 1984), passim, and Willi Marxsen, *Introduction to the New Testament,* tr. G. Buswell (Philadelphia: Fortress, 1968 [Oxford, U.K: Blackwell]), 217. Frederick D.V. Narborough, *The Epistle to the Hebrews* (Oxford, U.K.: Clarendon, 1943), 23–27, on the other hand, believes the readers were proto-gnostic Jews.

6. See George H. Guthrie, *Hebrews: The NIV Application Commentary* (Grand Rapids: Zondervan, 1989), 19–20; and Kummel, *Introduction to the New Testament,* 398–400. Guthrie would see a stronger Jewish element, Kummel a stronger Gentile element. We would follow Guthrie's position.

7. See F. F. Bruce, "'To the Hebrews' or 'To the Essenes'?" 217–232; and George E. Ladd. *A Theology of the NewTestament* (Grand Rapids: Eerdmans, 1974), 577f.

8. Willi Marxsen, *Introduction to the New Testament,* 219.

In this epistle, Christology is presented from a soteriological perspective, i.e., with a soteriological purpose. Indeed, it is the writer's overriding soteriology that determines the contents of his epistle. His purpose has been defined in various ways: to demonstrate the superior priesthood of Christ, to warn Jewish Christians about apostasy, to demonstrate the universalism of Christianity as a world religion, to show that the Christian life is a pilgrimage, and to establish the finality of the gospel.[9] All of these, which are legitimate purposes, reflect the writer's soteriological concern.

He views the Christian life as a dynamic process, and salvation is seen to be a day-by-day walk with Christ. The believer dares not lapse into an apathetic Christianity, for his very "life" is at stake. This theology will be the focus of this study. Before we can proceed further, however, we must determine the spiritual condition of the readers: were they actual Christians or not? Many have argued they were not believers. Calvin, for instance, believed they were outward followers but were not among the "elect,"[10] and Kosmala says they were members of Qumran who had not yet accepted Jesus as Messiah. However, it seems far more likely in light of 3:1f.; 6:4f.; 9f.; 10:23, 26; 12:22f. that they were believers.

They showed every evidence of being Christians, were called "brothers" (2:11, 12, 17; 3:1, 12; 7:5; 8:11; 10:19; 13:22, 23) and were in danger of apostatizing "from the living God" (3:12). It is doubtful that a good case can be made for denying the reality of a faith described in such terms as 6:4–6 (see below).

I. SOVEREIGNTY AND FREE WILL

W. C. Linss[11] has noted the presence of divine necessity in the terms of 2:1 (*dei*), 2:10 and 7:26 *(heprepen)*, 2:17 and 5:3 *(ōpheilie)*, 9:26 *(hedei)*, and 8:13 and 9:16, 23 *(anagkē)*. He also finds traces in the warning passages (6:4, 18; 10:4, 11; 11:6) which discuss the impossibility of reconversion for the apostate. When we examine the passages teaching sovereignty, we find that

9. See, respectively, Alexander Nairne, *The Epistle to the Hebrews* (Cambridge: Cambridge University Press, 1922), lxxxvii; F.F. Bruce, *The Epistle to the Hebrews New International Commentary on the New Testament* (Grand Rapids: Eerdmans, 1964), xxx; William Manson, *The Epistle to the Hebrews* (London: Hodder & Stoughton Ltd., 1951), 23–46; Kasemann, *The Wandering People of God*, 24f; and I. Howard Marshall, *Kept by the Power of God* (London: Epworth, 1969), 132–133.

10. See his commentary on Hebrews, especially ch. 6; and his *Institutes of the Christian Religion* (Grand Rapids: Eerdmans, 1957) 1: 608–609.

11. W. C. Linss, "Logical Terminology in the Epistle to the Hebrews," *Concordia Theological Monthly* 37 (1966), 365–369.

the overwhelming majority concerns the necessity of Christ's sacrifice. The only exceptions are 5:3 (on the old covenant practices) and 2:1 (on the need for "greater attention" on the part of these apathetic Christians).

There is no mention of predestination in a Pauline sense. As Marshall says regarding 11:40, "The idea here is not that of the predestination of particular people to salvation, but rather of the fulfillment of God's promises in due time. . . . The key word in Hebrews is not predestination but promise. Such promises may be pre-temporal, but their fulfilment depends, in each case, upon the faith and obedience of the recipients (Heb. 4:2; 6:11f.; 10:36)."[12]

In this epistle we see the God of the covenant, the God who is faithful to his promises. The keynote is reflected in 13:5, which uses Deut 31:6, 8, "I will never leave you or forsake you," as the basis for Christian contentment. There, God's faithfulness is seen to be more precious than riches; in v. 6 this becomes the antidote to fearful anxiety. At the same time these promises can only be realized by those who take them by faith. The sovereign power is available, but only to those who appropriate it for themselves. On this basis we see here a perfect balance between sovereignty and free will, with the emphasis being placed on the latter due to the particular problem to which the epistle is addressed, namely the willful apostasy of some from the faith.

II. THE POSSIBILITY OF APOSTASY

The key to the purpose of this epistle is 13:22, which describes it as a "word of exhortation." The extensive passages on the superiority of the person, ministry and death of Christ all point to this and set the scene for the "exhortation" or warning passages. Bornkamm argues that a familiar baptismal confession has been employed to highlight the present privileges of the readers (cf. 3:1; 4:14; 10:19f.),[13] and he may be right. At the very least these are catechetical elements used to stress the foundation of the readers' faith and to provide a further backdrop to the warning passages.

---

12. I. Howard Marshall, *Kept by the Power of God*, 147. Against Michel's claim that the "firstborn enrolled in heaven" in 12:23 teaches election, he asserts (148) that it simply speaks of the "burgess role of the citizens of Zion" and says nothing about election.

13. Gunther Bornkamm, "Das Bekenntnis im Hebrartntirg," *Studien zu Antike und Christentum* II (Munchen: C. Kaiser, 1959), 188f. However, we would not go so far as Philip Hughes, who says the danger was the repudiation of the converts' baptism, also a once-for-all event (to repeat it would be to repeat Christ's crucifixion and thus to mock the cross). There is no basis for such an extensive reinterpretation of the apostasy passages.

Pay attention, lest you drift away, 2:1–4—The first chapter had shown that Christ was superior to the angels, who possibly had been objects of worship among at least a segment of the addressees.[14] These verses draw the conclusion from this (*ouv*) and show that the purpose for the exalted Christology of chapter 1 was exhortatory. The overwhelming preeminence of the Son demands decision, and the readers must change their lives accordingly. They dare not allow themselves to "drift away" from the teaching of the gospel regarding such a One. This warning is important enough that the author includes himself in it, "We must pay more attention to what *we* have heard, lest we drift away. . . . How shall *we* escape if we neglect so great a salvation."

"Drift away" is a nautical term which metaphorically pictures indifference as an uncharted boat drifting out to sea and death on offshore rocks.[15] Apathetic "neglect"[16] of the Christian truths, which were confirmed by eyewitnesses, "signs and wonders," "mighty works," and "gifts of the Holy Spirit" (vv. 3b, 4), lead to a condition from which there is no "escape." The tone is eschatological, looking to the final judgment, and the believer is warned that present indifference will result in final retribution. "Salvation" here is similar to that in 1 Peter rather than Paul (see further below), looking to the future reward of the people of God. As such, its attainment is based on persevering growth in the truths of the gospel; this is seen in the "pay more attention" of v. 1.

Do not harden your heart, lest you fail, 3:1–19—This passage follows the discussion of Jesus's high priestly activity and begins by asserting Jesus's superiority to Moses (vv. 1–6), implying thereby that rejection of Jesus is correspondingly more serious than Israel's rejection of Moses. In keeping with this theme, the author uses the wilderness wandering as an illustration of the danger (vv. 7–19). At the outset, the writer stresses their position as the true Church, the New Israel—"holy brethren" (v. 1), "partakers of Christ" (vv. 1, 14), Christ's "house" (v. 6), and "brethren" (v. 12). These are called upon to persevere, to "hold fast . . . firm unto the end" (vv. 6, 14), and this is to be accomplished by "hardening not your hearts" (vv. 8, 15) and by "exhorting one another daily" (v. 13).

14. See Manson, *The Epistle to the Hebrews*, 49–51; Bowman, *Hebrews, James, 1 Peter, 2 Peter Layman's Bible Commentaries*, 24–25; and Montefiore, *The Epistle to the Hebrews*, 50–54.

15. Another metaphorical use of the same verb pictures a ring "slipping off" a finger and being lost.

16. This question (v. 3) is used by those who wish to deny that the readers were Christians. However, the use of "we" throughout plus the data already discussed favors the interpretation here.

He also emphasizes that as a result of "unbelief" one can "fail to enter God's rest" (v. 19). One must conclude that the reward is conditional[17] upon perseverance in "confidence and the boast of our hope" (v. 6) and in "the beginning of our assurance" (v. 14). The danger envisaged here is that the deceitfulness of sin can progressively harden one's spiritual resolve and that this evil, unbelieving condition can cause one to "fall away from the living God" (vv. 12–15). In this context this denotes the results of active rebellion against God.[18] Wilderness typology was quite prevalent in the early church as illustrative of both judgment and reward. Both 1 Cor 10:1–13 and Jude 5 make it a warning against the dangers of sin.

The obvious inference in all three passages is that one dare not trust his original "deliverance" from sin and lapse into apathy, but must persevere in his walk with Christ. Ps. 95:7b-11, used by the writer as the basis for his splendid *midrash* here, was sung by Jews as part of their sabbath worship in the temple. The readers probably understood it in this fashion, especially since vv. 1–7a of the psalm consist of a call to worship. The obvious inference is that one must listen to God—"Today if you shall hear His voice" (vv. 7, 15)[19]—and that this listening includes obedience.[20]

Fear, lest you fall short, 4:1–13—This passage is an extended explanation of the "rest" theology of 3:11, 19. Here the writer adds the "reward" imagery from the "wilderness" typology of 3:1–19.

To the Jew, the "rest" of God referred to his "promises" which were still "open" to his people, i.e., they extended beyond the "Promised Land" of Canaan. Israel failed to appropriate these promises and so failed to "enter" God's "rest." This is an eschatological concept which implies that the believer proleptically shares the "rest of God," i.e., the kingdom blessings of peace and security promised for the "last days." This rest is still promised to God's people, but they must "enter" it themselves (4:9, 10). In Jewish exegesis, the

<hr>

17. The conditional particles in vv. 6, 14 are, respectively, *ean* and *eanper*, which provide further evidence that the writer considers apostasy to be possible.

18. "Provocation" and "trial" in v. 8 and Ps 95:8 (LXX) look back to Exod 17:1–7, where Moses, exasperated at Israel's revolt because there was no water, renamed the place *Massah* (tempting) and *Meribah* (striving), because their "strife" "tempted" Yahweh's patience.

19. Bruce, *Epistle to the Hebrews*, 65, points out the messianic interpretation of this phrase in TB Sanhedrin 98a, where it is used to explain the coming of the Messiah to the gates of Rome. Messianic salvation is conditional upon hearing and obeying.

20. Both the Old Testament and New Testament concepts of "hearing" precluded one's obedience to the message. See Gerhard Kittel, "akouo," Gerhard Kittel, Geoffrey Bromiley, eds., *Theological Dictionary of the New Testament* (Grand Rapids: Eerdmans, 1964), 1:218–220.

"Sabbath rest" referred to "the world to come" (Gen R 17:12a).[21] Here the writer uses it in the sense of inaugurated eschatology, for the believer lives in a state of tension between the present promise and future realization. It is meant for "today" for those who obey and do not "harden" their hearts (4:6, 7 repeating 3:7–8, 15), and yet it is a heritage they can only claim by faith and which points forward to the next life.[22]

The believer is responsible for his perseverance in that "rest." Therefore in this epistle salvation merges with the concept of rewards, and the realized aspect of the reward (present faith) merges with the final aspect (future hope). Eschatology becomes a part of soteriology.

Press on, lest you fall away, 5:11—6:12—After a further section on Christ's high priesthood, this time centering on his superior qualifications and Melchizedekian office, the writer discusses his readers' immaturity and need for spiritual growth. Verses 5:11 and 6:12, combined with the plea for hearing/obedience in 3:7–8, 15; 4:7, shows that the problem had not yet gone so far as apostasy. What we see here is a spiritual deafness which may be called "spiritual laziness."[23] The readers were not listening to God or seeking to grow nearer to him. This would fit the picture of spiritual apathy we noted in 2:1–4.

Though they had been believers for some time, they were still "babes" in Christ who had not learned even the "fundamentals of the first principles" (5:12). Far from being ready for the advanced doctrine of Jesus's high priestly ministry, they needed to be retaught the ABCs of the faith. They had retrogressed rather than progressed and so are given a strong rebuke.

With this in mind, the author lays down the "foundation" teachings from which they must advance (6:1–3).[24] The doctrines mentioned in these verses are taken by many[25] to represent early prebaptismal catechesis, and

21. See Montefiore, *Epistle to the Hebrews*, 85f.; and Bruce, *Epistle to the Hebrews*, 77f.

22. See Charles K. Barrett's excellent discussion in his article, "The Eschatology of Hebrews," W. D. Davies and D. Daube, eds., *The Background of the New Testament and its Eschatology*, (Cambridge, U.K.: Cambridge University Press, 1956), 363–393.

23. The word *nōthroi* in 5:11 and 6:12 refers to a "dullness" of hearing which may well denote disobedience to God, in light of the "hearing" metaphor.

24. Marshall, *Kept by the Power of God*, 135, notes that the writer does not deny the possibility of further attention to these rudimentary doctrines but says they must advance beyond them.

25. See Bornkamm, "Das Bekenntnis im Hebrartntirg," 188f.; Montefiore, *The Epistle to the Hebrews*, 105; Hughes, *A Commentary to the Hebrews*, 193–206 ; George W. Buchanan, *To the Hebrews, Anchor Bible* (Garden City. N.Y.: Doubleday, 1972), 103–105; Otto Michel, *Der Brief an die Hebraer* (Gottingen, W. Germany: Vandenhoeck & Ruprecht, 1951), 19. Bruce, *Epistle to the Hebrews*, 113f., argues that it refers to Jewish

it seems probable that this is so. The similarities between the doctrines and Jewish teaching (see fn. 24) may be a deliberate attempt by the writer to remind them that they were little different from Jews in their current state.

The danger itself is described in vv. 4–6. There have been many attempts to explain this from the Calvinist perspective, and these fall into two major categories: 1) Calvin himself (fn. 10) believes the "tasting" was only partial, and these people were not among the elect; they exhibited many of the characteristics but only externally, never internally.[26] 2) Others believe the warning is only hypothetical and is not actually possible; due to the severity of the issue, the author overstates his case in order to help them remain steadfast.[27]

Both of these are doubtful. First, the powerful phraseology used of the endangered ones makes it certain that he believed they were true believers: 1) "once enlightened," a strong phrase describing conversion, with both terms used in the New Testament of the salvation which Christ wrought;[28] 2) "tasted the heavenly gift," which must mean they had fully experienced[29] the salvation blessings (cf. 2:9); 3) "partakers of the Holy Spirit," which could hardly describe anyone other than believers (cf. 1 Cor 12:13; 2 Cor 13:13; Phil 2:1);[30] 4) "tasted the goodness of the Word of God and the powers of the age to come," which must mean an experience of both the Word and the kingdom blessings. "Age to come" is part of the eschatology of this

---

doctrines used as a foundation for Christianity (seen especially in the plural "baptisms," which he believes refers to "ablutions" in a Jewish sense). However, Buchanan and Montefiore explain this in terms of Jewish Christianity, as seen in examples like the Baptist's disciples (Acts 19). Whatever the explanation, it is doubtful in this context if it refers to anything but catechetical instructions.

26. See also John Owen, *An Exposition of Hebrews,* 4 vols. (Evansville, Ind.: Sovereign Grace, 1960), 3:66–91; and Henry C. Thiessen, *Introductory Lectures in Systematic Theology* (Grand Rapids: Eerdmans, 1949), 390–391.

27. William Manson, *The Epistle to the Hebrews,* 106f.; John W. Bowman, *Hebrews, James, 1 Peter, 2 Peter Layman's Bible Commentaries* (Richmond: John Knox, 1968), 42f.; William Barclay, *The Letter to the Hebrews* (Philadelphia: Westminster, 1976), 57–59; W.G.T. Shedd, *Dogmatic Theology,* 3 vols. (Grand Rapids: Zondervan, 1969 [originally 1894]), 2:558; and Kenneth S. Wuest, "Hebrews Six in the Greek New Testament," *Bibliotheca Sacra* 119 (1962), 45–53.

28. "Once"—1 Pet 3:18; Jude 3, 5; and a key word in Hebrews (see below); "enlightened"—2 Cor 4:4, 6; Heb 10:32.

29. See the discussion in Marshall, *Kept by the Power of God,* 137–138, of John Calvin and John Owen on this phrase. J. Behm, *"geuomai"* in Kittel, Bromiley, *Theological Dictionary of the New Testament,* 1:675–676; and Robert Shank, *Life in the Son* (Springfield, Mo.: Westcott, 1960), 177f., favor this interpretation.

30. Those who argue against this, like Owen and Wuest, do so in the sense of Calvin's "common grace," that some are given the blessings of the Spirit who have never been the "temple of the Spirit."

epistle (see below and on 4:1–13) and speaks of the present possession of messianic glory.

In conclusion, we must say there is no more powerful or detailed description of the true Christian in the New Testament. Against the "hypothetical" theory of many Calvinists, we must note that there is no hint of such a possibility in this epistle (nor in the New Testament as a whole!). The language could hardly be more explicit; and while hyperbole is a possibility, this is not equivalent to a hypothetical, imaginary danger. The participial structure of vv. 4, 6 favor the translation of the NASB, "For in the case of those who. . .and *then* have fallen away. . . ." The best interpretation is to take the Greek directly, as expressing an actual possibility;[31] in fact, some think the language favors the theory that the writer is speaking of something which had already occured (although, as we have already pointed out, this is doubtful).

The question of reconversion is related to the two parallel participles in v. 6b, which are usually taken to be causal, i.e., reconversion is impossible "because they recrucify[32] to themselves the Son of God and expose Him to public shame." The usual explanation by those who accept the possibility of both apostasy and reconversion is reflected in the RV's margin, "the while they crucify. . . ." The present participles are taken to mean "as long as they continue" in such apostasy.[33]

However, this reads too much into the passage, and Bruce correctly says the author "distinguishes (as did the Old Testament law) between inadvertent sin and willful sin, and the context here shows plainly that the willful sin which he has in mind is deliberate apostasy."[34] The point the author makes is that such a person will continue in that state and will enter such a condition that he cannot repent.[35] He says nothing regarding whether such a person can ever cease his apostate state.

31. Marshall, *Kept by the Power of God*, 140, says "The element of hypothesis in the passage is not in that the danger is an imaginary one but in that it is only a possibility and not yet a reality in the lives of the readers."

32. We agree here with Marshall and Michel, *contra* Bruce, that the *ana* prefix of this verb in this context means "again" rather than "up" (i.e., reinforcing "crucify").

33. See Shank, *Life in the Son*, 309–329, for this view.

34. Bruce, *Epistle to the Hebrews*, 124. This is supported by the parable of vv. 7–8, where the land which refuses to yield a good crop, no matter what attention is given it, is considered derelict and meant for the "fire."

35. As to the oft-debated question as to the implied subject of "be renewed to repentance," whether God or man, Spicq believes it refers to man, Marshall to God. In light of the implied teaching of 12:17 (see below), we believe the most probable meaning to be that God will not renew them to repentance.

Finally, the writer proceeds to a point of encouragement (vv. 9–12), showing his confidence that the readers are headed for "better things." However, he is not overconfident, for this assurance includes his "desire" that each one persevere "in the full assurance of hope" so they "will not be sluggish" and become "imitators" of those who have already "inherited the promises." The eschatological language of this epistle continues the theology of the Christian life as a future-oriented perseverance. The language of chapters 3–4 is repeated in a context of encouragement rather than exhortation.

Hold fast, lest you die, 10:19–39—This follows the strong doctrinal section (6:13—10:18) on Jesus's high priestly activity both in his person (7:1–28, the Melchizedekian priesthood) and in his work (8:1—10:18, the perfect sacrifice). Again, the conclusion is drawn in terms of strong admonishment. As is common in the New Testament (especially Paul), didactic passages are followed by ethical commands. The same is true here, though the imperatives are couched in stronger modes due to the more serious problem to which the epistle is directed.

Many of the same themes seen in 5:11—6:12 are reintroduced here. The believer's confidence is again combined with his need for perseverance, and the danger of apostasy is repeated, here in the language of Old Testament sacrifice. Also, we once more have the readers described as actual believers. The first person plural (cf. ch. 6) dominates the exhortatory introduction (vv. 19–25), introduces the warning section (v. 26), and concludes the closing section on the past suffering for Christ and present need for a steadfast faith (v. 39). Moreover, they are described as having "received knowledge of the truth" (v. 26) and "enlightened" (v. 32).

The first phrase is found often in the pastorals (1 Tim 2:4; 2 Tim 2:25, 3:7; Tit 1:1) and the Johannine corpus (John 8:32; 1 John 2:21) and certainly refers to experiencing the salvific force of God's revelation.[36] Moreover, they are described as "sanctified" by the "blood of the covenant" (v. 29).[37] Both terms in the context of this epistle speak of Christian regeneration. "Sanctified by the blood" in 9:14 speaks of the power of Jesus's redemption; in 10:10, of Jesus's "once-for-all" sacrifice; in 10:14, of the believer's perfection; and in 10:19, of Christian worship (see further on the discussion of "perfection"). It is obviously a key phrase in the author's concept of salvation and stems from the *verba Christi* (Mark 14:24; Matt. 26:28; Luke 22:20; cf. 1

---

36. See Bruce, *Epistle to the Hebrews,* 258f.; and Montefiore, *Epistle to the Hebrews,* 177; *contra* Kosmala, *Hebräer-Essener-Christen,* 137, and Thomas Hewitt, *The Epistle to the Hebrews Tyndale Commentary* (London: Tyndale, 1960), 165f.

37. See Marshall, *Kept by the Power of God,* 148–149, for his arguments against Hewitt's claims that sanctification here is merely external rather than internal.

Cor 11:25). Indeed, the whole previous section (vv. 19–25) speaks of the believer's confidence in entering God's presence *via* the High Priest.

Interlaced within this summary statement are a series of exhortatory passages, encouraging the believers to "enter the holy place" (v. 19), "draw near" to God in worship (v. 22), "hold fast the confession of hope" (v. 23), and constantly "encourage" each other in the faith (v. 24). Verse 22 is especially crucial, speaking of both outward and inward cleansing in language reminiscent of levitical ceremonial ablutions (Exod 29:4 for priests, Lev 16:4 for the high priest) and also of the messianic promise in Ezek 36:25, which also combines the two: "I will sprinkle clean water upon you, and you will be clean; I will cleanse you . . . . A new heart I will give you, and a new spirit I will put within you." The author undoubtedly considers his readers to be actual believers who had a vital experience of the living Christ.[38]

The apostasy itself is described in very strong terms as a willful turning to sin.[39] Three phrases stress the severity of the act (v. 29): 1) "trampled under foot the Son of God," a phrase which shows open contempt and deepest scorn (cf. Zech 12:3 LXX; Matt 5:13, 7:6); 2) "considered the blood of the covenant an unholy thing," which may involve eucharistic sins[40] but more likely refers to the attitude of the apostate, who makes Jesus's blood a "common" thing, i.e., of no account; 3) "insulted the Spirit of grace," which is at least as strong as "grieving the Spirit" in Eph 4:30 and may well refer to the "unpardonable sin" of Mark 3:29 and parallels.

One must say that such a sin involves the complete rejection of Christ, and so the conclusion, like 6:4, is that "no further sin-offering remains." In this epistle this must mean that no further forgiveness is possible; the apostate has become an "adversary of God" and all that "remains" is "a fearful expectation of judgment," and "a fierceness of fire" (v. 27).[41] Again the writer turns after this powerful warning to encouragement (as in 6:9–12). Verses 32–34 provide the setting for this warning (and probably for the others as well). Under threat of persecution[42] they were being pressured to renounce

38. This is favored by the present tenses used throughout the hortatory passages here, which adjure continuing in their present state.

39. This is described in language reminiscent of sinning "with a high hand" (Deut 17:12, Num 15:30), which act resulted in being "cut off" from God without forgiveness.

40. "Blood of the covenant" was a eucharistic phrase (the passages mentioned above are all in eucharistic contexts) and may refer here to the same situation reflected in 1 Cor 11:25f. See Michel, *Der Brief an die Hebraer,* 236; Montefiore, *Epistle to the Hebrews,* 179.

41. In the Old Testament there was no forgiveness for willful sins, and Qumran made apostasy an unpardonable sin (1QS 2:13f.; 3:4f.).

42. This, along with 12:4, is a major text in dating the epistle. It is not possible to enter this difficult discussion at this time. However, Bruce, *Epistle to the Hebrews,* 267f.,

their faith. They had come through one such experience and were being asked to persevere through another.

However, in v. 39 he shows his confidence in them: "We are not among those who draw back to perdition; we are of the faith and obtain life." This is taken by many (see fn. 27) as further evidence for hypothetical thrust of the warnings (cf. 6:9f.). However, again this hardly supports such a view, since the argument is simply, "You haven't done this yet; I don't think you will," rather than a prophecy regarding their final perseverance.

Be careful, lest you fall short, 12:1–17—The best-known passage in this epistle is found in the intervening material between these two exhortation passages. Chapter 11, of course, contains the famous discussion of faith. Again, the doctrinal section has a soteriological purpose; the conclusion is that in the face of the data, one must persevere. Most scholars agree today that the "cloud of witnesses" in 12:1 refers back to the list of faith-heroes in chapter 11. So "faith" also has an exhortatory thrust (see below for the writer's view of faith). Heb 12:1–11 calls for a general submission to God's disciplinary process, and 12:12–17 is a call for action. The warning passage itself is found in 12:15–17, but the exhortations in vv. 1–14 build up to it. Verse 3b concludes the section on Jesus's example for perseverance (vv. 1–3a) and commands that they "not tire, losing heart" (Montefiore's translation).

The imagery continues the athletic metaphor of v. 1, picturing the runner collapsing before the end of a race. The following ten verses compare the sufferings of the readers to the discipline of a father (God) for his children (the Christian). The theology of the passage teaches that God does not superficially allow trials but does so out of love, for the good of his children, so that they may learn discipline. He always has our best in mind, desiring that we might "share his holiness" (v. 10) and that this might "yield the peaceful harvest of righteousness" (v. 11). This section also closes with a general exhortation (vv. 12–14), again based on athletic imagery but couched in Old Testament language (Isa 35:3f.).

The idea is that the spiritually crippled should brace themselves first and then help the "lame" to come for healing. There is added here the concept of responsibility, not only for one's self but also for fellow believers. These general exhortations point to a danger which they must avoid. Again that danger is apostasy (v. 15—"fall away"; v. 17—"rejected"). The possibility that some will do so is strongly suggested[43] and there are three areas within

---

uses it to argue for an early 60s date, and this would fit the eschatology of the epistle.

43. The phrasing says, "Be careful to make certain that no one falls away from the grace of God."

this danger: 1) "falling away from the grace of God," which echoes the active apostasy of 6:4f. and 10:29f.; 2) "root of bitterness," which "springs up and troubles you," looking back to Deut 29:18 (cf. 1QH 4:14) and stressing the dangerous results of apostates in the community who "defile" many others;[44] 3) "immoral and unspiritual people, like Esau," which draws upon Jewish tradition regarding his immorality and profane character[45] in selling his birthright as an example of the finality of apostasy (he "had no opportunity to repent"[46]). Therefore, we must again conclude that the writer considers apostasy to be not only a viable possibility but also a definite danger for his readers. Again the severity of the danger is presented in the strongest terms.

Conclusion—Several points have been clarified in this discussion: 1) the writer was addressing actual believers; 2) these believers were in danger of apostatizing from the faith, probably as a result of pressures placed upon them in the form of persecution; 3) such apostasy, if experienced, is irredeemable, for the person involved places himself beyond the possibility of repentance;[47] 4) the only remedy is a constant perseverance in the faith, and a continual growth to Christian maturity. This latter antidote must be accomplished not only individually but also corporately, i.e., every member must help and encourage one another in the faith; 5) the author is convinced that they would not become apostates and encourages them thereby to further growth in Christ.

In terms of the last two points, we must note that the major soteriological purpose of the epistle is not warning but encouragement. As Marshall notes, this is accomplished in three major ways: First, they are reminded of

44. See Bruce, *Epistle to the Hebrews*, 365ff.; and Marshall, *Kept by the Power of God*, 143f., who demonstrate that the imagery of the Deuteronomic passage speaks of a man who leads Israel into idolatry, saying that person will not find forgiveness but only "the curses written in this book," and "the Lord will blot out his name from under heaven" (Deut. 29:20).

45. We might note the degree of vilification in the Jewish allegory of Esau. He becomes the symbol not only of immorality (Gen. R. 65, 70d, 72a) but also a prime example of unrepentant sinners (Philo's Leg. All. 3:2 and de Migr. Abr. 153).

46. The metaphor itself does not mean God refused to forgive Esau but rather that the decision, once made, was final. Esau was "disqualified" and lost his "birthright." "Repentance," then, as in the NEB, would refer to "second thoughts," i.e., Esau found no way to rectify the situation and regain his birthright. See R. T. Watkins, "The N.E.B. and the Translation of Hebrews xii. 17," *Expository Times*, 73 (1961–1962), 29–31 and also fn. 47.

47. Note here that the author in 12:17 went even further into this question. In the case of a person actively "seeking" reinstatement, the author seems to say God may deny him the "opportunity," i.e., may not allow him to be reconverted. However, it must be kept in mind that the author speaks throughout of active rather than passive apostasy. It is the one who "willfully" apostatizes who is discussed.

the basic gospel truths which they had learned, to which they must cling, and from which they must develop (2:1–4; 3:6, 14; 10:35–39). Second, a living faith is made the earnest of the future hope (see further below) and leads to an obedient perseverance which triumphs over sin. Third, he calls on them "to assist each other by mutual exhortation on their pilgrim journey" (3:13; 10:24f.; 12:12f.; 13:17).[48] These are all given as means of encouraging them to ensure their perseverance in light of the threat of apostasy.

III. THE ATONEMENT AND REPENTANCE

In this epistle the atonement is seen as a radical, once-for-all provision given by the sovereign God. This is seen especially in the writer's use of *hapax* (found here in eight of the fourteen New Testament occurrences) and *ephapax* (found here in three of its five New Testament occurrences). Four of the former and one of the latter occur in chapter 9 (vv. 7, 26, 27, 28; and v. 12), which centers on Jesus's "once-for-all" sacrifice in contrast to the continuous "once a year" sacrifices of the high priest. "Eternal redemption,"[49] according to v. 12, came through Jesus's "once-for-all" entrance into the Holy Place with "his own blood."

Here and in 11:35 redemption is seen as the eternal gift[50] procured by Christ's once-for-all sacrifice.[51] The connection between atonement and repentance is seen in 6:4f., where the once-for-all provision is connected to the impossibility of a second repentance. J. Behm says Hebrews "emphasizes the seriousness of the total change implied in conversion when this is considered in relation to the obvious danger that Christians will grow slack in their Christianity and sink into dull indifference."[52] The conclusion is that Hebrews makes repentance a total commitment, a total surrender of the whole person at conversion, and that this can only be negated by a

48. Marshall, *Kept by the Power of God*, 146–147. See also Kasemann, *The Wandering People of God*, passim.

49. "Redemption" here is *lutrōsis*, part of the New Testament "ransom" terminology. The synonym *apolutrōsis* occurs in 9:15 and 11:35. The basic meaning is seen in 11:35, where it speaks of "deliverance" from torture. Christ has procured man's deliverance from sin. As noted by J. Behm, "*lutrōsis*" *Theological Dictionary of the New Testament*, 4:351, there is no real "ransom" force in the use of this word here.

50. For the eschatology involved in the "promise" aspect of this provision (cf. 9:15) see the next section.

51. This is also seen in the "once for all" theology of 7:27 and 10:2, 10.

52. J. Behm, "*metanoeō*," in Kittel, Bromiley, *Theological Dictionary of the New Testament*, 4:1005f. He believes 6:4f states man cannot "bring them back" and 12:17 adds that God will not allow them the opportunity. As is already said in this study, we believe 12:17 gives the implied subject of 6:4.

total apostasy. In light of the finality and vast superiority of the redemption Christ provided, repentance must also be a once-for-all decision.

Due to the nature of the epistle—it addressed believers in danger of apostatizing—it says little regarding the "first" repentance; e.g., it does not comment on the nature of repentance, whether or not man's free will plays a part, and whether or not he is sovereignly "elect" of God. All the attention is given to Christian exhortation, and the author's soteriology as a whole must be found in his view of faith and implied from his view of repentance.

IV. SALVATION AND ESCHATOLOGY

This epistle, like 1 Peter, gives salvation an eschatological orientation. It therefore must be seen in light of the inaugurated eschatology already discussed (cf. p. 7). Many have noted the primitive Jewish-Christian apocalyptic seen throughout the epistle and have argued that it provides the fundamental perspective of the epistle.[53] There is indeed a futuristic apocalyptic here; Christ awaits the day of victory over his enemies (1:11; 10:13, 25) when he will "appear a second time" (9:28), and God has already "subjected the world to come" unto him (2:5). The writer expected the imminent return of Christ (10:25, 37) which would see the fulfillment of God's promises for his people.

Indeed, the word "promise" provides a bridge between eschatology and soteriology, showing that the basic eschatological perspective is indeed "inaugurated" and is seen in a soteriological sense. "Promise" occurs fourteen times and is connected with the rest of God (4:1), the inheritance of the saints (6:12; 9:15), Abraham and the old covenant (6:15, 17; 7:6; 11:9, 13, 17), faith (11:33, 39), and the salvation Christ has provided (8:6; 10:36). It is therefore a soteriological term which looks to salvation as a present possession of the future hope. It is a "heavenly" promise (11:16) which links "the longed-for homeland of 11:16 and the heavenly Jerusalem of 12:22," "the unshaken Kingdom (12:28) and the city to come (13:14)."[54] This is both a future promise and a present experience; Christians "have come" already to these (12:22f.). A second word that connects the two doctrines is "hope," which adds the present aspect to the futuristic "promise"; the believer ac-

53. See Barrett, *"Eschatology of the Hebrews,"* 363f.; Ladd, *Theology of the New Testament.,* 572f.; and William Robinson, *The Eschatology of the Epistle to the Hebrews* (Selly Oak, U.K.: Overdale College, 1950), *passim.* They argue that the apparent Philonic dualism between the heavenly and earthly realms, seen in chs. 8 and 9 is subservient to eschatology; when properly understood it is not Philonic as such.

54. Ladd, *Theology of the New Testament,* 574.

cepts the promise as a living hope. As a "better hope" (7:19) it is especially
connected to the command to persevere in the "confidence of our hope"
(3:6; 10:23) or "full assurance of hope until the end" (6:11; cf. 6:18). "Hope"
is both a present possession and a future possibility; in it there is a tension between the "already" and the "not yet"[55] which illustrates perfectly the
problem discussed in the epistle. In our discussion of chapters 3 and 4, we
pointed out the present and future aspects of the "Sabbath rest."[56] It appears
also in the warning section of chapter 6, where the believer is described as
experiencing the "heavenly gift" and "the powers of the age to come" (6:4,
5). The heavenly realm, or eschatological reality, has entered this age and
becomes a part of the believer's life.

It is in this light that we will examine the writer's soteriology. It must
be understood as the present possession of a future inheritance. W. Foerster
says "*sōteria* denotes coming salvation. . . . In content this *sōteria* is defined
by *doxa*. . . but it is typical of Hebrews that the coming *sōteria* is viewed as
already present."[57] It is seen as both a future inheritance (5:9) and a present
reality (7:25). It is linked to the past provision of redemption through Christ
(2:10), the present experience of its benefits (6:9), and the future finalizing
of its rewards (9:28). Above all, it is connected with the encounter of Jesus's
proclamation of eschatological salvation (2:3).[58] Foerster connects it explicitly with *doxa*; this is especially true when one combines 2:3 with 2:10, in
which *archegos tes sōterias* is connected with the "glory" which God brings
his sons.[59] Note again the juxtaposition of past (Christ as "pioneer"), present
(sonship)[60] and future (glory) in salvation.

---

55. See Oscar Cullmann, *The Christology of the New Testament* (London: SCM,
1963), 98f.; and Ladd, *Theology of the New Testament*, 574f.

56. Barrett, "The Eschatology of Hebrews," 372, says, "The rest, precisely because it
is God's, is both present and future; men must enter it and must strive to enter it."

57. Werner Foerster, "*sōteria*" in Kittel, Bromiley, *Theological Dictionary of the New
Testament*, 7: 996. See also Charles E. Carlston, "Eschatology and Repentance in the
Epistle to the Hebrews," *Journal of Biblical Literature* 78 (1959), 296–302, who notes this
same connection, though he takes a hypothetical view of the warning passages.

58. E. M. B. Green. *The Meaning of Salvation* (Philadelphia: Westminster, 1965),
204, says salvation here "retains the characteristic New Testament eschatological tension. It is used as a general description of the Christian way (1:14; 6:9), but as both of
these verses suggest, the emphasis is primarily future. Salvation belongs to the eternal
world which our author contrasts with the empirical."

59. Montefiore, *Epistle to the Hebrews*, 60, defines this "glory" as the "splendour of
ultimate salvation, which awaits the consummation of all things."

60. We might notice the presence of "many sons" here, which qualifies the universal atonement of Jesus "on behalf of all men" (v. 9). Christ died for "all," but only the
"many" are sons.

Thus, while there is security in our salvation (6:9, 10; 10:39) there is no guarantee. It is ours by virtue of repentance but can only be secured finally by means of perseverance. Moreover, salvation in Hebrews is not separated from the life of holiness. The writer would agree with James's "faith without works is dead" theology. This is seen especially in the writer's use of *hagiaxo* in the epistle. Throughout (9:13; 10:10, 14, 29; 13:12) the term has its Jewish force of "purify,"[61] speaking of the process by which the ceremonially defiled were "cleansed" of their impurity. The Christian's present state as believer is spoken of as a consecration act. As Bruce says, "By His death they are consecrated to God for His worship and service and are set apart for God as His holy people, destined to enter into His glory. For sanctification is glory begun, and glory is sanctification completed."[62] Therefore the major motif is the present status of the believer as a consecrated one.[63] It is synonymous with, yet also builds upon, *sōteria*. At the same time there is a dynamic element in it. The presence of salvation within must lead to a "holy life" without. In 12:10, 14, the term is given the meaning it has in the Pauline corpus (cf. Rom 8:18f.; 2 Cor 1:12; 1 Thess 5:23, etc.), i.e., holiness of life and conduct. To secure the final salvation, one must continue in a day-by-day holy walk with God.

V. FAITH AND SALVATION

H. N. Huxhold has written that faith in Hebrews, especially in chapters 11—12, is more like Pauline hope than Pauline faith.[64] In this he is essentially correct, for the concept has an eschatological character in the epistle. No better definition of faith in this epistle could be given then that found in 11:1: "Now faith is certainty regarding things hoped for, evidence for things not seen."[65] The term *hupostasis* translated "certainty" here, has both an objective and a subjective side in its other two occurrences in Hebrews. In 1:3 it is used objectively of God's "essence" and in 3:14 it is used subjectively of

---

61. Buchanan, *To the Hebrews*, 32, uses this meaning of the term as major evidence that the epistle was directed to Jewish believers.

62. Bruce, *Epistle to the Hebrews*, 45.

63. This is probably the meaning of "holy brethren" in 3:1 and "saints" in 6:10.

64. H.N. Huxhold, "Faith in the Epistle to the Hebrews," *Concordia Theological Monthly* 38 (1967) 657f. . In this same sense, Gerhard Delling, "*teleioō*," in Kittel, Bromiley, *Theological Dictionary of the New Testament*, 8:86 n3. says, "In Hb. *pistis* is not to be equated with *sōteria*, since it does not specifically denote the content of Christian faith."

65. The form of the Greek shows that this is a formal definition of "faith."

the believer's "confidence." Here it has nuances of both,[66] though the latter predominates, and "certainty" seems the best translation. And *elegchos* "evidence," employs the metaphor of eyesight to illustrate spiritual faith. In the same way that our eyes provide "evidence" for physical reality, "faith" produces evidence for spiritual reality.[67]

In Paul, while faith and hope are similar and closely connected (cf. Rom 4:18; 8:24), the basic meaning is personal trust and union with Christ. In John, it is faithcommitment and personal belief (John 1:12; cf. 20:29). "In Hebrews faith is the faculty to perceive the reality of the unseen world of God and to make it the primary object of one's life."[68] The whole of chapter 11 relates to the writer's concept of salvation as a future-oriented gift. He uses the Old Testament faith-heroes as examples of his basic definition in v. 1 and as illustrations of his concept of salvation. They too had to persevere in accepting the future-thrust of salvation as a promise from God. They lived as though the future state was a present reality. Faith was simply accepting God's word, believing it, and living in that light.

The lesson is therefore obvious. Salvation must be secured by a persevering faith which grasps the future salvation and makes it a present reality. Faith must take hold of his promises in the midst of trials and suffering,[69] trusting God in light of the blessings Christ has wrought. The danger was that they might allow their faith to slip, lose sight of God's promises, and therefore fail to "keep their souls" and be "destroyed" (10:39). This last warning is couched in the language of encouragement and has led some to conclude that the author is actually certain that his readers will see the end of their faith whatever the persecution, i.e., that he teaches the final triumph of their faith.[70]

While this is somewhat true, it cannot detract from the persevering aspect of this faith and the reality of this danger. This comforting thought

66. Faith accepts a future possibility as if it had present "substance" (AV). Therefore it is both objective and subjective in thrust. See Bruce, *Epistle to the Hebrews*, 277–279; Michel, *Der Brief an die Hebraer*, 98–100, Marshall, *Kept by the Power of God*, 148.

67. Similarities between this definition and Hellenistic thought led Crasser and Kasemann to conclude that the concept of faith here is taken from gnostic teachings. Others, like Bruce, see similarities with Philo. In light of previous conclusions regarding the Jewish background, the latter is much more likely.

68. Ladd, *Theology of the New Testament*, 584.

69. *Ibid.*, 585, shows how the writer was careful to make his list apply to the present situation. In vv. 35–39 he lists those who had faith in the midst of torture, "refusing to accept release, that they might rise again to a better life." These are seen in 12:1 ("witnesses") as an example for the present situation.

70. See Paul M. Bretscher. "Faith Triumphant—Echoes from the Epistle to the Hebrews," *Concordia Theological Monthly* 31 (1960), 728–739.

must be read in the light of the warning passages, not vice versa. The whole pattern of soteriology in this epistle demands the absolute necessity of perseverance for final salvation.

VI. PERFECTION AND FAITH

One of the important teachings of Hebrews centers on the development of perfection, first in Christ and consequently in the believer. Heb. 12:2 links the two concepts—perfection and faith—in Jesus himself. He is called "the Pioneer[71] and Perfecter of our faith." The problem is how Jesus could be the "perfecter" when he himself was "perfected" (2:10; 5:9). Kasemann takes a literal view and interprets it in gnostic fashion that the redeemer needed to be perfected himself before he could bring others to perfection.[72] However, as Marshall shows, the dominant idea in both verses is suffering, not perfection.[73] It is not that Christ was imperfect but that he entered completely into the believer's experience of "perfection" through suffering. This was part of his high priestly ministry.

Behind this whole idea is the pattern of "obedience," a key part of the writer's perfection theology, as seen in 5:8–9.[74] Obedience to the Father can only be learned through "discipline" (12:5f.), and this is the path to maturity or perfection. Jesus was "perfected" by becoming "obedient unto death" (Phil 2:8) and suffering as the one sacrifice. It is in this sense that he is "Pioneer and Perfecter." By his perfect sacrifice[75] he brought man to the possibility of perfection (10:14). He was both perfect provider and perfect example in bringing men to sonship and glory.[76]

---

71. On this term, see the discussion of 2:10 earlier. In this context it probably means that Jesus has pioneered the new age of faith. As Marshall, *Kept by the Power of God,* 149, says, he "supplies the impetus" and example for faith (see 12:3).

72. Kasemann, *Das wandernde Gottesvolk,* 82f; Spicq, *L'Epitre aux Hebreux* 1:64f., notes Philonic parallels; and Michel, *Der Brief an die Hebraer,* 76f., sees a cultic flavor.

73. Marshall, *Kept by the Power of* God, 150. See also Bruce, *Epistle to the Hebrews,* 44.

74. "Learned obedience through suffering" (5:8) was a favorite saying in both Hellenistic (where it was a popular aphorism) and Jewish circles. In its application to the Son of God, however, it speaks of incarnation and divine purpose (cf. Phil 2:8).

75. This is seen in 12:3, where he is "Pioneer and Perfecter" in the sense that he "endured the cross." Delling (fn. 64) says "the two terms refer primarily to the passion of Jesus on its personal side."

76. This does not dispute the sense seen by B. F. Westcott, *The Epistle to the Hebrews* (Grand Rapids: Eerdmans, 1973 [originally 1892]), 397; and Bruce, "'To the Hebrews' or 'To the Essenes'?" 352, that it means "in Him faith has reached its perfection." Rather, both ideas are present; one has reference to him, the other to his followers.

A strong debate ensues over the question whether *teleioō* and cog-nates[77] are cultic[78] or ethical[79] in thrust. Actually, it is best to note both ideas in the concept. The cultic religious implications are seen in the tabernacle dualism of 9:9f.; the Melchizedekian priesthood emphasis (5:9); the imper-fect law (7:19), and the mature-immature contrast (5:14). Yet within these very categories there are ethical implications; implicit within these is an ethical-moral sense. This is seen especially in the theological concept of the "pilgrimage" of believers, who are on a "wilderness journey" in search of God's "rest." This is also indicated in the general soteriology of the entire epistle. A march-forward (6:1f.), a perseverance in the essentials of Chris-tian development, is at the heart of the writer's exhortation.[80] Salvation is the eschatological possession of a forward-looking faith.

Of course, this does not mean there is a total flux in salvation, for there is a once-for-all foundation (7:27; 9:12) for the Christian's sanctification (10:10). Nevertheless this foundation is not a static fact but rather a dy-namic, life-producing force in which the believer must be actively involved "now" (2:8; 8:6; 9:24; 12:26). Therefore perfection is more than an external, cultic experience; it is an internal life-changing "goal."[81] Wikgren defines the concept thusly: "The response of faith by the believer" is "in a sense proleptically *teleios* through initiation and participation in that community of faith which also constitutes this ideal goal (cf. xi. 40)."[82] The end is not fi-nally attained or obtained; one must reach it by suffering as he suffered. The idea is the attainment of "complete-ness" or "maturity," and the Christian is pictured as one in progress toward that end.

77. *Teleioō* (2:10; 5:9; 7:19. 28; 9:9; 10:1, 14; 11:40; 12:23), *teleiōs* (5:14; 9:11), *teleiōtes* (6:1), *teleiōtes* (12:2), *teleiōsis* (7:11).

78. See Olaf E. Moe, "Der Gedanke des allgemeinen Priestertums im Hebraerbriefe" *Theologische Zeitschrift* 5 (1949), 161–169; Delling, "*teleioō*" 8:82–83; Michel, *Der Brief an die Hebraer*. 76f.

79. See Allen Wikgren, "Patterns of Perfection in the Epistle to the Hebrews," *New Testament Studies* 6 (1960), 159–167; Cullmann, *The Christology of the New Testament*, 92; Marshall, *Kept by the Power of God*, 150. All, however, recognize the presence of the cultic in the term.

80. Note Kasemann's title, *Das wandernde Gottesvolk*, which is an excellent example of a key element in Hebrews. Kasemann describes the readers as "pilgrim people of God" who are traveling the road of salvation. While his discussion of origins is highly suspect, his insight into theology must be applauded.

81. Wikgren, "Patterns of Perfection," 160, takes this sense of *telos* to be the basic use of the concept in this epistle.

82. Ibid., 162

He must "press on toward perfection" (6:1)[83] on the basis of the "greater and more perfect tabernacle" (9:11; cf. 9:9). It is the promise which leads to perfection (11:39–40). Heb 12:23 seems to connect this with the believer's death, which is the "completion" of his earthly pilgrimage.[84] Therefore we might conclude that perfection, as one of the major terms for salvation in this epistle (see also "repentance" and "sanctified": earlier), has a twofold thrust: 1) it speaks of the crisis experience of salvation, in which one receives the salvific gifts;[85] and 2) it speaks of the eschatological "goal" by which the Christian strives *via* his spiritual pilgrimage to enter that final "rest" with God. This latter element, identified with the doctrine of perseverance in Hebrews, is predominant in this epistle.

CONCLUSIONS

Many might argue that the soteriology of this epistle, as presented here, is given a semi-Pelagian coloring.[86] This, however, is to misunderstand the perspective from which the author wrote, as well as the "word of exhortation" (13:22) within which his purpose is found. The readers were believers who were in danger of failure and apostasy, and so the writer does not spend time discussing their faith-decision. This is presupposed in his *hapax* theology, which provides the background for his view of salvation as a pilgrimage, i.e., both a present possession and a future hope. His perspective, then, is the other side of the salvation-coin, salvation as the eschatological goal, not only a present experience but also a future gift, which can only be obtained by perseverance in Christian development.

83. The verses just before this (5:13–14) contrast the "mature" to the "babe"; the mature are those who by "practice have their senses trained to discern good and evil."

84. See Bruce, *Epistle to the Hebrews*, 376; and Wikgren, "Patterns of Perfection," 160. The application is to the whole community of saints in the Old Testament and now, who are united through Christ. It especially has in mind the Old Testament saints of ch. 11 (cf. vv. 39–40). Wikgren points to its use for martyrdom in IV Macc. 7:15; cf. Wisd. 4:13, Luke 13:32.

85. Green, *Meaning of Salvation*, 204, says, "Whilst, however, the main thrust of the teaching of Hebrews on salvation points to the future, it does not do so exclusively. In 5:9 we are told that Jesus became 'the procuring cause' of salvation. Clearly this is something that is already achieved."

86. One of the tragedies of our current situation in evangelicalism is the emotive code-words or labels which we attach to certain positions and enable us to automatically reject the totality of that position on the basis of the label. One of the worst of these "code-words" is "semi-Pelagian" which means automatically that the position is a-biblical, and that the data within need not be studied further. To many strong Calvinists any Wesleyan-Arminian Position is automatically "semi-Pelagian."

The writer argues against a static Christianity that is content to dwell in the assurance of final inheritance. Such a faith is not faith at all; it inevitably stagnates into immaturity (5:13–14; 6:1) and leaves itself open to apostasy (6:4f.). Some might also charge that such a doctrine teaches salvation by works; but here we must note that Hebrews presupposes the faith-decision and relates to perseverance in that new condition.

Moreover, we would add that there is no sense here of a perseverance by works. The writer frequently connects perseverance with the sovereign power of God, and there is a definite sense of security (see above). However, this security itself is a present possession rather than a future guarantee. Verses 10:14 and 2:11 use "timeless present" participles to describe the perfecting and sanctifying work of Christ. Verse 12:28 says we have received "a kingdom which cannot be shaken" and 9:12 says Christ obtained "eternal redemption." However, this must be seen as present "promise" rather than as absolute certainty (9:15) and as subject to the dangers discussed in the epistle. Therefore, we would conclude that for the writer perseverance is not a "work" but is rather a yielding to the sovereign power of the Holy Spirit within.[87]

Hebrews and John—A comparison of these two key works will help clarify the doctrine of perseverance as we have defined it, for the two represent opposite sides of the same truth. Both teach a combination of security and responsibility in salvation, with John stressing the former and Hebrews the latter. In John 6:37–40 and 10:29–30 the believer's security is stressed in emphatic language (but note responsibility in the present participles of 6:35, 40 and in the "hear-follow" terminology of 10:27),[88] while in Hebrews the believer's responsibility to persevere is stressed (but note security in the passages just mentioned as well as in 6:9f. and 10:39). The promise of God's support provides security, but the Christian must avail himself of this promise "lest he fail to enter God's rest."[89]

New Testament passages on apostasy—If this epistle was the only place in the New Testament where the doctrine of perseverance and the possibility of apostasy were taught, we would wonder if our exegesis might be

---

87. The Holy Spirit is seen in this epistle as giver and witness; 2:4 and 6:4 look to the believer's experience of the gifts of the Spirit at salvation (cf. 10:29); and 9:18, 10:15 (cf. 3:7) look to him as witness, speaking through Old Testament fulfillment and testifying to the efficacious sacrifice of Christ (cf.9:14).

88. See the discussion of these and other Calvinist texts in "Exegetical Notes on Calvinist Texts," also within this volume.

89. Green, *Meaning of Salvation,* 206, says God "will certainly keep the trusting soul. . . . But that does not mean that he will keep the man who does *not* want to be kept."

wrong or if Hebrews perhaps was not a part of the canon. However, it agrees with many other passages in the New Testament, and we must see it in the light of the theology of the New Testament as a whole. Several passages teach what we may call "conditional salvation," i.e., salvation which can only be received finally when man meets certain God-ordained conditions. Rom 8:12–14 makes sonship conditional upon our continual participation in the leading of the Spirit; while the Spirit does the work (so Owen) the believer must continually yield to it. 1 Cor 15:1–2 says that one must "hold fast" to the truths of the Word, lest his belief be "in vain"; this must mean persever-ance is the only guarantee against an "emptying" ("in vain" is "to no avail" rather than "thoughtlessly" or "rashly") of one's salvation in apostasy. John 8:51 makes obedience to his Word the condition for eternal life ("never see death").

Col 1:21–23 says the believer will be presented "blameless" only "if [he] continues in the faith" and is "not moved away from the hope of the Gospel" (cf. Acts 14:22). Second Pet 1:8–11 warns against forgetting the sal-vation experience (apostasy) and exhorts the readers to "make your calling and election certain." Perseverance is also seen in the phrase, "as long as you practice these things, you will never stumble." Finally, 1 John 2:23–25 says that one will only abide in the Father and have eternal life "if what [he] heard from the beginning abides in [him]."

There are also several passages stating the danger of apostasy. Matt 24:4, 5, 11, 13 and 2 Thess 2:3 prophesy a general apostasy that will precede the tribulation period. Only "he who endures to the end" "will be saved." It should be noted that this speaks of the time preceding the tribulation and not of the tribulation itself. First Tim 4:1, 16 says some will apostatize and exhorts Timothy to persevere so as to ensure his salvation and that of his flock. Second Pet 3:17, 18 calls for diligence and exhorts the readers to guard themselves against the error of those who "fall from [their] own steadfastness"; the phrases "led away" and "fall from" show this is a real, not hypothetical, danger. In 1 Cor 9:27, Paul's statement that he may become "castaway" must mean "rejected" rather than just "disqualified"; in Rom 1:28; 2 Cor 13:5; 2 Tim 3:8; and Titus 1:16 it means "reprobate" and refers to those who are outside the kingdom of God. James 1:14–16 and 5:19, 20 warn against the danger of "erring" and thus "dying" and equate "erring" with "straying."

The death here is more than just physical death but must refer to eternal condemnation. And 2 Pet 2:20, 21 is quite similar to Heb 6:4f. and 10:29f. Those who have "escaped the pollutions of the world by the knowledge of the Lord" and "are again entangled and overcome" are in a worse state than before. Again these must be believers, and again they have apostatized from the faith. Finally, Rev 22:19 shows that some can have their names "removed from the book of life." These passages show that the position of the writer to the Hebrews with regard to apostasy fits the mainstream of New Testament teaching

Subject Index

ethics, 117
"Evangelical Arminians" (Horton), 1
evil
  Calvinist problem of, 138–139
  existence of, 136, 137, 141
  God and, 30
  responsibility for, 144
  sin and, 30, 30n3, 46–47
Examination of Perkins's Pamphlet
  (Arminius), 158
exegetical notes on Calvinist texts
  book of Acts, 206–208
  1 Peter, epistle of, 218–219
  Johannine writings, 200–206
  overview, 197–198
  Pauline writings, 208–218
  synoptic gospels, 198–200
external knowledge, 78

F

Faber, Frederick W., 51
faith
  aspects of, 205
  Augustine on, xix
  Christian, 106
  as condition, 81
  defined, xx
  foreseen, 86–88
  grace and, 99–107
  man's nature and, 105–106
  obedience of, 225
  objective, 106
  ordinary, 106
  overview, xix–xxi
  perfection and, 293–295
  salvation and, 291–293
  subjective, 106n3
false gods, 78–79
false prophets, 36
fatalism, xxii, xxiin18
federal headship, 166n68
Finney, Charles, 4
1 Peter, epistle of, 218–219
Fisk, Samuel, 84
five-point Calvinism, 4, 197
Fletcher, John, 179, 187, 191
Flew, Antony G.N., 137n8

Foerster, Werner, 290
foreknowledge by God
  Boettner on, 214
  conditional election, 77–82, 157–162
  forelove versus, 78n20
  grace and, 86–88, 208
  human responsibility, 90–91
  of individuals, 80n21
  Pauline writings, 211–212
Foreman, Kenneth J., 26
forgiveness, 137
Forlines, F. Leroy, 189
"Free Grace" (hymn), 27–28
Free Grace (Wesley), 48–49n35
free will
  Arminianism and, 6–9, 16, 31n6
  Calvin on, 30
  conditional election and, 90–91
  God's sovereignty and, 84
  in Hebrews epistle, 277–278
  human inability and, 168–171
  predestination and, 159–162
  Wesley on, 186–187
  See also will
freedom, 2, 137, 160n46, 189–190, 233–238
  See also compatibilistic freedom; human freedom; libertarian freedom

G

Geisler, Norman, 245n12
general call, 34n11
general grace, 34, 34n11, 38
Genevan Calvinism, 153
Gerig, Wesley, 255n38, 256n41, 259n52, 260n53
glory of God, 5–6, 14–17, 48
God
  Adam, parallel, xvi, 24
  atonement, intention for, 51–52, 63–67, 170
  attributes of, 99–100
  believer's and, 33–34
  beneficence of, 97
  as cause of sin, 7, 11–12, 23

cosmic purpose of, 225–226
covenants of, 14, 162, 217
daily work in the life of believers, 33–34
desire for relationship, 49, 105, 141
desire for vs ordaining salvation, 41
double predestination and, xvii
God *(continued)*
enemy and will of, xxii–xxiii
as eternal, 78
evil and, 30
false gods, 78–79
foreknowledge. *See* foreknowledge by God
free-will. *See* free will
glory of, 5–6, 14–17, 48
goodness of, 97
grace of, 86–88, 181–182
as gracious being, 136
grief and anger over sin, 40n20
justice of, 7, 88
love of, 212–213
making his Son to be sin, 59
mediatorial work and, 158–159
nature of, 83
omnipotence of, 10–13, 137n8
as personal being, 136
personhood of, 93–95
promise of, 113–114, 224–226, 238–240
providence of, 12, 13
purpose of, 211–212
relationship with, 49, 105, 141
restrictions on, 84n36
salvation. *See* salvation
salvific grace and, 18–28, 47, 136
self-limitation of, 10–11, 13
self-revelation of, 47–48
sin and, 7, 11–12, 23, 30, 40n20, 85
Sonship and, 59, 211
sovereignty of. *See* sovereignty
ultimate concern of, 228–232
universal purpose of, 226–227
universal salvific will of, 40–41, 47
voluntary self-limitation of, 10–11, 13
will of, xxii–xxiii, 98–99, 131

world history events planned by, 124–125
God-centered theology, 1–17
"God's Universal Salvific Grace" (Grounds), xx, 18–28
Gomarus, Franciscus, 151, 152
goodness of God, 97
governmental view of atonement, 64, 172, 176
grace
as antithesis to sin, 20–21
Christocentric personalism of, 21
common, 96, 187
defining, 96–97
divine, 169–171
effective grace, 32n7, 34, 34n11, 38, 187
faith and, 99–107
general grace, 34, 34n11, 38
irresistible. *See* irresistible grace
justifying, 188–192
love as, 98, 101
New Testament affirmations, 96–97
objective, 103
perfecting, 192–196
predestination and, 22
preliminary grace, 185–189
prevenient, 8, 103–104, 185–189
saving, xix, 104–105
sovereign, 87
special, 96
sufficient grace, 32n7
universal, 18–28
See also Spirit of Grace
Grace and Responsibility (Cobb), 179
grace encounter, 180–181
grace-enabled libertarian freedom, 33–34, 49
Grantham, Thomas, 174n107
Greathouse, William M., 185
Greek grammarians, saving faith and, 268–273
Green, Michael, 209
Grider, Kenneth, 185
Griffith-Thomas, W. H., 22
Gromacki, Robert, 206
Grounds, Vernon C., xx, 18
guilt, 209

by imputed righteousness of Christ,
171–176
in Old Testament, 99
Pauline writings, 208–209
sanctification and, 15
saving grace and, 103–104
justification *(continued)*
by works, 86
"Justification by Faith" (Wesley), 191
justifying grace, 188–192
Justin Martyr, xix, 95

K

Käsemann, Ernst, 56, 293
Keathley, Kenneth, 161
Keener, Craig S., 255n39
Koolhaes, Jasper, 154, 156
Kosmala, Hans, 277

L

Ladd, George Eldon, 209, 214,
215–216
Laney, J. Carl, 262n59
Leclerc, Diane, 186
Lenski, R.C.H., 253–254, 260n54, 261
"A Letter Addressed to Hippolytus A
Collibus" (Arminius), 9, 11, 173
Letters to Malcolm (Lewis), 85
Lewis C. S., 85
libertarian freedom, 15, 30–34, 37,
48–49, 160, 160n46, 181
Life in the Son (Shank), 242f
life principles, 211
Limborch, Philip, 10, 147
limited atonement, 212, 213n53
limited election, xviii–xix, xviiin10, 22
Lindström, Harald, 183
Linss, W. C., 277
Lloyd-Jones, Martyn, 189
logic, rules of, 138, 138n10
Long, Elmer, 177
Lord's prayer, 39
Louw, Johannas P., 53, 56, 59
love
of God, 212–213
grace as, 98, 101

M

Maben, Alan, 2
MacDonald, William G., xx, 93
MacKay, Donald M., 135
Maddox, Randy, 178, 193
man-centered theology, 1–3, 13–14
Marshall, I. Howard, xxi, xxiii, 129,
198, 203, 205, 212, 212n49, 278,
287–288
Martenson, Clement, 154
Marxsen, Willi, 276–277
McCall, Thomas, 193
*The Meaning of Pentecost in Early
Methodism* (Wood), 179
Meeuwsen, James W., 167, 167n70
mercy, 139, 163–164, 232, 232n18,
235–237
merit, 143
Methodist Articles of Religion, 183
Michaels, J. Ramsey, 253
middle knowledge, 161
Mikolaski, Samuel, 19, 21
Modern Reformation (magazine), 1
Mohler, Al, 2, 10
Molina, Luis de, 161
monergism, 171n93
Moo, Douglas, 60, 189
moral exhortations, 31–32
moral outrage, 40
moral will for humanity, 45–46
morality, 108
morally justified reasons for sin, 47
Morris, Leon, 202
Mother Teresa, 6
motivational effectiveness of New Testament, 45
Mounce, Robert H., 262n59
Mounce, William D., 269
Mueller, Richard A., 2–3, 13, 146,
150n12
Mullins, E. Y., 25–26
Murray, John, 201, 210–212, 247
mystery, 46–47

N

natural headship, 166n68
nature of God, 83

Scripture Index

Printed in Great Britain
by Amazon.co.uk, Ltd.,
Marston Gate.